To my darling wife, Ruth, who has generously given her support, advice and understanding over the years.

Jeffrey Sherwin

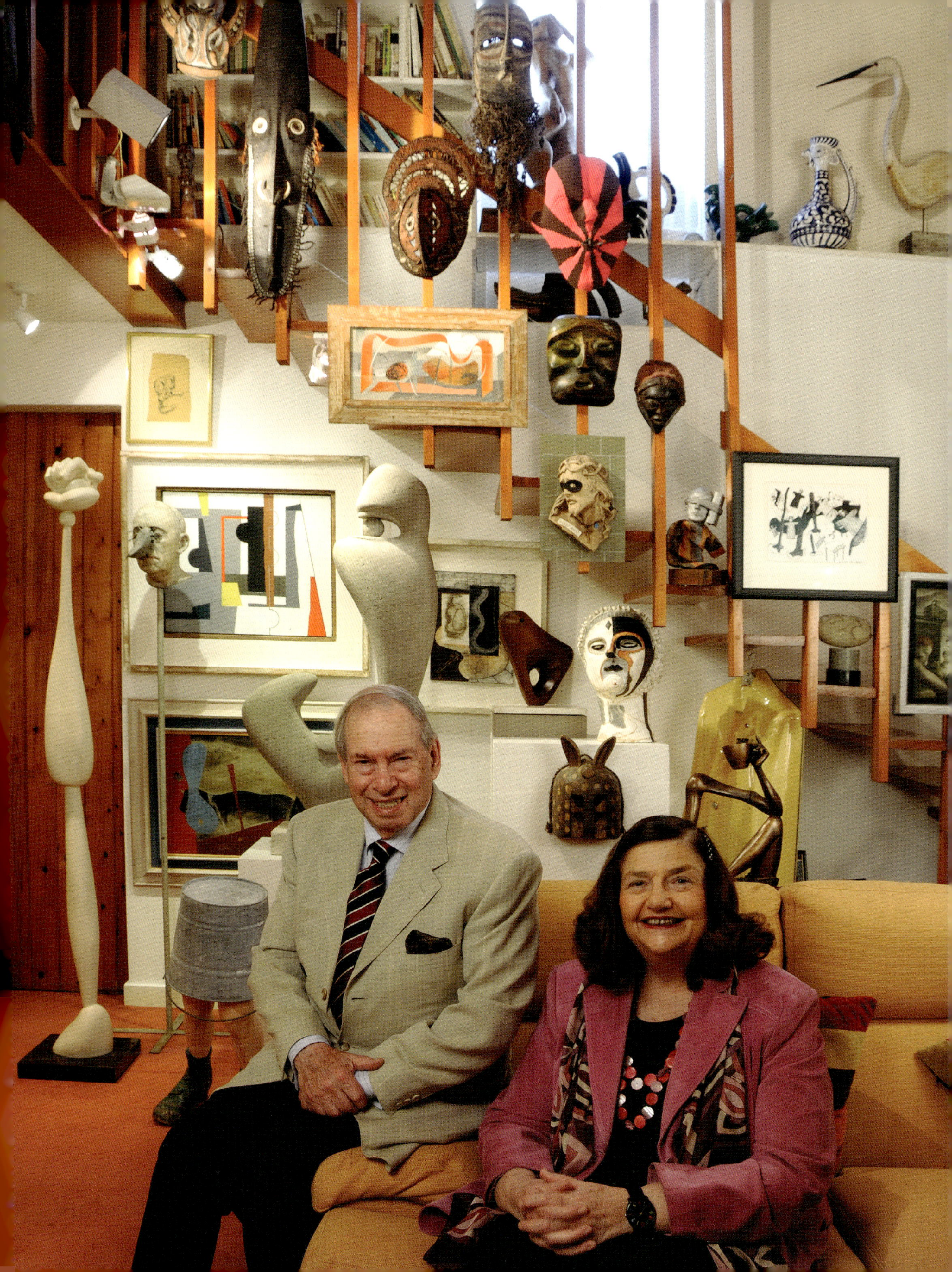

BRITISH SURREALISM IN CONTEXT

A COLLECTOR'S EYE

THE SHERWIN COLLECTION

BRITISH SURREALISM IN CONTEXT – A COLLECTOR'S EYE

All colour photography by Norman Taylor, and additional illustrations provided by Dr Sherwin unless otherwise stated.

Every attempt has been made to contact the holders of copyright in the works illustrated and anyone believing an omission has been made should contact the Commercial Office, Leeds Museums and Galleries, Discovery Centre, Carlisle Road, Leeds, LS10 1LB.

This book has been published to accompany the exhibition:
British Surrealism in Context – A Collector's Eye
Leeds Art Gallery 10th July to 1st November 2009

Front cover: *The Playground of Salpêtrière* by Conroy Maddox
Back cover: *October 2, 1938–2* by Reuben Mednikoff

Published 2009

ISBN 978-0-901981-82-0

All text edited by Silvano Levy and Tanja Pirsig-Marshall

Designed by FDA, Huddersfield 01484 861611
Printed in Yorkshire by J W Northend 0114 250 0331

For sales, distribution and rights enquiries, please contact:
sales@jeremymillspublishing.co.uk or visit www.jeremymillspublishing.co.uk
telephone 01484 463340

CONTENTS

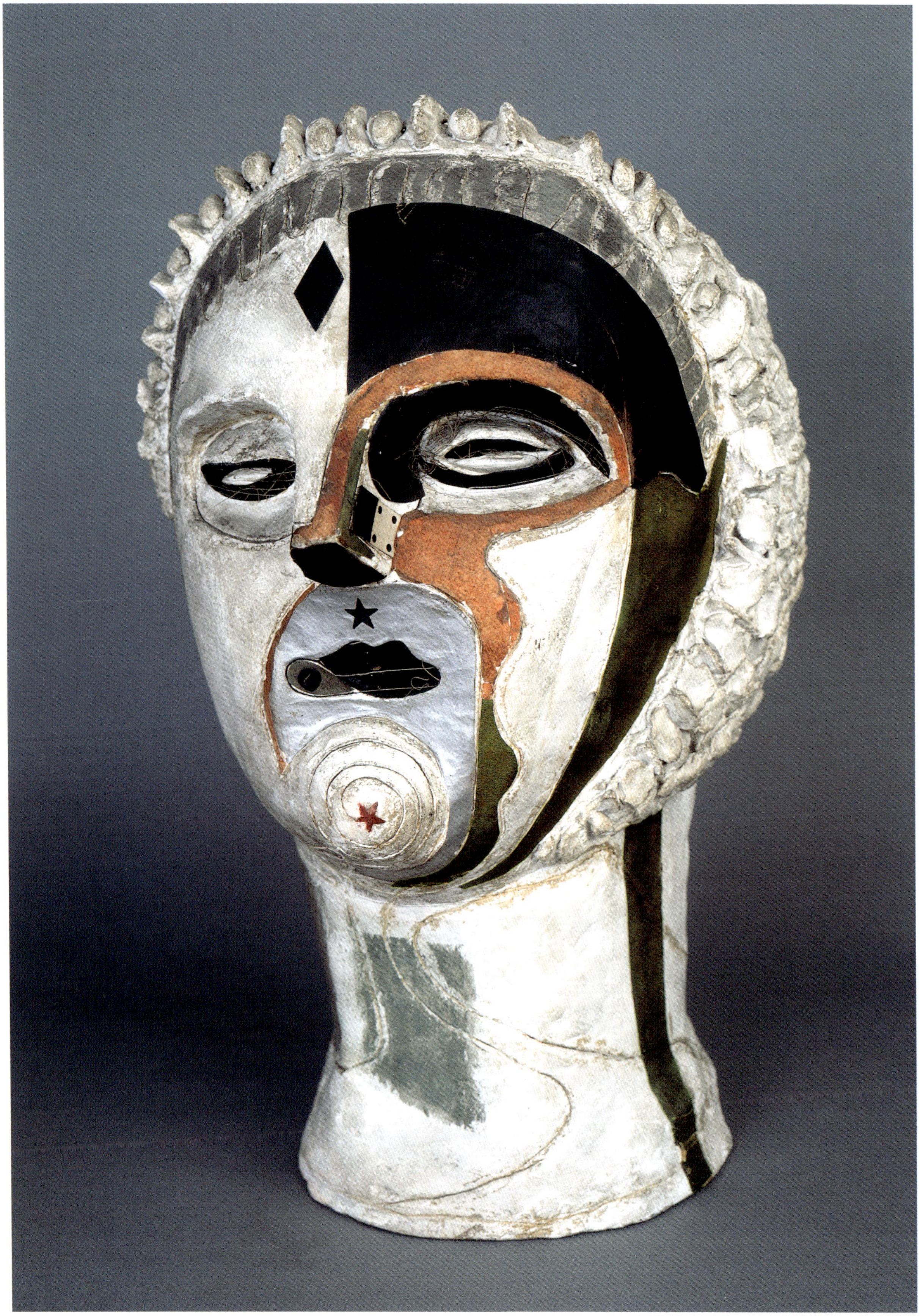

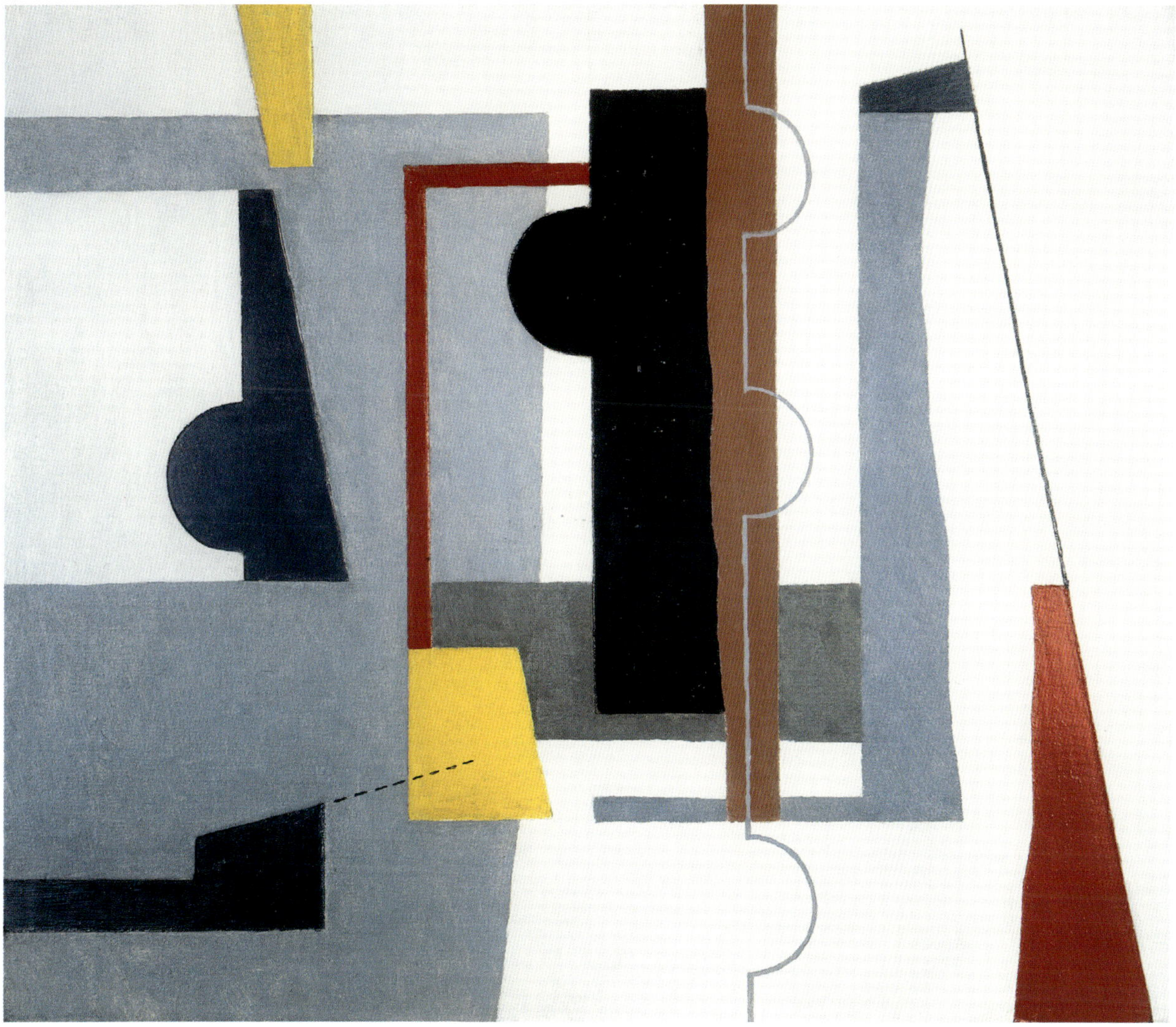

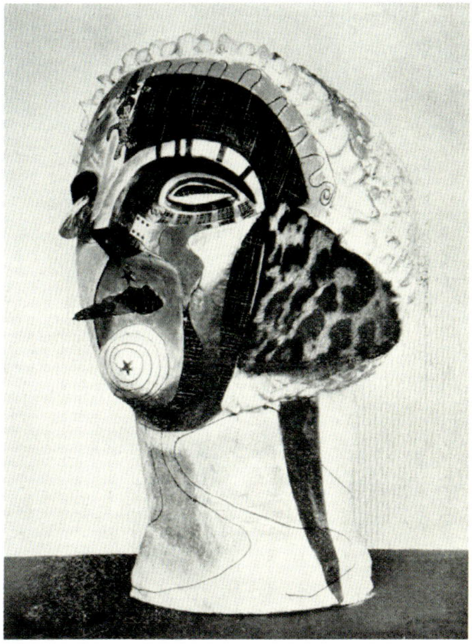

Angel of Mercy
Eileen Agar, 1934

Reproduced as The Politician
in Arson, 1942

Forms on a White Ground
John Piper, 1935

PREFACE

JOHN PROCTER

Leeds Art Gallery is delighted to host the exhibition 'British Surrealism in Context: A Collector's Eye' drawn from the Ruth and Jeffrey Sherwin Collection, the largest collection of British surrealism in the country. The presentation of this collection brings to the gallery something of the excitement, the adventure of private collecting with all the doubts, the questions, and happy coincidences that it involves. For Leeds Art Gallery, it is an opportunity to explore the collaboration between the institution and the private collector.

Thanks go to Dr Jeffrey Sherwin and his wife Ruth for sharing their enthusiasm with us and giving us the opportunity to display their unique collection. The collector was actively involved in the curation of the show and opened up interesting aspects of his collecting. In his essay, Jeffrey talks about the motives behind his collecting and shares some of his recollections of the process of collecting. He enjoys not only acquiring artefacts in the context of their time, but also placing them in a broader social context. The exhibition is organized in groups – an important aspect of Sherwin's collecting: groups of sculpture and related preliminary drawings; of works with visual connections; of the diverse output of one artist. Certain parts of this extensive collection, including artefacts from Papua New Guinea and Africa, and his kinetic art collection had to be omitted.

Our thanks go to Michel Remy, University of Nice, for his comprehensive and insightful essay on British surrealism, to Jon Wood for exploring relationships between sculptures and works on paper in Sherwin's collection and Silvano Levy for his interesting work on Toni del Renzio. Peter Farmer designed the catalogue and the printed material for the exhibition, Norman Taylor photographed over five hundred art objects and ephemera. Our thanks go also to Lizzie Docherty, Tara Sibson, Alex Robertson and Nigel Walsh.

We are deeply grateful for the generous financial contribution and support we received for this catalogue from Leeds Metropolitan University. Additional support for the exhibition was also received from Sotheby's, London.

INTERNATIONAL SURREALIST EXHIBITION 1936

It was not until 1936, when the first *International Surrealist Exhibition* was held in the New Burlington Galleries in London, that a British Surrealist Group was officially formed and that surrealism was introduced to Britain.

The exhibition, held at the Burlington Galleries from 11 June to 4 July 1936, was organized by Humphrey Jennings, Henry Moore, Herbert Read, Roland Penrose, David Gascoyne, Diana Brinton Lee, Hugh Sykes Davies, Rupert Lee, Paul Nash, E.L.T. Mesens, Andre Bréton, Paul Éluard, Man Ray and Georges Hugnet.

André Breton and poet Paul Eluard helped choose the European exhibits, which included works by Dali and Ernst as well as examples of primitive art. The show was the first of its kind in Britain, attracting international critical acclaim and inciting both the interest and outrage of the sceptical British public.

In terms of attendance figures, the exhibition was an outstanding success. The crowds were so large on opening day that traffic in Piccadilly was brought to a standstill. During its three-week run, over thirty thousand people visited the exhibition.

Throughout the exhibition, the show's organizers delivered lectures on the theories and intentions of surrealism to large audiences. Salvador Dali gave the most famous of these lectures on the 1st July. The eminent surrealist caused a furore when he stepped on stage and began to deliver his lecture in a full deep-sea diving suit. Only minutes later, a shocked audience watched with a mixture of horror and disbelief, as he began to suffocate and had to be released from the helmet with pliers.

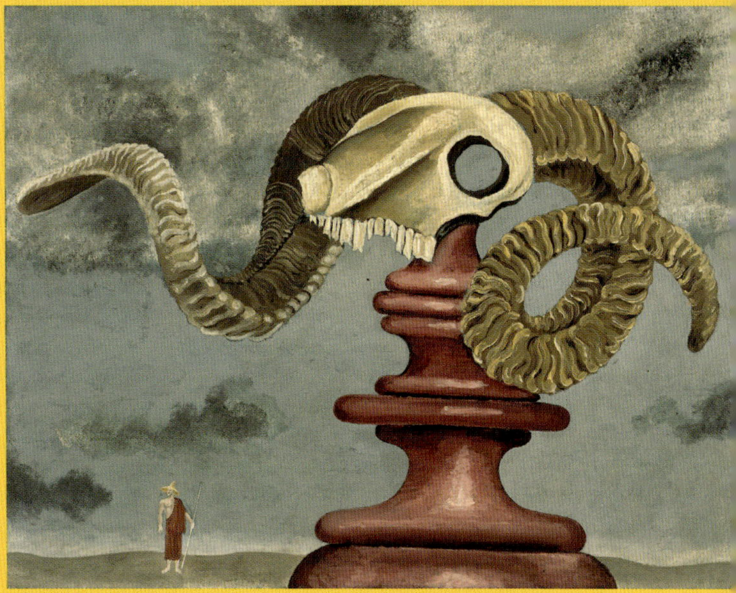

Aries
John Banting, 1935

Abdication of Edward VIII, *Daily Express*, December *1936*
The Berlin Olympics, August 1936

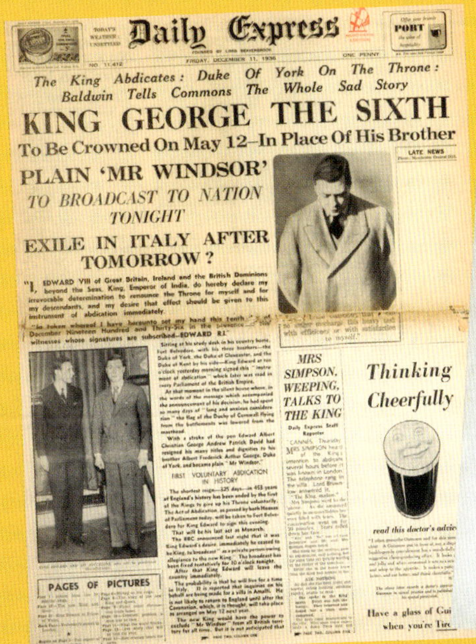

Daily Express

FRIDAY, DECEMBER 11, 1936 — ONE PENNY

The King Abdicates: Duke Of York On The Throne: Baldwin Tells Commons The Whole Sad Story

KING GEORGE THE SIXTH

To Be Crowned On May 12—In Place Of His Brother

PLAIN 'MR WINDSOR'

TO BROADCAST TO NATION TONIGHT

EXILE IN ITALY AFTER TOMORROW?

"I, EDWARD VIII of Great Britain, Ireland and the British Dominions beyond the Seas, King, Emperor of India, do hereby declare my irrevocable determination to renounce the Throne for myself and for my descendants, and my desire that effect should be given to this instrument of abdication immediately.

"In token whereof I have hereunto set my hand this tenth ... of December Nineteen Hundred and Thirty-Six in the presence ... witnesses whose signatures are subscribed—EDWARD R.I."

MRS SIMPSON, WEEPING, TALKS TO THE KING

Thinking Cheerfully

PAGES OF PICTURES

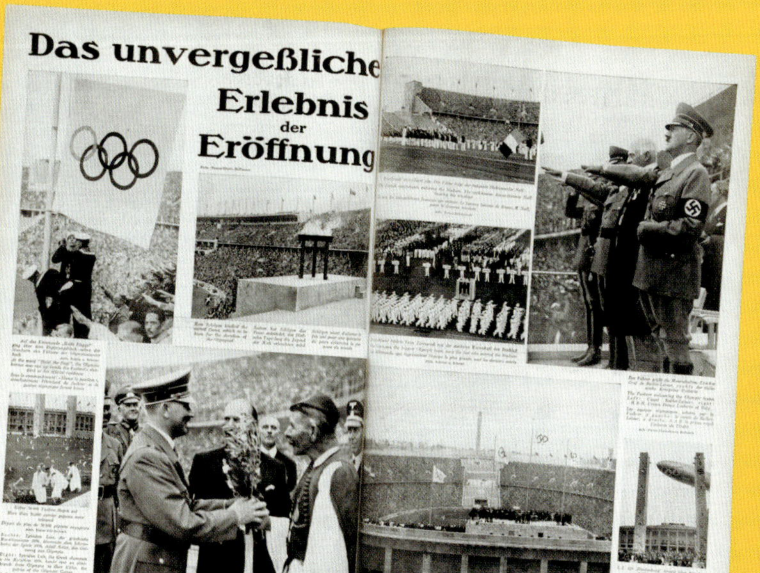

Das unvergeßliche Erlebnis der Eröffnung

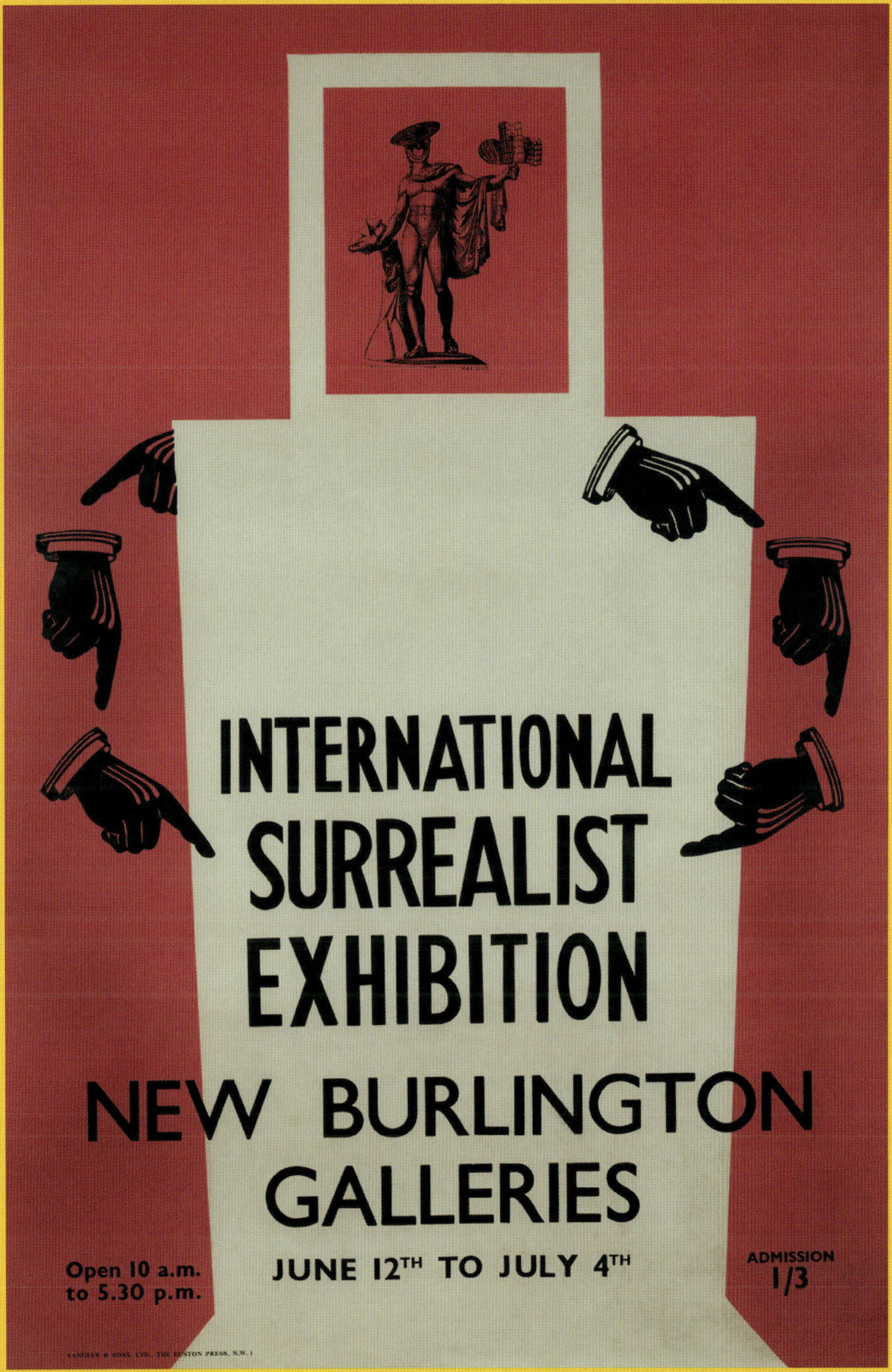

International Surrealist Exhibition Poster
Max Ernst, 1936

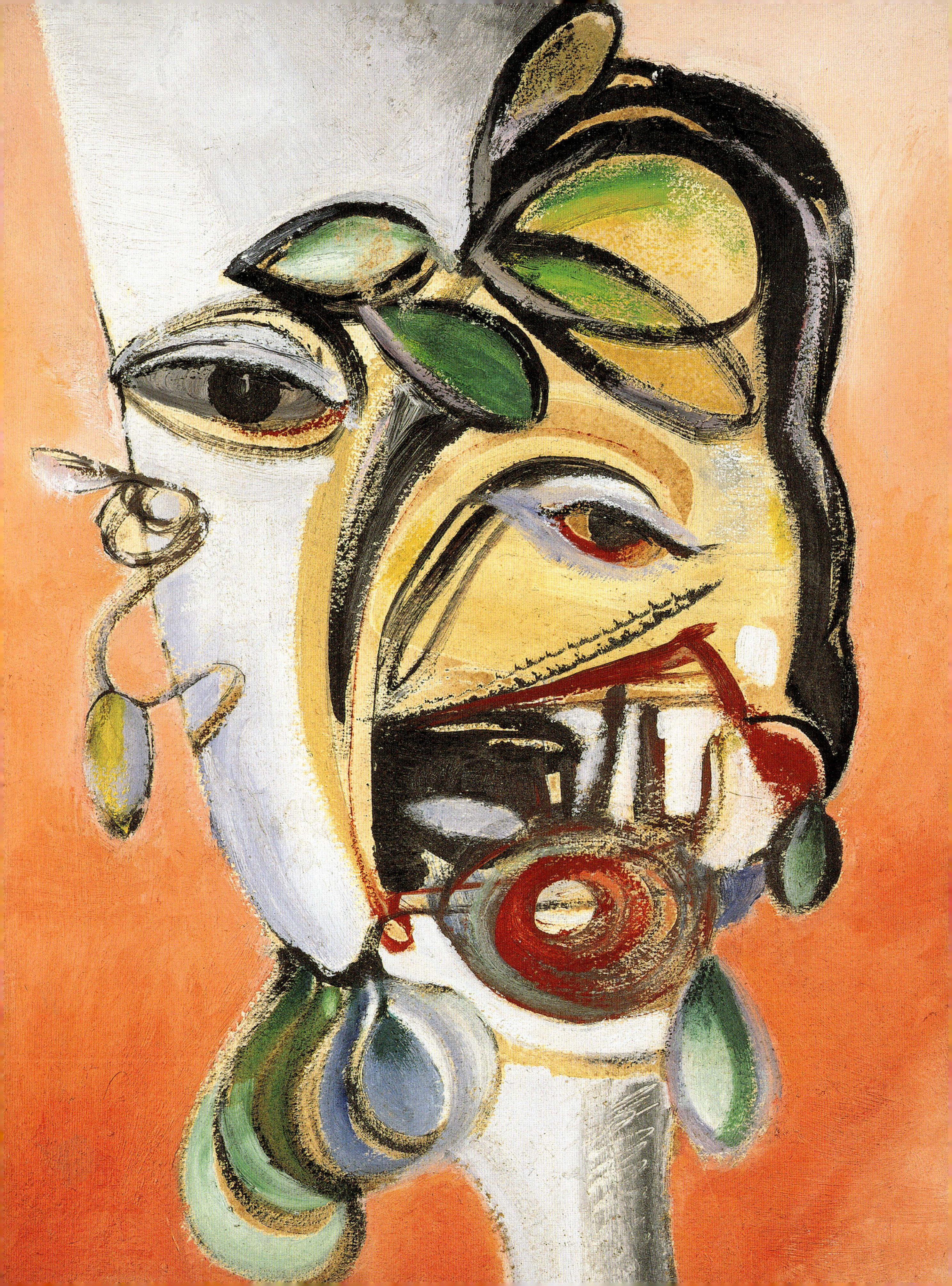

IRRUPTIVE, DISRUPTIVE, UNSWERVING SURREALISM

A CONTRIBUTION TO THE REASSESSMENT OF SURREALISM IN BRITAIN

MICHEL REMY

There was no dada movement in the England of the twenties to deliver Britain of any surrealist offspring. Not that surrealism is strictly speaking heir to dadaism, but it did arise from the ashes of the First World War through the iconoclastic ramblings of dada – a most fertile ferment. While 1924 can easily be taken as marking the beginning of deliberate, organized surrealist activity in France, it is much more difficult to give a precise date to the birth of the surrealist movement in this country. June 1936 is the year when the International Surrealist Exhibition, organized by Herbert Read and Roland Penrose, took London by storm, but more than heralding surrealism the exhibition confirmed that surrealism was already here. As André Breton put it in *Frontiers not Limits of Surrealism*, surrealism was here showing that it drew together 'the fertile resources of the literature and art of the past', that it had 'to pay a very major tribute to English literature and art' and that London was thus becoming the centre of 'the objectification and internationalization of surrealist ideas'.

Could we say, then, that the way had been paved? From an art historical point of view, there is no doubt that one can find harbingers of such radical revolt, but one must absolutely bear in mind that however rebellious they might seem, those occurrences in no way shared what will be at the core of the surrealist proposition: a pure, across the board form of uncompromising refusal in the name of the totality of the human being. It is interesting to notice that, however deeply shocking and disorientating the exhibition of post-impressionism organized by Roger Fry in 1910 might have been for a large part of the public, it boiled down to the affirmation of one simple specific aesthetic principle: the importance of structure independent of contents. Roger Fry's famous statement that the point was now 'to think form' heralded a totally disinterested art, an art of the timeless, not of the anecdotal, an art of the intellect, not of action. The breakthrough was of great importance, there is no denying it, but there was nothing which engaged the individual as a whole, least of all Fry's search for 'pure form'.

Transplanted
Emmy Bridgwater, c.1942

Among those who threw the conservative English art establishment into panic were Matisse and Picasso, the former for his unequalled use of colour and the latter for his disruption of conventional shapes and planes. They were both unwittingly at the origin of the great divide, which split English art until the advent of surrealism: Matisse was 'recuperated' by the Bloomsbury group with Roger Fry at its prow, while Picasso became the emblem of the imitators of cubism and inspired the development of English futurism, later called vorticism.

VORTICISM

During the first ten years of the 20th century, there undoubtedly emerged a questioning of artistic forms and, at a deeper level, a questioning of aesthetic criteria. The place of the viewer, in other words, was challenged and a sense of irreversible dislocation introduced, as vorticism emblematized.

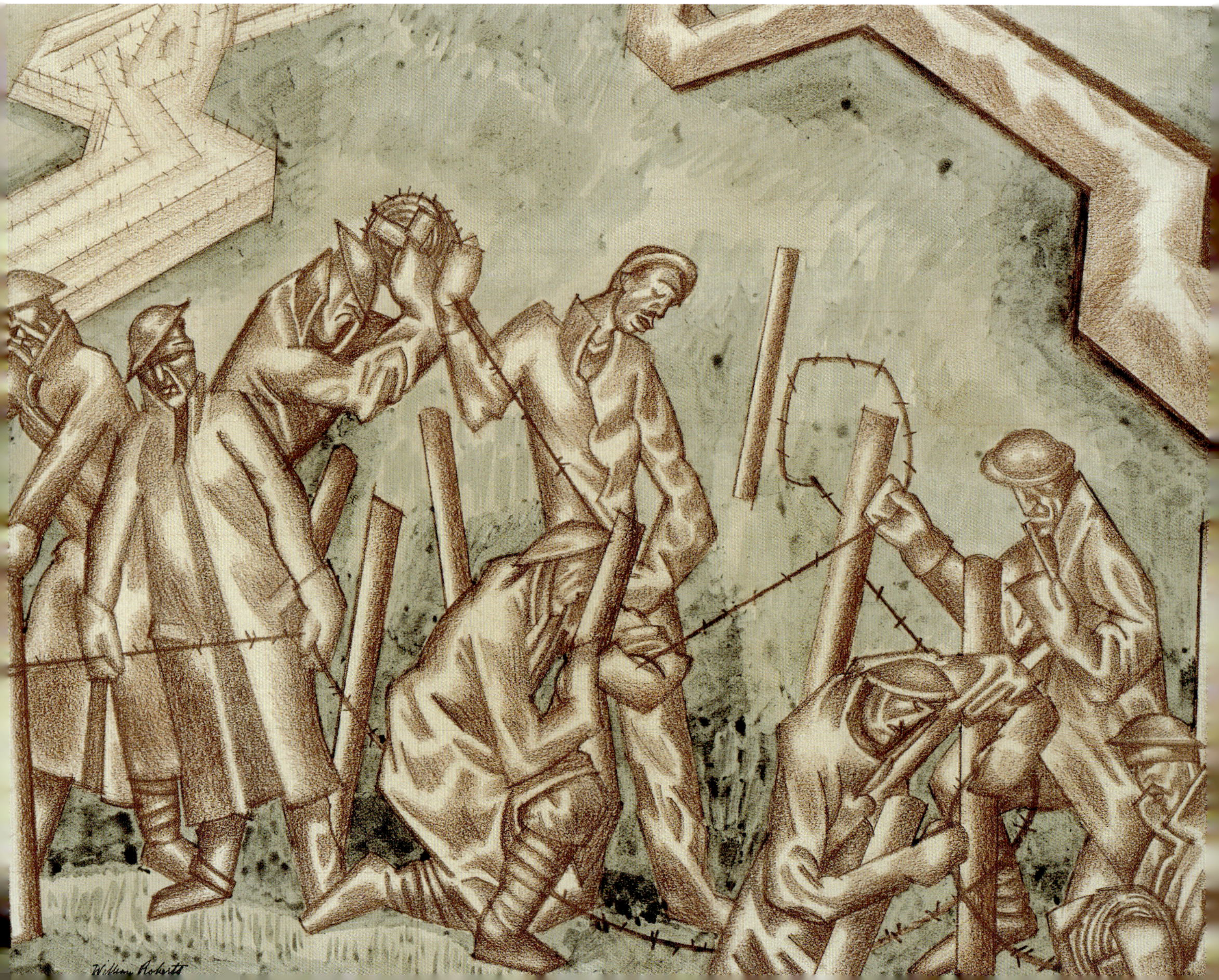

The Wiring Party
William Roberts, c.1915/18

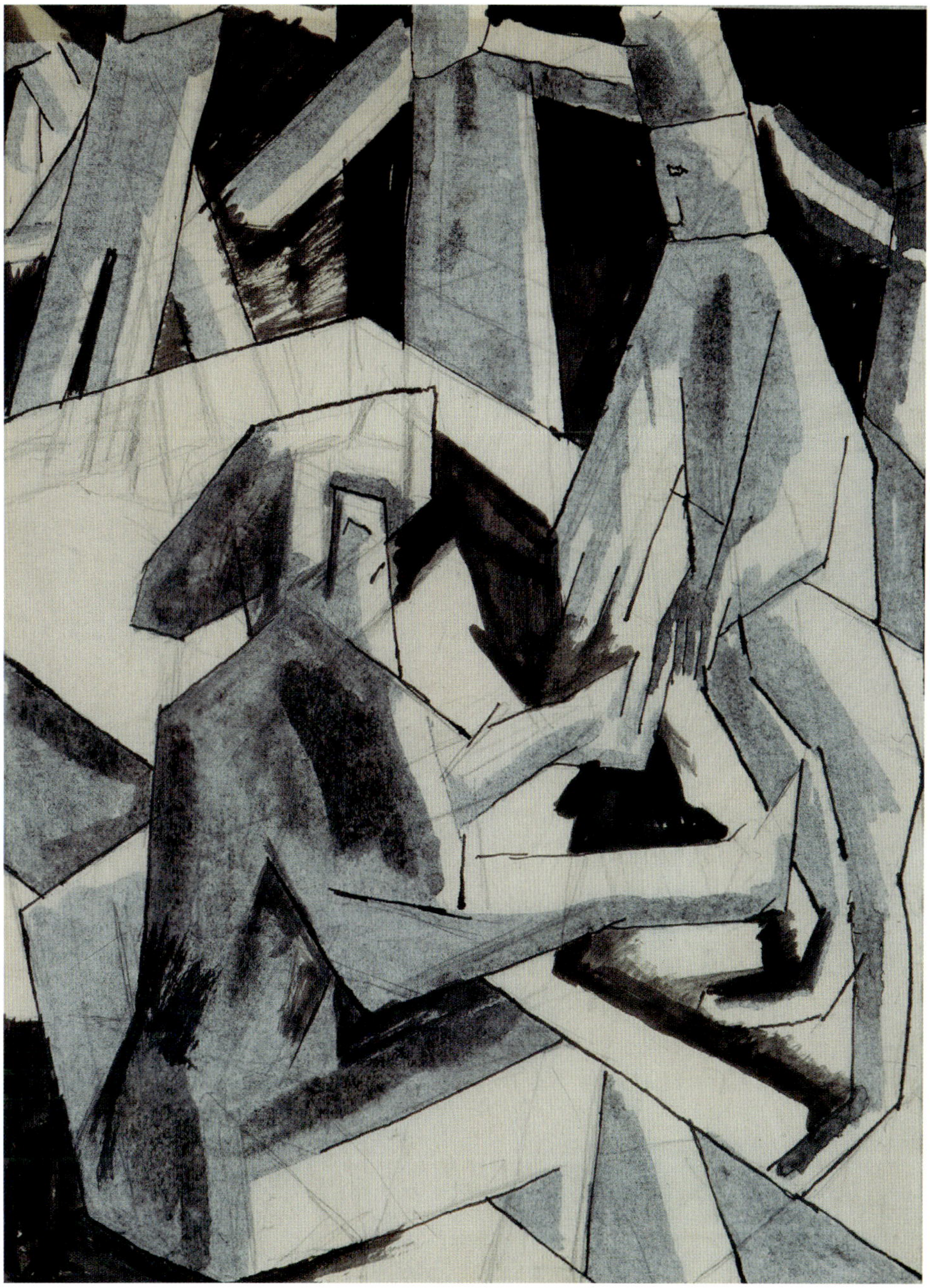

From the Players' Series
David Bomberg, 1913–1919

It dislocated the position of the viewer even before, paradoxically, resituating it within the development of the art world in a respectable manner, just like any other movement. However, on the whole, vorticism may well be seen as revolutionary not only in the sense that it had a political dimension – which is probably the only common point with surrealism, even if its political standpoint was almost at the opposite – but also in the sense that it brought to the fore the energy of the artist as an individual, an energy hailed as having to be proselytizing and iconoclastic. Vorticism tolled the knell of the organic and the naturalistic in favour of the mechanistic, which meant that any notion of morality was superseded by the notion of muscular energy and strong will. David Bomberg's *Players' Series* (1913–1919) and William Roberts' *Wiring Party* (1915–1918) exemplify this upsurge of reality-transforming energy and testify to how the vorticist revolt centred on a re-channelling of art into processes of heroicization (of the sailor, the worker, the soldier, the car driver, etc), which really were processes of narcissization and authoritarianism. All these new values, which heralded not so much a new world as new aesthetic priorities, were at the opposite of what was then brewing in France.

In other words, there was a belief in England that it was at the forefront of new aesthetic treatments of reality, but the other more dramatic reality which was to fall upon everybody, the reality of the war, soon demystified the celebrations of the Machine and the Will to Power. This, to a great extent, explains the decline of the vorticist messages and the simultaneous re-emergence of the Bloomsbury spirit which dominated the aesthetic life of England in the next ten years or so after the war. It is true that the radicalism of Wyndham Lewis, David Bomberg and William Roberts did open doors and disposed of any attachment to reality and mimetic aesthetics, but the failure of vorticism lies first in the paradoxical isolation of the artist, tied as he is to specific thematics and 'symbols' which actually bring him back into the social reality he wanted to leave, and secondly in the conviction that art was no longer to be seen as a militant form of activity and was no longer 'a matter of groups, programmes and manifestoes' (Wyndham Lewis). The paradox was to be solved by surrealism some fifteen years later.

This renewal would not come from groups which art historians see as landmarks in that troubled post-war period, the X Group and the Seven and Five Society. The former, created by Wyndham Lewis in 1916 with ex-vorticist members, returned to qualities of harmony, order and stability in an attempt to resist the growing influence of Bloomsbury – back to a certain kind of classicism in other words. The latter, formed in 1919, proclaimed 'that there has been of late too much pioneering along too many lines, altogether too much of a hurry, and themselves desire the pursuit of their own calling rather than the confusion of conflict.' Their inaugural declaration stipulated that they did not intend to 'demonstrate a theory nor to attack a tradition' and praised 'sincerity' in painting. All this, it is easy to realize, is timid, vague, over-cautious, and lacks ambition and, worse, it lacks working principles on which to elaborate a new *Weltanschauung*.

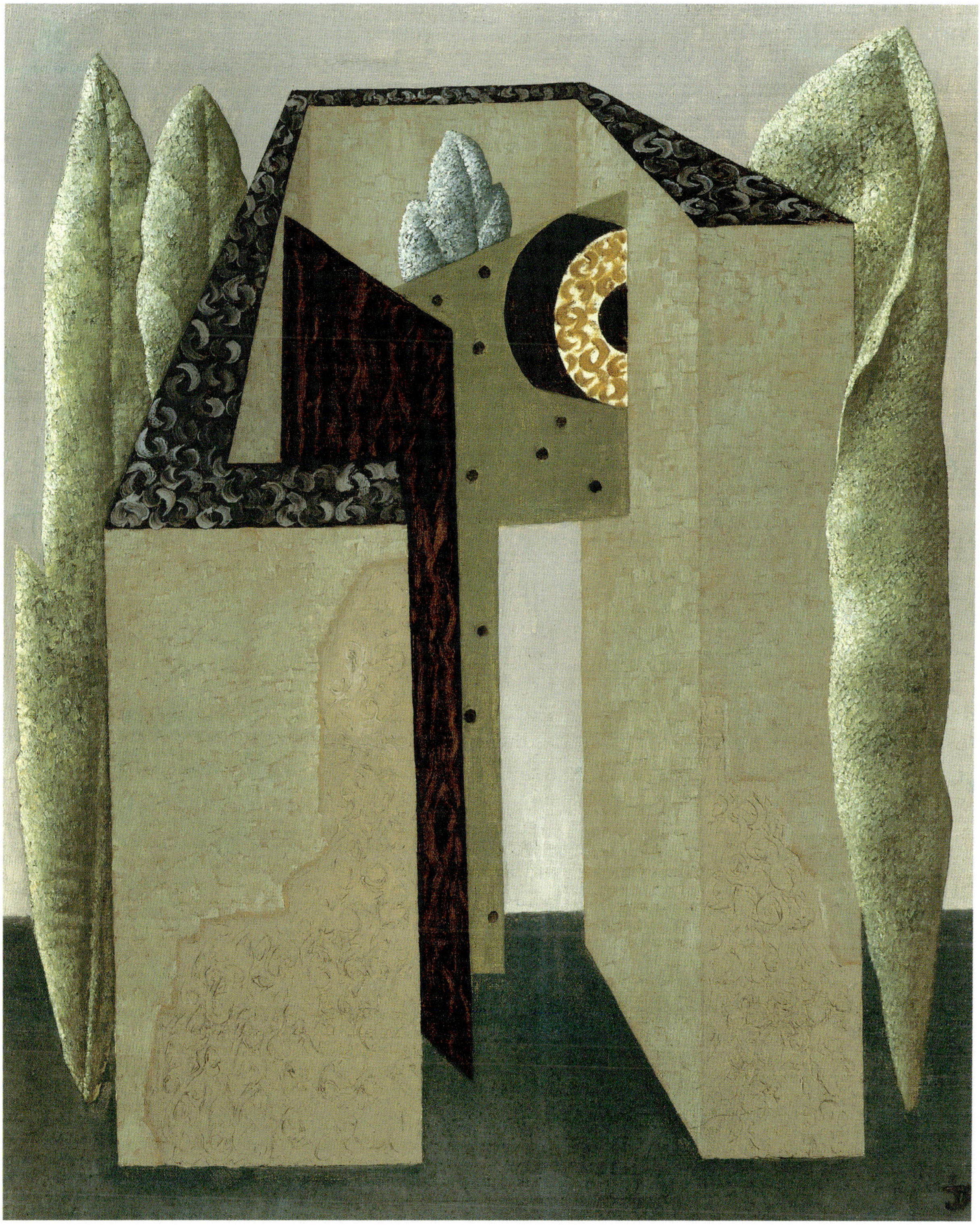

Unit One Composition
John Armstrong, 1933

UNIT ONE

The twenties, then, were perhaps 'roaring' in the field of fashion, but dull, withdrawn and uninspiring in the field of aesthetics. Only two artists seem to stand out, as is perceptively accounted for by Charles Harrison in his *English Art and Modernism*, Paul Nash and Ben Nicholson, who unwittingly represent the two trends which were to create a division in the artistic production of the thirties, with Paul Nash's work as the evocation of a mood of mystery and immanence in outdoor scenes devoid of human beings, places of encounters-to-be, and Ben Nicholson as the heir to cubism and the proponent of a formalist, frontal and flat presentation of abstract geometrical shapes involved in relationships strangely devoid of emotion. It is true that, however different they may be, Nash and Nicholson used the flat surface of the canvas as a place of subversion of that very flatness – possibly the only link one can see between them and surrealism. They also represent, however timorously, an opening of English art to European and, more specifically, French art, were it only through the connections they established with France and French artists.

Interestingly enough, these two trends – formally incompatible as they may appear – met again when Paul Nash and Ben Nicholson launched Unit One. As a movement it gathered seven artists chosen in the double name of 'Design and structural pursuit' and 'imagination explored apart from literature and metaphysics', a blending of forces – 'abstract art' and 'surréalisme' as Nash himself wrote - reducing Bloomsburyism to a passéist coterie. It let everyone believe, for a while at least, that those two forces were only mildly antagonistic, because, again in their founding declaration, there was no ethical principle which interrogated the place and status of man through the questioning of the place and status of the viewer.

At this stage, the decisive part played by Herbert Read should not be underestimated. Read, who, in a way, was challenging, if not replacing, Roger Fry as one of the gurus of the art world. The difference between the two was that Read had read Freud and Jung. Fry remained a formalist, while Read appeared as the upholder of the symbolizing activity of the subconscious. And indeed, this was what Unit One was to suffer from: the fragility of the link between the objective and the subjective, which surrealism acclaimed, proclaimed and strengthened.

In 1934, Unit One organised its only exhibition at the Mayor Gallery and published, at Read's suggestion, a volume of declarations and photographs. Both events created a great stir and drew undivided attention especially to

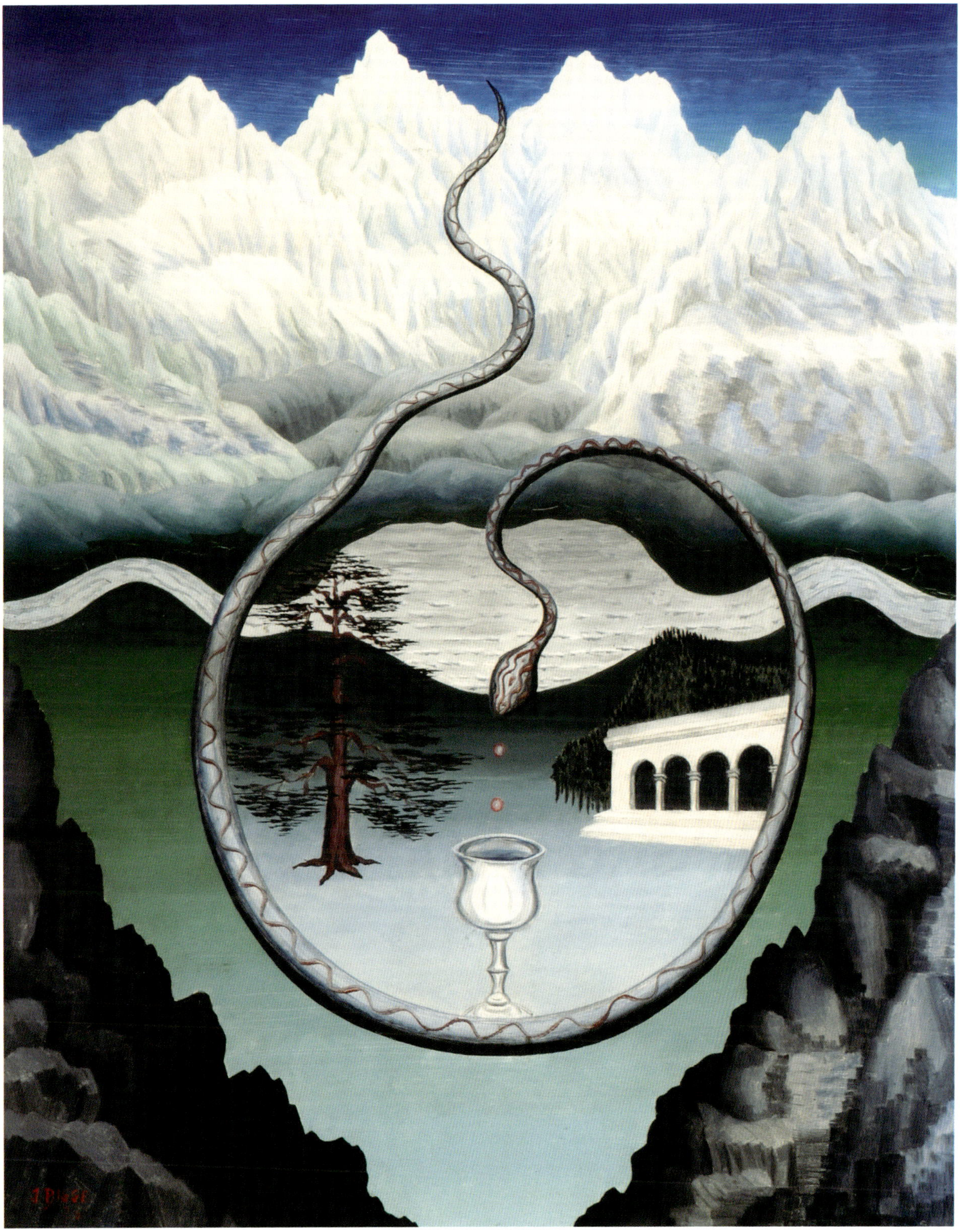

Tyrolean Dreams
John Selby-Bigge, 1935

the fact that all artists not only represented a kind of avant-garde but were all English, while previously key exhibitions had systematically included continental artists. Unit One gathered artists of completely different inspirations under the banner of the 'truly contemporary spirit', as Nash put it in his letter to *The Times* on June 12 1933, then in *The Listener* in July 1933, when he officially launched the group, adding that the activity of Unit One was 'the pursuit of form' and 'the pursuit of the soul' – clearly an attempt to bridge the gap between Fry and Freud, between abstraction and surrealism. Armstrong, Bigge and Burra represent this attempt to cross over and ignore differences just as Ben Nicholson, Hepworth and Wadsworth do. Towards that same goal, the former tendency adopted a veristic technique which could be called 'magic realism' with clear-cut forms, often out of proportion, enlarged, oversized compositions empty of human figures, a predilection for vegetable shapes often appearing monstrously, as in Armstrong's *Unit One Composition* (1933) and Bigge's *Tyrolean Dreams* (1935). The latter trend, under the influence of French cubism, evolved as an art based on abstraction, on impersonality and the collapse of finite forms into the infinite. On the whole, Nicholson and Hepworth stood for a purely technical approach to the essence of surfaces in relation to the former, and the essence of form to the latter, pointing to a kind of utopian dream of unity and harmony. The aim was to make the viewer feel the purity of surface and form as a key to a fundamental universality yet to be discovered. In her contribution to *Circle* in 1937, Hepworth wrote that 'these formal relationships have become our thought, our faith, waking or sleeping – they can be the solution to life and living. . . The language of colour and form is universal and not one for a special class. . . it is a thought which gives the same life, the same expansion, the same universal freedom to everyone'.

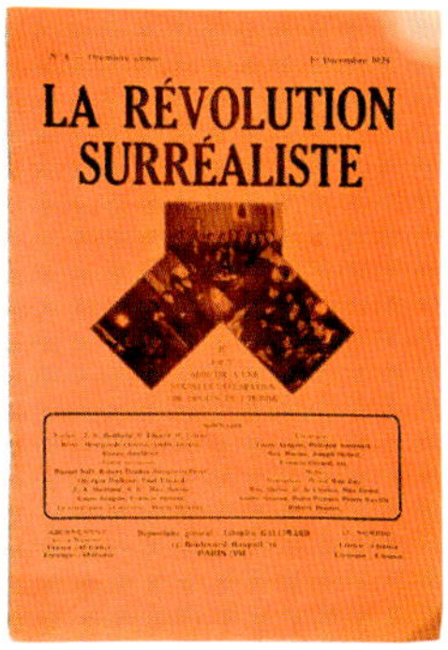

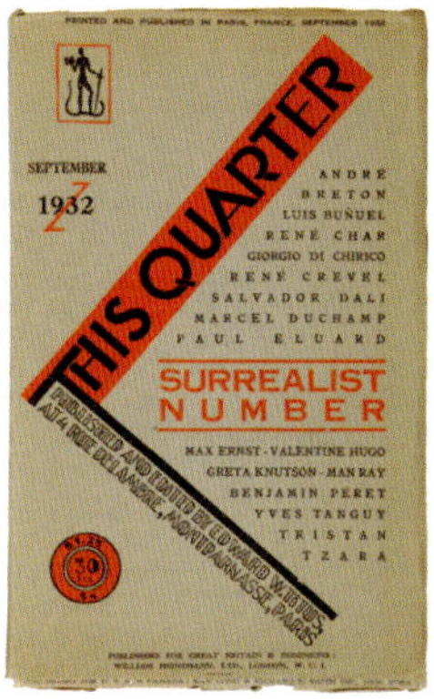

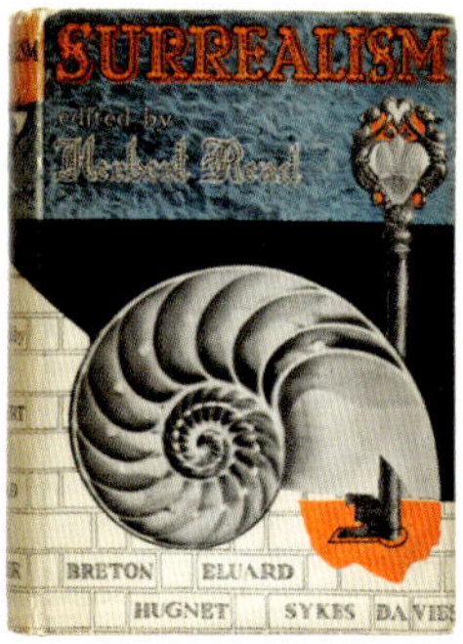

La Révolution Surréaliste
André Breton *et al*, 1924

This Quarter
Edward W. Titus, 1932

Surrealism
Herbert Read, 1936

This being said, could these differences between imaginative and abstract be erased or ignored? The historical unification of the two trends by Unit One did assert the existence of modern art in England, and this is an essential fact to remember, but the same two forces were bound to go into different directions and the unity so strongly affirmed by Nash and Read couldn't last. Unit One could only split, and the participation of Nicholson and Hepworth in the Seven and Five Society exhibition in 1935 sealed the split. A new 'spirit' was needed.

Symptomatically enough, 1935 was the year Herbert Read published a resounding essay entitled 'Why the English have no Taste'. It was also the year when several young artists who had reacted against the teaching they had received in the London schools of art and had left for France, were

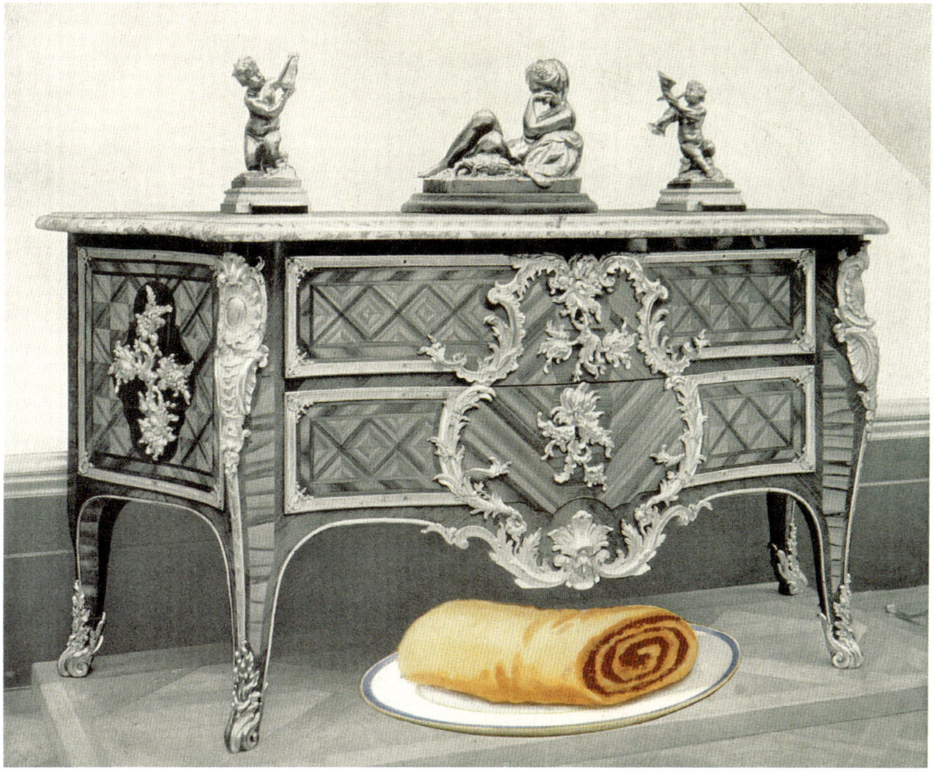

Commode with Swiss Roll
Humphrey Jennings, 1936

coming back from Paris. Eileen Agar, Roland Penrose, Julian Trevelyan, David Gascoyne and Humphrey Jennings, most of them on their second or third visit to Paris, brought back with them a determination to re-orientate their rebellion against conventionalism and traditionalism in art and were on the cusp of playing a crucial part in the development of surrealism in England. Coincidental with this, the publication of David Gascoyne's *A Short Survey of Surrealism* in November 1935, his translation of Breton's *Qu'est-ce que le surréalisme?* and, in February 1936, the publication of a collection of his surrealist poems *Man's Life is This Meat*, testified to the inevitability of the introduction of surrealism into England. The ground had been prepared, but in an unwitting and un-concerted way. Indeed, surrealism in England is the result of a necessity, emphasized by the fact that it was also the result of chance. Surrealism was born of the marriage of the heaven of chance and the hell of necessity.

In his essay 'Why the English have no Taste', published in the June 1935 issue of the French surrealist review *Minotaure*, Herbert Read provides a possible reason for the length of time it took surrealism to penetrate England when he co-figures the origin of the lack of taste in two historical facts, one religious; the emergence and dominance of Puritanism; the other, economic; the emergence of capitalism, the former as in-dissociable from, and

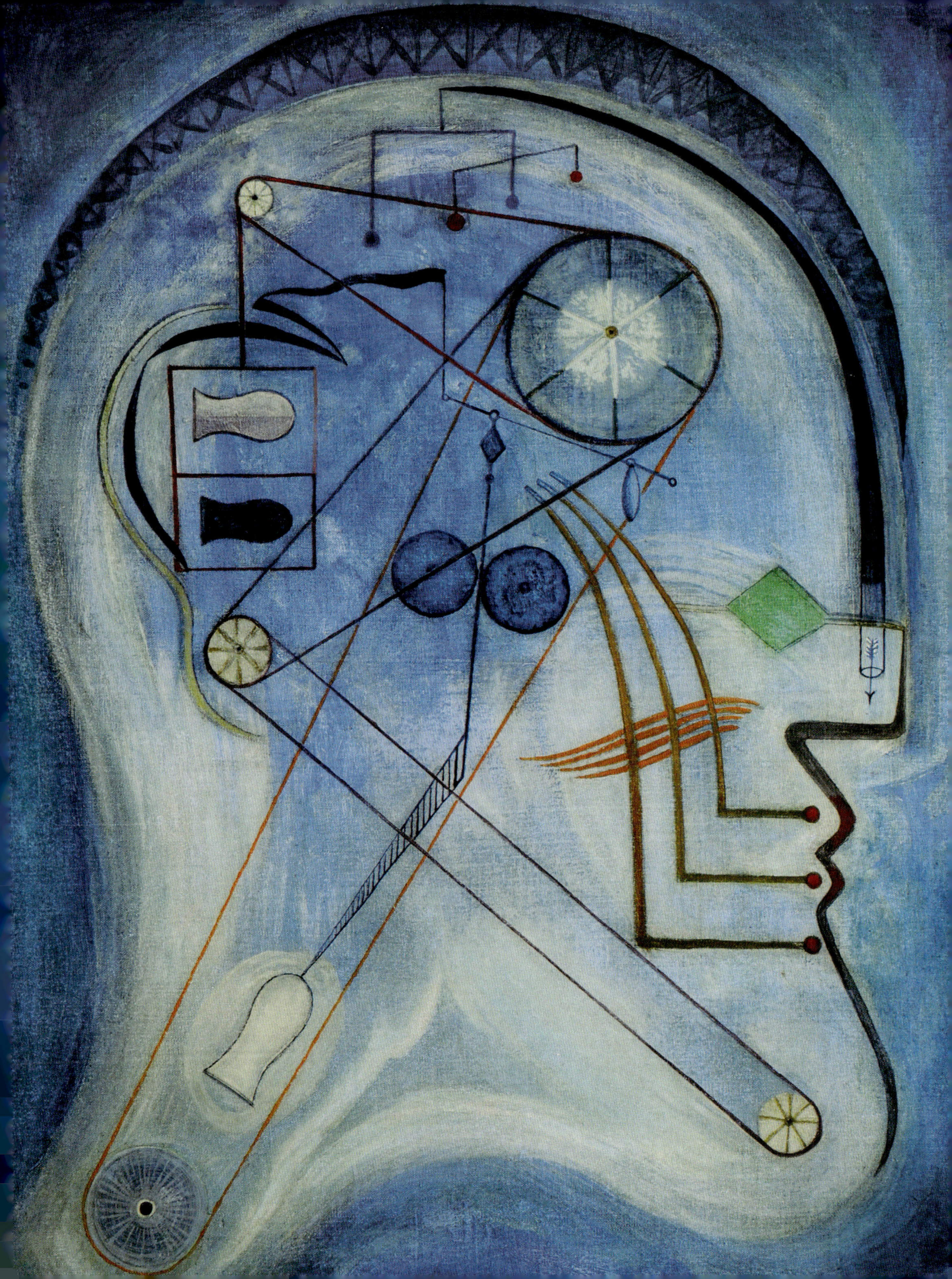

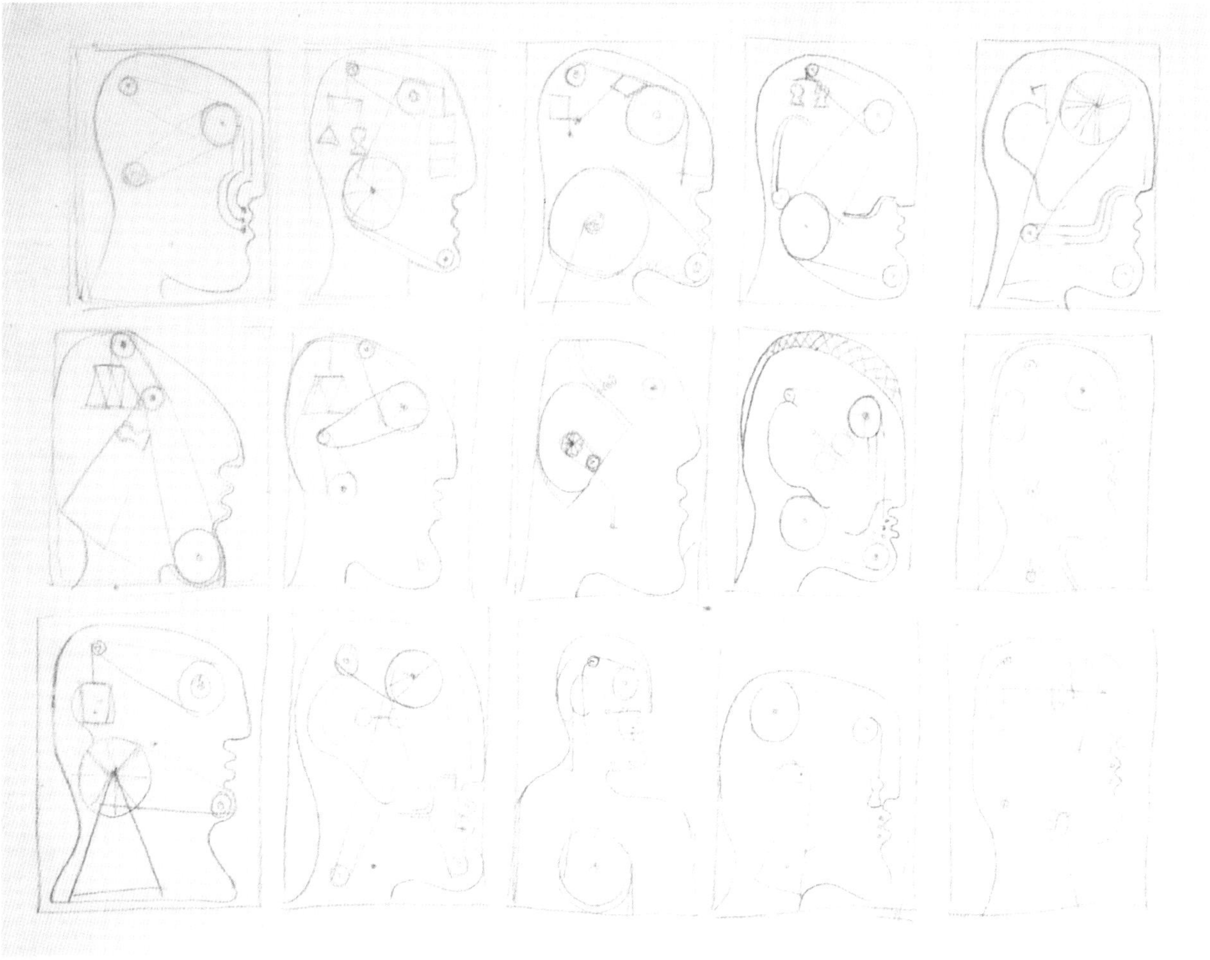

Hypnosis
Julian Trevelyan, 1935
with preliminary drawings

answerable for, the latter. The English ideal, he argues, is one of normality which, in itself, is a neurosis, a mask revealed as such by the famous English sense of humour, neither more nor less than an acute awareness of, and diffidence towards, what deviates from conventions and social codes. As a consequence, Read goes on, the fear of infringing upon the limits of normality deadens sensitivity, inhibits artistic expression and results in the lack of taste as well as the lack of mental and social freedom. Consequently, Read realised that any form of unconventional art, such as Unit One and, obviously and most superlatively, surrealism, was an unsurpassable antidote.

POLITICAL ACTIVISM

Now it is easy to understand how all the agitation and throes of aesthetic change in the art world over those years were transcended by surrealism, not only through an attitude which meant rising above dualisms and divisions between artists and movements, but also through, we might say, the magic of political commitment. For this is a crucial element to bear in mind: aesthetics, it was then felt almost as unavoidable, had to relate to politics. At any rate it is at the core of the surrealist proposition. Aesthetics could no longer be isolated from the world, artists could no longer ignore the socio-political situation around them and had to clearly state their positions here and now, as happened after the Spanish Civil War broke out when artists were invited to get together and publish their opinions. Since this should in no way be at the cost of what art is about, i.e. the emancipation of the mind, surrealism came as the answer: neither the magic realism of Bigge or Armstrong or Hillier, nor the abstract formalizations of Nicholson or Hepworth could satisfy the new needs of man, his hankering after both imaginative, free-wheeling visions and strict, structured compositions in a world which needed social transformation. A form of art was needed which would short-circuit the dualism between objectivity and subjectivity, the political and the non-political, the conscious and the subconscious, negation and affirmation, the ephemeral and the permanent. Surrealism was that movement.

In 1933, the Artists' International Association was founded, based on Marxist readings of society and the role of artists within it. The A.I.A.'s rather sketchy opinion on the significance of modern art – hesitating between seeing it as a means to defy bourgeois conservatism and seeing it as too remote from the social preoccupations of the proletariat – was balanced by its constant efforts to link up with various contemporary artistic events and even create those events, as when it invited the surrealist group, after it was formed, to its yearly exhibitions. This was made easier by the broadening of the A.I.A.'s aims when the Communist Party changed its policy and chose to prioritize opposition to Fascism and thus to ally with, and invite, all those who stood against Fascism, regardless of their opinion of Soviet politics. In 1934, the *Left Review* was launched, with contributions by Marxist celebrities such as Anthony Blunt, James Holland and James Boswell. These obviously challenged the idea that art might be 'pure form' by claiming that it was a human activity like any other, taking place in a given society at a given time in given social, political and economic conditions. Historical materialism was dealing the last blows to formalist aesthetics.

When the International Surrealist Exhibition opened in London on June 11, 1936, these aesthetic and political forces were brought together, as well as transcended if one may say, by another kind of force: 'a vertiginous descent into the dark, hidden territories' of the mind (André Breton in the *Second Manifesto*). In other words, it is the exploration of the subconscious. This definitely lent scope, depth, perceptiveness and a kind of radical self-questioning to art, placing the new irruptive movement high above, and at the margin, of all the others. Almost immediately after the exhibition and the launching of a properly constituted group, the movement in England independently of France, published a solemn and scathing *Declaration on Spain*, a simple broadsheet inserted in *Contemporary Poetry and Prose*, Roger Roughton's poetry review sympathetic to surrealism, which welded art and politics, by clearly emphasizing the similar goal of the two, the liberation of man's mind from the shackles of conservatism and its repressive quality. Through 1936 and 1937, a fierce debate took place in the pages of *Left Review* between surrealists and left-wing theorists, the latter reproaching the former with still behaving and thinking like bourgeois-minded artists. Nevertheless, in 1937, 43 English surrealists were invited by the Marxist Artists' International Association to exhibit in defence of the 'Unity of the Artists for Peace, Democracy and Cultural Development'. In 1939, the *London Bulletin* published a broadsheet 'To All the Workers in England' to unite against the war.

FULL FORCE AHEAD

The ten years or so which correspond to the official, constituted existence of surrealism in England from 1936 to 1947 (before it re-emerged twenty years later) saw a formidable concentration of strategies all aimed at bypassing sterile discussion or argument about the validity of the abstract or the figurative, of objective or subjective art forms. Emblematic of surrealism's deep disregard of such issues is the collaborative work of Reuben Mednikoff and Grace Pailthorpe for which André Breton confessed his unbounded admiration at the June 1936 exhibition. Together, they worked

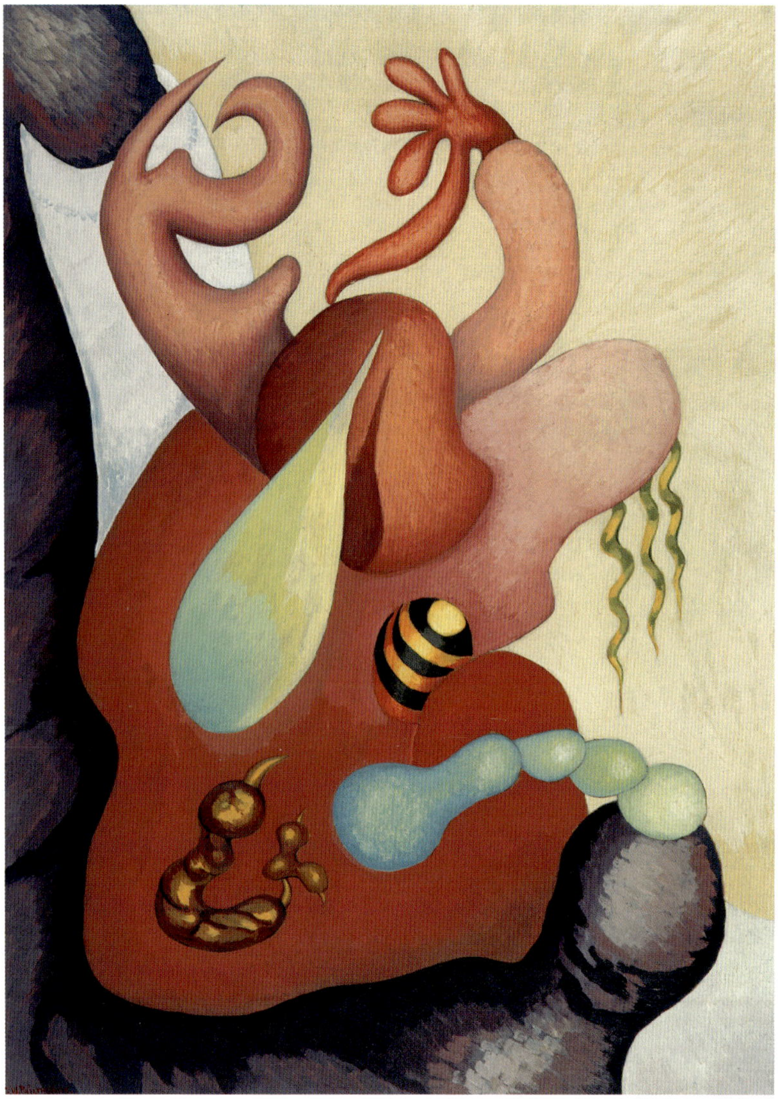

April 1922, 1940
Grace Pailthorpe, 1940

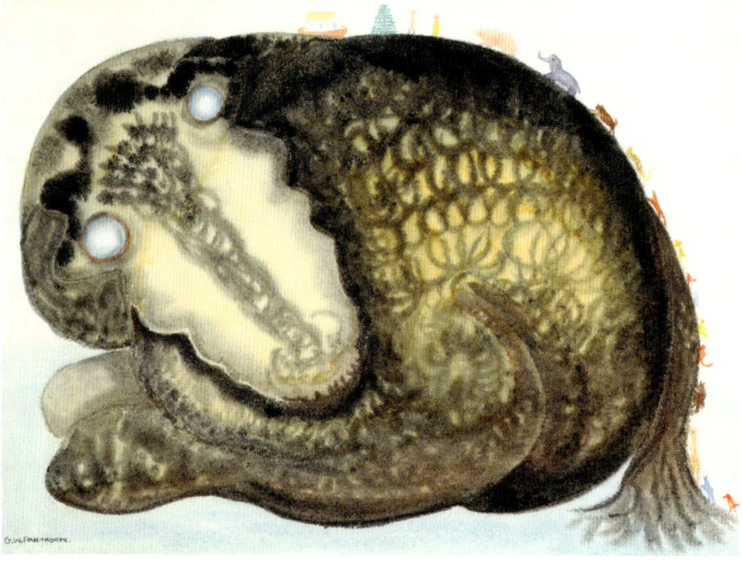

November 3, 1937
Grace Pailthorpe, 1937

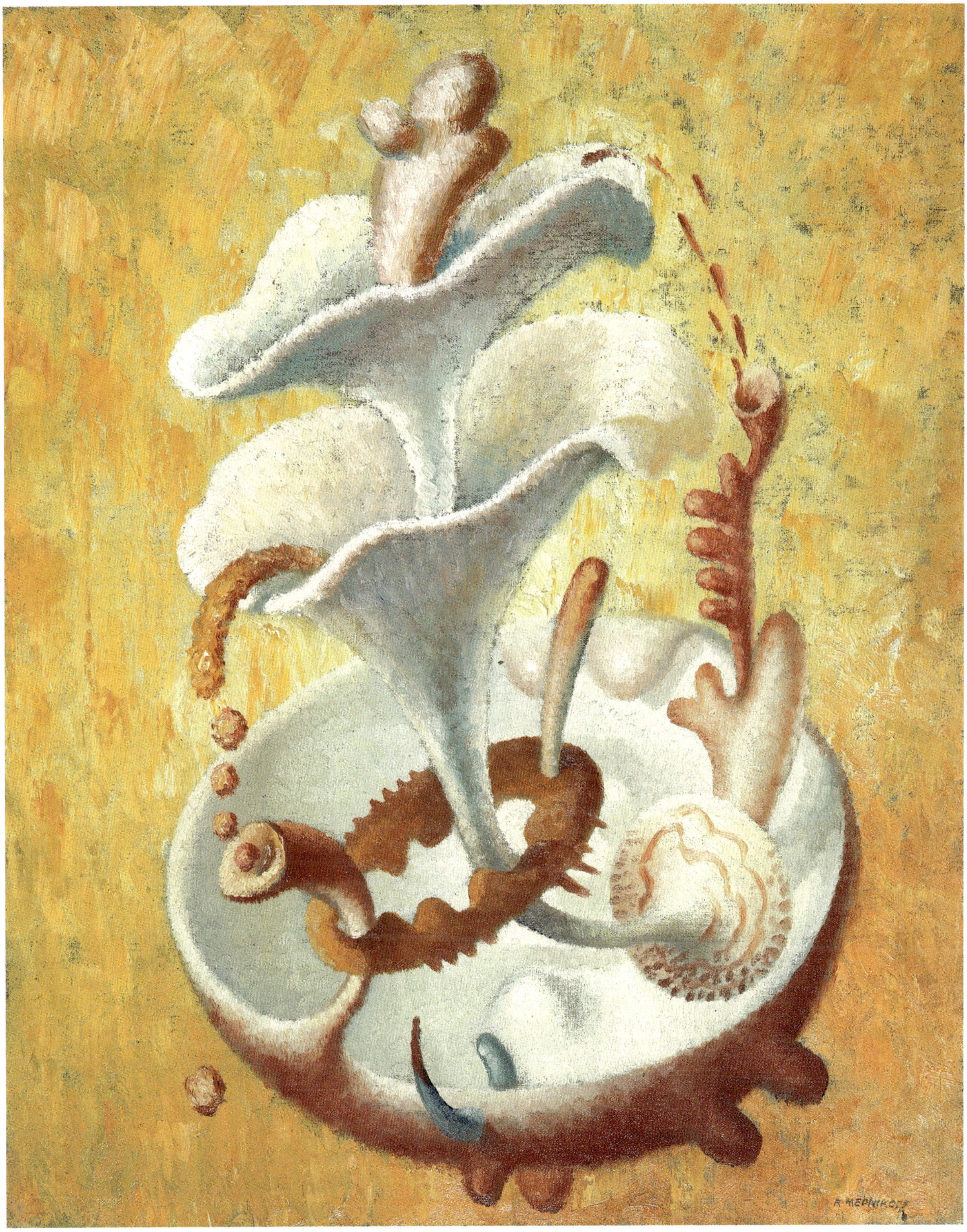

April 23 and 24, 1935 (Arborial Bliss)
Reuben Mednikoff, 1935

intimately on their respective drawings and paintings, cross-psychoanalyzing each other, and delivering the delicious and delirious creatures which haunt our subconscious. Even more emblematic of this is the title of Pailthorpe's drawings exhibited there, *Ancestors*, a hint at, and tribute to, what founds our mental lives. The result of the automatic, spontaneous outpouring of subconscious pulsions, hard severe faces, masculine jaws, breasts and wombs – nipple-eyes opening on top of protuberances – rush forth from the depths of the mind. Both Mednikoff and Pailthorpe attempted to explore the origins of the images which haunt us and constitute the deep layers of our Being and to establish a grammar and narrative of those images. Pailthorpe's *November 16, 1937* manifests the drama of birth, the foetus-like arthropod seeking protection under the mother's armpit as it discards the eggs it comes from. All Pailthorpe's works are torn between protection and separation in a straightforward, uncompromising confrontation with the trauma of birth and the relation with the mother. Mednikoff's own research into his own repressed impulses is revealed in every single drawing and painting, as in *Arboreal Bliss* (April 23 and 24, 1935), which he himself described as 'an orgy of sucking milk and faeces out of mother with my penis and mouth'. Sadistic treatments of oral and anal images abound in Mednikoff's production in an attempt to confront the liberation of repression and, in their endless process of self-division and emergence of shapes, they chart a fluid space of ever-renewed dissemination, which, we soon realize, is also a space lying deep down in us. These are our enigmas. Indeed, what is fundamental to understand is that Mednikoff and Pailthorpe situated themselves right away at the aboriginal place and moment of the creative urge, the place and moment when man is liberated, for a fraction of second, from what represses him, socially and psychologically, and creates. This is why there is much more than what psychoanalytical descriptions may reveal, there is an exuberance, an energy, an expansiveness in their works which projects them outside the scope of any rationality, authority or truth, even theirs. Mednikoff and Pailthorpe are the superlative surrealists who proved the radical irreducibility of the surrealist undertaking – and therefore their, and its, permanent validity beyond any aesthetic consideration.

Collage is a powerful way of challenging aesthetic criteria whilst placing the viewer in an intermediary position, between acquired beliefs and the refutation of those beliefs. The minimalist quality of Jennings's collages, for example, forcefully increases their disruptive quality. *Commode with Swiss Roll* and *Hospice de la Bernina* are cases in point: the photographs used for the collages, cut-out and glued together, oppose and contradict each other in the most obvious way. In so doing, they suspend their

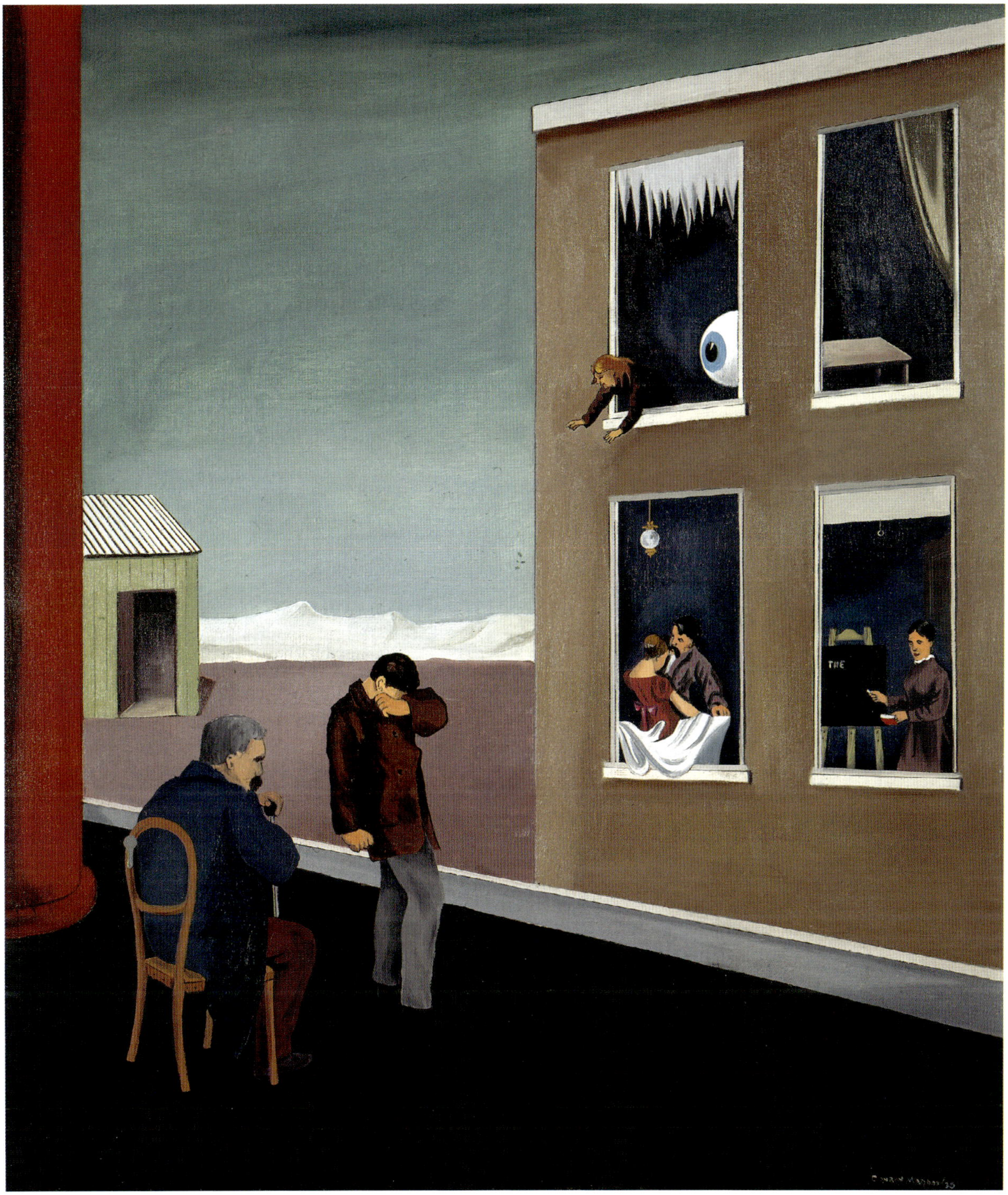

The Lesson
Conroy Maddox, 1938

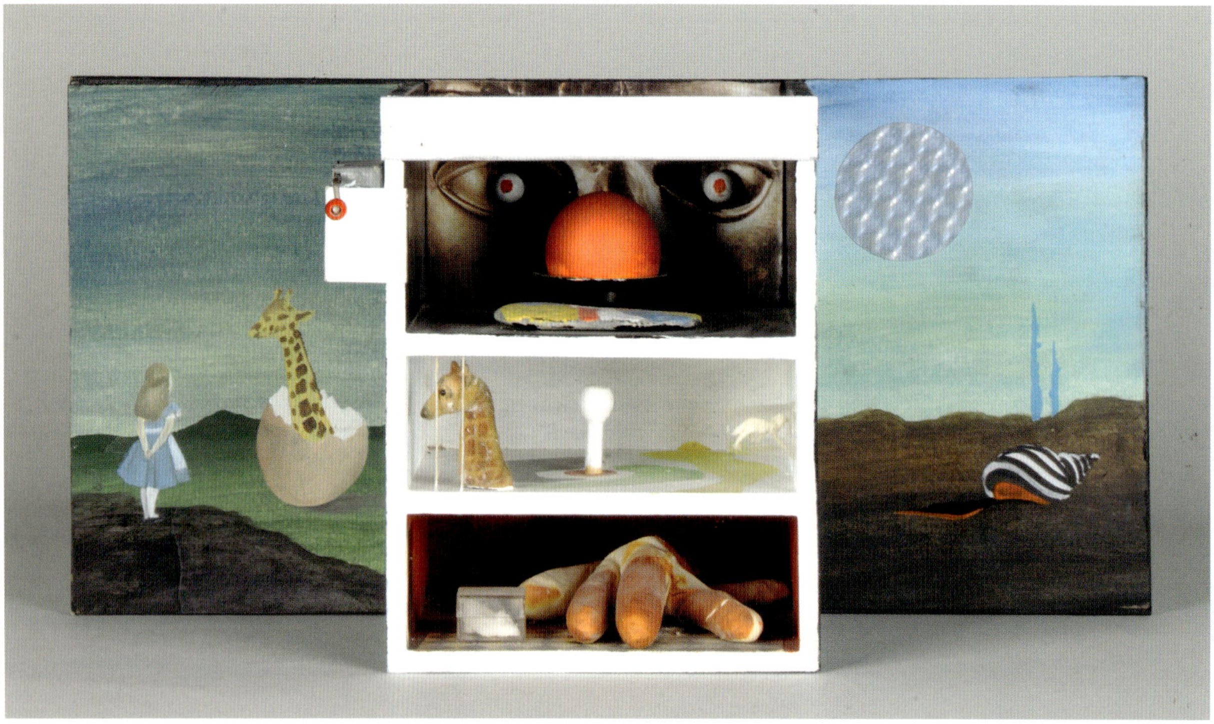

A Secret Doll's House
Conroy Maddox, 1994

representationality, their mimetic quality, to enter a space in which they can no longer be identified only as what we have learnt they were, but are made to tend towards something radically different. Each of the collaged elements is dis-placed from itself, literally dis-located in a frontal, straightforward way. The trick does not actually stem so much from a deliberate choice of the artist – this is only the first stage – as from elements from reality, the artist being a mere instrument and the viewer, the one who is led to conceive the relationships at work in the collage against all preconceived laws of reality. In other words, reality throws doubt upon itself and puns on itself. Here again, one realizes the active role given by surrealism to the viewer – the eventual maker of the work.

The principle of collage, as we have just seen, lies at the origin of Maddoxian aesthetics. Conroy Maddox's paintings – in which Magritte seems to meet Chirico under the aegis of Sade, Lautréamont, Bataille and Freud – are encounters which precipitate everyday life objects into a world of desire. In *The Lesson*, the scenes which the young man refuses to see at the windows of the house – in other words the symbolic body – are the visual expression of the unnameable, of the obscene, as is indicated by the missing word on the blackboard of the schoolmistress, which she is about to teach. The viewer, the young man's alter ego, can only add up all the clues given in the windows – a woman threatened by phallic icicles and an eyeball, the sign of castration, a dancing couple engaged in the prelude to lovemaking, a curtain drawn on a scene/ stage about to be peopled – in the hope of finding a meaning, but, in so doing, he yields to a general short-circuiting of relationships and enters the dark territory of fears, complexes and desires, which one cannot fully face although highly tempted to. In his powerful collage *Reflections on Prince Vibescu*, an homage to Apollinaire, the obscene sexual pun in the French name of the prince (cock, fuck, arse) is rendered through the disjunction of sexual images which force the viewer to piece them together and, in so doing, gradually reach deeper layers of meaning. In his objects, the *Onanistic Typewriter* (1940), in his *A Secret Doll's House* (1994) or in *Denouément* (c.1946), Conroy Maddox insists on hinting at un-avowable stories, 'mysterious and ineluctable' as he said, whose successive elements take us to the limits of desires and taboos. There also lies the origin of his interest in the manifestations of hysteria, first depicted by Dr Charcot in Paris at the end of the 19th century and then by Freud and Breuer in their joint studies, as appears in *The Playground of Salpêtrière* (1975), in which, as he said in the eponymous text he wrote in 1940, we are faced with 'an image of exquisite anonymity, of imperturbable contradictions, an image so uncertain that it seems to forever tremble between the believable and the unbelievable and phantom-like questions the validity of all that surrounds you'.

Maddox's friend in Birmingham, John Melville, is another of the surrealists who was first influenced by Max Ernst's collages and Picasso's cubist works, but also went beyond those two influences right into surrealism, joining the English group in 1938. This move is announced in his *Reclining Woman* of 1934 in which a body is seen in its un-making. Later on, Melville's gloriously surrealist *The Museum of Natural History of the Child* (1937) – an acquisition of the Leeds Art Gallery – is one of the cult works of the movement, a sexually-haunted fantasy developing between animal and vegetable forms from the upturned head of a boy.

Toni Del Renzio's mindscapes invite us in the same way into the regressive and repressed zones of the subconscious. In *Paranoiac Regression* (1941), he is actually breaking through the barrier of repression in the 'devoutly to be wished' regression into the hinterland of the face, now empty of its features, where desired encounters take place; this would mean the end of all external authority, especially paternal. Does it signify that only paranoia can liberate us, however painful that may be?

Inventiveness is the word which best defines Roland Penrose. Not only as regards to the crucial part he paid in the introduction of surrealism into

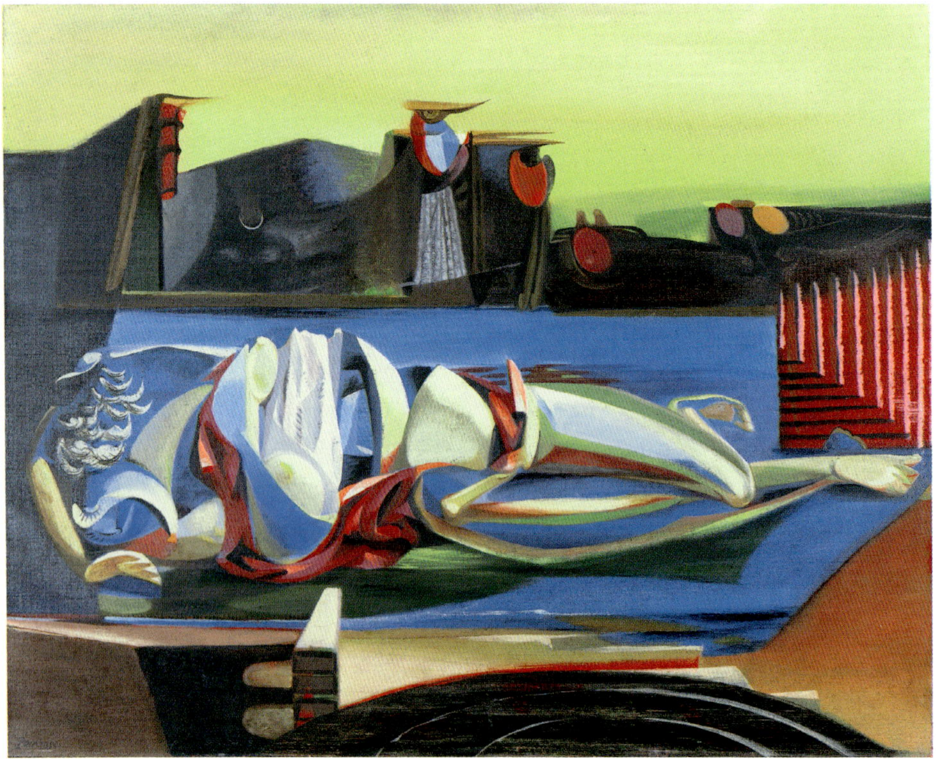

Unsleeping Beauty
Roland Penrose, 1946/47

England, but also as regards his versatile and thought-provoking techniques. Again, his approach is essentially that of collage, but a collage which is aimed at the radical revision of the status of the image itself and of the body as a place of deconstruction, in other words, a place where fragmentation is a way to reveal a fundamentally self-dividing unity, a unity which is clearly postulated, and not ascertained. This is exactly what his extensive production of a new, original, kind of collage from 1937 onwards, based on the use of colour postcards, testifies to. This technique, celebrated by Nougé and Magritte in an article published in the *London Bulletin*, takes collage beyond the limits Max Ernst had so splendidly given it: by juxtaposing and overlapping, as the case may be, a set of exactly identical postcards into fan or butterfly shapes, the figurative contents of the cards are made to recede, other images born of those on the cards are liberated, the unpredictable product of the repetition and specific arrangement of the cards. This means that those images were always already there, virtually, potentially, lying beneath, and they emerged from behind, at the simple visual contact with the viewer's eyes. It is this potentiality which also defines surrealism, a potentiality which, contrary to the previous artistic movements, engages the whole of the subject.

Interestingly enough, the same idea of an impossible whole which is merely hinted at by fragments, but fragments never sufficient to complete that whole, fragments always operating as fragments and not as parts of a construction,

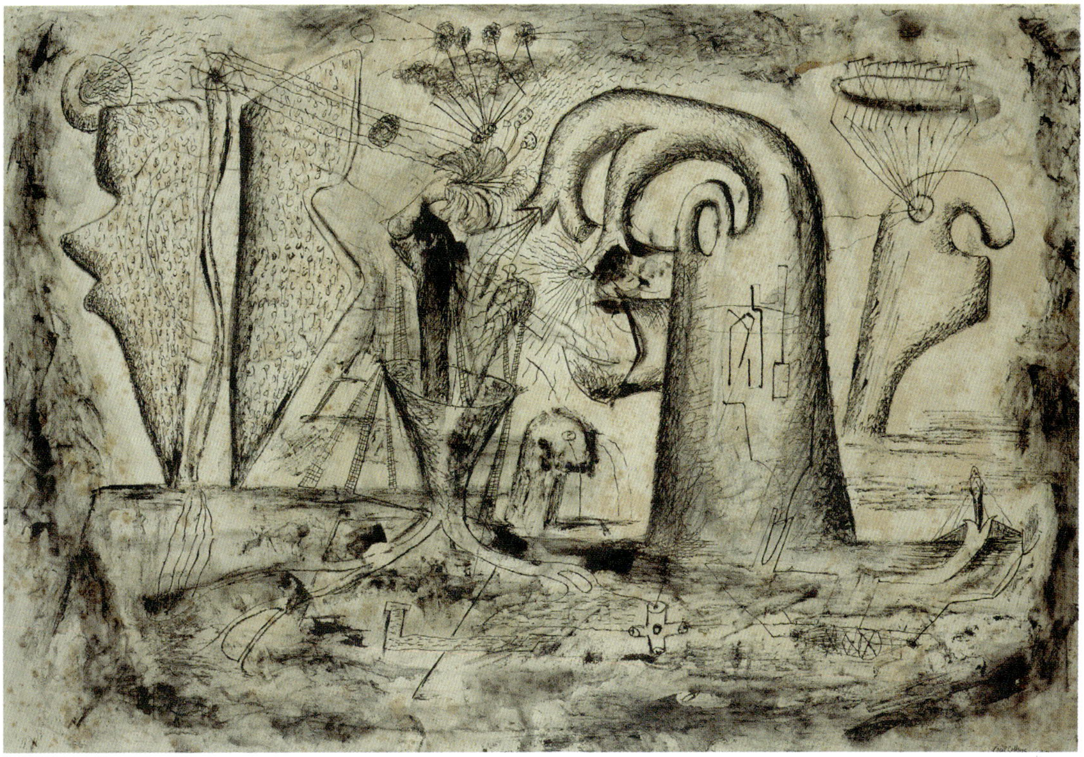

Obsequies of Time
Cecil Collins, 1933

is at the origin of Penrose's astonishing vision of Lee Miller in *Unsleeping Beauty* (1946) in which the body, seen to be reclining on a couch of some kind, is dis-membered before being re-membered by the viewer's erotic desire, as through a magic life-giving ritual. The painting stages the awakening to a new life, a gradual coming into existence again – as in the fairy tale – under the many eyes of a totem-faced mountain ridge, that of Arizona, where Lee Miller and Roland Penrose were staying at Max Ernst and Dorothea Tanning's place in Sedona, near Phoenix. The deconstruction at work, i.e. the undecidable operation of destruction and construction experienced by those fragments, is brilliantly expressed in the title – indeed, between sleeping and awakening, there lies the beauty of insatiable desire and of the impending act of love, the prince's kiss! In relation to this approach based on the notion of renewal, we should not underestimate Penrose's political militancy, especially when he went to Spain in November 1936 with his first wife, Valentine, David Gascoyne and Christian Zervos, the editor of *Cahiers d'Art*, to answer critics and check that, in spite of revolutionary acts of violence, 'monuments had been revered and protected in some cases more efficiently by the Republicans than by the Church'. Later, Penrose was active in organizing the 1st of May 1938 demonstration against Chamberlain and the opening of the Guernica exhibition at the Whitechapel Gallery in 1938 with Labour Party leader Clement Attlee, giving to Picasso's masterpiece its full, uncompromising political meaning.

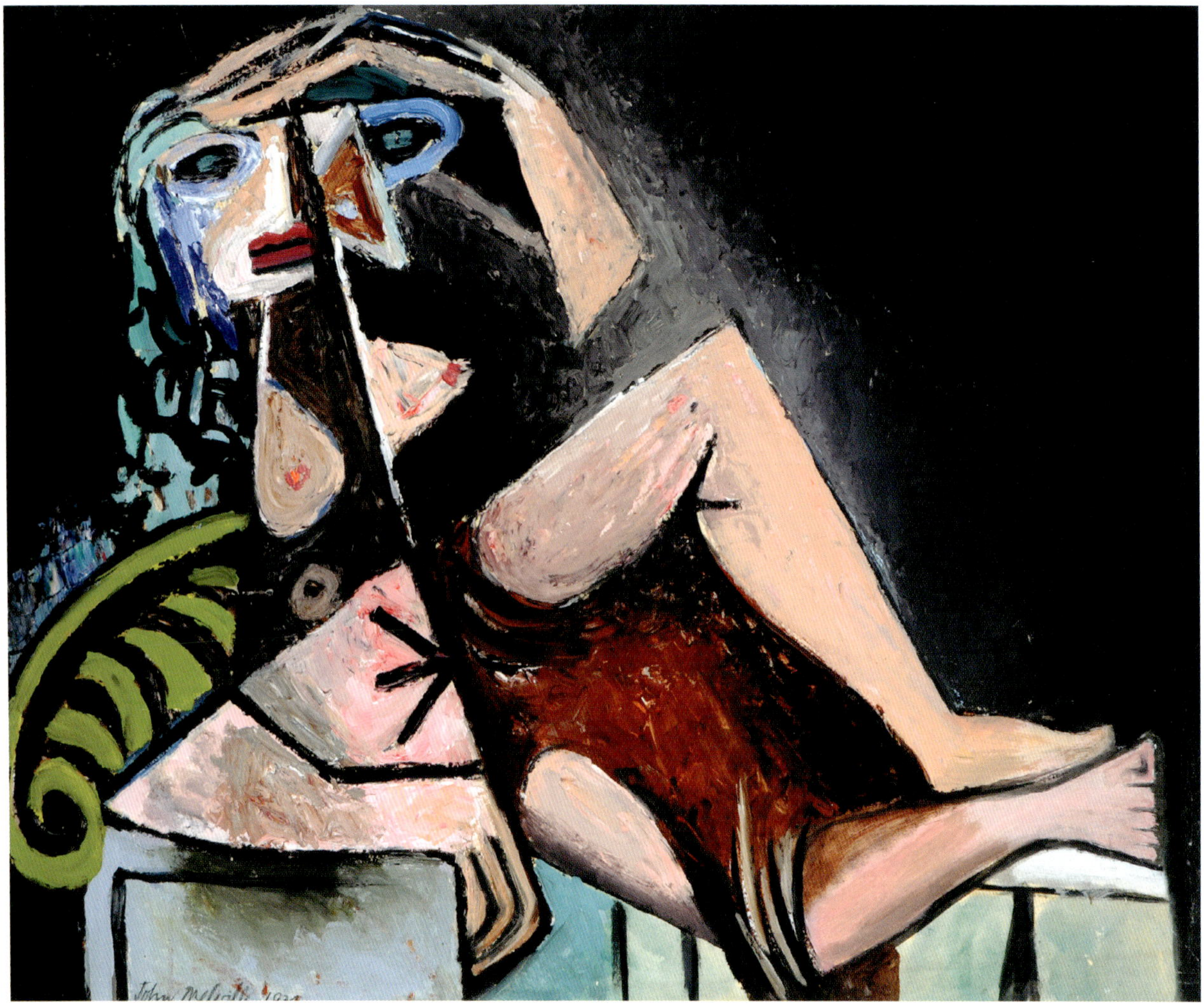

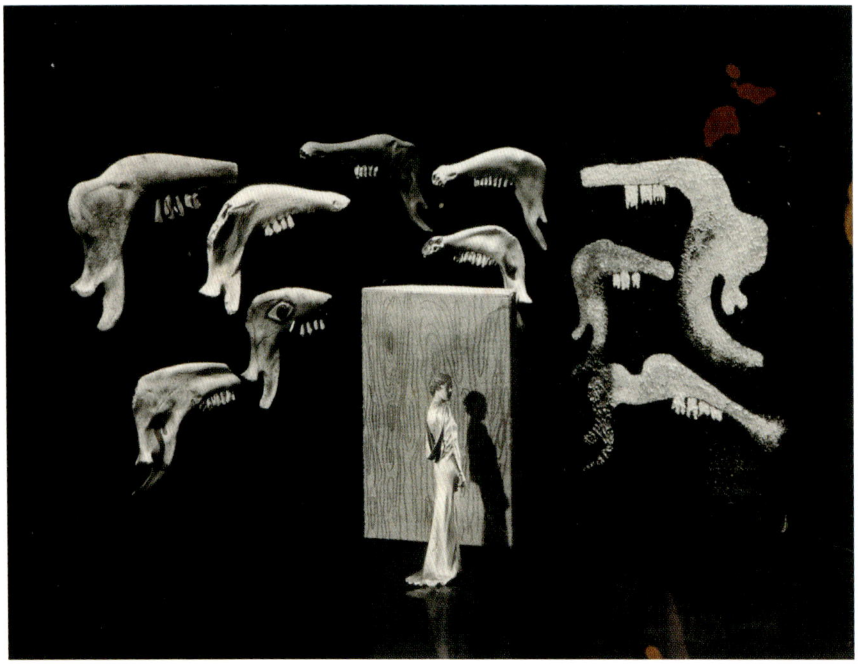

Reclining Woman
John Melville, 1934

A photograph taken by Humphrey Spender for the *Vogue* magazine and a 'montage' by John Banting for a *Vogue* display

WOMEN SURREALISTS

British surrealism has probably been the only surrealist movement in which women came powerfully to the fore and played a crucial part, thus giving the lie, if need be, to what critics, like Whitney Chadwick, too easily caricatured, namely the submission of women by their fellowmen within the surrealist ranks. In England, five women stand out – to whom should be added Grace Pailthorpe, dealt with above – exerting their full independence within the group. The history of Eileen Agar, Emmy Bridgwater, Edith Rimmington, Ithell Colquhoun and Lee Miller is strongly marked by a total absence of exploitation by 'male desire and dominance', and demonstrates their claim – tacit or not – to both aesthetic and individual freedom, these two aspects being inseparable.

Eileen Agar's *Angel of Mercy* (1934) is not strictly speaking a surrealist work, but it opens the way to the ironical play with aesthetic formalism. Indeed, here, the plaster cast surface turns into a kind of playground, combining, and distancing itself from both modernity and ancient artistic forms – fluid spiralling lines and more or less geometrical areas of colour – and playing with dualities. This apparent lightness of tone makes us understand why collage became Agar's main means of expressing the deep, intimate relationships between the mineral, animal and vegetable kingdoms by overlapping and juxtaposing and distributing in her works, as in *Foot in Hand*

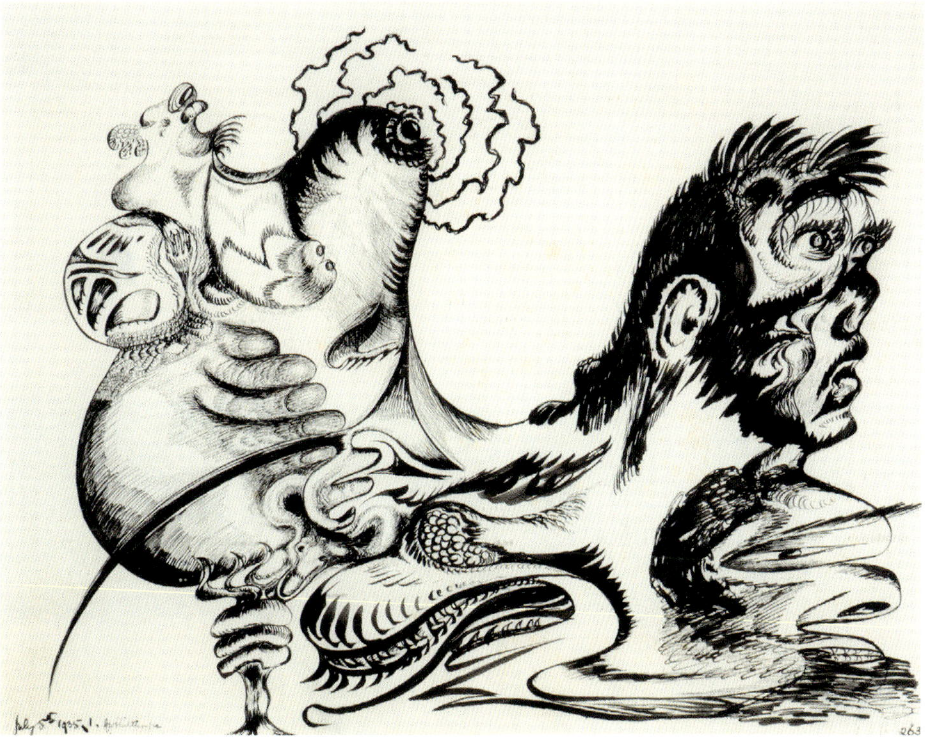

July 5, 1935-1
Grace Pailthorpe, 1935

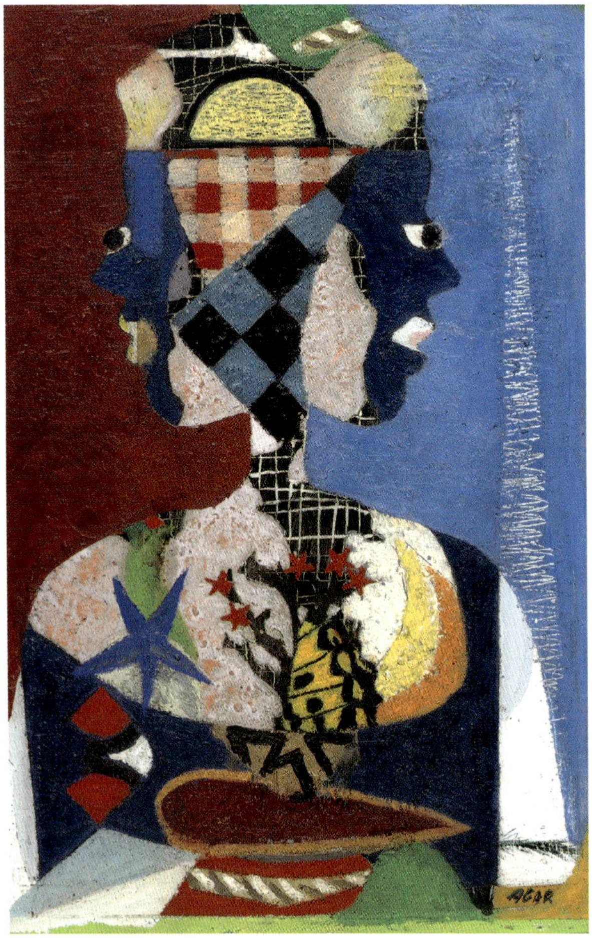

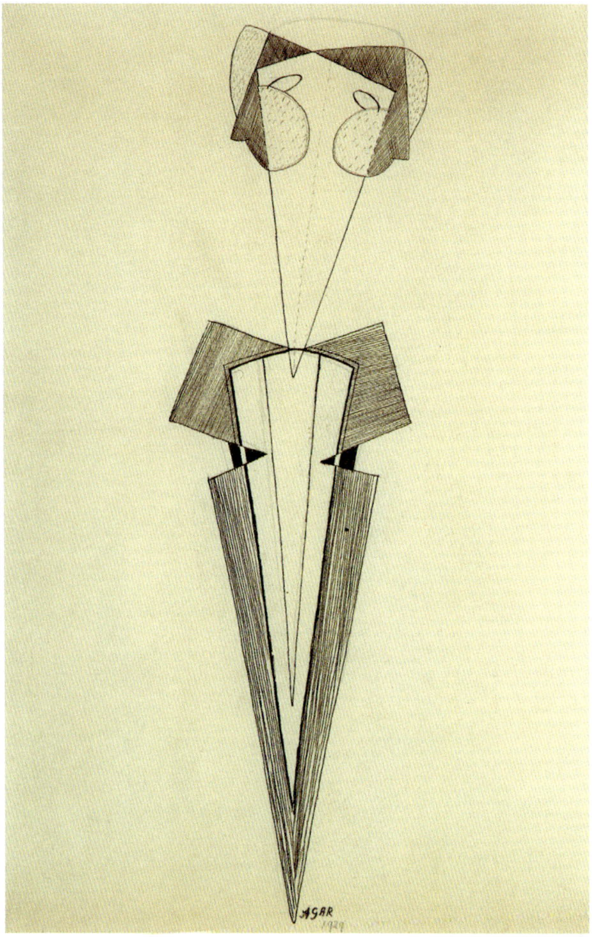

Happy Breakfast
Eileen Agar, 1937

Oscar Wilde
Eileen Agar, 1929

(1939) fragments of hands, faces, leaves, ropes and fish forms. . . Never trying to hide the successive layers of the material used – the eventual source of her humour – she invites the eye to manifest all its playful desire to make accepted reality literally turn over.

In their own ways, Emmy Bridgwater and Edith Rimmington achieve the same unstoppable slipping of meaning. Their works are places of gaping intervals, between life and death, creation and destruction, Eros and Thanatos, places of processes of mutation and transformation. In Bridgwater's *Transplanted* (1947), we grasp the very moment of metamorphosis of a face into a plant, unless it be the reverse. It is a face whose eyes slip into leaves, whose mouth opens onto dark secret forces and whose nose becomes the stem of a flower, unless it is the beak of a bird. In *Brave Morning* (1942), the bird, flying between the scared-eyed girl and the top-hatted stern masculine father-figure, seems to unleash forces of liberation and destruction, as seen in the breaking of window frames on the right, and forces of life in shapes reminiscent of eggs and ovaries, all signs of the desire to break away.

As regards, and in relation to, the haunting presence of desire and death, Edith Rimmington's *Sisters of Anarchy* (1941) seems to act as one of the tutelary figures of British surrealism. All Rimmington's paintings are scenes which divide the eye, places of loss and re-origination, places of conjunction and disjunction, of non-contradictory contraries. 'I am also the other', somehow, somewhere, Edith Rimmington's figures seem to claim. Together with this, the expected, impending transformation taking place in her visionary scenes is entrusted, if one may say, to the animal world. As in Bridgwater's paintings, the bird holds the deep truth inaccessible to man's consciousness, a truth revealed nowhere but in the space between figures and objects, i.e. nowhere specific but in the actual anarchic leap from one to the other. That truth resides in the slipping process from one field of reality into another and in the ability of the mind's eye to fuse with it. These visions, then, basically take place between relentless desire and its accomplishment, between memory and actualization, between the past and the future, in an attempt to retrieve the gaze we have lost.

Ithell Colquhoun's reckless descent towards primordial images is further evidence of the richness of the surrealist exploration of the other side of the mirror. Her challenging of morals and established values in her own life and her interest in the Hermetic tradition as well as in the Celtic lore of Cornwall crystallized in all her works, more especially in *Dance of the Nine Opals* (1942) based on the Merry Maidens, a magic Druidic circle of stones near Penzance. Feeling a mysterious current of energies issuing from between the stones and herself, she saw them as opals, her own birthstone and in a kind of process of translation of outside forces into inside forces, she transformed the nineteen stones into nine, her birth number, thus visionarily blending the objective and the subjective into a simultaneously chthonic and mental choreography – the entrance into another order, a kind of extra-reality within this, our reality. Colquhoun's early interest in the occult, although it meant in the early forties her exclusion from the group by E.L.T. Mesens who saw something too overtly religious in it, emphasized this determination to pass beyond and into oneself, thus transforming the status of the subject, just as she anthropomorphosized a tree trunk in *Tree Anatomy* (1942), in which the distinction between a hollow in a tree trunk and the feminine sex is blurred in the name of a life to come at a superior level.

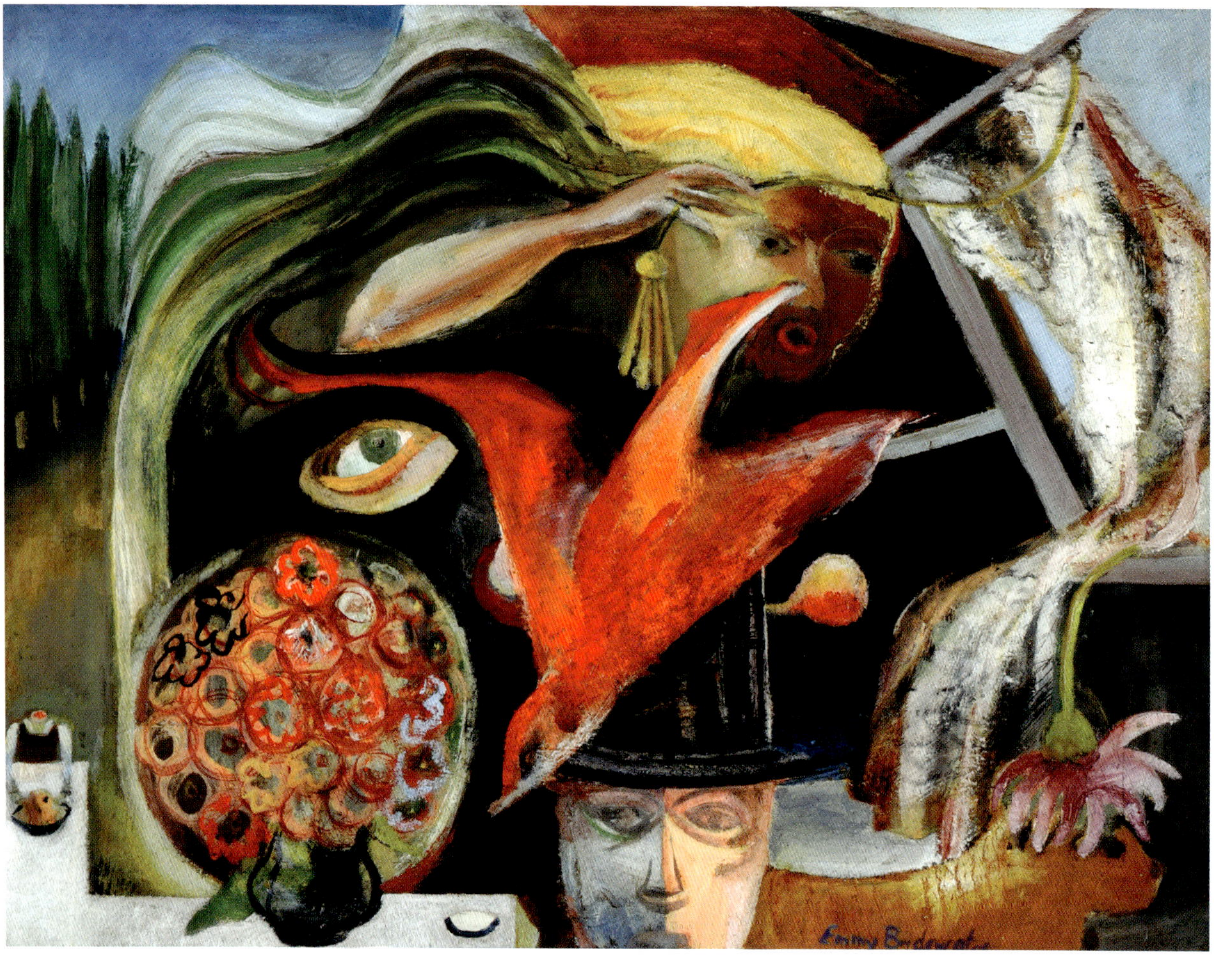

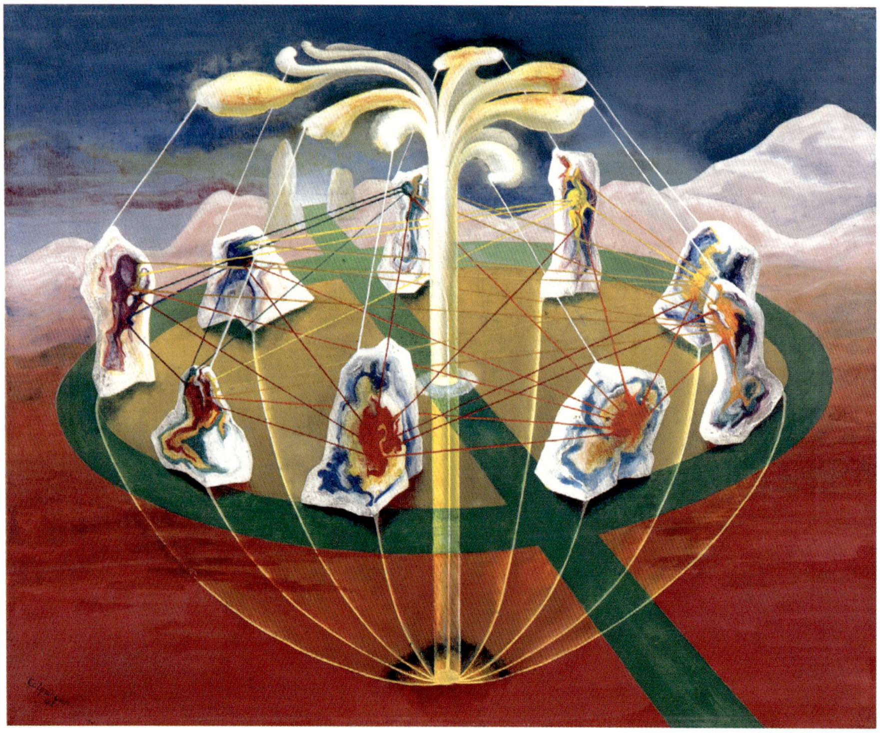

Brave Morning
Emmy Bridgwater, c.1942

The Dance of the Nine Opals
Ithell Colquhoun, c.1942

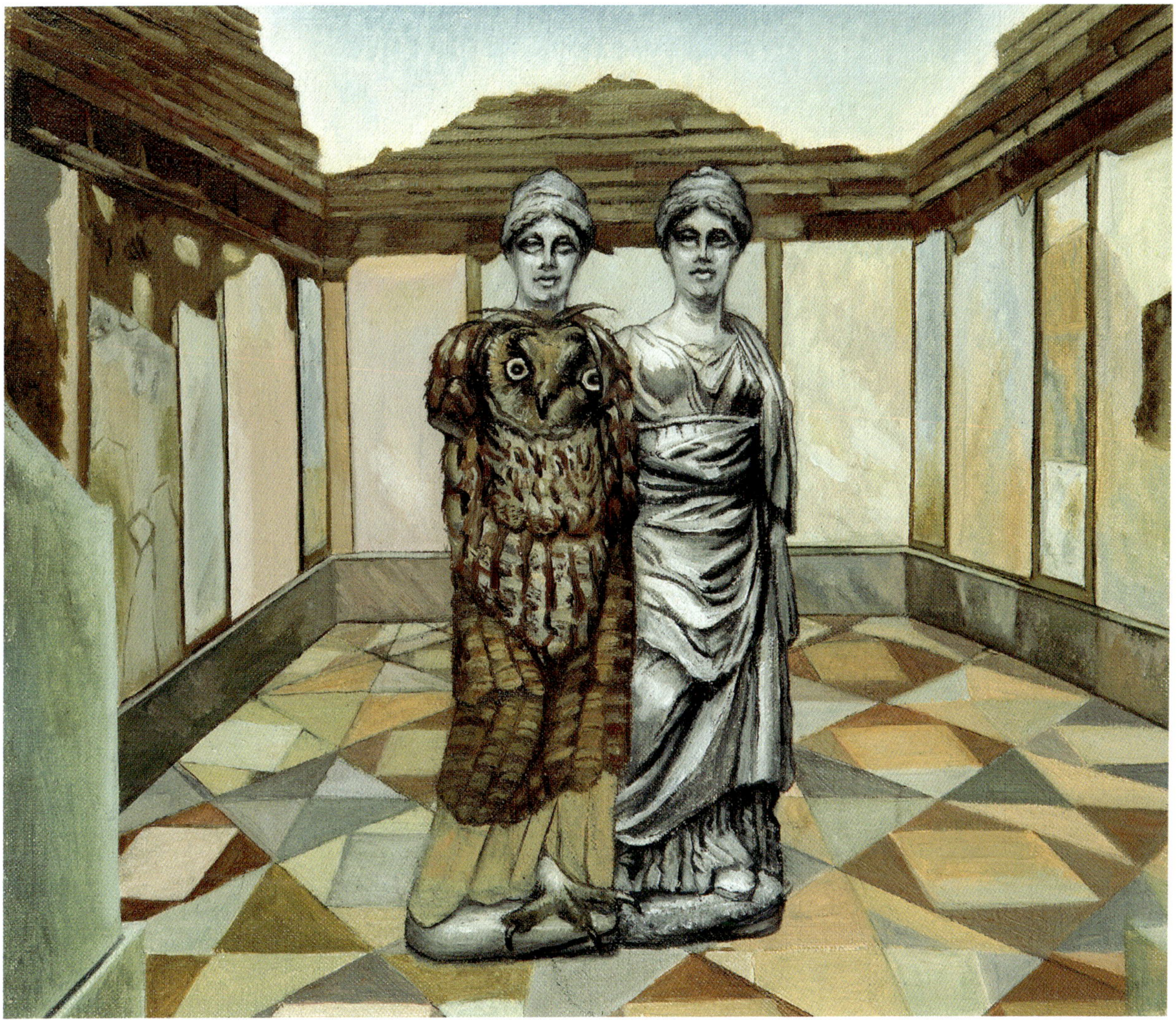

Sisters of Anarchy
Edith Rimmington, 1940/41

MILITANTISM CONFIRMED

One now realizes the formidable, not only aesthetic, but also philosophical and even ontological upheaval signified by surrealism. To this, one should add another dimension, the concern with social issues and the situation of man in this world. Indeed, the conjunction of art and politics, of aesthetic and political intransigence is latent in the works we have seen, and could not be fully understood independently of a politically militant background. Significant of this rising above categories, the December 1938 to January 1939 exhibition *Living Art in England*, organized by E.L.T. Mesens gathered surrealists and constructivists and abstractionists in protest against the government's foreign policy and to help Jewish and Eastern Europe refugees. This attitude, in point of fact, is to be found at the very core of the work of John Banting and Samuel Haile.

One of the most committed is certainly John Banting, a Stalinist communist, who never ceased to stigmatize the artificiality of man and especially the snobbishness and moral collapse of high society and socialites. The photo of Banting deriding the Nazi flag in Austria in 1938 – where he happened to stop over at a hotel at which Himmler himself was staying – is obviously anecdotal but, given the risk he took, it is emblematic of his provocative and overtly scathing pictorial statements: if we take a bird's eye view of his whole output, we could say that it shows a continuous tension between the humorous and enthusiastic creativity in man, as evidenced by music (*The Accordion Player*, c.1933) – Banting played jazz – and man's self destructive impulses, as if the Muse of Music was orchestrating the Dance of Death. This reaches a kind of point of no return in his series of *Jaws* (*Battle of the Jaws*, 1929) with its skeletal remnants of the human face whose repetitive insistence confronts man with his elemental reality, which looms large at the back of all his so-called civilized activities. The rope which often recurs in his works, corresponds to his urging man to re-connect with a deeper reality, a reality before forms are socially stereotyped, to find Ariadne's thread. . .

In a sense, Samuel Haile, a painter, a potter, a staunch anti-colonialist and a pacifist, was more radical, albeit more discreet and less 'public'. Evidence of this is given by his not returning to England when the war broke out, and he and his wife Marianne de Trey were in Switzerland and made the decision to go to and stay in the United States all through the war – an exile, like that chosen by André Breton, whose point was, as he said, 'to keep enough freedom to continue his craft' seeking 'to warn his contemporaries when he sees their spiritual gropings'. In his case, the

John Banting with Nazi Flag
Humphrey Spender, 1938

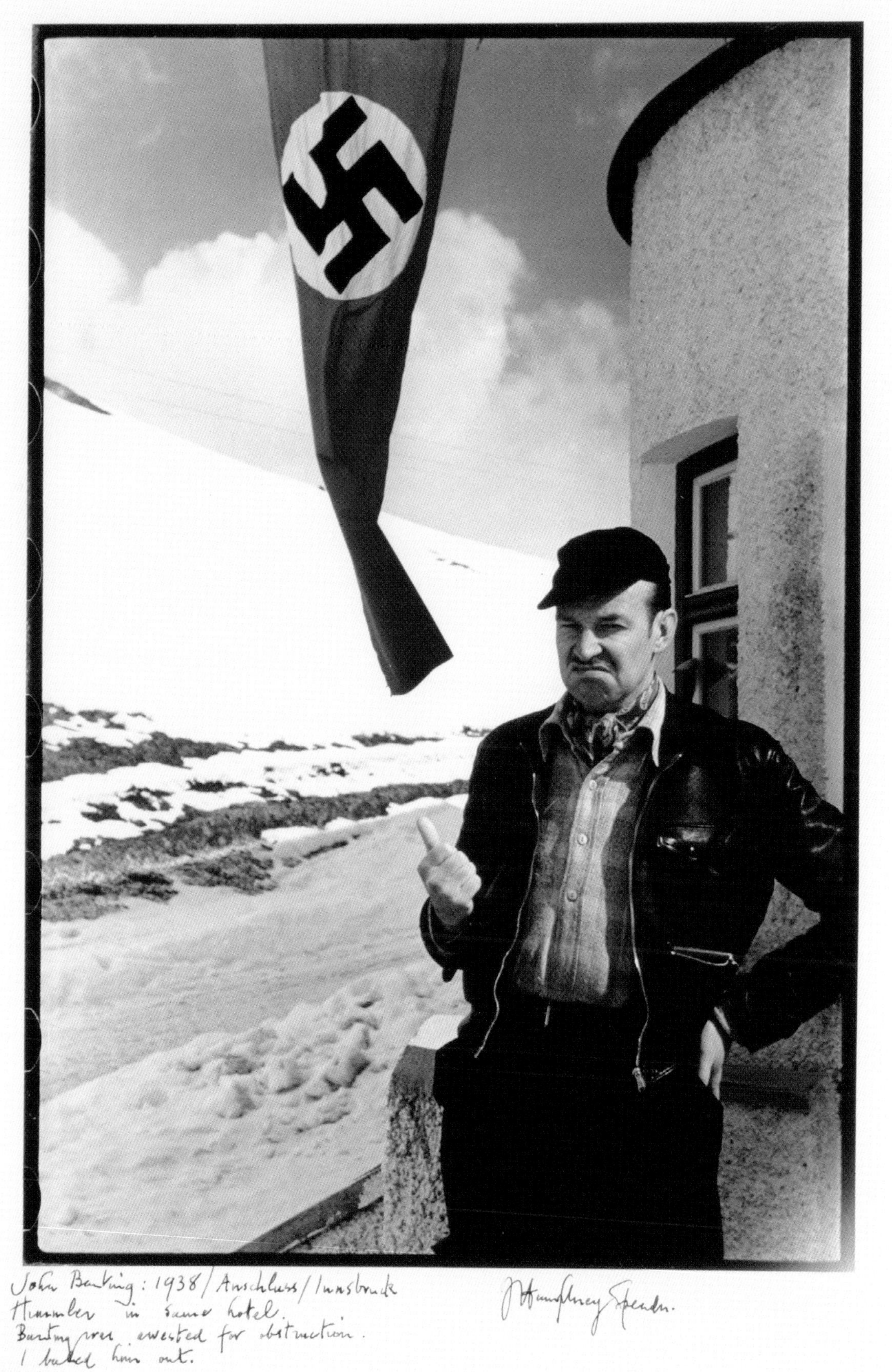
John Banting: 1938/Anschluss/Innsbruck
Himmler in same hotel.
Banting was arrested for obstruction.
I bailed him out.
Humphrey Spender.

resistance to any submission to values imposed on the artist in the name of entities such as Flag, Fatherland or even Freedom, linked up with the denunciation of man's abdication of his creative forces. *Shop Windows in Trinidad* (1938) confronts man with his exploitation of colonized populations and the moral degradation it implies, as is powerfully conveyed by the general confusion and dislocation of lines and figures in the painting. Here, Haile tries to make our eyes retrieve some primary, direct vision by following the various intersecting lines of force which carry the eye to another 'plane of existence', as he termed that state of mind in which man is liberated from dualities and is ready to resist all forms of oppression. But deep down, beneath the despair which haunts Haile's work, there is another message full of hope and opening: that the viewer and the painting entertain a mutual relationship, the artist being only an intermediary who works towards a liberation of the viewer's eye; in that sense, a surrealist painting means nothing but ceaseless exploration and the confrontation with the instability of meaning. *Brain Operation* (1939) catches the eye between the two branches of a pair of scissors held by a human hand. Who is operating upon man if not man himself? Again, Haile denounces man's self-destructive behaviour in these pre-war times. This, which is deepened by his statement that 'as the discoveries of surrealism react on our world, so will the ensuing reality react on surrealism', is further evidence of the maturity reached by British surrealism at the end of the thirties and of surrealism's very commitment to the dialectics of mind and body.

To Banting and Haile, one could add Merlyn Evans, present at the International Surrealist Exhibition in 1936 although he did not consider himself as a surrealist and did not want to be politically involved with the group then. This being said, he nonetheless made undeniably political paintings, railing at the soullessness of political economy in *Tyrannopolis* (1939), painted when he moved to Durban, in South Africa, of which he himself said that it showed 'the beginnings of megalometropolitan exodus. . . the cessation of productive work in the arts and sciences'. Influenced both by abstraction and Freudian surrealism, he depicts here the disappearance of the organicity of cities, which entails the severance of all links between human beings.

SCULPTURE

In the field of sculpture, what is essential to remember is the shift, provoked by surrealism, from works made in more or less conscious reference to the classical tradition and humanist principles, what Wilenski called the 'Greek prejudice', to works which decisively brush aside classical, primitive and modernist influences altogether by combining and transcending them.

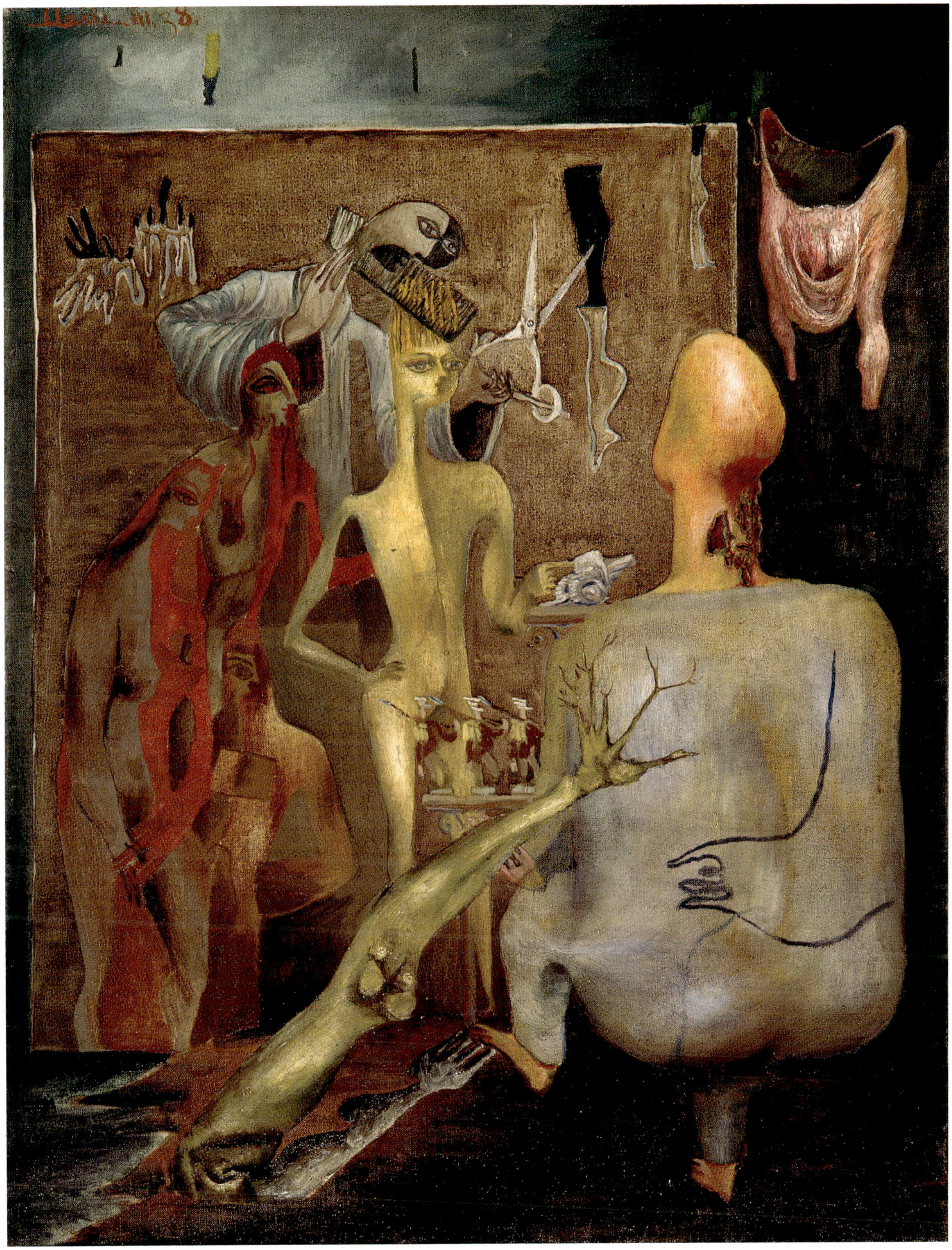

Shop Windows in Trinidad
Thomas Samuel Haile, 1938

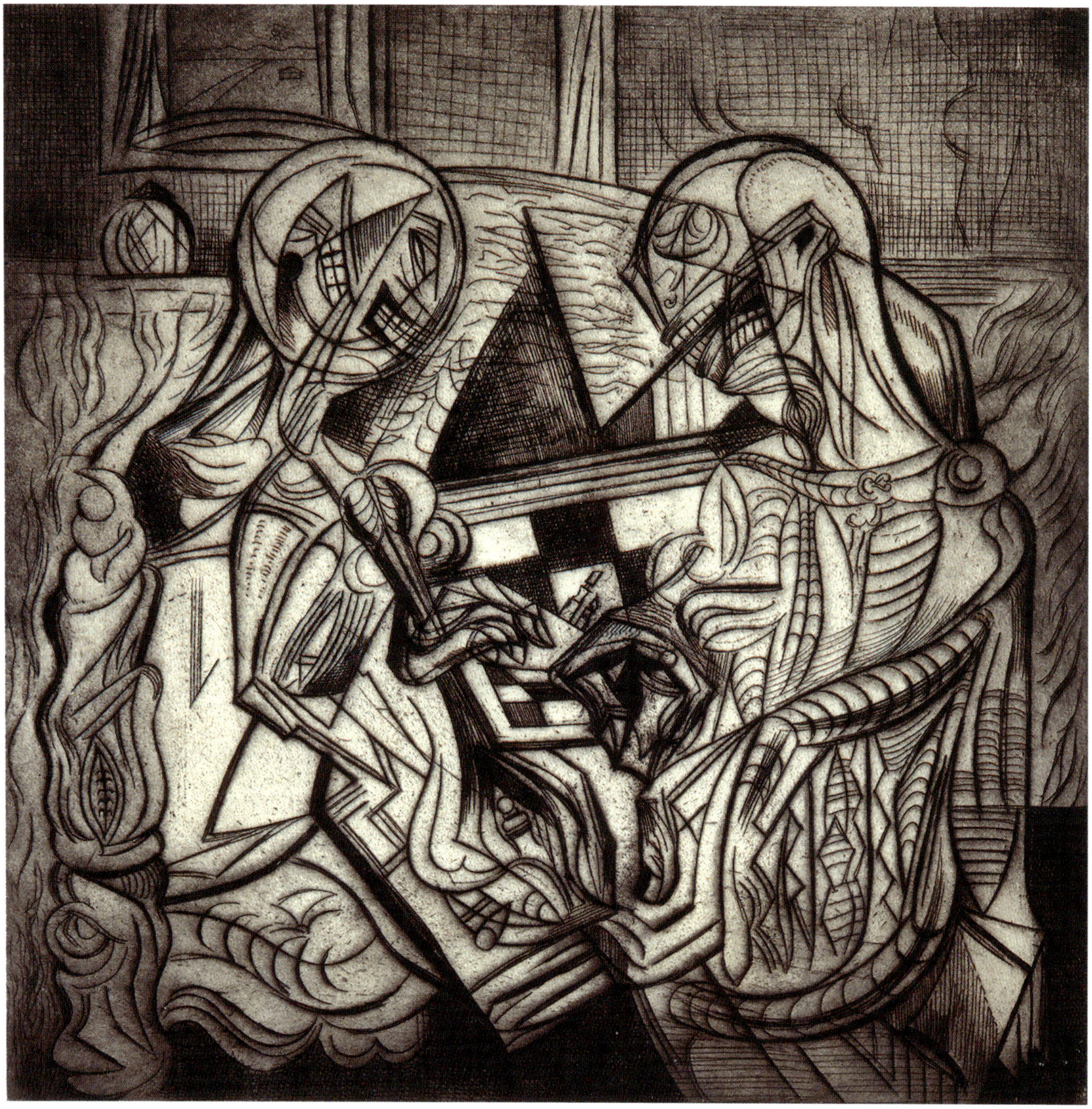

The Chess Players
Merlyn Evans, 1948

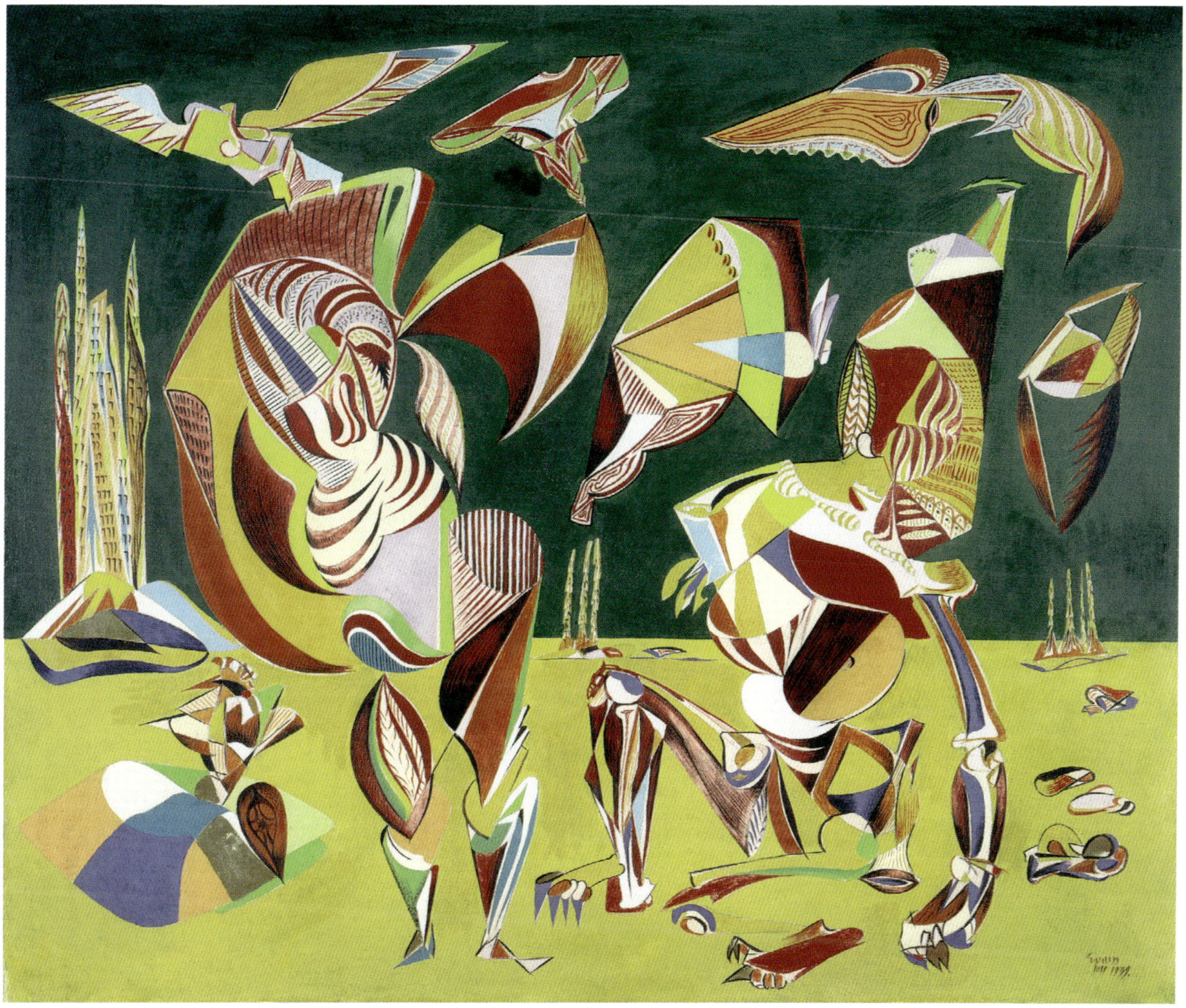

Tyrannopolis
Merlyn Evans, 1939

Moore's sculptures, definitely surrealist between 1936 and 1939 – he was excluded from the group for his yielding to officialdom and sculpting Madonnas – achieve this slippage by referring above all to natural forms from landscapes, those being simultaneously indistinguishable from forms of the human body, thus not devoid at all of erotic undertones. The piercing of holes through matter, one of the most pleasurable, if not erotic, moves of the sculptor, as Moore himself confessed, is evidence of a position which evolved from a certain abstraction towards what we might call biomorphism. The stone or the wood used for the sculpture is seen not as intended for a body, but as a body in all its physicality. In that sense, sculpture stands half way between the organic and the mental, furthering the blending of the two. Inspired by Brancusi's 'purified', 'rarefied' conception of sculpture, but also by the found objects – stones or wood fragments found by chance in nature – so dear to surrealism, Moore preferred to create a space invested with libidinal intensities. Works like his *Helmet* series, or what we see in his serigraphies in this exhibition, are figures in the making, leading the viewer's eyes on, around and into the undulations of the surface, into a definitely maternal matter.

McWilliam's approach has the same kind of provocation of the sense of unity of the human figure – so much of a dogma throughout the history of Western art – but, contrary to Moore, instead of plunging into a multipolar space where the organic and the inorganic fuse, he detaches forms from the whole which they belong to and lets them create their own space from, not with, the material. This obviously means the subversion of organicity, especially as McWilliam only deals with the human face and body, parts of the body we probably feel most related to. By isolating fragments and excluding others, he gives to the viewer the experience of what is missing and this lends great dramatic quality to his sculptures. The isolation of the lower mandible from the human face in *Mandible* (1938) is a case in point, which reveals the underlying aggressiveness contained in forms once they are grasped as forms and not as part of a whole. In *Spanish Head* (1939) it is clear that the eye is first and foremost fascinated by the empty space it risks falling into, by its own vulnerability as it risks rolling out of its position, into an emptiness which has become the real subject of the sculpture. The face is seen at the margin of itself and the work is seen as a place of intense, ultimate conflict between what was and what is, between predatory forces of destruction and resistance of matter, an obvious reference in the case of this work, to the desperate struggle of the young Spanish Republic against the Fascism of General Franco. McWilliam's sculptures confront us then with a monstrous dislocation of what is most precious to us, our face, our body, with the impossibility of achieving comfortable, reassuring completeness. He thus emphasizes the fate which is that of the eye, to be ever unsatisfied and be the place of unrelenting desire, the desire to stand up and resist – as is starkly emblematized by his *Long Arm* (1939) a tribute to the raised fists of the anti-Fascists in the Spanish Republic and elsewhere! When he declared that he 'believed in the words of the Queen of Hearts when she said it takes all the running you can do to keep in the same place', one feels like adding that another favourite character of his must have been the Cheshire Cat.

Mention must be made here of the surrealist outsider, Scottie Wilson who represents pure automatism. Through the compulsive alignment of small strokes of his ink pen, images are built up, created, emerging from the visceral-looking shapes which those strokes delineate, obeying the dictation of the subconscious since there is no really predetermined intention. In his *Greedies* series, the sinister-looking figures threaten peace and serenity and seem to record personal secrets. The almost mythopoetic vitality does try to exorcize those monsters which emerge from an unfathomable interior space somewhere between the individual subconscious and the collective unconscious. *Town with Greedies, Moon and Bird* (c.1945) and *Untitled* (c.1945) are powerful interior visions unwittingly liberated. Wilson then tried his hand at drawing on crockery but, to my mind, with much less imaginative power and more flatness.

Helmet, Head and Shoulders
Henry Moore, 1952

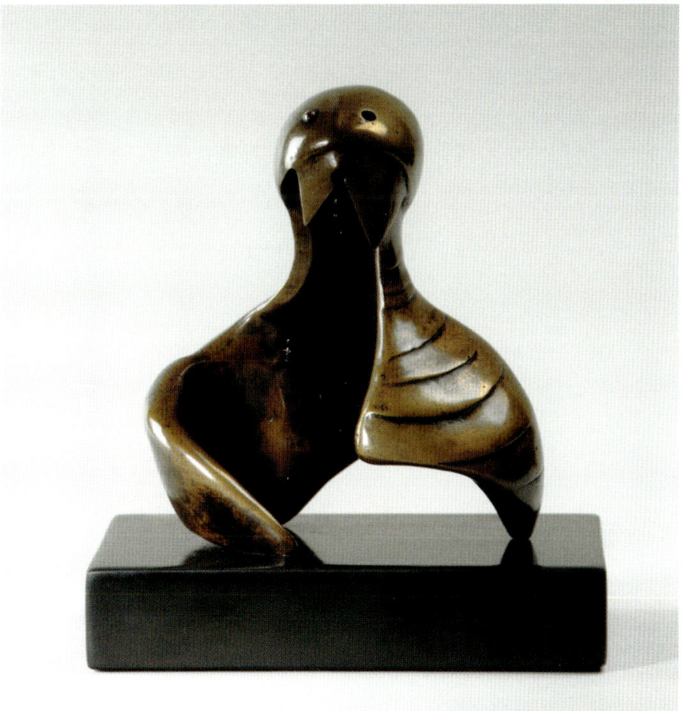

HERE AND NOW

Beyond all we have said so far, i.e. the reaffirmation by this exhibition of the tenets of the most consequential movement in art and thought of the twentieth century, the great interest of the Leeds exhibition resides in the irrefutable evidence it provides for the continuation of the surrealist proposition. The presence of contemporary surrealists, one might say of the fourth generation, gives it a singularly atemporal quality. Indeed, is there a single young contemporary vorticist, or cubist, or post-impressionist? This apparently absurd question says it all about the permanent validity of the surrealist spirit, founded on an ever-renewed, ever-self-challenging, theory-diffident approach, rooted in the essence of man and never losing sight of its ontological status. Every surrealist work protests and refuses reduction, explanation, interpretation and self-satisfaction, leaving it to the individual to decide, however temporarily.

Contemporary surrealist works, so perceptively chosen for this exhibition, by Desmond Morris, John Welson – together with those of Anthony Earnshaw, Tony Pusey, Oscar Mellor and Paul Hammond – are ample signs of surrealism's capacity to renew itself and project itself ahead. In the same way as indelible traces of its rebellious, value-challenging spirit sustain the visions of Hieronymus Bosch, Sade, Victor Hugo's mediumnistic drawings, Arcimboldo, Blake and many others, countless proofs of the same spirit are to be found, very much alive and defiant, in contemporary artists and it is to the credit of Jeffrey Sherwin to have brushed aside any historical consideration, any stereotyped belief in the value of past works because they are past, in the course of the development of his collection. Surrealism escapes time and the docketing craze of art historians. The public shouldn't fall into their traps: the energy and interrogative power of surrealism does not need the sanction of time. It simply is – and will be unmistakably.

Glen Baxter's subtle work on the disproportion introduced between the caption given to an image and the content of the image, gives to humour a de-stabilising power in an almost Magrittian way, challenging thus the size of things and its reliability. Tony Pusey's eccentric hybridizations of the organic and inorganic, the sexual and the mechanistic, are the children of Tanguy's apparitions and claim a life of their own, shocking to anyone who still believes in the unity of the Being. Oscar Mellor's frontal parades of nude women are scenes of held-up eroticism whose blunt frankness nonetheless hides and indicates darker voyeuristic or sadistic motives, as in his *Marriage of Convenience* (1984). Hammond's punning works involve our most solidly established beliefs in the absolute validity of certain values

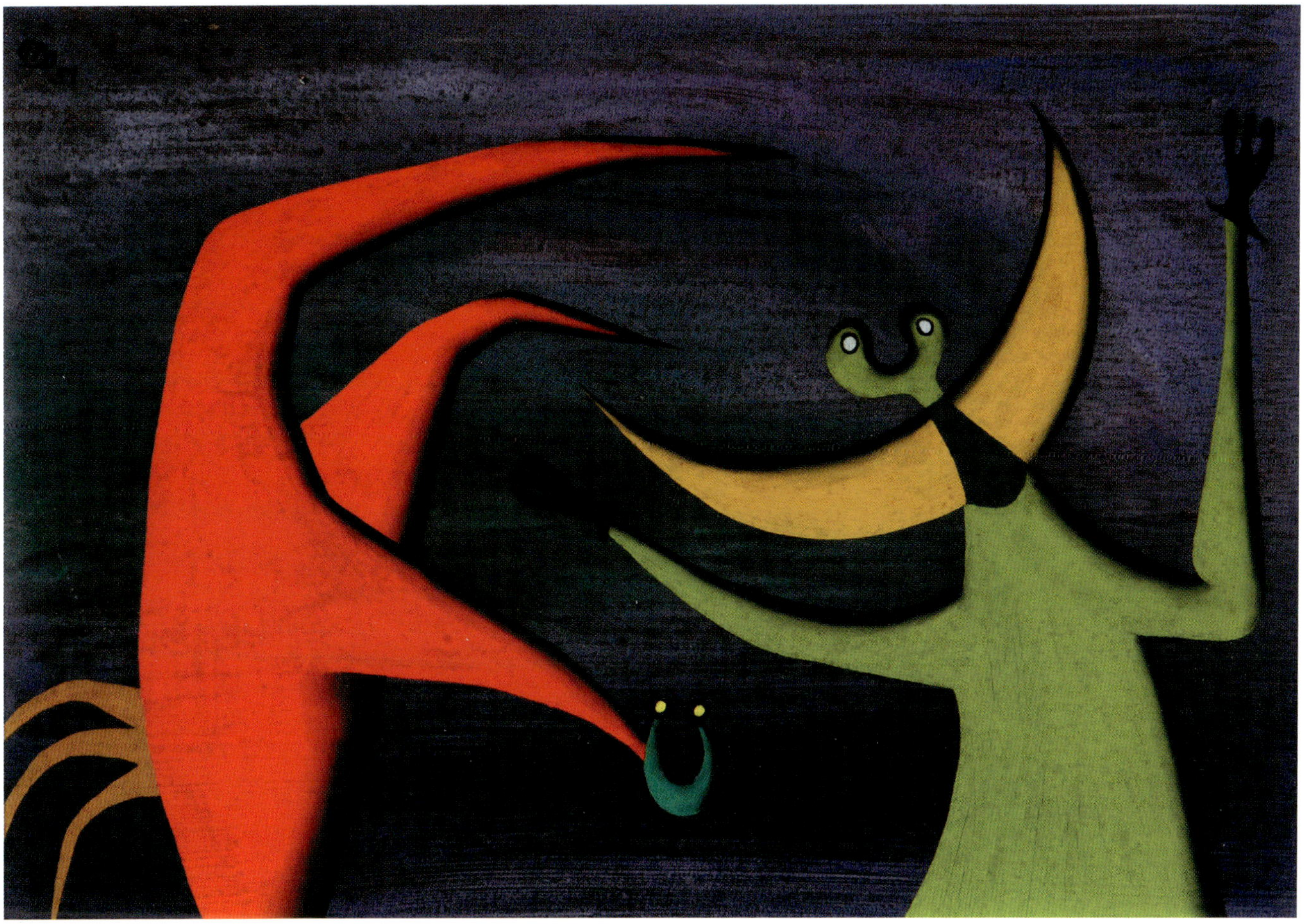

The Greeting Ceremony
Desmond Morris, 1957

and the same goes for Patrick Hughes, a one-time companion of surrealism. Anthony Earnshaw, who came to surrealism through a passion for jazz and blues – also the rebellious forms of expression of an oppressed minority – has evolved strategies of deflation and demystification of the surface reality of objects and words. His ironical, profoundly anarchistic standpoint is most vividly revealed in his poetic object *Homage to Jason* (1985), in which the globe is reduced to a ball of string and Jason's Argos is a mere paper boat attached to the globe by the string, a demystifying echo of the Golden Fleece. His *Mickey Has Cut Off Dumbo's Left Ear* (1999) signifies a debunking of icons – as he did with Jason, Newton, Don Juan and Walter Raleigh – a process by which eventually the object laughs at us and at our assumptions and our fossilized cultural heritage.

Infusing the movement with fresh, inspirational force, Desmond Morris, whose official entrance into the movement was a joint exhibition with Joan Miró at the London Gallery in February 1950, selected by E.L.T. Mesens, has created an ever-expanding universe of organs and organisms detached from the bodies they are supposed to belong to and living, all of a sudden,

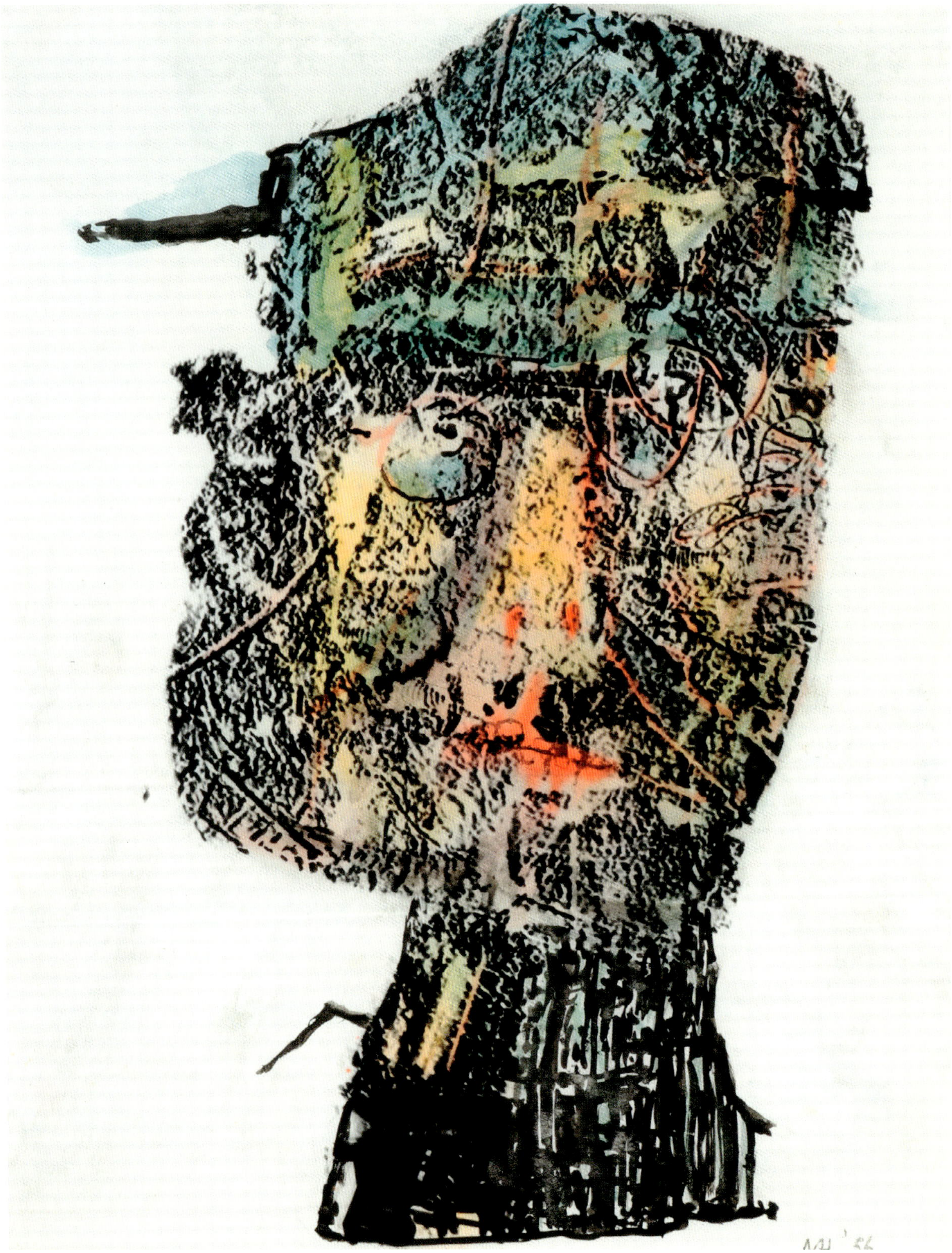

Japanese Head
Nigel Henderson, 1956

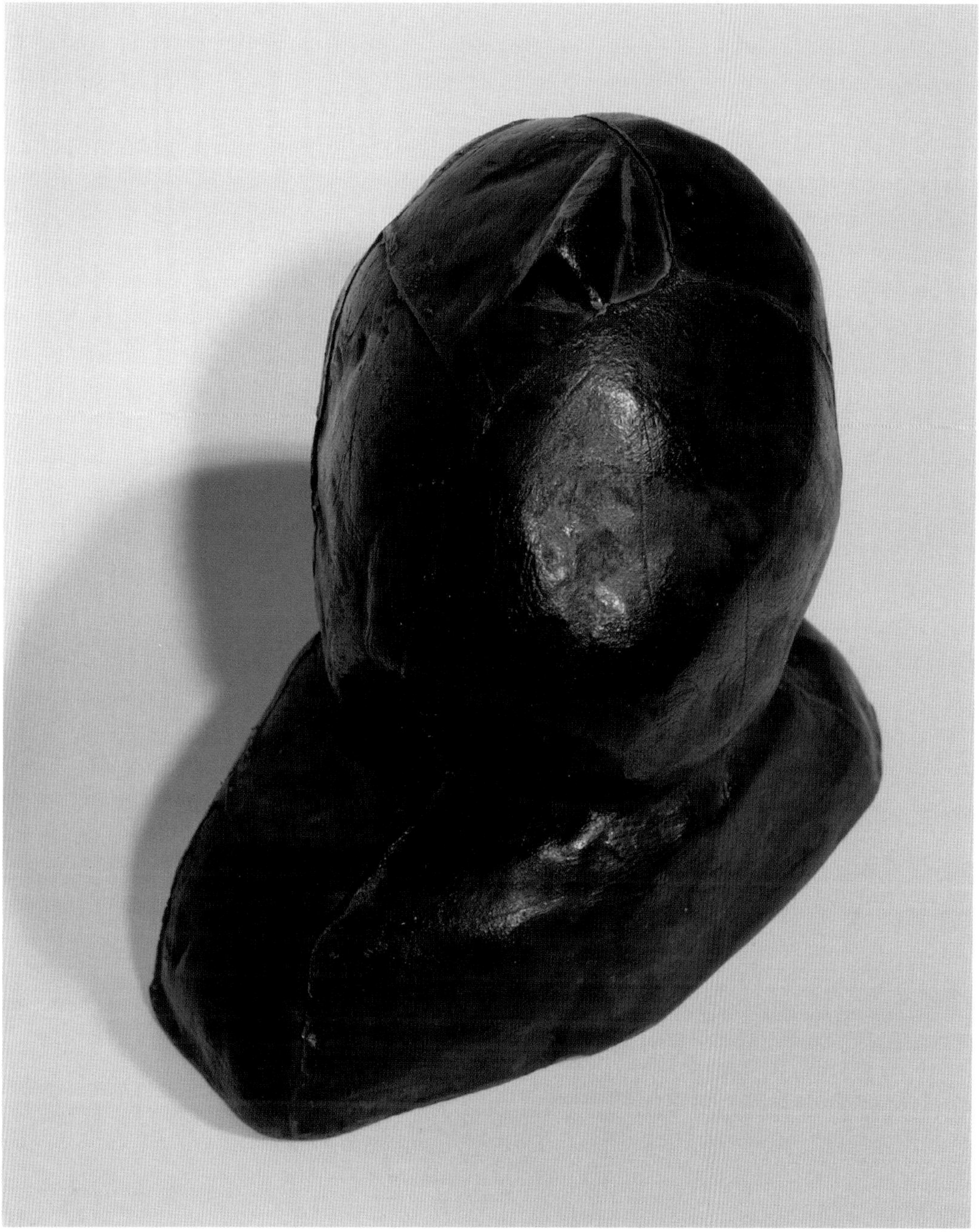

Bandaged Head
Eduardo Paolozzi, c.1953–56

properly independent lives of their own. Figures are scarcely identifiable – except, possibly, by biologists or surgeons! – but imply a secret ritual, sending the viewer back to primitive life in the hope of retrieving the original moment of creation, the secret of the artistic gesture, between the scientific and the aesthetic, the biological and the artistic, the organic and the totemic. Desmond Morris's activity is unrelenting to this day. Morris's creatures coax us into initiating dialogues with what lies deepest in ourselves. They are the mirrors of our past history as much as of our future conscience, playing and jousting almost sarcastically with what may be found in all rational systems of thought, developing a heightened consciousness of the emergence of forms. *Family Group* (1960) presents us with three enormous tubercles in the making, on whose surface mouths, noses, lips, ears and nostrils proliferate – matter is seized at the moment of an intense mutation, as if these were giant foetuses, the sites of monstrous mitoses. *The Greeting Ceremony* (1951) and *The Serpent's Choice* (1958) create scenes of playfulness not devoid of some latent drama that of predation shown here in contrast to the elation of forms confronted with their own life and growth.

One of the 'leading lights' – lighthouses, André Breton would have said – of surrealism in England at the moment this is written, is undoubtedly John Welson, who has never ceased, silently but vibrantly, to disperse the darkness into which British surrealism has at times lapsed. Welson started off by being one of the most thorough carvers of reality, as if he made us see all objects through the jagged splinters of a broken window pane, celebrating then a radical process of metamorphosis and the transmutation of objects, delivering 'a never-ending cadavre exquis', as Conroy Maddox put it, but undeniably alive! In his early paintings, objects, bequeathed to us by family, social class, education and personal beliefs, are torn apart, quartered and submitted to monstrous encounters, couplings and concatenations, thus simultaneously putting in question the status of matter itself and celebrating the deep-lying logic of pure desire. *Brittle Evening* (1977) and *Interior* (1978), are emblematic of the violent forces of deconstruction at work in us.
In the past few years, Welson has internalized his quest and reached – physiologically and imaginatively – down to the viscera at the level of which gestation and creation actually take place. The intestinal and organic soft forms in his drawings and paintings, which seem to salute Desmond Morris's biomorphs, map out places of incipient growth, places of imminence, where the rupture with a consensual conception of the respective places of the body and the mind has always already started. We are already inside, the witnesses of a monstrous ballet, or battle, or lovemaking of pre-organic forms, the matter of the mind.

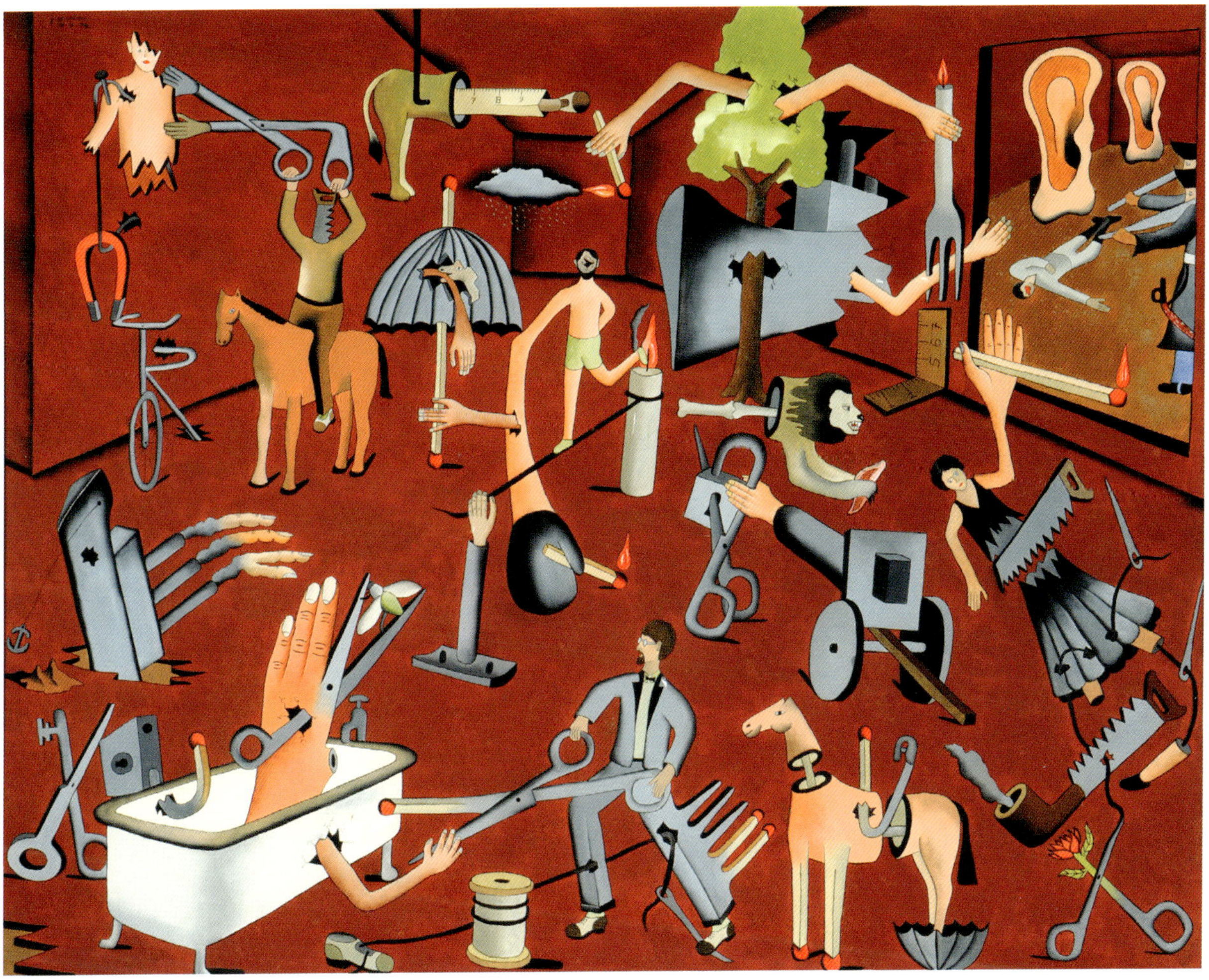

Interior
John Welson, 1978

A last word about present-day surrealism: all hopes are permitted when one realizes the energy of groups here and there all over the world, in Portugal, in South America, in France with the forthcoming rebirth of the Phases movement, after the tragic death of Edouard and Simone Jaguer, in the Czech Republic, in Canada with Gregg Simpson, in Sweden around Tony Pusey, in the United States around Franklin and Penelope Rosemont in Chicago and, last but not least in England, in Leeds very precisely, around Kenneth Cox and *Phosphor* (which succeeded the highly challenging *Manticore*) and an informal group around John Welson, Kathy Fox, Bill Howe and many other young torchbearers. It is impossible that such an exhibition does not herald, in one way or another, a renewed gathering of surrealist forces.

What has to be borne in mind is that the commitment required by surrealism of the subject is a total immersion, not only of one's mental faculties but also of social, political, aesthetic, metaphysical and ontological values. The subject's estrangement from himself and herself brings about a radical revision of long-held beliefs, a suspension of judgment especially. This, we see thanks to Jeffrey Sherwin's collection, marks its stark difference from all the other artistic movements which are allegedly seen as its forerunners or its heirs. Whether we like it or not, this is the question we will ask ourselves when looking at Bryan Kneale, Kenneth Armitage, John Piper, Eduardo Paolozzi, Tom Phillips, Victor Reinganum and even Damien Hirst, but the answer is simple and the difference easy to establish: in surrealism, the viewer is eventually confronted not with the work, but with himself, or rather with what is other in him, other than what he ordinarily goes by. 'I am other, too', the subject is led to wondering when in front of a surrealist work, remembering Rimbaud's famous statement *'Je est un autre'*. It is this, the conjuring up of the unavoidable 'other-in-me', together with the urge to debunk and go beyond accepted values, which defines the surrealist approach and its permanent validity.

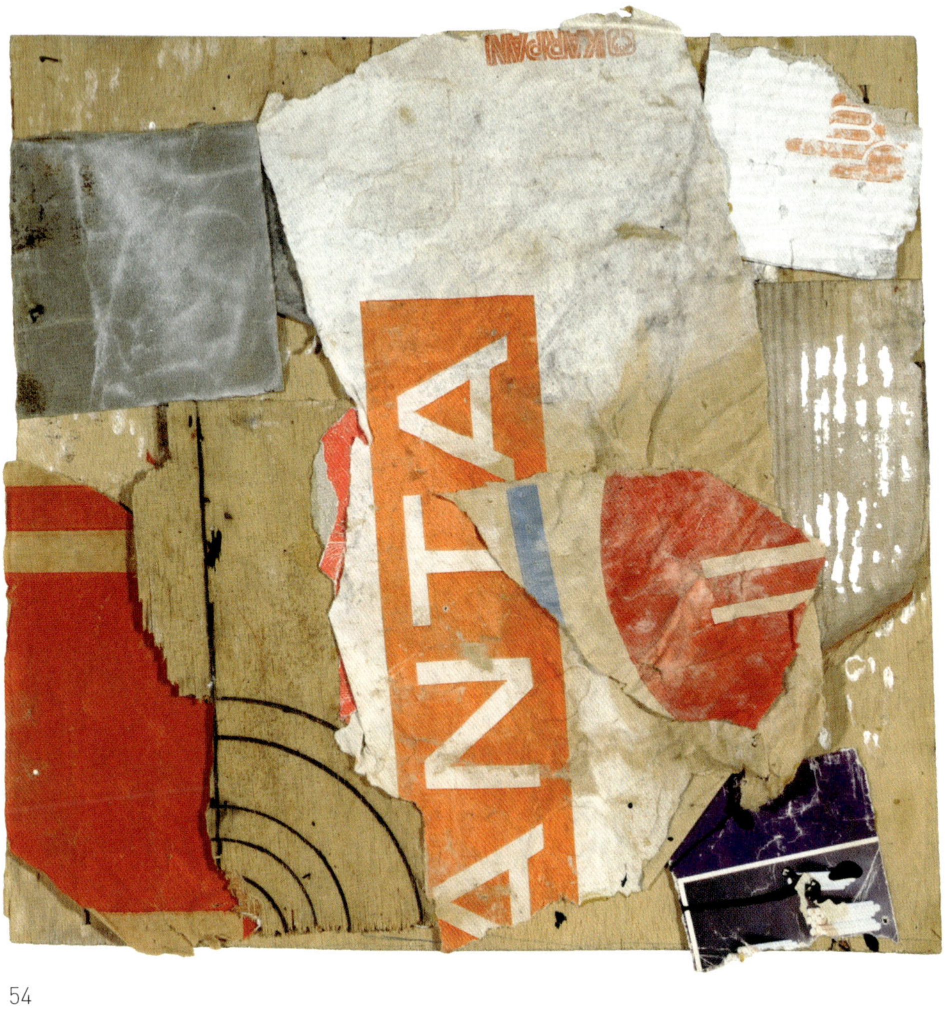

Fanta
Harry Thubron, undated

Mr Churchill is 71
Kurt Schwitters, 1947

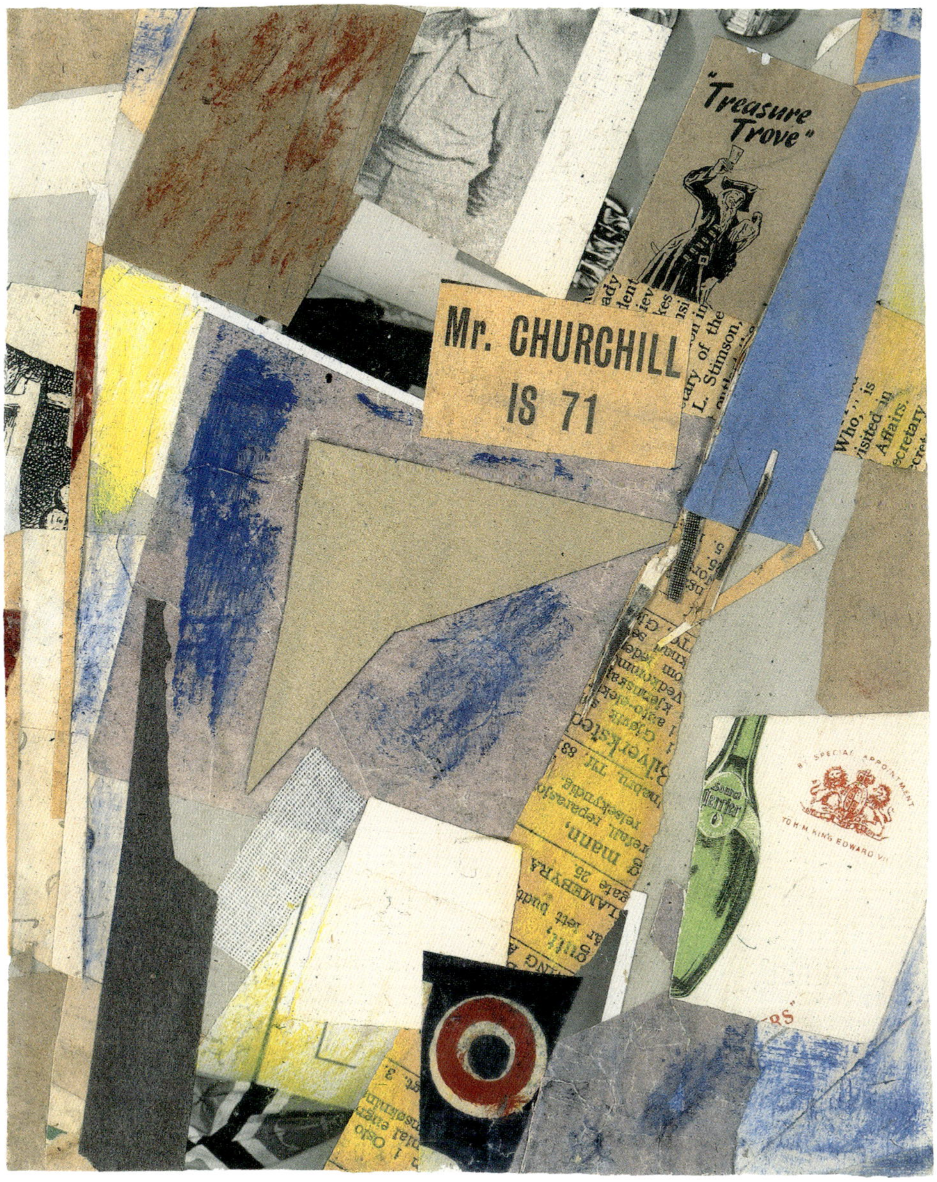

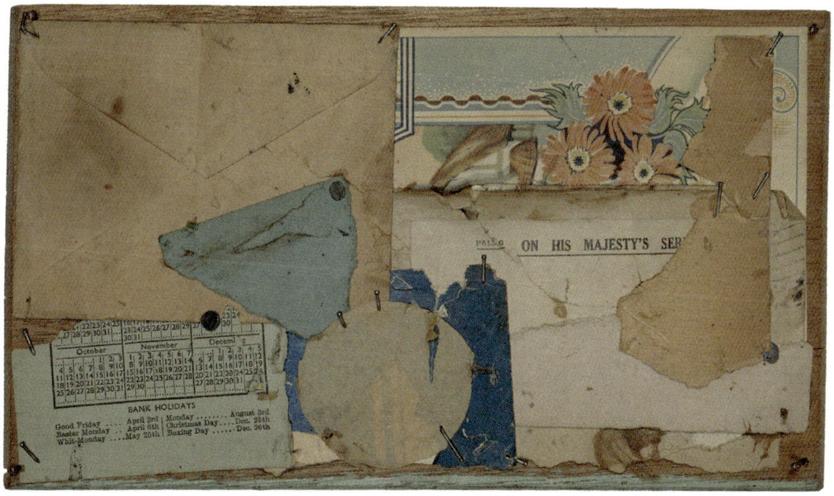

On His Majesty's Service
Damien Hirst, 1983–86

THE SPANISH CIVIL WAR

The French surrealists had welcomed the election of the Spanish Republican government in April 1931, which brought an end to the dictatorship of General de Rivera, and they were convinced that Spain's working class would provide a shining example of proletarian revolution for France. Yet until the outbreak of the Spanish Civil War in July 1936, when Spain's immediate political situation forced itself into surrealist consciousness, there is little sense that the surrealists paid much attention to the intricacies of Spanish politics.

In 1936 they published several frantic tracts calling upon the French people to support the Spanish Republican Army's struggle against General Franco's fascist military forces. Surrealism's faith in the psychically and socially transformative power of aesthetics was being radically questioned by political events such as the Spanish Civil War, the rise of fascism and the instability of French and Spanish leftist governments.

In 1938 Picasso's painting *Guernica*, was exhibited at the Burlington Galleries, London, in Leeds and Oxford before it was displayed for a further two weeks at the Whitechapel Art Gallery. For Roland Penrose, who had organised the tour, and other radical artists the painting represented all that they had tried to achieve in the late 1930s: the perfect combination of powerful activity, political impact, the connection to a working-class audience and to raise funds for the Republican cause. The uniqueness of the era was underlined by political confusion and disillusionment that immediately followed it, with the Nazi-Soviet Pact and 'Phoney War'.

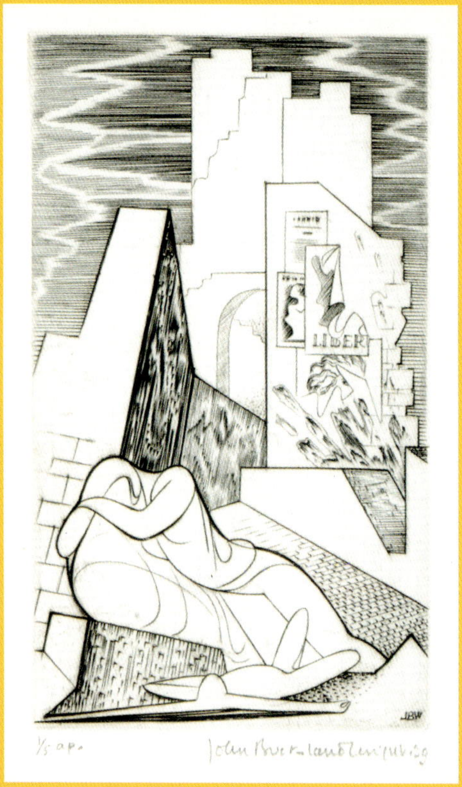

Fraternité
John Buckland Wright, 1939

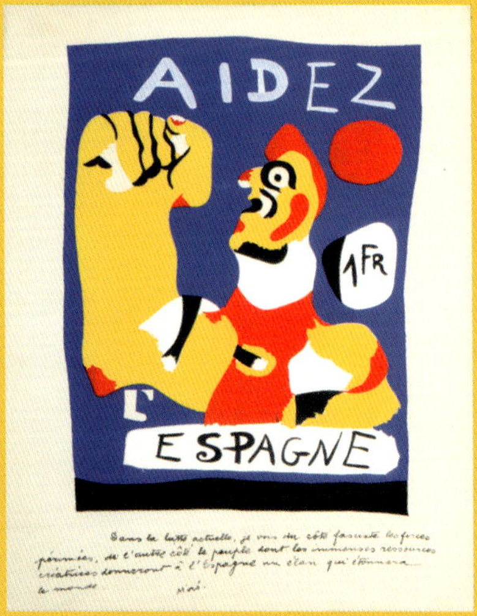

Aidez Espagne, Pochoir
Juan Miró, 1937

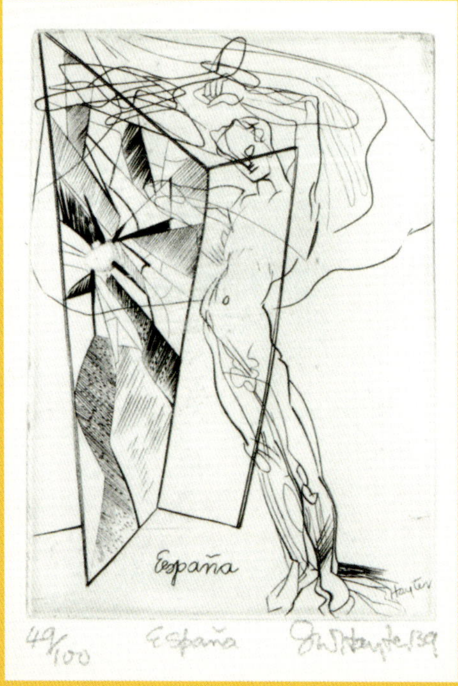

España
Stanley William Hayter, 1939

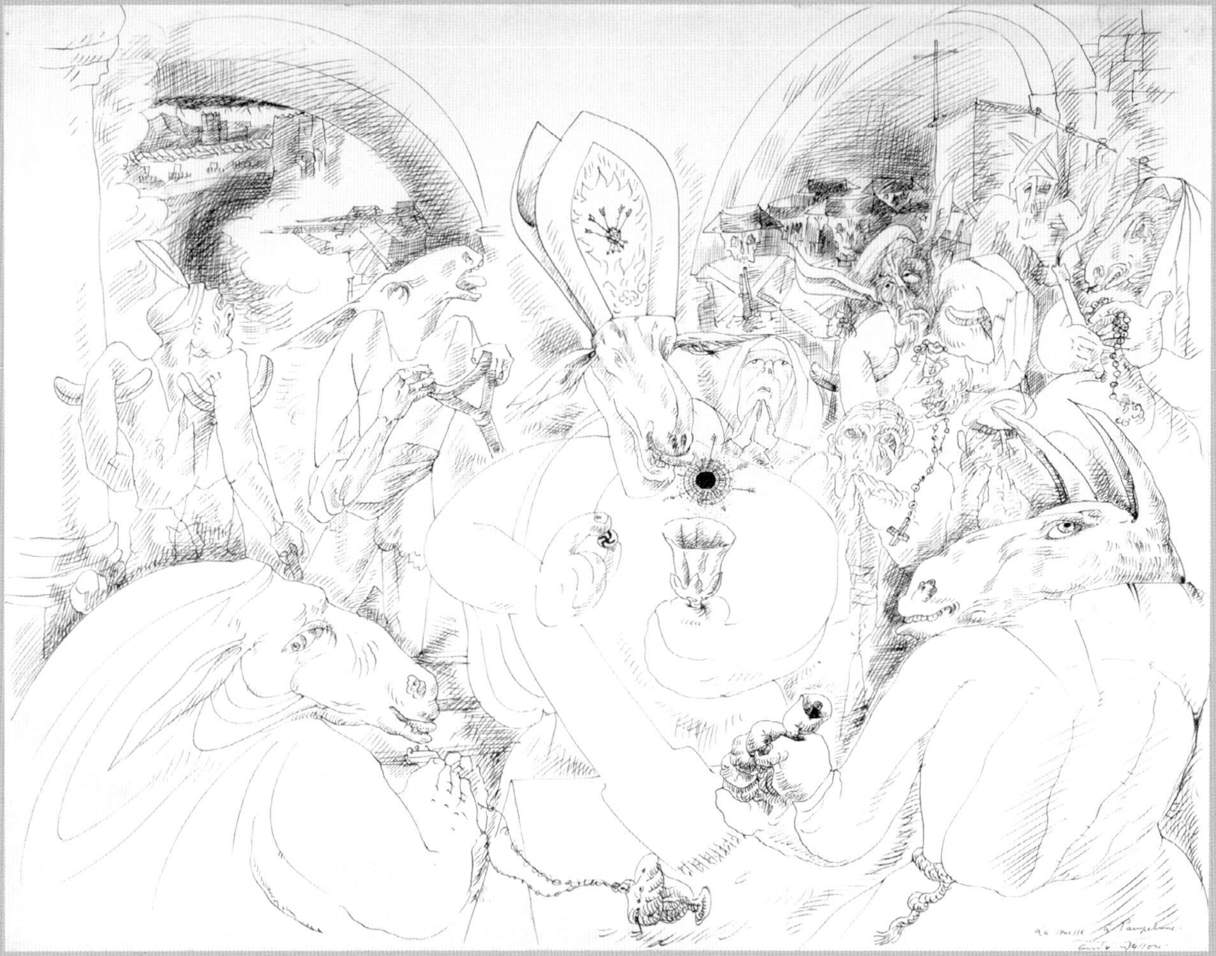

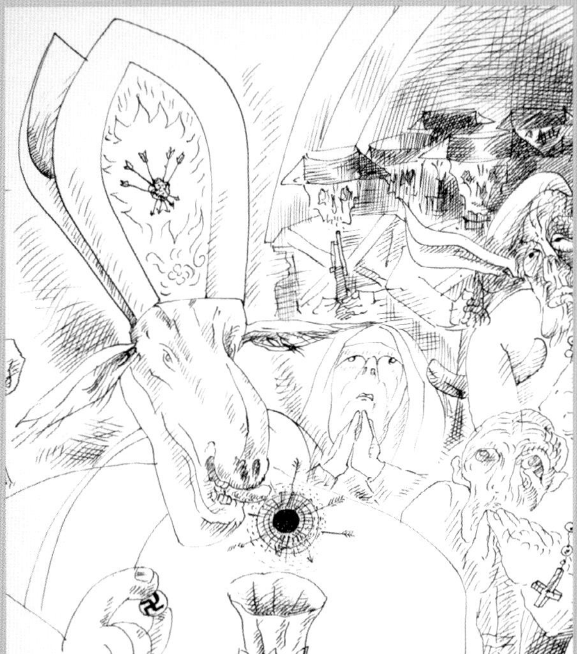

La Messe á Pampelone/Mass at Pamplona
André Masson, 1937

La Messe á Pampelone/Mass at Pamplona (detail)
André Masson, 1937

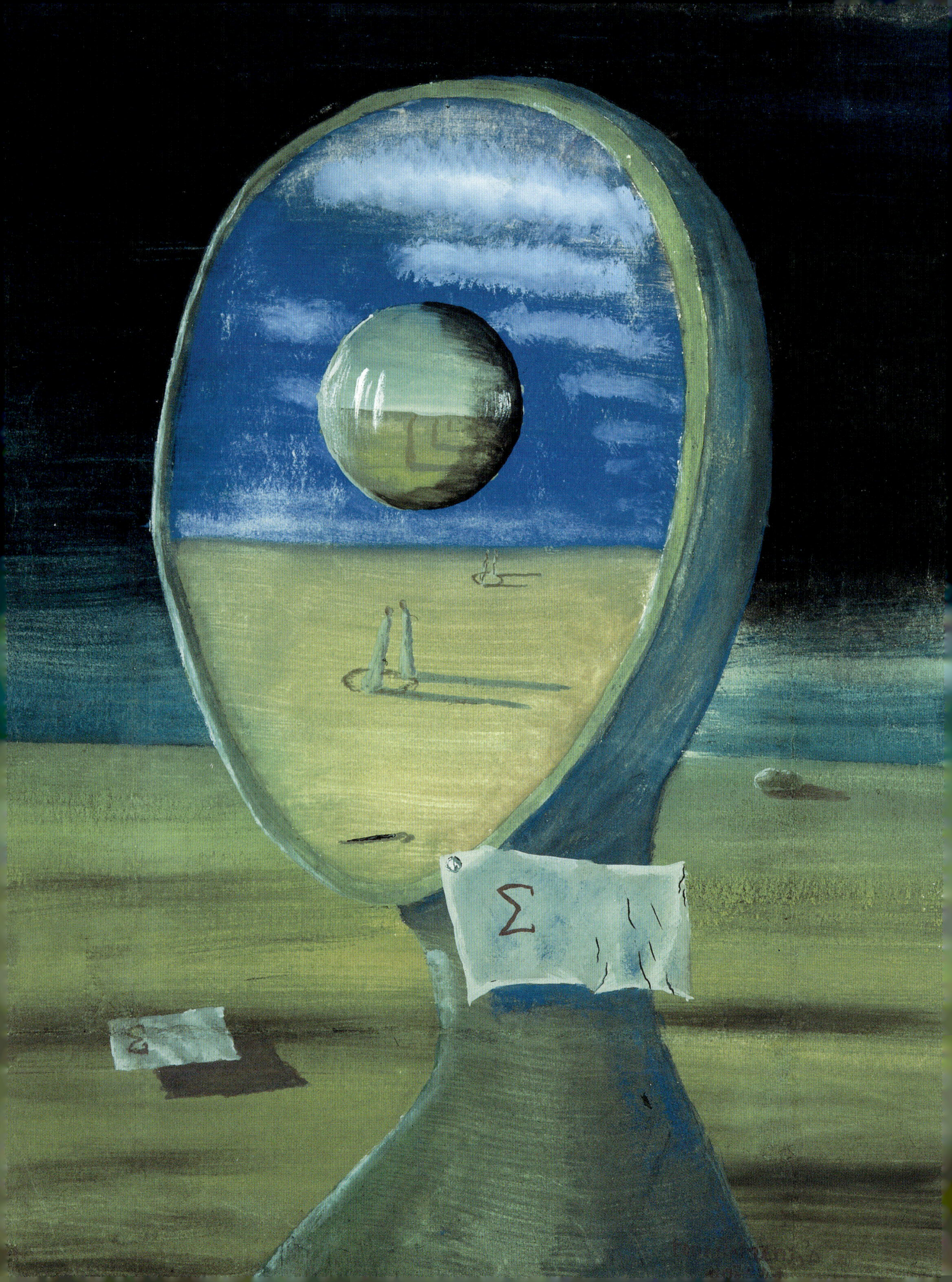
Σ
Σ

TONI DEL RENZIO: SURREALIST CHAMPION OR ANTAGONIST?

SILVANO LEVY

The Second World War brought an unprecedented indolence to the surrealism movement in Britain. The activities of 'The Surrealist Group in England', as it came to be known, had flourished during the latter 1930s, particularly from 1938, when E.L.T. Mesens, former secretary of the Brussels Palais des Beaux-Arts, assumed the role of group leader. Once war broke out, however, this impetus diminished. The *Surrealism Today* exhibition at the Zwemmer Gallery in 1940 did, it must be said, create a brief focus for surrealism. But, after this culmination, surrealism in Britain lay silent. The following year, 1941, marked a lull in British surrealist activity that was so apparent that it prompted Breton to write from New York to urge 'collective' action in London.[1] His entreaties, however, fell on deaf ears: Penrose, to whom the letter was addressed, had become engaged in experimental work in camouflage design, as had Julian Trevelyan. S.W. Hayter, Gordon Onslow-Ford and Sam Haile had left for the United States, whilst F.E. McWilliam had joined the Royal Air Force. The actor Jacques Brunius had, somewhat fittingly, taken a position as head of BBC French programmes. Mesens had already closed the London Gallery, which had acted as a nerve centre for surrealism in Britain at the end of July 1939, and in June 1940, he stopped publishing *London Bulletin*, which had become the British surrealist mouthpiece. He began to divert his energies to war work and took up a position at the BBC, where he was involved in broadcasting Allied propaganda to Belgium. The mood was sombre in the early 1940s, with the war becoming only too real.

It was into this climate of artistic inactivity that a 24-year-old aspiring surrealist of Italian and Russian origin, Toni del Renzio, arrived from France and soon set about animating the waning surrealist group. Rather than creating stability and direction, however, his efforts gave rise to an unforeseeable turbulence that left a trail of split loyalties, betrayal, violent outbursts and public humiliation. The tumult culminated in a virulent and passionate leadership struggle in which no holds were barred, even the most iniquitous. Perhaps inevitably, the sensationalism of these events has dominated and clouded their appraisal in the annals of surrealism.

Paranoiac Regression
Toni del Renzio, 1941

1 Letter dated 7 November from Breton to Penrose. SNGMA archives GMA.A.35.RPA.703.

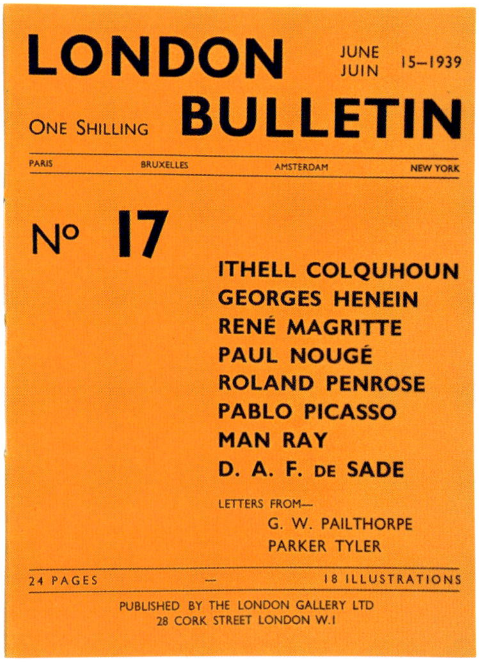

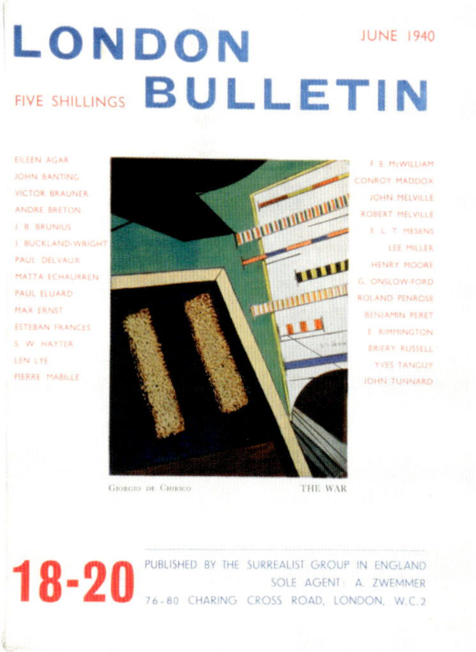

London Bulletin number 17 (June 1939), number 18–20 (June 1940)

What is indisputable is that, soon after the Zwemmer exhibition, artistic inertia seemed to prevail. 'Nothing', del Renzio complained, 'was proposed by Mesens and Penrose in the way of action or any publication or discussion of developments in surrealist theory and principles.'[2] Del Renzio had felt that Mesens' stance on surrealism was 'indeterminate' and was alarmed by the fact that the Belgian had contemplated establishing links with the mystico-religious 'Apocalyptic Movement' that had been founded by Henry Treece, G.S. Fraser and J.F. Hendry in 1938 and had published its first anthology, *The New Apocalypse*, in 1939.[3] Mesens, according to del Renzio, had even toyed with the idea of drawing Dylan Thomas into the surrealist group. Del Renzio's principal concern about Mesens was that, unlike Onslow-Ford, he provided neither mediation with Breton, nor an allegiance to his principles.

In this doctrinally nebulous climate, as he saw it, del Renzio strongly felt that 'a pure surrealist alternative ought to be presented if the movement was to stand any chance of staying alive'.[4] Intensely aware by the beginning of 1942 that surrealist activity had been allowed to dwindle into insignificance for a whole year by what he regarded as Mesens' ineffectual leadership, del Renzio decided to take the bull by the horns and revitalise the movement himself:

War or no war, there was nothing being done about surrealism. Hitler had to be defeated, yes, but surrealism also had to carry on.[5]

2 Toni del Renzio, *The Absent Text – The Third Manifesto of Surrealism or Else*, catalogue of the exhibition *Surrealism in England 1936 and After*, the Herbert Read Gallery, Canterbury College of Art, 1986, pp. 59.
3 *The New Apocalypse*, edited by J.F. Hendry and Henry Treece, Fortune Press, London, 1939. Robert Melville was a contributor.
4 Email to the author, 2004.
5 Email to the author, 2004.

At no time had del Renzio joined the surrealist movement officially but, during a brief period, he found himself at the centre of its fight for survival, an endeavour undertaken in response to Breton's pronouncement that continued action was necessary despite the war.[6] In March 1942, after a year of preparation and with financial help from Ithell Colquhoun, del Renzio published the sole issue of a magazine entitled *Arson*, with the intention of giving a clear focus to surrealism and of re-establishing the group.[7] His intention was 'to provoke authentic collective surrealist activity'.[8] Robert Melville, whose writings had impressed del Renzio, played a key role in the conception of the journal. The publication placed itself at the heart of surrealist discourse, announcing itself as 'An ardent review. Part One of a Surrealist Manifestation'. *Arson* was, in effect, the first surrealist publication since the demise of *London Bulletin* and had all the trappings of a manifesto, particularly in that it appeared to mark a new beginning. It professed to be 'a testimony of vital life lived among the ruins, not only of bombed houses, but of exploited people'. Conroy Maddox, Robert Melville, John Melville, Eileen Agar, Edith Rimmington, Emmy Bridgwater, Breton, Nicolas Calas, Giorgio de Chirico, Esteban Francés, Pierre Mabille, Onslow-Ford, Marguerite Salle, del Renzio himself and Roberta, Robert Melville's daughter, were listed as the 'collaborators'. Conroy Maddox, officially a member of 'The Surrealist Group in England' since 1938 and principal activist of the Birmingham group since 1936, was represented by his violently anti-religious text 'From The Exhibitionist's Overcoat', as well as reproductions of two drawings and his painting *Anthropomorphic Landscape* (1941). Del Renzio's own mastery as a painter was exemplified by a reproduction of *Paranoiac Regression* (1941). Breton's inclusion took the form of a reprint of an interview with Calas, first published in *View*, whilst de Chirico was represented by an extract from *Hebdomeros*. Robert Melville provided a text on Masson.

Arson made a point of demonstrating its allegiance to French surrealism: it not only printed texts by Breton but also promised its readers a future publication of Breton's poem 'Fata Morgana' in French. Del Renzio's own fidelity to the movement was evinced, even before the publication of *Arson*, by his writing to Maddox to say that he had decided to forego exhibiting at the Leicester Galleries 'because of the need to adopt an unequivocal position in opposition to everything outside surrealism'.[9] The standing of Mesens within the surrealist movement was certainly acknowledged in *Arson*: the editorial, 'For André Breton. . .', addressed to the various surrealists throughout the world, included the name of Mesens in its enumeration and Mesens was quoted on the front cover.[10] In addition, an advertisement for his *London Bulletin* occupied half a page. At the same time however, these

6 André Breton in the *View*, no. 7–8, surrealist double number, October–November 1941.
7 The title *Arson* was inspired by del Renzio's reading of excerpts from Nicolas Calas' Foyers d'Incendie (1939) in *The Partisan Review*, New York, October–November 1941.
8 Toni del Renzio, 'Memories of Polemics Past', unpublished lecture given at a symposium in conjunction with the exhibition *Surrealism in England 1936 and After*, Herbert Read Gallery, Canterbury College of Art, 1986.
9 Letter to Maddox dated 31 March 1942. The exhibition in question was due to be organized by Ithell Colquhoun, whom del Renzio regarded as 'essentially a mystic, and therefore individualist, conscious of being an artist'.
10 Del Renzio had no idea at the time that Brunius was in London. He first met Brunius through John Banting in the winter of 1942.

gestures also excluded the Belgian from first-hand involvement in the *Arson* venture and thereby indirectly pointed to fissures in his leadership. Del Renzio insisted that he had never had the intention of challenging Mesens, but in his enthusiasm to revive and invigorate surrealism in Britain, he, unwittingly perhaps, expressed a criticism that rang true with many around him. The reproach implicit in *Arson* probably had the tacit consensus of many of the group. According to Maddox, there was certainly a mood of frustration at the time: 'we felt that he (Mesens) was doing very little, that he was lethargic'.[11]

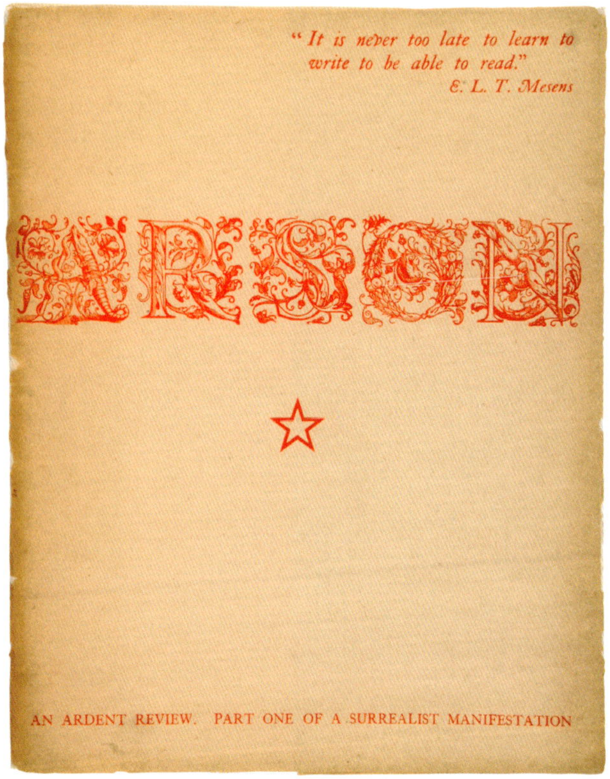

Arson (March 1942)

Del Renzio's second surrealist endeavour, an exhibition entitled *Surrealism*, held between 27 November and 15 December 1942 at the International Arts Centre in London, alienated Mesens once again. The participants were Maddox, who exhibited an oil painting entitled *Knight and Devil* (1942), Colquhoun, del Renzio, John Melville and Agar. Penrose became involved by lending some paintings by French surrealists. Mesens, however, consciously decided not to be connected with the event and actually refused a request for his help.[12] The gesture was highly significant and, together with his deliberate absence from the exhibition, marked the beginning of a split in the group. For the first time Maddox and John Melville found themselves involved in surrealist activity that had not been initiated by Mesens.

11 In conversation with the author, 1996.
12 Letter dated 28 April 1943 from del Renzio to Maddox.

As a result of his two ventures, the publication *Arson* and the International Arts Centre exhibition, del Renzio became known as an active proponent of surrealism, and it was not long before the editors of *New Road 1943*, John Bayliss and Alex Comfort, invited him to contribute a surrealist section to their publication.[13] With texts solicited from Ithell Colquhoun, Maddox and Robert Melville, in addition to his own contribution, del Renzio compiled an anthology that appeared in the spring of 1943.

Del Renzio had also wanted to include a poem by Mesens but, once again, the Belgian distanced himself from del Renzio's venture and vetoed the text. Faced with such hostility, del Renzio found it impossible to continue his acquiescent attitude towards Mesens. 'As much as I wanted to accept Mesens' authority', del Renzio recalled, 'I refused to concede on the point of the anthology'.[14] It was this clash that gave rise to 'the beginning of a sharp disagreement' between the two.

The eventual appearance of the *New Road 1943* compendium provided just the excuse that Mesens may have been seeking to launch a discrediting attack on del Renzio. Mesens addressed his disapproval to the October 1943 issue of *Horizon*, which, in any case, carried a caustic review of *New Road 1943* as a whole. This condemnation, written by Ivor Jacobs, was total: 'I cannot discern in their poetry the slightest hint of promise or in their critical prose a single iota of critical sensibility'.[15] It was immediately after this harsh reproof that *Horizon* printed a virulent letter to the editor written by Mesens, Brunius and Penrose, all of whom had been excluded from the *New Road 1943* anthology.[16] The trio denigrated the anthology by alleging not only that it had no sanction from the official English movement, that Mesens, Brunius and Penrose insist they represented, but also that it was inconsistent with and invalid as surrealism: 'We in England formally refused to associate ourselves with this caricatural and bewildering publication'. The invective was turned into a personal attack on del Renzio himself, 'a spam-brained intellectual', a 'buffoon'.

Del Renzio responded publicly with a communiqué in the December 1943 issue of *Horizon*.[17] Firstly, he accused Mesens of supporting 'that dismal renegade Eluard, with whom, as long ago as 1939, Breton and the surrealists found it impossible to continue any dealings', and secondly, he accused the principal proponents of English surrealism of years of procrastination. Del Renzio goes on to identify Mesens with 'senility' and proposes that 'younger and livelier men with reputations neither to make nor to lose should become the voice of surrealism'.

13 *New Road 1943*, edited by Alex Comfort and John Bayliss, The Grey Walls Press, Billericay, 1943.
14 Email to the author, 2004.
15 Ivor Jacobs, 'Auden Aftermath', *Horizon*, vol. 8, no. 46, October 1943, pp. 286.
16 J.B. Brunius, E.L.T. Mesens, Roland Penrose, 'Correspondence', *Horizon*, vol. 8, no. 46, October 1943, pp. 289, recto of back cover. Del Renzio had been shown the letter by Cyril Connolly, the editor, before its publication and had been offered the opportunity to veto its inclusion in *Horizon*. Del Renzio allowed the letter to be published, believing that it would provoke the intervention of Breton in support of the *Arson* and *New Road 1943* initiatives.
17 Letter dated 31 October 1943 from del Renzio and published as 'Correspondence', *Horizon*, vol. 8, no. 48, December 1943, pp. 433–4.

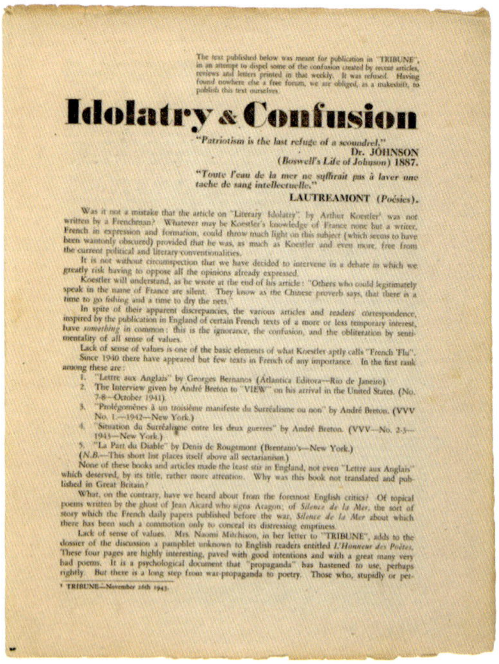

The text published below was meant for publication in "TRIBUNE", in an attempt to dispel some of the confusion created by recent articles, reviews and letters printed in that weekly. It was refused. Having found nowhere else a free forum, we are obliged, as a makeshift, to publish this text ourselves.

Idolatry & Confusion

"Patriotism is the last refuge of a scoundrel."
Dr. JOHNSON
(Boswell's Life of Johnson) 1887.

"Toute l'eau de la mer ne suffirait pas à laver une tache de sang intellectuelle."
LAUTREAMONT (*Poésies*).

Was it not a mistake that the article on "Literary Idolatry", by Arthur Koestler[1] was not written by a Frenchman? Whatever may be Koestler's knowledge of France none but a writer, French in expression and formation, could throw much light on this subject (which seems to have been wantonly obscured) provided that he was, as much as Koestler and even more, free from the current political and literary conventionalities.

It is not without circumspection that we have decided to intervene in a debate in which we greatly risk having to oppose all the opinions already expressed.

Koestler will understand, as he wrote at the end of his article: "Others who could legitimately speak in the name of France are silent. They know as the Chinese proverb says, that there is a time to go fishing and a time to dry the nets."

In spite of their apparent discrepancies, the various articles and readers' correspondence, inspired by the publication in England of certain French texts of a more or less temporary interest, have *something* in common: this is the ignorance, the confusion, and the obliteration by sentimentality of all sense of values.

Lack of sense of values is one of the basic elements of what Koestler aptly calls "French 'Flu".

Since 1940 there have appeared but few texts in French of any importance. In the first rank among these are:

1. "Lettre aux Anglais" by Georges Bernanos (Atlantica Editora—Rio de Janeiro).
2. The Interview given by André Breton to "VIEW" on his arrival in the United States. (No. 7-8—October 1941).
3. "Prolégomènes à un troisième manifeste du Surréalisme ou non" by André Breton. (VVV No. 1—1942—New York.)
4. "Situation du Surréalisme entre les deux guerres" by André Breton. (VVV—No. 2-3—1943—New York.)
5. "La Part du Diable" by Denis de Rougemont (Brentano's—New York.)

(*N.B.*—This short list places itself above all sectarianism.)

None of these books and articles made the least stir in England, not even "Lettre aux Anglais" which deserved, by its title, rather more attention. Why was this book not translated and published in Great Britain?

What, on the contrary, have we heard about from the foremost English critics? Of topical poems written by the ghost of Jean Aicard who signs Aragon; of *Silence de la Mer*, the sort of story which the French daily papers published before the war, *Silence de la Mer* about which there has been such a commotion only to conceal its distressing emptiness.

Lack of sense of values. Mrs. Naomi Mitchison, in her letter to "TRIBUNE", adds to the dossier of the discussion a pamphlet unknown to English readers entitled *L'Honneur des Poètes*. These four pages are highly interesting, paved with good intentions and with a great many very bad poems. It is a psychological document that "propaganda" has hastened to use, perhaps rightly. But there is a long step from war-propaganda to poetry. Those who, stupidly or per-

[1] TRIBUNE—November 26th 1943.

Idolatry & Confusion
(March 1944)

Mesens' next offensive appeared in March 1944, when he and Brunius published *Idolatry and Confusion*, which attacked Eluard, Aragon and Vercors' so-called 'resistance' poetry for its 'conformismes'.[18] But the pamphlet was also a vehement and personal response to del Renzio.[19] It claimed that it was only on the basis of rumours and hearsay of a disagreement between Breton and Eluard that del Renzio had launched his attack on Eluard. *Idolatry and Confusion* accused del Renzio of being an opportunist and ridiculed his name; 'Ranci del Conno', 'Vomi du Pinceau'.

When, in 1944, del Renzio arranged a poetry reading with Ithell Colquhoun at the International Arts Centre, Mesens and his supporters, including George Melly, Simon Watson Taylor and the anarchist Ken Hawkes, took the decision to sabotage the spectacle.[20] As the performance progressed, the saboteurs became increasingly clamorous and unruly. The disruptive behaviour escalated and culminated in the throwing of food and detritus. Del Renzio felt nothing but scorn for the 'loutish gang Mesens brought to the Centre'.[21] With Ithell Colquhoun, he ended up suffering the indignity of having to take refuge behind a piano that was on the stage. The incident was colourfully reported in November 1944 in *Message from Nowhere/Message de nulle part*:

Mr del Renzio's vulgar little poem 'Morgenroth (to darling Ithell)' . . .bore no conceivable connection with surrealism. After reading this nonsense one was forced to the conclusion that the only link between del Renzio and surrealism

18 Vercors was the pseudonym of the novelist and essayist Jean Bruller. He wrote *Le Silence de la mer*, which launched the *Éditions de minuit* in 1942.

19 J.B. Brunius and E.L.T. Mesens, *Idolatry and Confusion*, London Gallery Editions, March 1944, 6 pages. The tract was written originally for publication in *Tribune*, but it had been refused.

20 Del Renzio has written of Hawkes: 'I had come across Ken Hawkes through a little group of radical pacifists with strong anarchist tendencies and we collaborated in various projects. He retained all the prejudices of his petty bourgeois origins and held me responsible for his own failings. As part of the anarchist rent-a-mob that Mesens enlisted he achieved a sort of notoriety and recognition in anarchist circles. He never grasped what surrealism was, as examination of the few feats he contributed to the publications of the era demonstrates'.

21 Toni del Renzio, 'Memories of Polemics Past', unpublished lecture given at a symposium in conjunction with the exhibition *Surrealism in England 1936 and After*, Herbert Read Gallery, Canterbury College of Art, 1986, pp. 3.

was that of a tape-worm in a man's intestines. When, therefore, during the early spring, Mr and Mrs del Renzio were advertised to give a 'surrealist' poetry reading at the International Arts Centre, Bayswater, the meeting was attended by a number of French, Belgian, American and British surrealists who were determined to prevent the further discrediting of the movement by the quaint couple. . . Mr del Renzio. . . referred, in his opening remarks, to 'his friends' Pierre Mabille and Aimé Césaire! The remainder of his address was inaudible, due to the fact that the brave couple were cowering behind a grand piano, until, after half-an-hour, three quarters of his audience left the meeting in protest... As we left the room, Mr del Renzio's white silk tie flapped symbolically.[22]

Del Renzio's rapid response to Mesens and Brunius' *Idolatry and Confusion* of March 1944 was the eight-page manifesto *Incendiary Innocence*, which appeared on 'Lautréamont's Day April 4, 1944'.[23] In the six pages of text of this '*Arson* pamphlet' del Renzio declares total allegiance to Breton and redefines the surrealist position with a fresh and vigorous vision for the group in Britain, which, clearly, he regarded himself fit to provide.[24] The piece goes on not only to question the appropriateness of Mesens' leadership, but also to criticise the Belgian's continued support for Eluard, whose 'war poetry', del Renzio insists, is doomed to be included in Péret's condemnatory *Le Déshonneur des poètes*.[25] In this thinly veiled reference to Mesens, del Renzio accuses the incumbent leader of a 'failure of nerve' that has allowed surrealism in Britain to become debased into 'just a series of pedestrian puns and

Incendiary Innocence (April 1944)

Message from Nowwhere/ Message de nulle part (November 1944)

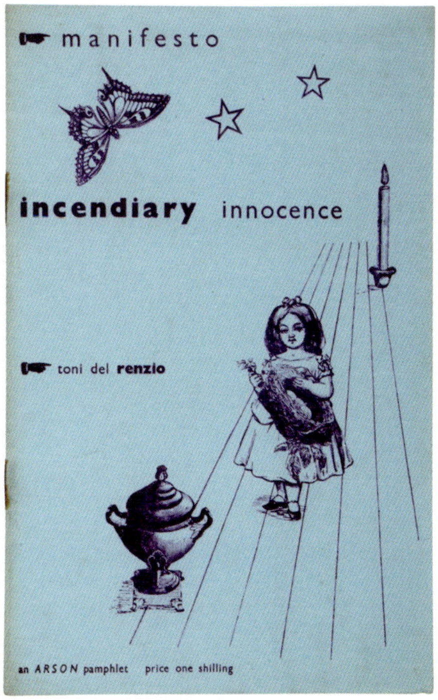

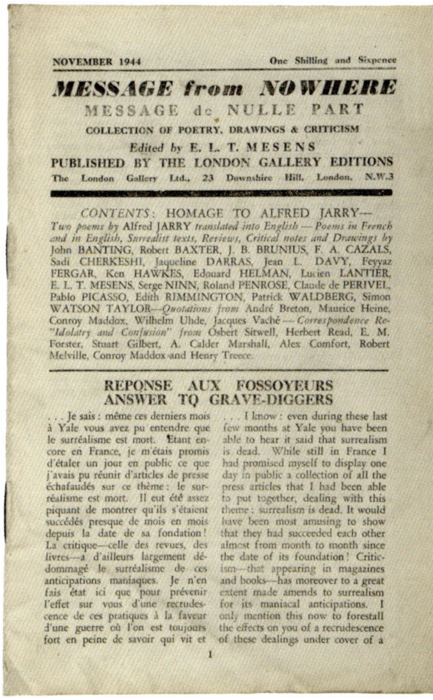

NOVEMBER 1944 One Shilling and Sixpence

MESSAGE from NOWHERE

MESSAGE de NULLE PART

COLLECTION OF POETRY, DRAWINGS & CRITICISM

Edited by E. L. T. MESENS

PUBLISHED BY THE LONDON GALLERY EDITIONS

The London Gallery Ltd., 23 Downshire Hill, London, N.W.3

CONTENTS: HOMAGE TO ALFRED JARRY— *Two poems by* Alfred JARRY *translated into English — Poems in French and in English, Surrealist texts, Reviews, Critical notes and Drawings by* John BANTING, Robert BAXTER, J. B. BRUNIUS, F. A. CAZALS, Sadi CHERKESHI, Jaqueline DARRAS, Jean L. DAVY, Feyyaz FERGAR, Ken HAWKES, Edouard HELMAN, Lucien LANTIER, E. L. T. MESENS, Serge NINN, Roland PENROSE, Claude de PERIVEL, Pablo PICASSO, Edith RIMMINGTON, Patrick WALDBERG, Simon WATSON TAYLOR—*Quotations from* André Breton, Maurice Heine, Conroy Maddox, Wilhelm Uhde, Jacques Vaché — *Correspondence Re- "Idolatry and Confusion" from* Osbert Sitwell, Herbert Read, E. M. Forster, Stuart Gilbert, A. Calder Marshall, Alex Comfort, Robert Melville, Conroy Maddox and Henry Treece.

REPONSE AUX FOSSOYEURS
ANSWER TQ GRAVE-DIGGERS

. . . Je sais : même ces derniers mois à Yale vous avez pu entendre que le surréalisme est mort. Etant encore en France, je m'étais promis d'étaler un jour en public ce que j'avais pu réunir d'articles de presse échafaudés sur ce thème : le surréalisme est mort. Il eut été assez piquant de montrer qu'ils s'étaient succédés presque de mois en mois depuis la date de sa fondation! La critique—celle des revues, des livres—a d'ailleurs largement dédommagé le surréalisme de ces anticipations maniaques. Je n'en fais état ici que pour prévenir l'effet sur vous d'une recrudescence de ces pratiques à la faveur d'une guerre où l'on est toujours fort en peine de savoir qui vit et

. . . I know : even during these last few months at Yale you have been able to hear it said that surrealism is dead. While still in France I had promised myself to display one day in public a collection of all the press articles that I had been able to put together, dealing with this theme : surrealism is dead. It would have been most amusing to show that they had succeeded each other almost from month to month since the date of its foundation! Criticism—that appearing in magazines and books—has moreover to a great extent made amends to surrealism for its maniacal anticipations. I only mention this now to forestall the effects on you of a recrudescence of these dealings under cover of a

1

22 Ken Hawkes, 'Epitaph', *Message from Nowhere*, pp. 17.
23 Isadore Ducasse was born on 4 April 1846 in Montevideo. He subsequently took the pen name 'Comte de Lautréamont'.
24 Manifesto. *Incendiary Innocence*. An *Arson* pamphlet, Toni del Renzio & The Favil Press Ltd, London 1944, pp. 7, unpaginated. Further unattributed citations from this publication refer to this note.
25 Mesens and Penrose had translated Eluard's *Poésie et Vérité 1942* and had published it through London Gallery Editions in 1944.

doubtful jokes'. In the place of this 'intellectual collapse' del Renzio insists on reinstating a vision of 'pristine clarity', a vision that he terms 'innocence'. For him, not only is 'innocence' an apposition to 'ignorance', but it also encompasses *'furor'*, the 'capacity for anger', which leads to 'revolt'. Whilst *Incendiary Innocence* can be viewed simplistically as an overview of surrealist activity in 1944, it was also, arguably, a valid and effectual vehicle for future revolt that confronted the internal conflict and dormancy that was stifling the surrealist group in England at the time.

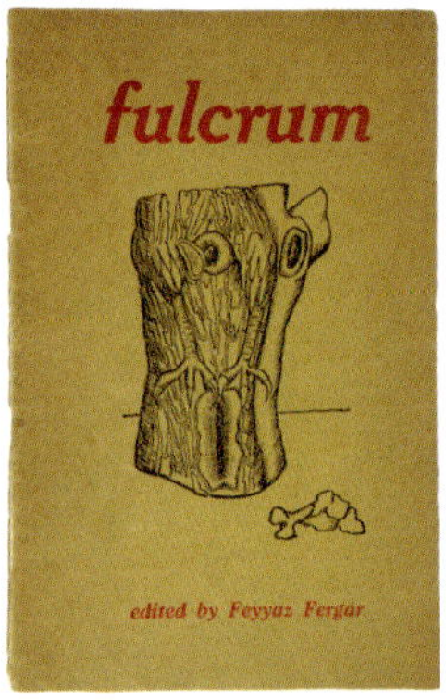

Fulcrum (July 1944)

But the intransigence that del Renzio was attributing to Mesens was, in reality, diminishing. In the first months of 1944, London Gallery Editions had published both Eluard's *Poésie et Vérité 1942*, in Mesens and Penrose's translation, and a bilingual collection of poems by Mesens entitled *Troisième front*.[26] Also, plans were announced for the publication of works by Valentine Penrose, Brunius, Breton and Aimé Césaire. Equally demonstrative of resurgent activity connected with Mesens was Feyyaz Fergar's *Fulcrum*, which appeared in July 1944 in an edition of 500 copies.[27] Sadi Cherkeshi and Fergar produced another magazine, *Dint*, that, in its second issue of autumn 1944, contained a surrealist poem by Watson Taylor, although surrealists did not otherwise contribute. In addition, Kurt Schwitters, who had arrived in London from Norway in 1940, held a solo exhibition in 1944 at Jack Bilbo's Modern Art Gallery.[28] Later, in March 1947, Mesens was to involve Schwitters in the programme of the London Gallery, where he gave two public recitals of his poetry.

Del Renzio's onslaught continued regardless, and in *Tribune* of 14 July 1944 he published 'Surrealism, or else. . .' in which he criticised the two recent London Gallery Editions publications, Eluard's *Poésie et Vérité 1942* and Mesens' *Troisième Front*, along with two other texts.[29] Mesens' poems are condemned in an openly sardonic manner for their imagery 'drawn from the privacy of the author's bathroom and watercloset', for 'feeble jokes' and for 'extreme pettiness'. What emerges most strongly in this review is del Renzio's unrelenting allegiance to Breton. The publication of this critique was seized upon very rapidly by the circle consolidating around Mesens as a further opportunity to condemn del Renzio. In the August 1944 issue of *Tribune*, Watson Taylor engages in a virulent attack, which, as well as opposing the ideas expressed in the July review, sets out to humiliate del Renzio personally: 'Mr del Renzio's comments on the surrealism of today are themselves so obviously "sapless variations on a threadbare theme" that one is surprised that *Tribune* should be so gullible as to give him the opportunity of making a fool of himself'.[30]

26 E.L.T. Mesens (trans.) Paul Eluard, *Poésie et Vérité* 1942, London Gallery Editions, 1944; E.L.T. Mesens, *Troisième Front, poèmes de guerre, suivis de Pièces Détachées*, London Gallery Editions, 1944, translated by the author and Roland Penrose.
27 Feyyaz Fergar was head of the BBC's Turkish service during the war.
28 Schwitters kept a low profile during the Third Reich and emigrated to Norway in January 1937. In 1940 Nazi troops invaded Norway and he was forced to flee for his life to England, where he was interned until November 1941.
29 Toni del Renzio, 'Surrealism or Else...', *Tribune*, 14 July 1944, pp. 17.
30 Simon Watson Taylor, 'I note that. . .', *Tribune*, 18 August 1944, pp. 14.
31 *Message from Nowhere*, November 1944, p. 22.
32 Email to the author, 2004.

The final nail in the coffin of del Renzio's surrealist aspirations was hammered home in *Message from Nowhere/Message de nulle part*, which secured a more resolute regrouping of the English surrealists around Mesens. The pamphlet described itself as a 'collection of poetry, drawings & criticism' and was, effectively, a stocktaking of surrealist enmities and hopes that called the roll of faithful once again. It marked the moment when allegiances had to be declared. Del Renzio's whole enterprise is rebuffed as 'the vomitus outpourings of a moral and aesthetic anxiety [. . .] dismal wreckage that wants clearing'.[31] For someone who saw himself as striving to rekindle a dying surrealist flame it was the ultimate aspersion.

Such unrelenting censure had, in the end, brought about its intended objective: the group's support for Mesens was now solidifying. *Message from Nowhere* marked the end of the 'del Renzio affair', with the definitive marginalization of the initiator of *Arson*. It would, however, be erroneous to discount del Renzio's role in the history of the English Surrealist Group. Arguably, the resurgence of Mesens' activity, together with all ensuing surrealist ventures, is attributable to del Renzio's spirited, albeit provocative, interventions. Without his enthusiastic attempts to salvage the remains of a former activity and to rally a diluted circle of individual surrealists, a resurgence of the surrealist group in England may never have occurred in late 1944. Justifiably, del Renzio regarded his role as pivotal: 'If I hadn't done something', he maintained, 'surrealism may not have been mentioned again'.[32] In the final analysis, however much del Renzio may have been attacked and belittled during the 1940s, it is undeniable that he filled an intellectual void. He may have been hated, betrayed and ridiculed, but he certainly was not and could not be ignored.

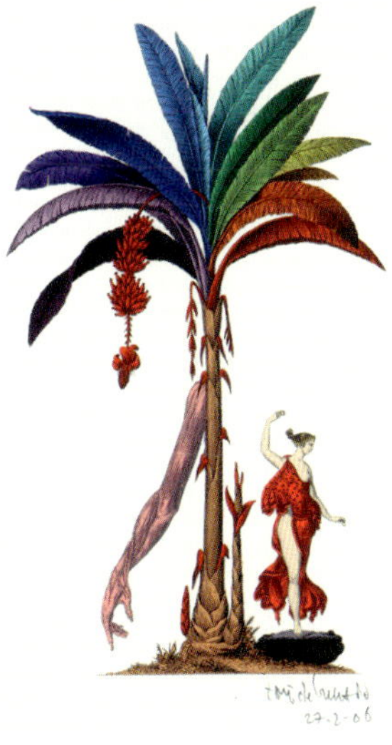

Untitled
Toni del Renzio, 2006

FOUND OBJECTS

A found object is a natural or man-made object found by an artist and kept because of some intrinsic interest the artist sees in it. The objects may be put on a shelf and treated as works of art in themselves, as well as providing inspiration for the artist. The sculptor Henry Moore, for example, collected bones and flints which he seems to have treated as natural sculptures as well as sources for his own work. Found objects may also be modified by the artist and presented as art, either more or less intact as in the dada and surrealist artist Marcel Duchamp's ready-mades, or as part of an assemblage. As so often, Picasso was an originator, from 1912, when he began to incorporate newspapers and such things as matchboxes into his cubist collages, and to make his cubist constructions from various scavenged materials. Extensive use of found objects was made by dada, surrealist and pop artists, and by artists such as Tony Cragg, Bill Woodrow, Damien Hirst and Sarah Lucas among many others.

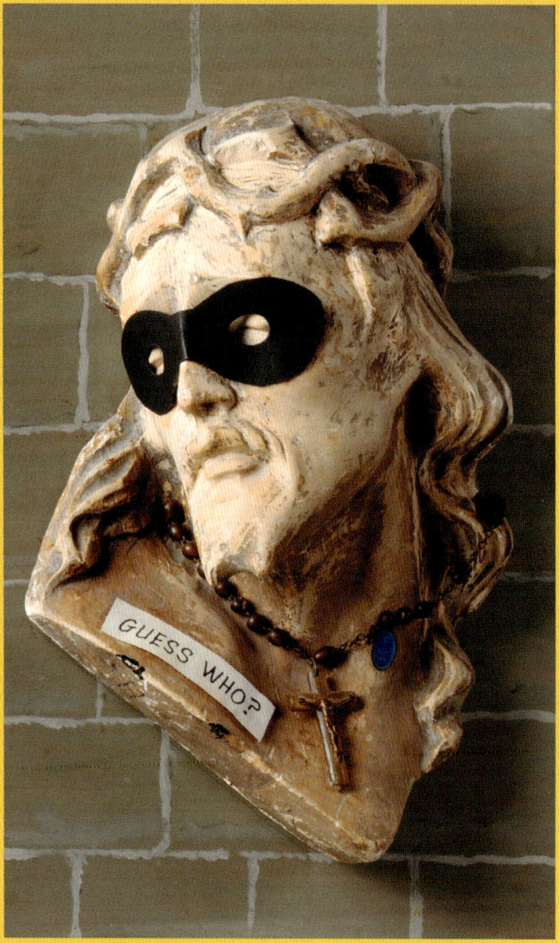

Guess Who?
Conroy Maddox, 1960

Make Mine a Quadruple
Anthony Earnshaw, 2000

The Glamorous Heart Attack
Anthony Earnshaw, 2000

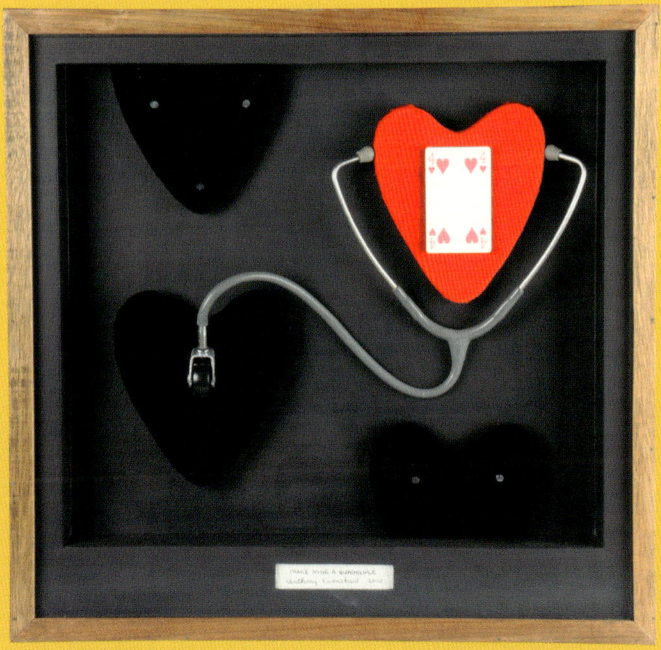

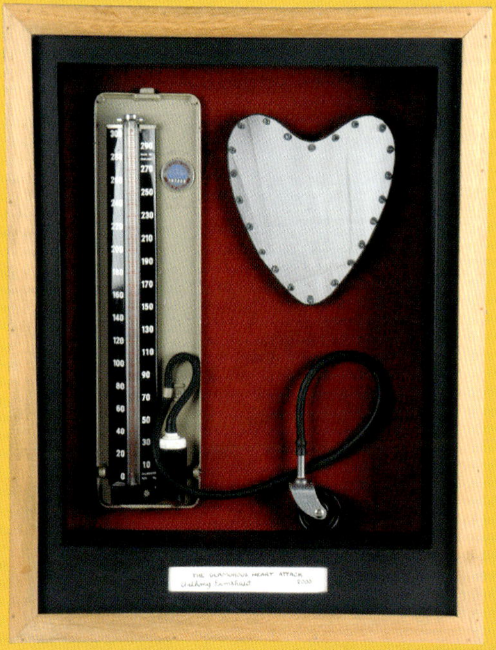

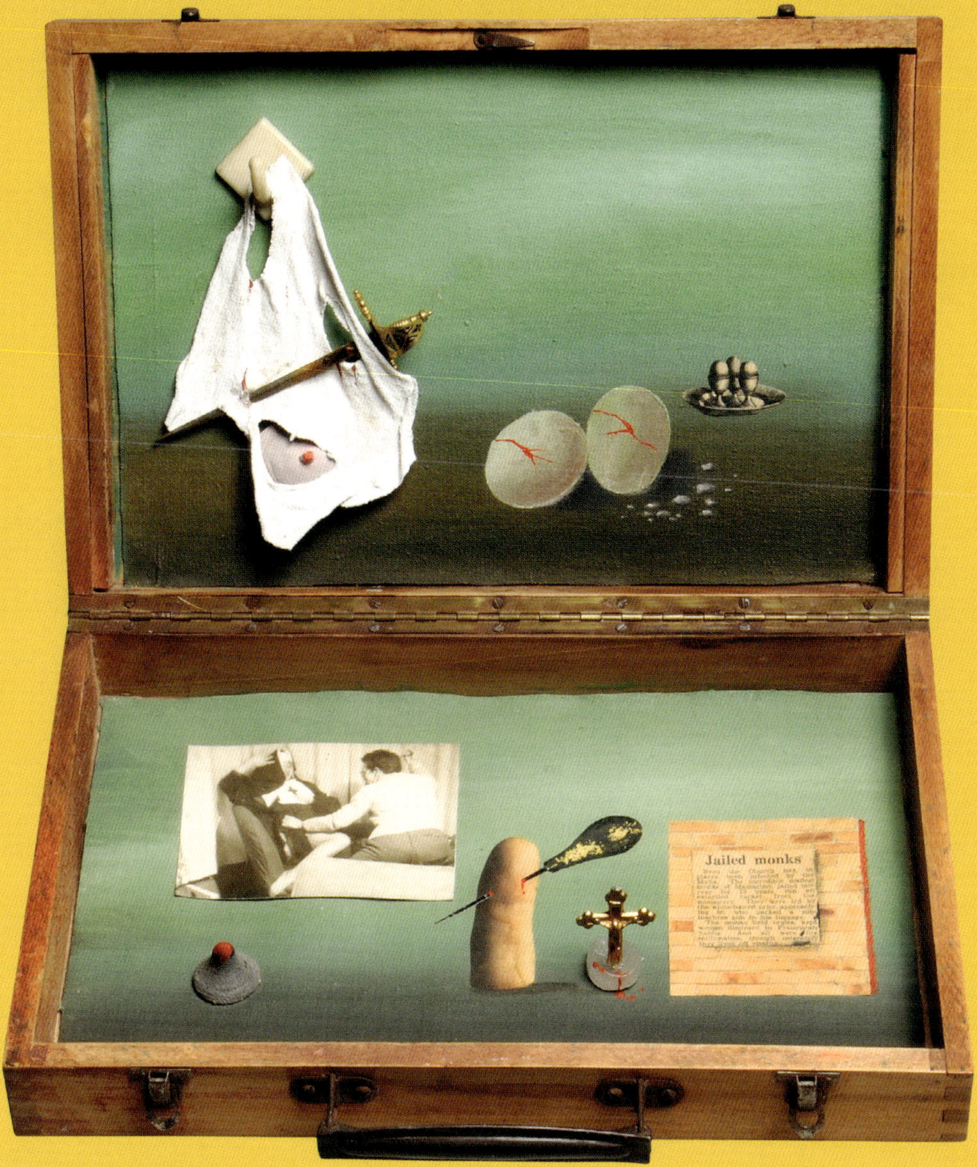

Denouément
Conroy Maddox, 1946

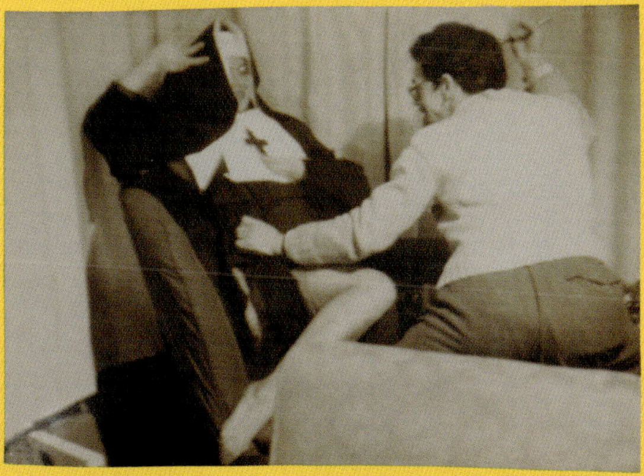

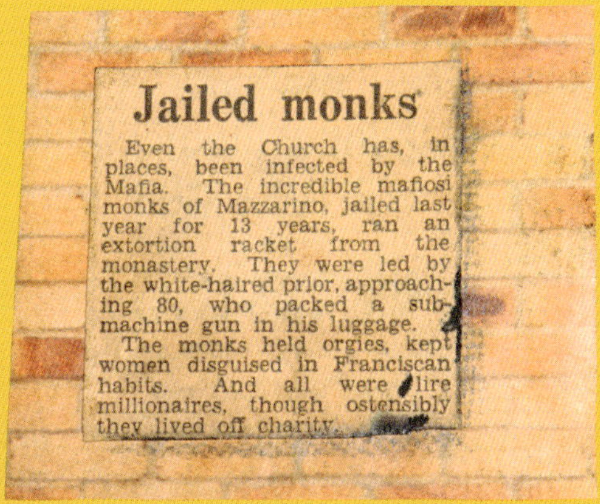

Jailed monks

Even the Church has, in places, been infected by the Mafia. The incredible mafiosi monks of Mazzarino, jailed last year for 13 years, ran an extortion racket from the monastery. They were led by the white-haired prior, approaching 80, who packed a submachine gun in his luggage.

The monks held orgies, kept women disguised in Franciscan habits. And all were millionaires, though ostensibly they lived off charity.

Denouément (details)
Conroy Maddox, 1946

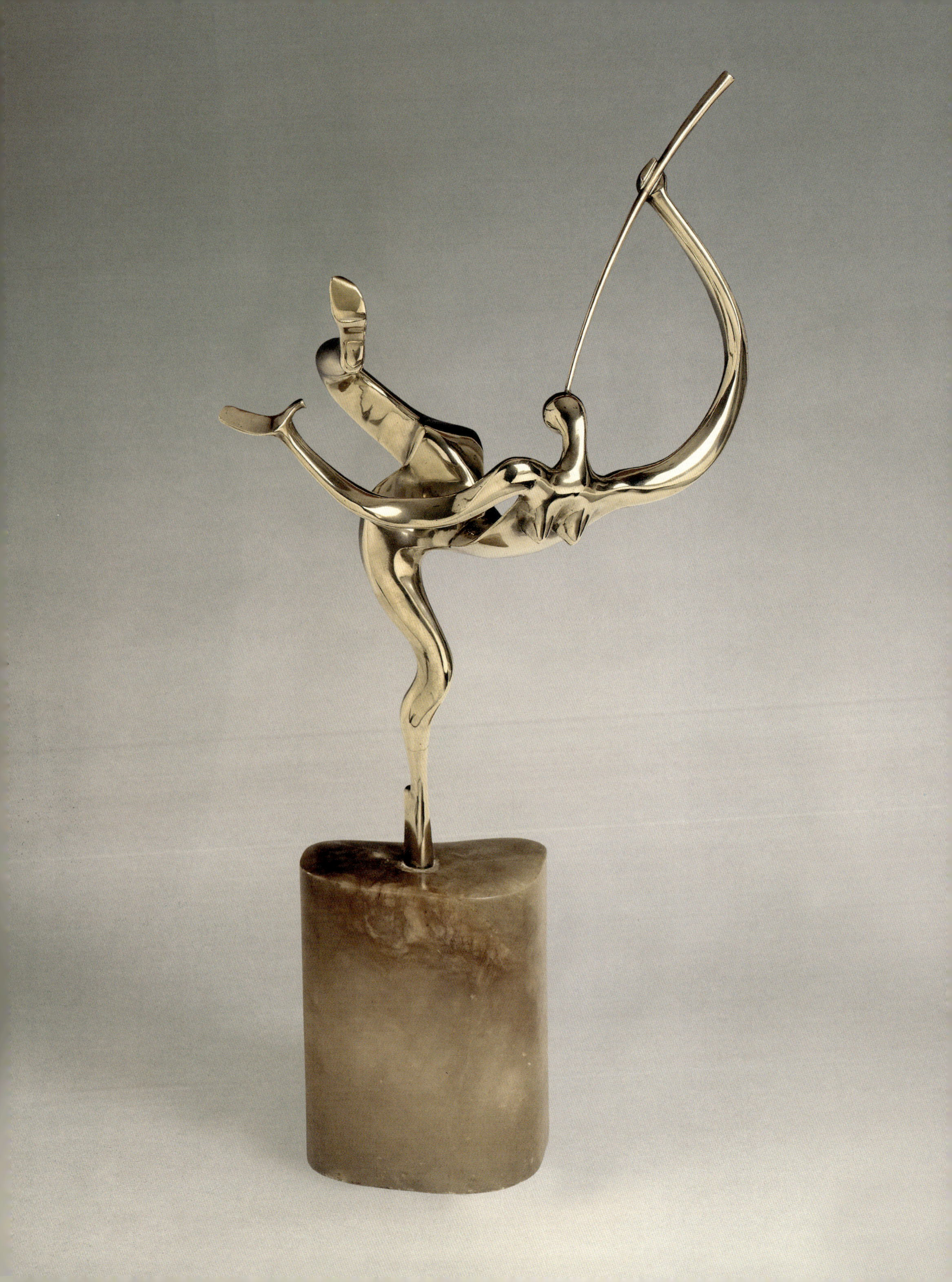

SCULPTURE AND ITS SHADOW

LOOKING AT SCULPTURE AND DRAWING IN THE HOME

JON WOOD

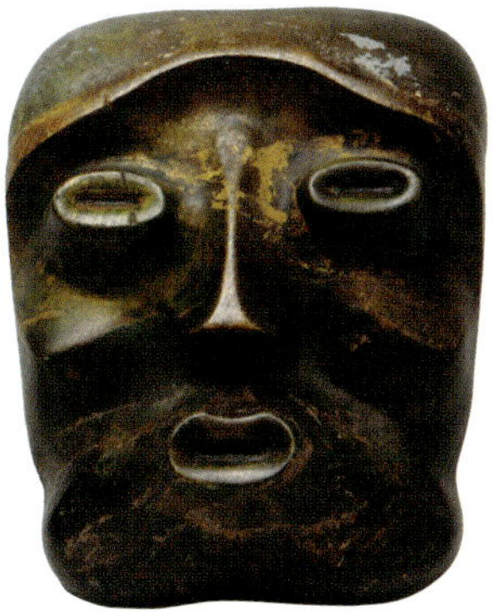

Anyone familiar with the Sherwin house and collection will know the significant place that British sculpture has in it. Over the last 25 years, Sherwin has been an avid collector of 20th century sculpture, with a keen and interested eye on the exhibitions and collections displays at Leeds Art Gallery and the Henry Moore Institute, carefully building up a collection of his own. Whilst surrealism lies at the heart of the Sherwin collection, his interest in sculpture is longstanding and has led him to acquire works that both pre-date and post-date the surrealists' activities, as well as to collect works which we might call 'surrealist sculpture'. . .[1] It has also led him to acquire works which, were made during decades in which surrealism was emerging as the dominant European art movement, but by artists without any direct affiliation with its ambitions.

One such item is Gertrude Hermes' extraordinary *Doorknocker* (c.1929), at once a bird and an abstract composition, it is both a sculpture and functional object. It is a subtle and elegant small-scale piece which very much reflects the richness of her work at this time. Throughout the early years of her career, Hermes not only worked as a wood-engraver and a sculptor, but also carried out a number of 'design' commissions, such as her fountain and door furniture for the Shakespeare Memorial Theatre in Stratford-upon-Avon in 1932.[2] Animals were frequently the subjects of her work at this time and Hermes often used polished surfaces to 'activate' her 'animalia', whether it be the sparkle of her aluminium *Moth* (1926) soaring towards the light or the shimmering surface of *Frog* (1930) poised to leap. The shiny surface of *Doorknocker* is designed to attract attention. The bird is a swallow and the shiny brass surface, which evokes the swift movement of this bird, is further activated when the work is held and the doorknocker used.

Moving this frontal work from vertical to horizontal changes the way it appears: first, we read an asymmetrical composition of spirals and arrows, hollows and cuts, curves and lines, and then, we are face to face with the beak and breast of a bird. Like a hammer hitting an anvil, the subsequent 'knock' on the door not only signals the transformation from abstraction to

Mask of Apollo in Autumn
Leon Underwood, 1933

Herald of the Day
Leon Underwood, 1934

1 This has sometimes been a two way process, with exchanges between collector and institution: Sherwin for example generously lent his polished version of Leon Underwood's *Herald of the Day* and Maurice Lambert's alabaster *Kneeling Figure* (1926) to the 2002 Henry Moore Institute exhibition *Shine: Sculpture and Surface in the 1920s and 1930s*; in return he was inspired by the exhibition to track down and acquire a version of Gertrude Hermes' *Doorknocker*.
2 For more on Gertrude Hermes, see the forthcoming publication: Jane Hill, *The Sculpture of Gertrude Hermes*, Aldershot: Lund Humphries, forthcoming.

figuration and back again, but it also announces the arrival of a visitor to the house. In addition, the choice of the 'swallow' for *Doorknocker* is highly significant, since it was this bird which was regarded as special in Roman mythology, sacred to the home and to the penates, the household gods. The original golden shine of Hermes' brass *Doorknocker* thus had sacred and auratic connotations, both celebrating and protecting the spiritual well-being of the domestic house.

Doorknocker
Gertrude Hermes, c.1929

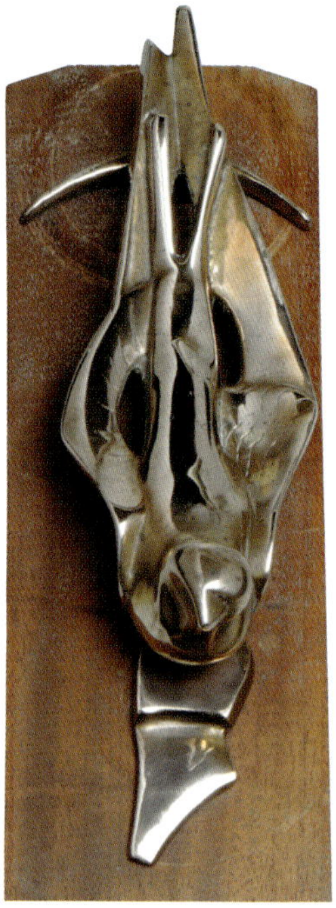

Once over the threshold and into the Sherwin house, you will be greeted by a large Hubert Dalwood sculpture, *Shield Screen* (1959–60), originally commissioned as a room divider for the St Martins' Place branch of the Ionian Bank, upon which, since it doubles as a sideboard, are seated small works by John Hoskin, Geoffrey Clarke and Laurence Burt. Here sculpture is placed on sculpture, in ways that only the collector or the artist is able to do, and some fascinating as well as playful cross-generational comparisons are afforded. Such ensembles generate reflections on the shared, rough and ready patina of metal sculpture in Britain in the 1950s. They also indirectly shed light on the subsequent 1960s fondness for colour and for the chic modern smoothness and colours of formica and plastics that Burt's work intimates, after all the 'Iron Age', Celtic existentialism of the previous decade.[3]

One of the consequences of Jeffrey Sherwin's approach to collecting and of the collection as domestic display, is that 'surrealistic' and 'surrealising' tendencies can be readily observed across work that we wouldn't usually specifically associate with the movement. Sometimes these tendencies, though surprising, are very real and historically precise, at other times they are more speculative and illusive. Alongside these axes of 'sculpture' and 'surrealism', the overall strength of the Sherwin collection resides in its blend of imaginative eclecticism, and the collector's age-old tendency to think and envisage objects in terms of pairs, groups and sets.

In the two main living rooms of the Sherwin house, there are more moments of 'creative curating' on view that can spark comparative thinking about the sculpture made in this country across the last century, through various pairings and juxtapositions. Gertrude Hermes' *Two Frogs (Copulating)* (1929), for example, sit poised next to Eduardo Paolozzi's *Copulating Grasshoppers* (one of a number of works by Paolozzi in the collection), reminding us of the saucy side of ('Carry on') British sculpture, as much as of the collector's own sense of humour. Such pieces can put the 's' back into 'sculpture'. 'Every bourgeois home should have one', the collector says, with a twinkle in his eye. What is particularly intriguing here is to find sculptors such as Hermes

3 Burt was an artist whose work quickly moved from one to the other, moving between helmet heads on the one hand and space men on the other, but always making work that subtly combined the archaic with the futuristic. See: Jon Wood, 'Laurence Burt's Space Odyssey', in *Things out of Mind: Work, Past and Present. An Exhibition of Objects and Images by Laurence Burt*, University of York, 2005.

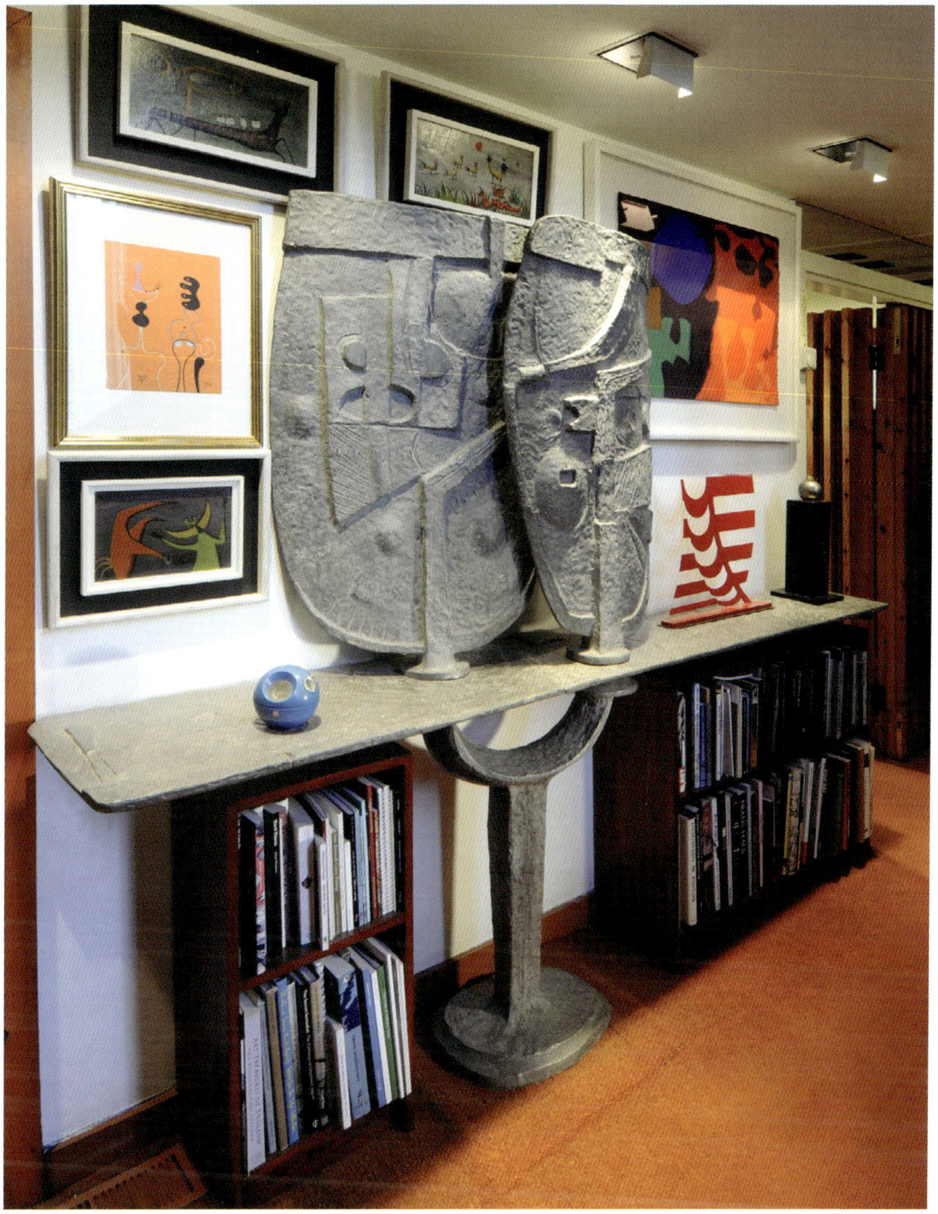

Hubert Dalwood's *Shield Screen* at the Sherwin's house

and Paolozzi sharing the same 'naughty but nice' joke and it reminds us how little we still know about the often playful shared sensibilities and concerns that charge and underpin the practices of sculptors in this country. Official histories will only give official stories and such lateral thinking might open imaginative and revealing ways into the subject, showing sculptors letting off steam, unhindered by academic and establishment mores. Such works, for example, might lead us to think of other such copulating couples in the work of Eric Gill, Jacob Epstein and more recently Bill Woodrow. . . and to questions about the sexual side of many British sculptors' interests, well expressed within some of its major oeuvres, in the sculptural articulation of erotic thought.

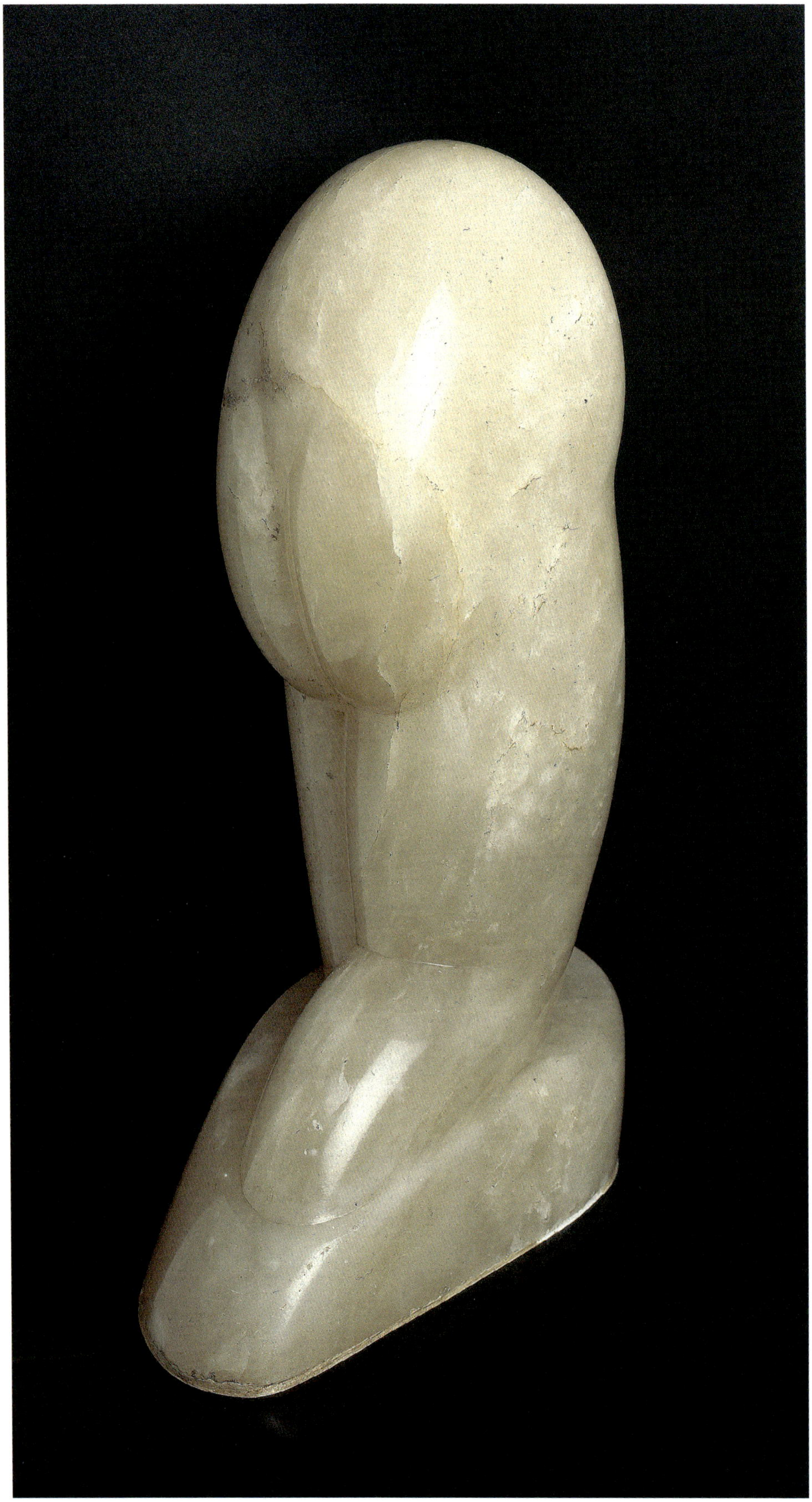

Kneeling Torso
Maurice Lambert, 1927

The Sherwin collection can thus reveal some surprisingly strange bedfellows and this continues elsewhere in highly revealing ways. We find a group of sculptures in the 'mother/father and child' genre, but without the usual child-nurturing posture. Two are by Maurice Lambert and where we might have expected to find another inter-war work by one of Lambert's peers, such as Underwood or Kennington, we find a 1980s sculpture by Glynn Williams making up the third item of this group. Together they serve to remind us how ubiquitous and dominant the child-bearing, child-nurturing 'mother and child' set-piece, much favoured by sculptors such as Henry Moore, would become across the last century. The fact that such departures continued to be made over a 50-year period, either side of the Second World War, underscores the cultural prominence of this 'mother and child' genre in this country. These carved modelled men and women don't sentimentally cradle their children, rather they juggle them acrobatically, balancing and supporting them on the heads, hands and shoulders.

Untitled (Foetus)
Leon Underwood, 1924–25

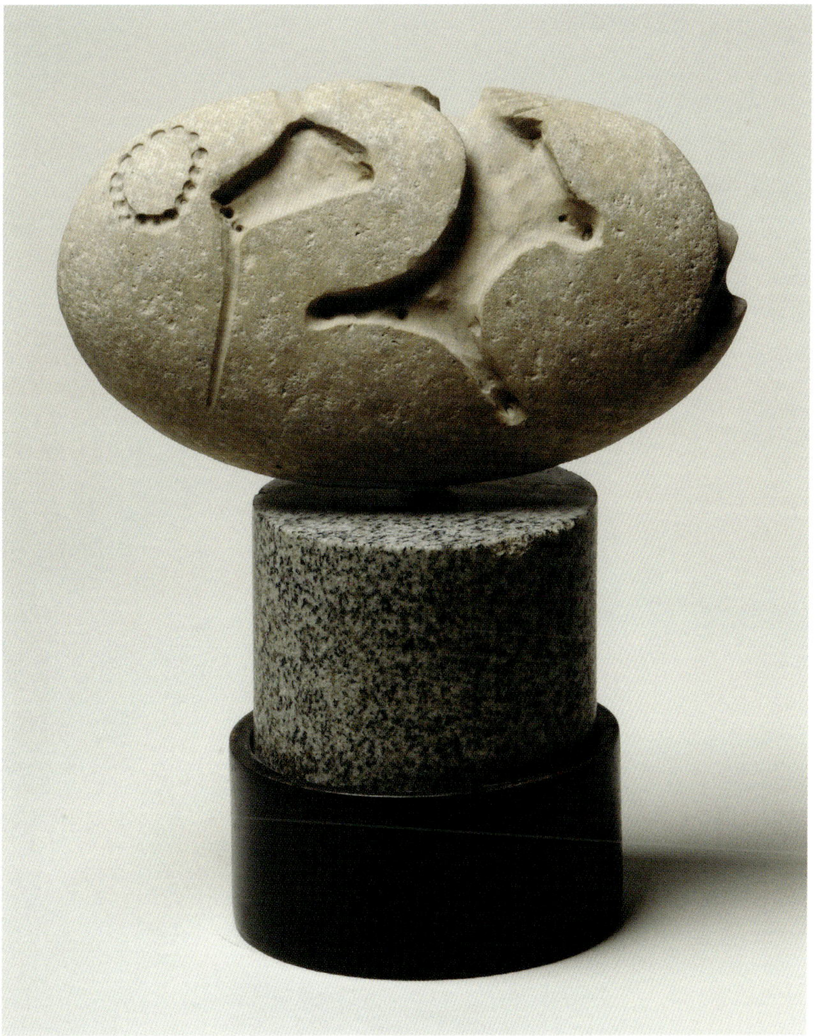

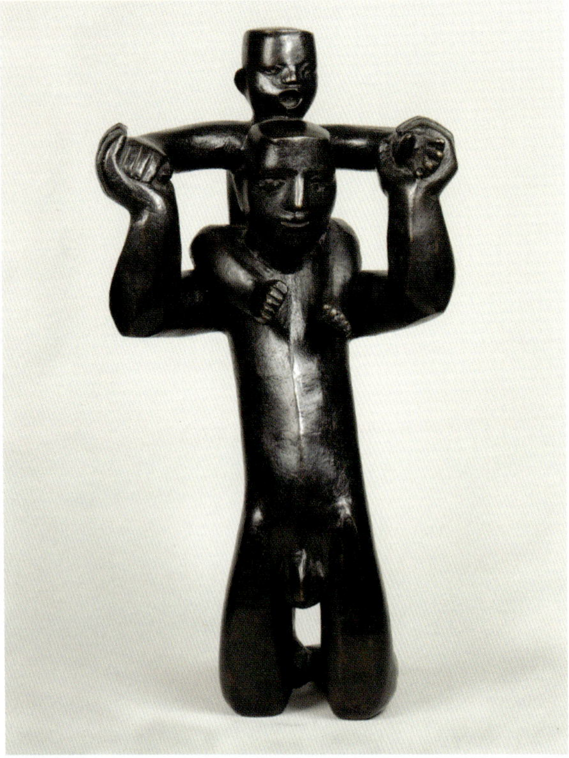

Kneeling, Holding, Protecting
Glynn Williams, c.1981

Woman Lifting Child
Maurice Lambert, c.1934

Brother and Sister
Maurice Lambert, c.1935

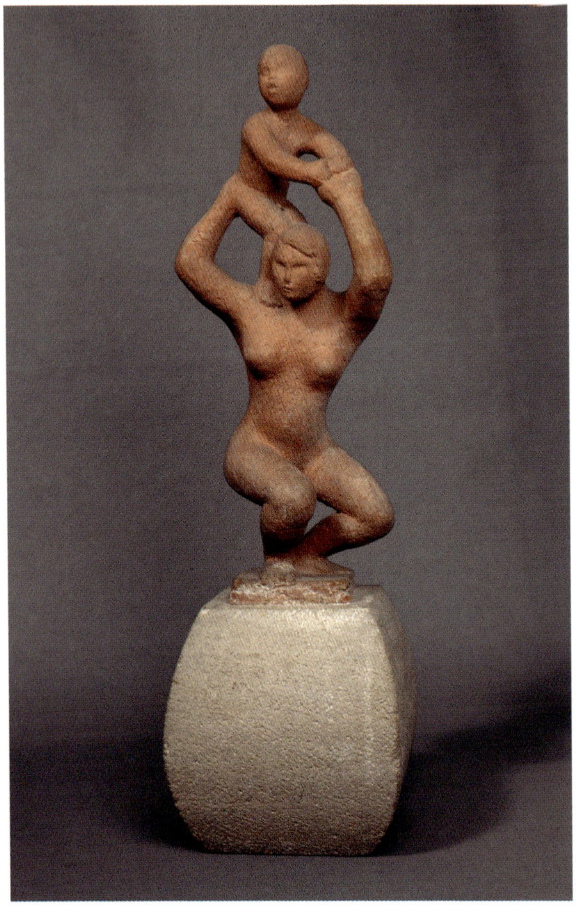

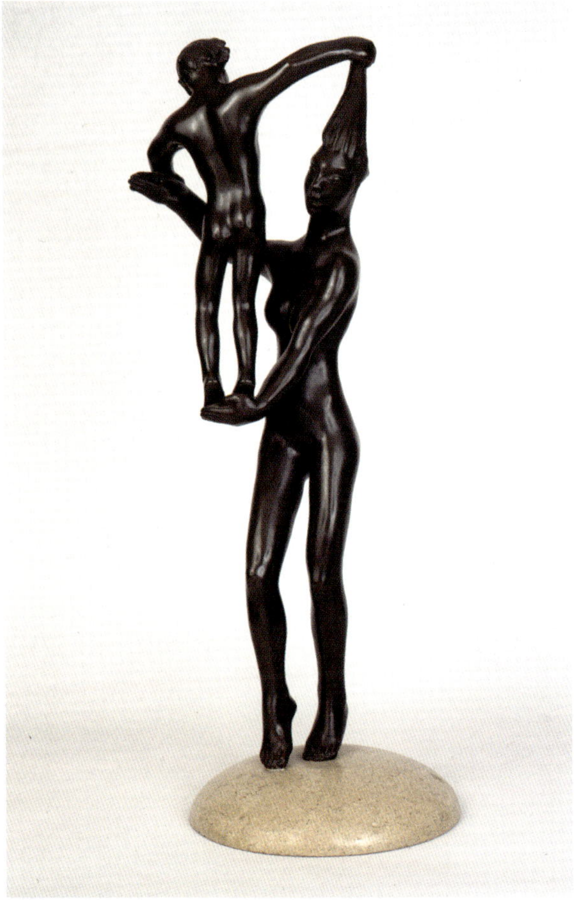

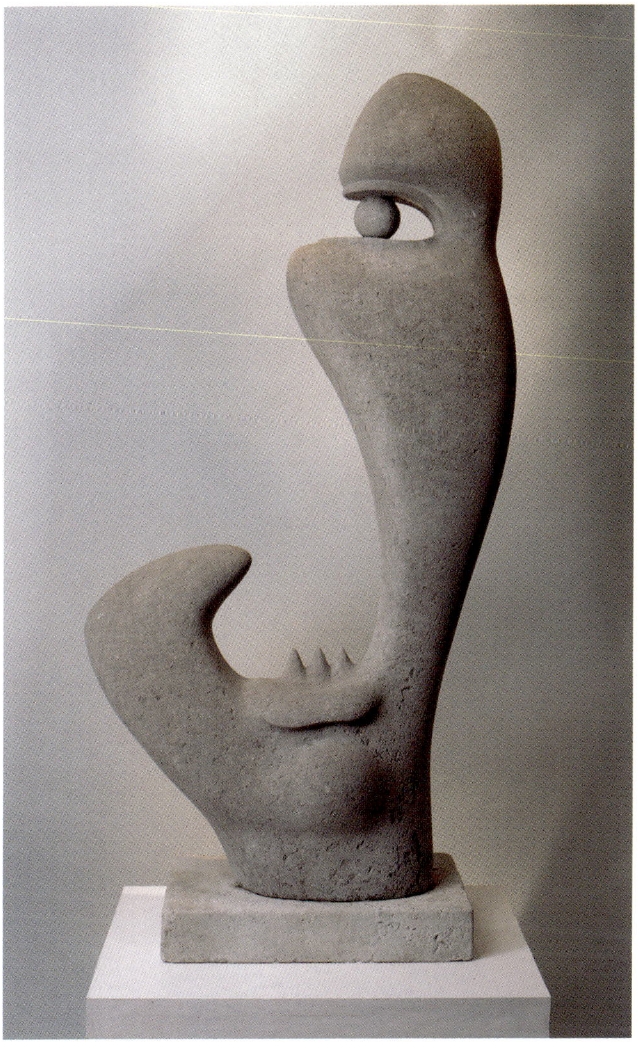

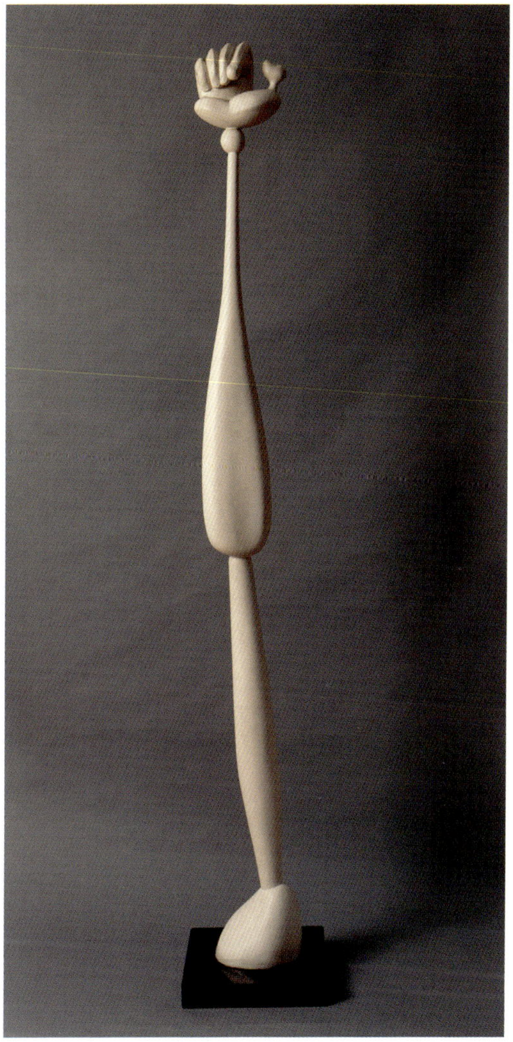

The more strictly 'surrealist' component of his sculpture collection also reveals some unexpected companion pieces. We find a good stock of Conroy Maddox works – sculptures and assemblages, as well as paintings – and others by Anthony Earnshaw. Most strikingly of all, however, are F.E. McWilliam's *Spanish Head* (1938–39), *Carving* (1936) and his Spanish Civil War work *The Long Arm* (1939), which sit in close proximity to Leon Underwood's amazing *Foetus* (1924–25) and *Mask of Apollo in Autumn* (1933). Between these works, important questions emerge involving our perception of how cultural politics were articulated by sculptors in three dimensions and in ways that blend modern biomorphic/skeletal form with political message. Underwood's work should be shown alongside McWilliam's more often and seeing them all alongside Eileen Agar's *Angel of Mercy* (1934), the curious sibling of her *Angel of Anarchy* and once reproduced as *The Politician* in Tony del Renzio's *Arson* magazine in 1942, casts new light into the shadows of their subtle political lives.

Spanish Head
F.E. McWilliam, 1939

The Long Arm
F.E. McWilliam, 1939

One of the most intriguing aspects of the Sherwin sculpture collection, however, resides in his consistent interest in combining sculptures with works on paper which relate in some way to them. 'British sculpture' in the Sherwin collection is thus revealed not just by sculptures, but also by works on paper and other 'flat' works. And, like other collectors and curators, he has an eye and mind for pairs and doubles. Sometimes the framed work behind the sculpture will be either a preliminary or a post-work drawing, at other times an autonomous drawing with a curious life and enigmatic relation of its own to the sculpture in front of it. This two dimensional/three dimensional combination is one that encourages the viewer to move between and across dimensions: from sculpture to drawing/painting and back again, comparing the flat and the shaped, and pondering again the processes and narratives of making (amongst other things) that might charge the spaces between the two objects. Such comparisons are afforded across a number of groups in the collection. They are exemplified most obviously by Henry Moore's small bronze *Reclining Mother and Child* (1979) seen alongside a crayon and white drawing of the same year and subject in the Sherwin collection.

Study for Reclining Mother and Child
Henry Moore, 1979

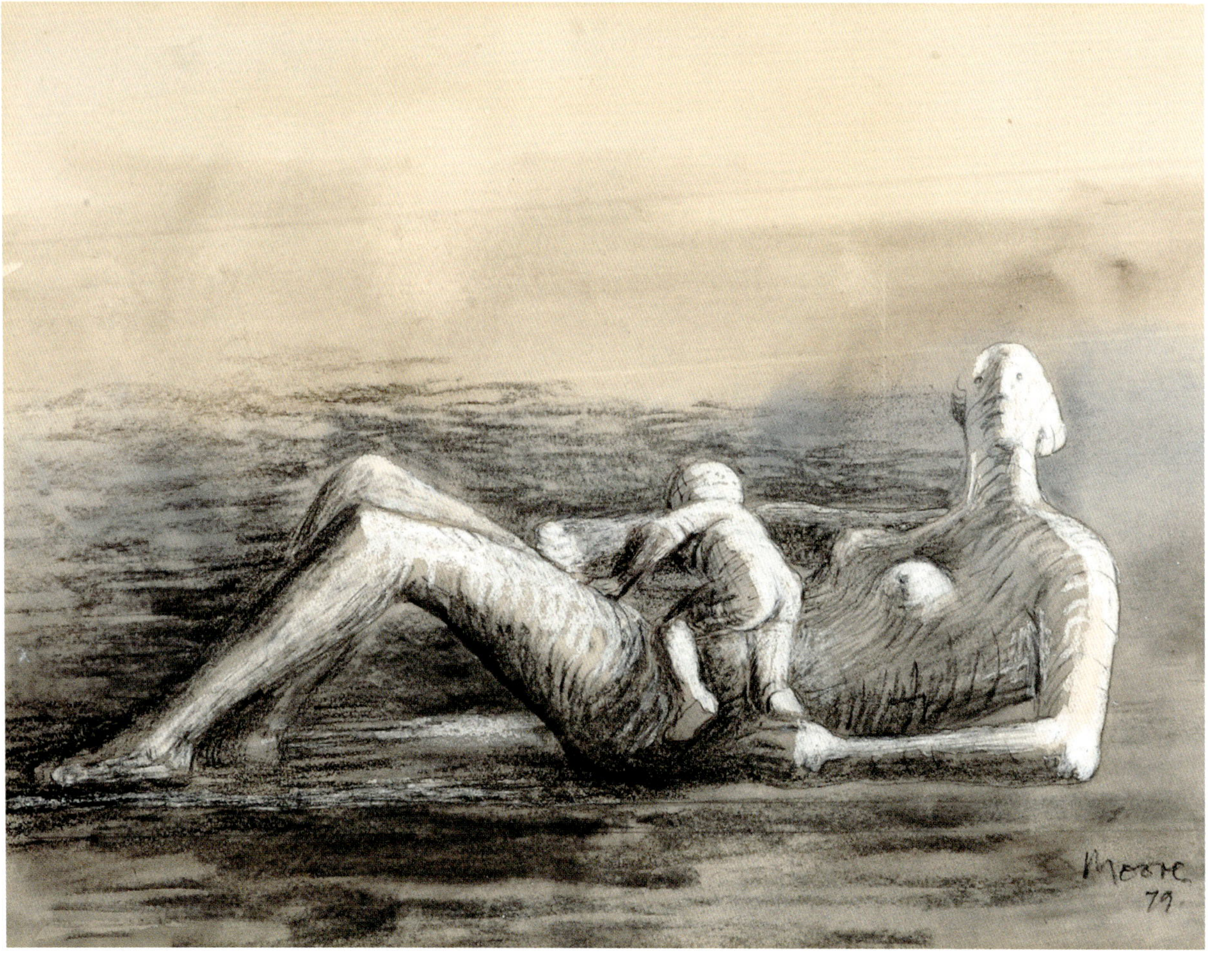

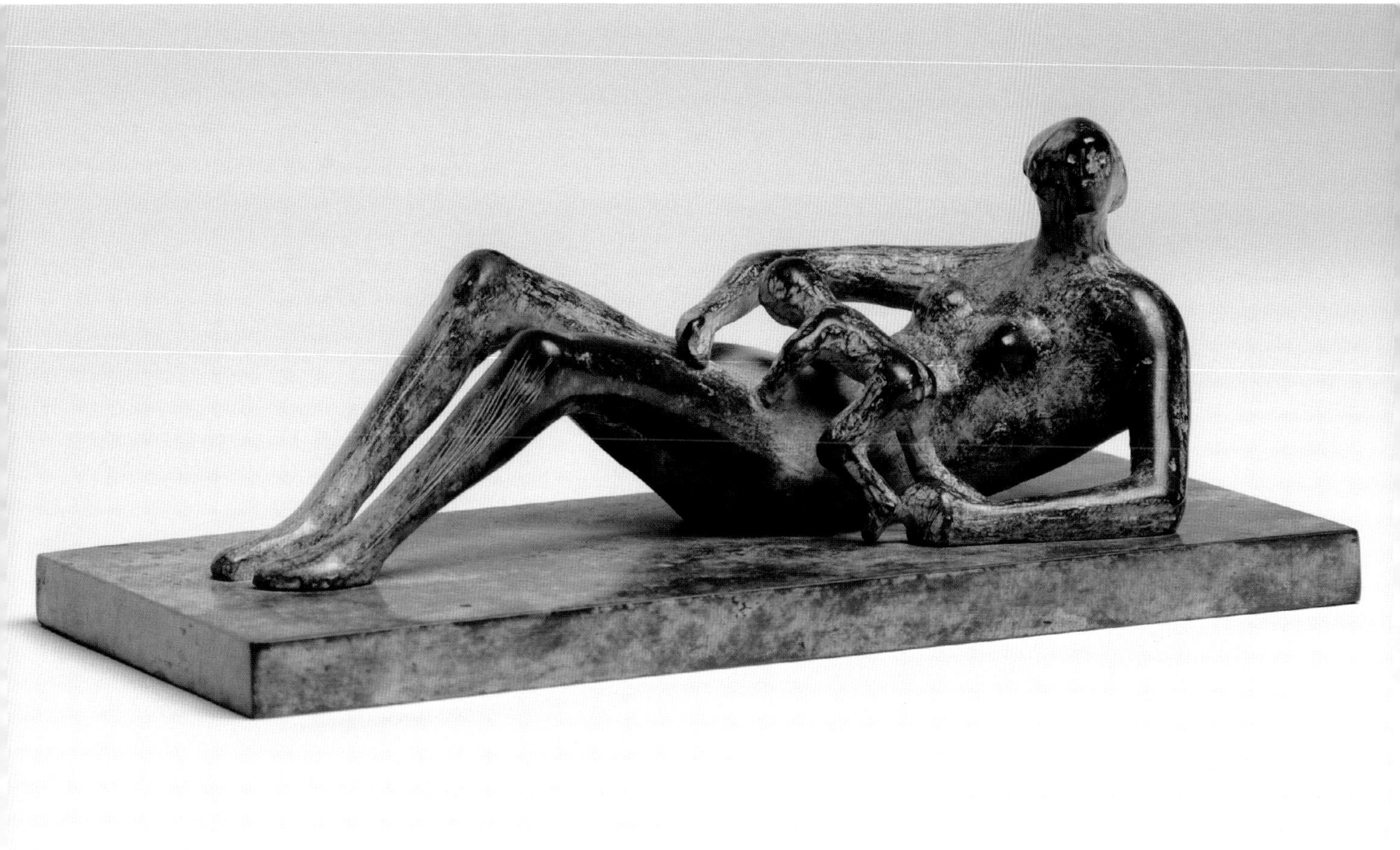

Reclining Mother and Child
Henry Moore, 1979

A number of works on paper have been acquired and accumulated around Gaudier-Brzeska's large relief sculpture called *Wrestlers*. This work was originally modelled and carved in plaster in 1913–14 (this original is in the Museum of Fine Arts in Boston) and Sherwin owns one of the nine herculite casts made in 1965.[4] Around this work he has gathered Gaudier's *Drawing for a Decorated Cupboard* (c.1913), a drawing of two *Wrestlers* (c.1913) and Gaudier-Brzeska's linocut of two *Wrestlers* (c.1913) pulled by his friend Horace Brodzky, as an edition of 50, a number of years after Gaudier's death in 1915.[5] What this group reveals is striking. His plaster relief has always been a difficult work to date (1913 or 1914) as well as to understand, but seen within this group of works a number of aspects become clearer. The *Wrestlers* were both a subject and a composition for Gaudier-Brzeska at this time that echoed across works and media. It also recurred with different kinds of figuration and different levels of abstraction. The linocut image, for example, is one of the most extreme versions of the latter and the drawing one of the more easily legible. The repetition of the subject might also suggest its commercial reproducibility and the fact that his *Drawing for a Decorated Cupboard* also used its forms, suggests that *Wrestlers* has strong

4 Evelyn Silber, *Gaudier-Brzeska*, London: Thames and Hudson, 1996, p.266.
5 This linocut, pulled by Horace Brodzky, was used for the cover of Ezra Pound's book on Gaudier-Brzeska, when it was reprinted in paperback by New Directions in 1970. Not only was the print reproduced the wrong way around, but it was a strange image to use, given Brodzky's own public disagreements with Pound and the American poet's account of Gaudier's life and work.

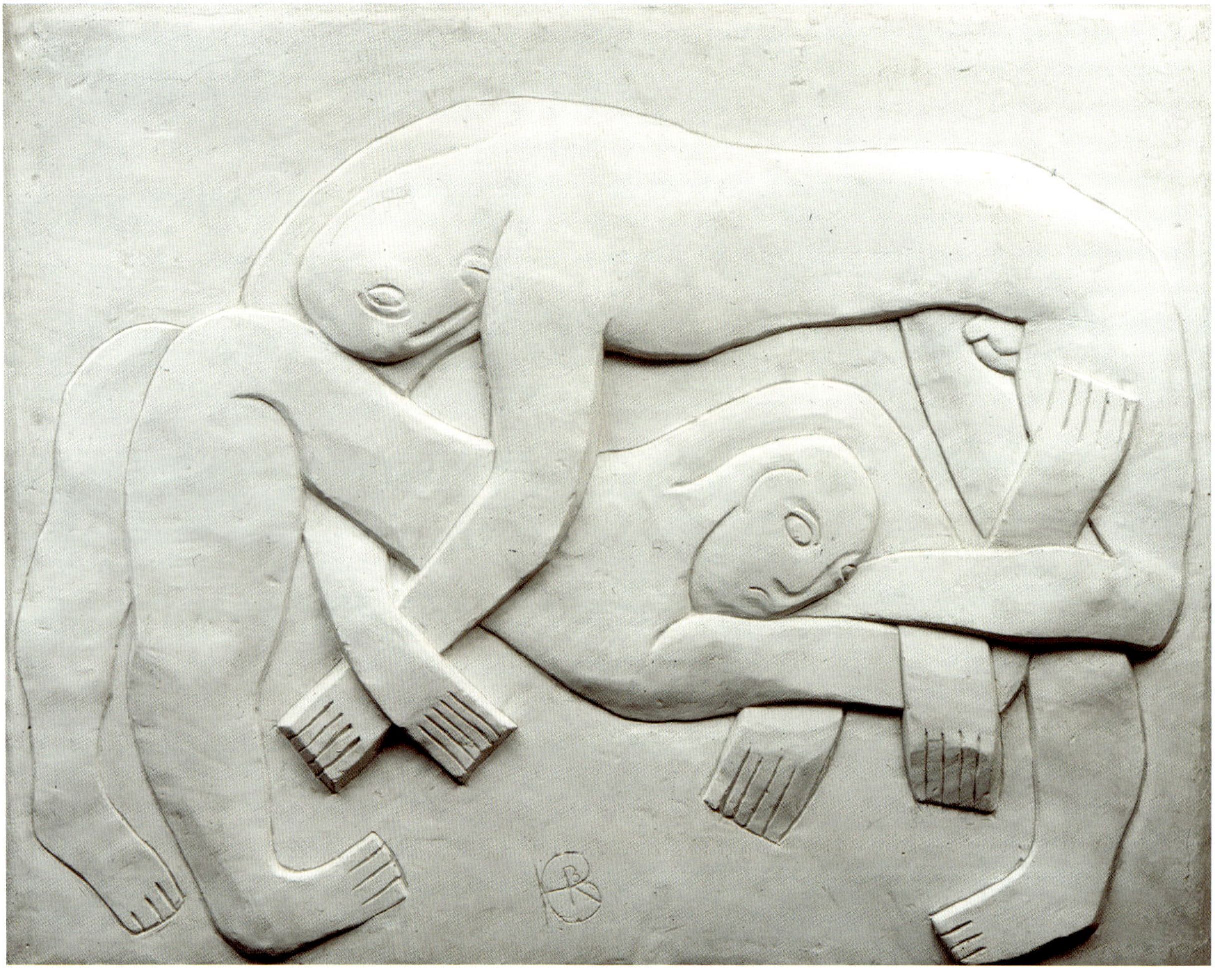

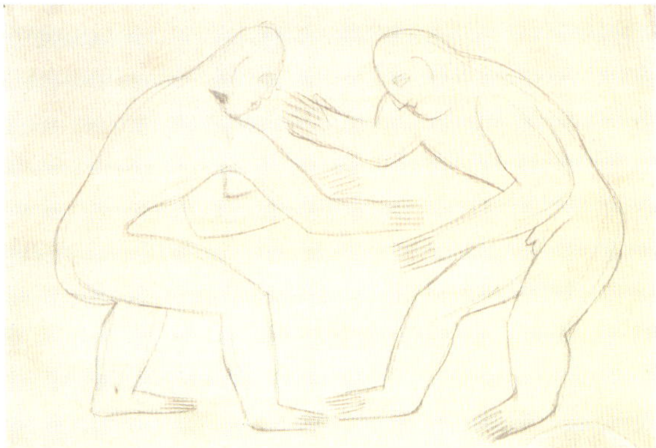

Wrestlers
Henri Gaudier-Brzeska, 1913 (cast in 1965)

Wrestlers
Henri Gaudier-Brzeska, c.1913

connections to his work with Roger Fry's Omega Workshops.[6] *Wrestlers*, the scale and format of which was unusual in Gaudier-Brzeska's oeuvre, was thus likely envisaged as part of a designed and decorated interior. This context might also help us grasp the changing degrees of figuration and abstraction that these interlocking figures experience: we find, for example, a similarly raised level of abstraction in Gaudier-Brzeska's two *Wrestlers*

6 For more on Gaudier and Omega and in specific relation to the work of Raymond Duchamp-Villon, see: Jon Wood, *Henri Gaudier-Brzeska: Artistic Identity and the Place of Sculpture in the Omega Workshops*, in Alexandra Gerstein (ed.), *Beyond Bloomsbury: Designs of the Omega Workshops*, 1913–19, London: Courtauld Art Gallery, 2009, pp.34–41.

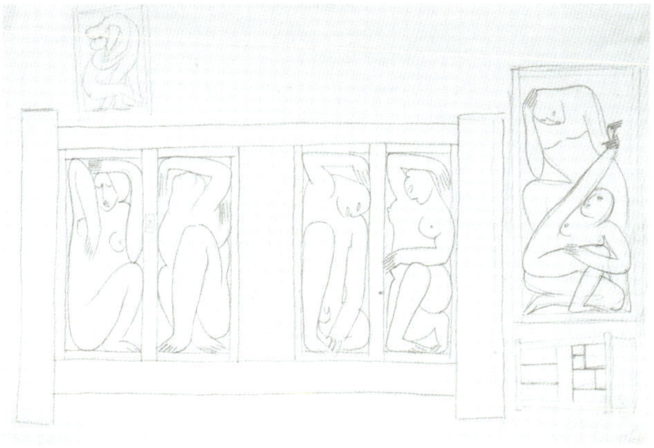

Drawing for a Decorated Cupboard
Henri Gaudier-Brzeska, 1914

which feature on one of his marquetry trays for Omega. Perhaps different items adorned by a number of variations on the wrestlers theme were likely to have featured in the same room in 1914. Finally, the different types of physical action represented – some are more resonant of figures in an embrace, more like Raymond Duchamp-Villon's *Lovers* – underscore the amenability of the work and its meanings for different kinds of viewer at the time. It has an Omega as well as vorticist appeal and has the potential to appeal to both men and women. *Wrestlers*, seen through the small group of works, appears as a deliberately open and ambivalent work: it is about either love or war, and about both together at the same time.

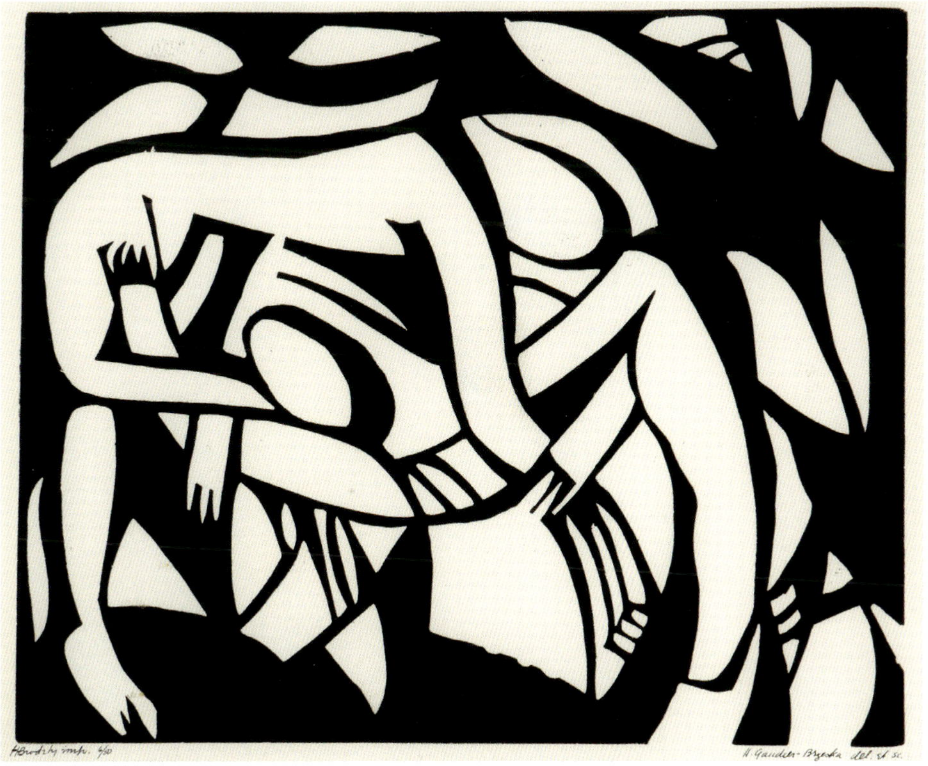

Wrestlers
Henri Gaudier-Brzeska, c.1914

Looking back and forth between Gaudier-Brzeska's relief sculpture and the drawings can offer some new interpretations for the sculpture in the light of the contexts of its production and reception. For another group of sculptures and related drawings – Bernard Meadows' *Black Crab* (1953) and *Study for Black Crab* (1952), and Kenneth Armitage's *Family Going for a Walk* (1951) and the work on paper of the same name and date – the works on paper go some way to provide a more poetic 'context': namely the imagined atmosphere and 'microclimate' of the finished sculpture. Such drawings, you might say, seem to carry the 'weather' of their respective sculptures with them: providing a context which, for the artist, evidently informs the meaning and associations of the sculpture.

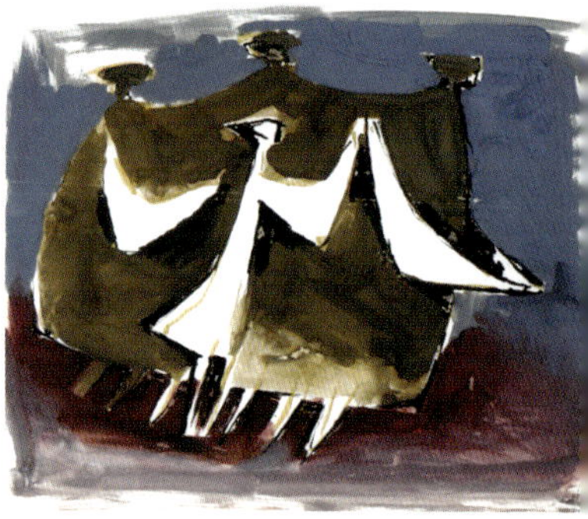

Study for Family Going for a Walk
Kenneth Armitage, 1951

Armitage's sculpture is the original small-scale model for a larger version which was exhibited at the Venice Biennale in 1952, when Armitage had come to light as a significant contemporary sculptor. The Sherwin sculpture collection has a particular strength in 1950s British sculpture, and includes Geoffrey Clarke's *Maquette for the Unknown Political Prisoner Competition* (1952) (the cone-like cage structures of which find an echo in his print on the same subject of that year), Eduardo Paolozzi's *Bandaged Head* (1953–56) and Mary Martin's *Expanding Form* (1955). Armitage's sculpture was thought to be a terracotta model, but conversations between the collector and the artist revealed the work to be made out of dental plaster, a tougher and

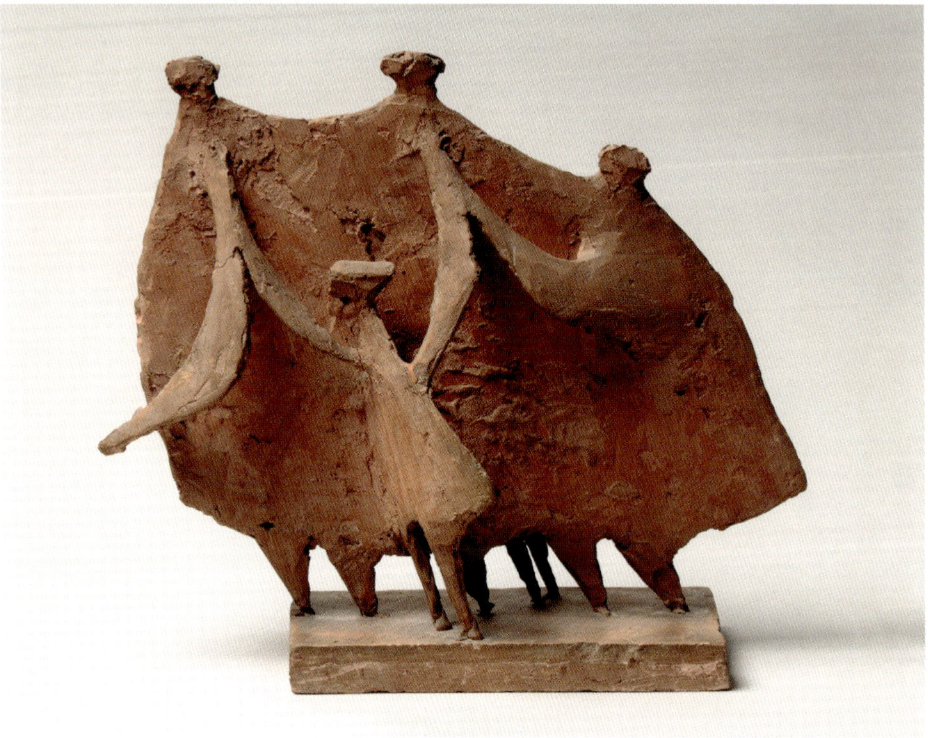

Family Going for a Walk
Kenneth Armitage, 1951

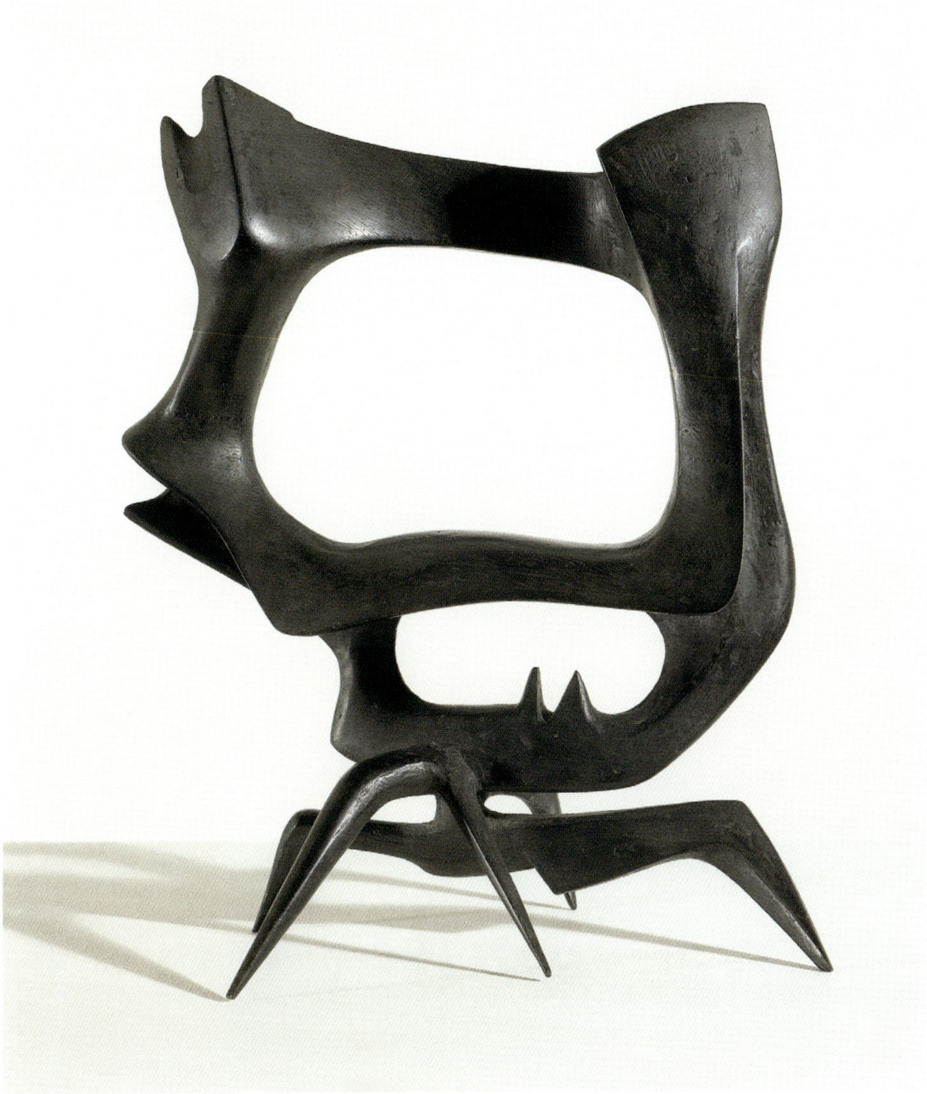

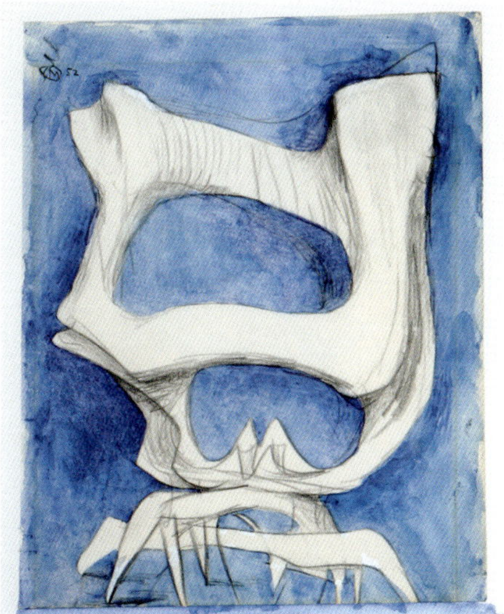

Black Crab
Bernard Meadows, 1953

Study for Black Crab
Bernard Meadows, 1952

more resilient material. Looking back and forth between sculpture and work on paper is to look at the evocation of two strikingly different temperatures and humidity levels juxtaposed. The sculpture is dry, arid even, whilst the work on paper – a painting as much as a drawing – is rain drenched. It presents a family – united, ground-bound, arm in arm and soaked to the skin, under blustery slate grey skies and, judging by those skies, under the promise of more torrential downpours to come. It's a walk in the park, a walk along the promenade, a walk with the Great British weather. . . and we watch this family group as it is blown along together like clothes on a washing line.

Whereas the Armitage works tell of an ordinary British scene with a familiar British weather, the two works by Bernard Meadows together evoke altogether more distant climes and stranger beings, shores and experiences. Meadows' series of crab sculptures of the 1950s and onwards were inspired by his experiences in the Second World War whilst stationed in the Coco Islands in the Indian Ocean.[7] Photographs of Meadows as a young airman show him crouching on a beach there surrounded by crabs, of which the artist had a fear. One of the preliminary pencil and wash drawings for *Black Crab* (1953) shows the exaggerated monstrous scale of the sculptor's crab. It shows it looming large – up, close and personal – and encourages the viewer to imagine the actual work even larger than it is as a sculpture. It also shows the brilliant bright sky blue that provides the creature with its backdrop and its sun, sea and sand habitat. Bronze is often seen as being colourless, but set within this luminous Asia Pacific context the hard blackness of his bronze black crab is powerfully accentuated, as are the smooth, curvy and spiky forms of this imaginary crustacean's armoured body. It is not difficult to imagine this creature darting sideways on the hot sands: at once a possible meal and the stuff of nightmares.

The 1950s sculptures of Armitage and Meadows work particularly well alongside their flatter, pictorial counterparts partly because the sculptures themselves were very frontally composed, with decisive fronts and backs. They are in a sense all image and outline, despite their respective surfaces and volumes, and particularly amenable to graphic representation. This makes it comparatively easy for the viewer to move back and forth, spotting differences and similarities – an activity that can afford insight into how the artists themselves envisaged the overall work and concept at different stages of its creation. With later combinations of works, made by Bill Woodrow and Edward Allington, where figures twist and turn and where fronts and backs become less easy to define, the relationship of the two and three dimensional is of a different, more complex order.

7 Alan Bowness (with an essay by Penelope Curtis), *Bernard Meadows: Sculpture and Drawings*, The Henry Moore Foundation in association with Lund Humphries Publishers, London, 1995, p.10.

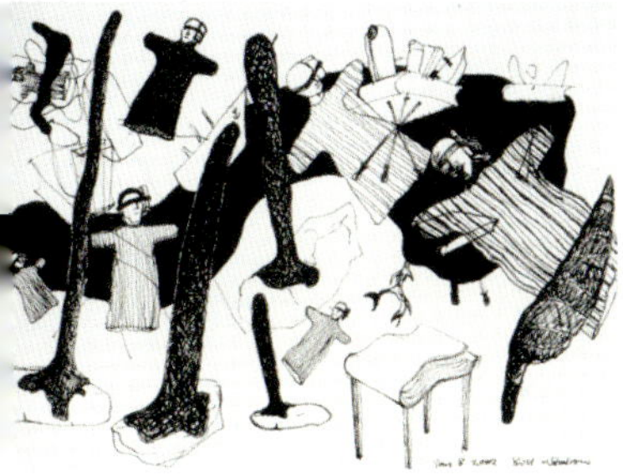

Playing with History
Bill Woodrow, 2002

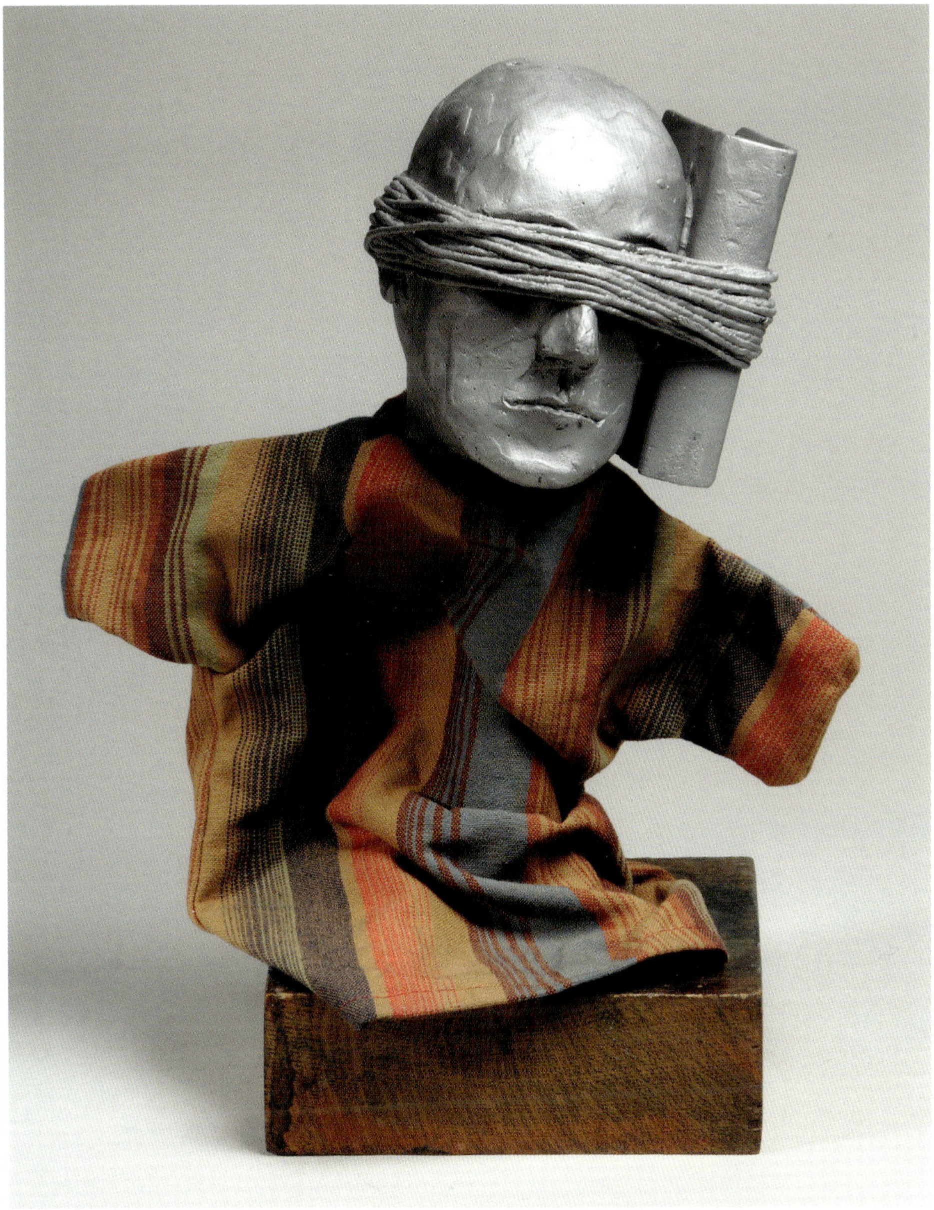

Playing with History
Bill Woodrow, 2002

Woodrow's *Playing with History* (2002) is difficult to display as a sculpture because, as a puppet, it is designed to be worn on the hand and played with. The movements and turns of the hand of the puppeteer thus determine its positions and, in part, its figuration. As sculpture and on static display, it has been shown both with its aluminium head on its side (as if asleep) and upright (as if awake). The drawing in the Sherwin collection relating to this piece animates the mobility of this puppet sculpture, for the work is shown in various states and positions, each floating in space. Although the drawing has something of a 'preliminary' relationship to the finished puppet, Woodrow's drawing is also a work in its own right and includes other items and sculptures as well as the puppet. The drawing thus sits in parallel to the sculpture, at once 'about it' and the broader visual and allegorical context within which Woodrow has imagined and made it. It provides an artistic and intellectual context which includes his Fourth Plinth commission in Trafalgar Square, *Regardless of History* (2000), and which relates to the artist's interest in giving sculptural shape and figuration to the ways in which the past is both stored and communicated, both shared and forgotten.

The relationship between drawing and sculpture in Woodrow's work is complex, with drawing often taking on an independent and autonomous life of its own. Within Edward Allington's practice drawings operate similarly, although Allington's sculptures often start on the page as drawings for possible sculptures, beautifully drawn and contextualised within some kind of architecturally structured domestic interior. This interior is often delineated

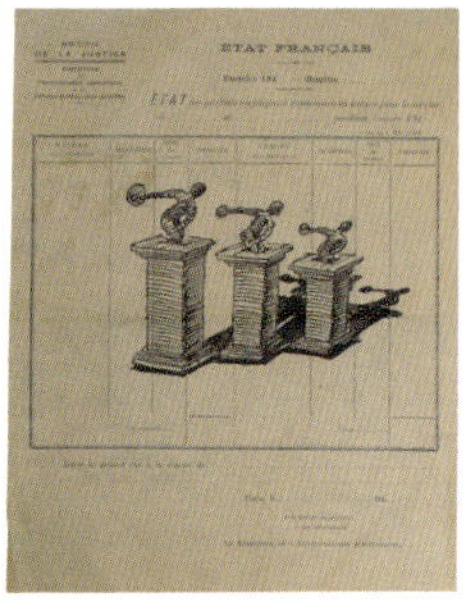

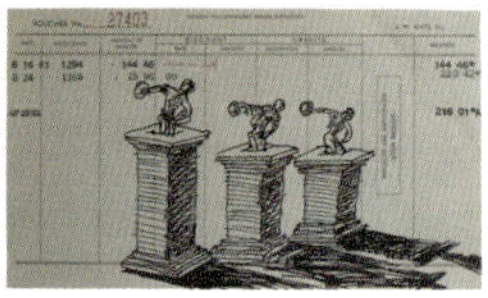

Study for Myron's Discobolus Diminished
Edward Allington, 1987

Myron's Discobolus Diminished
Edward Allington, 1987

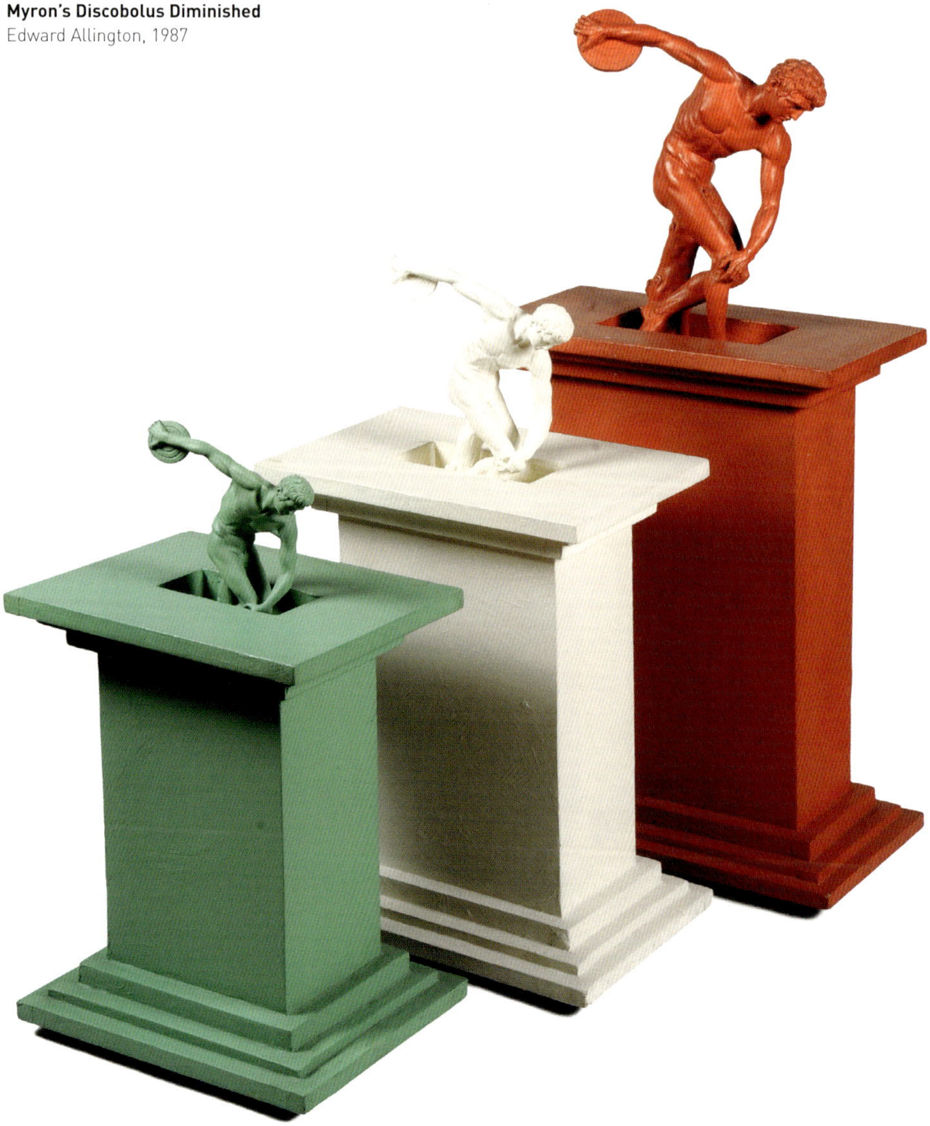

8 The artist in conversation with the author, 16 April 2009.

by doorways, skirting boards, plaster cornices, stucco ornamentation and most strikingly by wooden floorboards, which suggest one of those perspectivally disorientating rooms that we find in Giorgio de Chirico and then Max Ernst's surrealist paintings and graphic works. Allington's *Myron's Discobolus Diminished* (1987) is a three-part sculpture, which features the Roman disc thrower in three different sizes within three different sized plinths, each painted red, white and green, in keeping with the Italian flag. Whilst the subject is classical, Allington's rendition of the subject revamps it with post-modern pop, putting the 'disco' back in 'discobolus'. It is all about moves, both athletic and conceptual. The preliminary drawings which relate to this sculpture are intriguing. Both are drawn on old ledger sheets – one American and one French – which Allington had picked up from junk stores on his travels. Such 'scavenged' materials, as he calls them, are then used for sketches, quickly made in the studio whilst working on the sculpture. Asked if they were preliminary drawings, Allington's answer was telling: 'I can't really remember if they were made before, during or after. They were sketches that I made when thinking about the sculpture and how it might work'.[8]

Seen as a group in themselves, the sculptures and related works on paper in the Sherwin collection reveal some of the mutually informative, symbiotic relationships that can occur between media when the making of sculpture is at stake. They remind us that traditional narratives and time lines of making, understood in terms of 'before' the sculpture and 'after' the sculpture, are too simplistic to convey the complex life of such works. They are not simply drawings for sculpture or drawings from sculpture, nor are they duplicates, one mirroring the other, rather they are always drawings about sculpture and how it has, in one way or another, been imagined, shaped and staged. The space between dimensions, between the sculpture and the drawing, is thus a very rich and insightful as well as a shared one. In a sense this charged and resonant space has the potential to create a third work, in a way that brings the two works together, making them more than the sum of their parts: a third work which simultaneously inhabits the realm of the actual sculpture and its pictorial representation framed on the wall.

THE BRUNO HAT HOAX

AMAZING HOAX ON ART EXPERTS
UNKNOWN ARTIST WITH FALSE MOUSTACHE
Daily Express, July 23 1929

The 1920s and 1930s marked the heyday of The Bright Young Things. They threw extravagant parties and staged highly elaborate hoaxes – and all reported with relish in the gossip columns at the time. One such event was described by the *Daily Express* as 'An Amazing Hoax on Art Experts'. Reports also appeared in the *Graphic* and *Evening Standard*, *The Sunday Dispatch* and the *Daily Mirror*.

In the summer of 1929 a sophisticated hoax was played upon the world of modern art. Evelyn Waugh, Brian Howard, John Banting and a handful of Mitfords successfully held an exhibition in the London house of Bryan Guinness. They claimed to have discovered the brilliant new talent of artist Bruno Hat, working in obscurity in a village near Clymping.

The story was put out that Bruno Hat was discovered by Bryan Guinness in the general store in the village of Clymping, where Bryan Guinness had a summer cottage, and that the paintings were done by a thirty-one-year-old native of the German city of Lübeck and the stepson of the lady who owned the store. Self-taught he had never exhibited, but some of his work had been taken to Paris where it had been well received – so an exhibition had been arranged at the home of Bryan Guinness. Selected

The Adoration of the Magi
John Banting, 1929

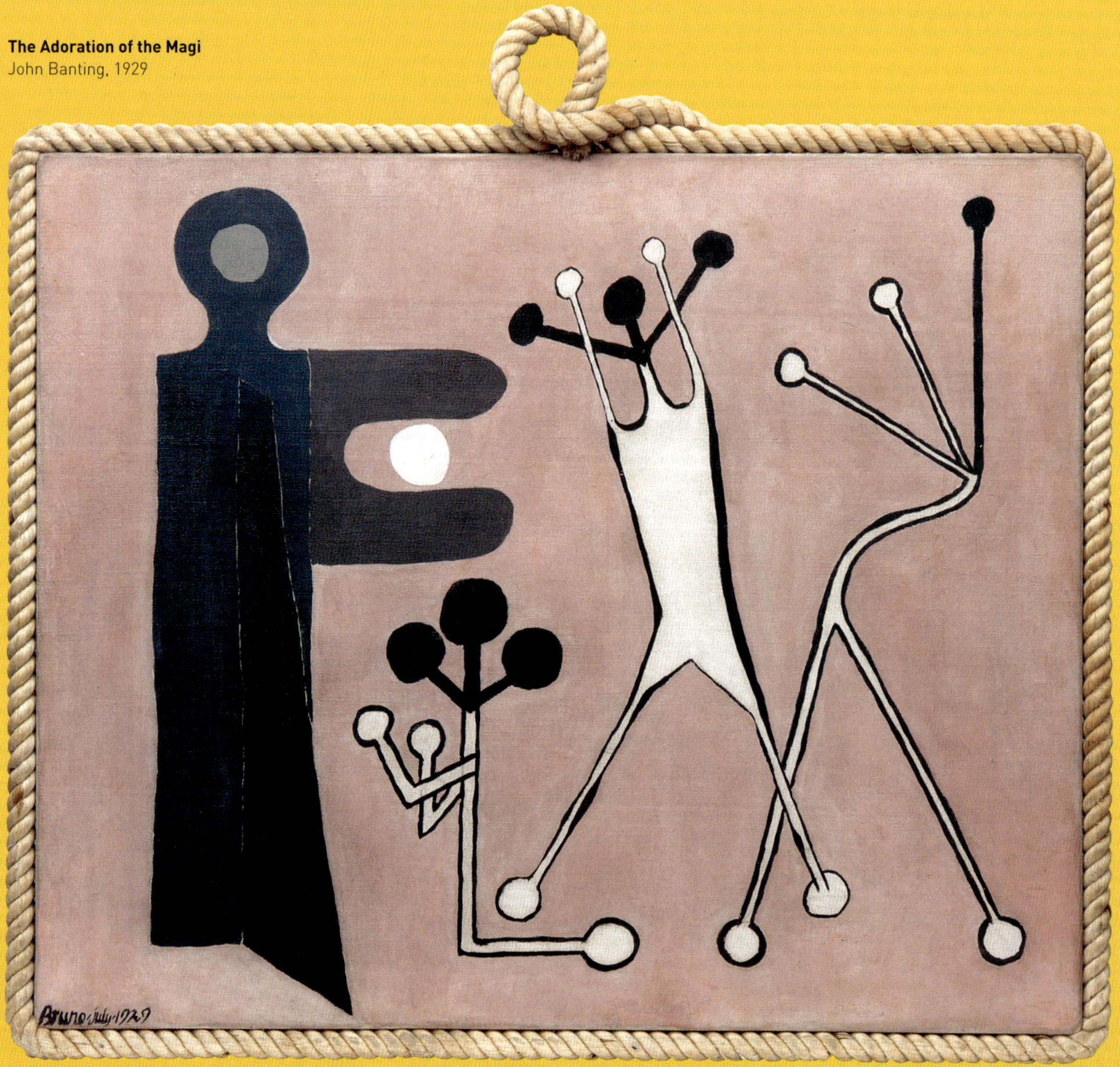

BRITAIN'S INVITATION.

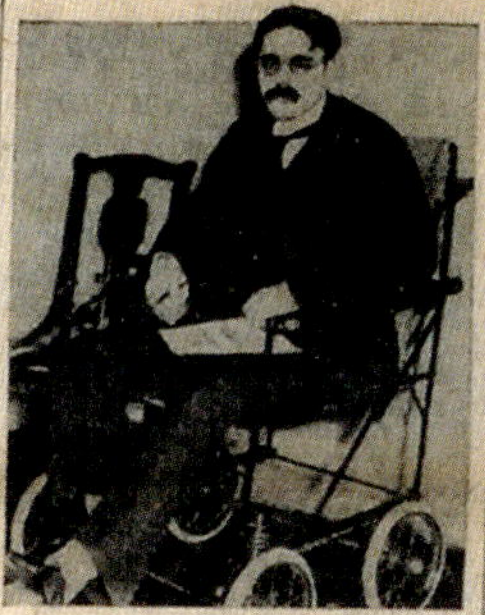

"Mr. Bruno Hat," whose "exhibition of pictures" hoaxed many guests at Mr. and the Hon. Mrs. Bryan Guinness' house in Buckingham-street, Westminster.

AMAZING HOAX ON ART EXPERTS.

UNKNOWN ARTIST WITH FALSE MOUSTACHE.

Half social and artistic London was the victim yesterday of an ingenious and amusing hoax at a cocktail party given by Mr. and the Hon. Mrs. Bryan Guinness at their house in Buckingham-street, Westminster.

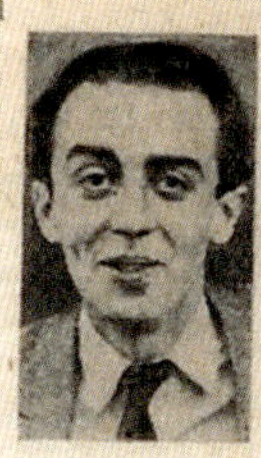

Mr. Brian Howard.

Mr. Bryan Guinness, a rich young Oxford graduate, is a son of the Right Hon. Walter Guinness, M.P., Minister of Agriculture in the late Conservative Government.

The guests included many eminent art critics and connoisseurs (though not the "Daily Express" critic). They had been asked to see the works of a hitherto unknown artist.

"FIRST EXHIBITION."

Their hopes had been raised high by the invitation which announced: "First exhibition of pictures by Bruno Hat," and bore the following biographical note:—

Mr. Bruno Hat came to England with his father in 1919 from Lubeck. After having lived in this country a short time, Mr. Max Hat married an Englishwoman, and bought a general dealer's shop in Sussex, where he lived until he died in 1923. The shop is now managed by Mr. Bruno Hat with the help of his step-mother.

Mr. Bruno Hat is now thirty-one years of age. Apart from some two months or so at a Hamburg art school, he is entirely self-taught. In frequent visits to London, exhibitions have provided him with little more than a glimpse of contemporary movements in painting. He has never, until now, exhibited a picture. A month ago, however, several examples of his work were taken to Paris, and the opinion there was so immediately favourable that successful arrangements have been made for an exhibition there in the early winter.

The pictures were, in fact, the "Daily Express" understands, painted by Mr. Brian Howard, son of Mr. Francis Howard, the distinguished collector and chairman of the National Portrait Society. They were of a kind familiar to all students of ultra-modern art, though some of them bore such titles as "Leda and the Swan," "Portrait of My Brother."

"Mr. Bruno Hat," wearing a false moustache, was seated in an invalid chair beneath "his" pictures, and received the congratulations of the company with becoming modesty.

GROUPS OF EXPERTS.

Reverent groups of experts moved about the room examining the pictures or gazing at "Mr. Bruno Hat," who, to make the hoax complete, was ably represented by a friend of Mr. Guinness and Mr. Howard.

Some of the guests knitted their brows over a leaflet lying on a table. It was headed, "Approach to Hat," and signed "A. R. de T.," and was a pompous parody of a "high-brow" artistic eulogy.

A final touch of verisimilitude was lent by a young woman seated at a table with a price-list and order-book before her.

The party lasted for some hours, and the majority of the guests left quite unaware of the good-natured hoax which had been played on them.

One of "Bruno Hat's" pictures has been purchased by Mr. Lytton Strachey, the author.

Amusing scenes at the exhibition are described by the "Dragoman" in today's "Talk of London."

LORD KINNOULL A SOCIALIST.

MRS. KATE MERRICK'S SON-IN-LAW.

The "Daily Express" understands that the Earl of Kinnoull has formally expressed a wish to join the Socialist Party, and that his application for membership has been accepted.

Lord Kinnoull succeeded his grandfather as the fourteenth earl in 1916.

He married last year, as his second wife, Miss May Merrick, daughter of Mrs. Kate Merrick, the ...

BRITISH CRUISER EXPLOSION.

ONE DEAD, 2 SERIOUSLY INJURED.

H.M.S. VINDICTIVE.

THE Admiralty issued the following late last night:—

"The Secretary of the Admiralty regrets to announce that the following casualties were caused by an explosion which took place on board H.M.S. Vindictive at Chat-...

THE GRAPHIC, August 3, 1929 221

AN ART HOAX OF THE WEEK

The Spoof "Abstract Works" of "Bruno Hat" Which Fooled Many Distinguished Visitors

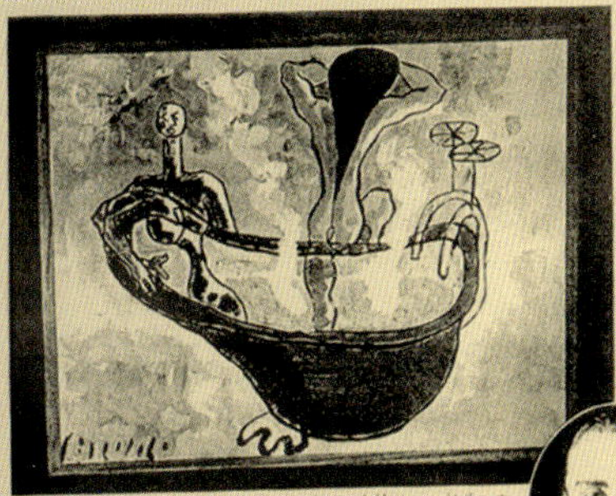

"THE BATH": Shown at the "spoof" art exhibition held at a cocktail party given by Mr. and the Hon. Mrs. Bryan Guinness, and attended by many well-known figures in social and artistic London. It was only next day that the guests, who included many eminent art critics and connoisseurs, learnt that they had been hoaxed

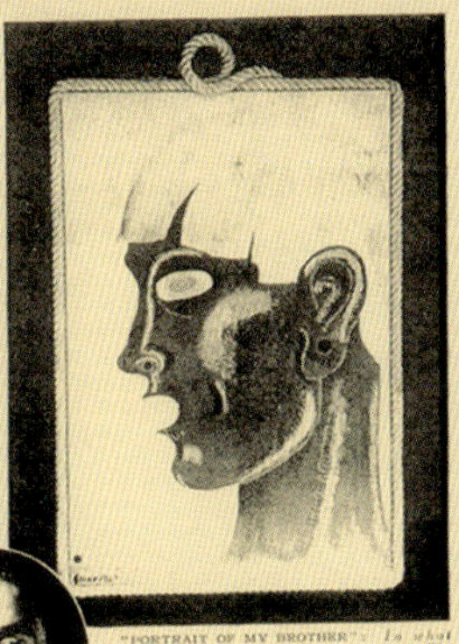

"PORTRAIT OF MY BROTHER": In what Mr. Bryan Guinness's catalogue described as "The exhibition of pictures by Bruno Hat, the first English abstract painter, a pioneer of pure form"

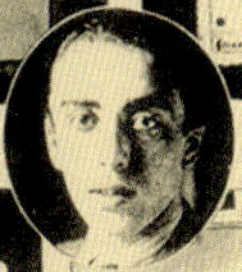

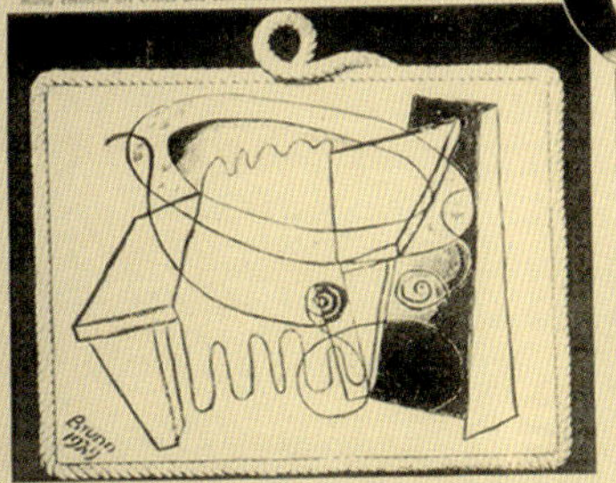

"ABSTRACT"—THE ARTIST'S FAVOURITE WORK: Such was the title to this picture in the hoax exhibition of "the shy artist, Bruno Hat," described in the catalogue as "uninfluenced, virtually untaught, and the first natural, lively, spontaneous flower of the one considerable movement in painting today." Mr. Lytton Strachey purchased one of the paintings

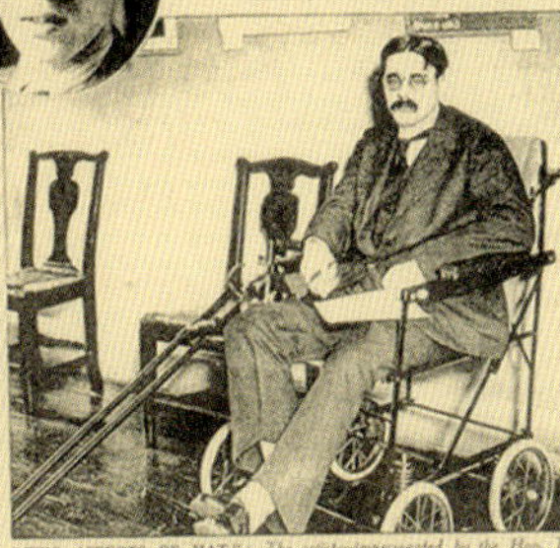

"TWO ASPECTS OF HAT": The artist—impersonated by the Hon. Tom Mitford—as he appeared at his exhibition, an invalid with smoked glasses and a false moustache; and (inset) as he really is. "Bruno Hat" has now been revealed as Mr. Brian Howard, son of the chairman of the National Portrait Gallery

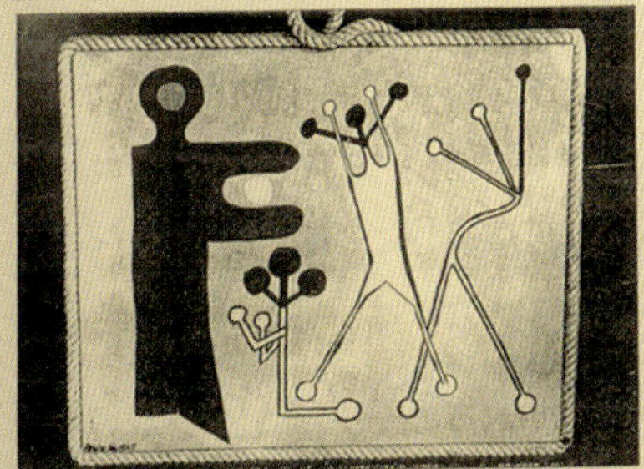

"ADORATION OF THE MAGI": According to one report of the "private view" last week, many people stood "in apparent rapture before some of the exhibits, and an eminent critic murmured his appreciation of the colour values." It should be noted that, though the exhibition was a rag, Mr. Howard is a young artist of genuine promise, and many of the pictures have intrinsic merit

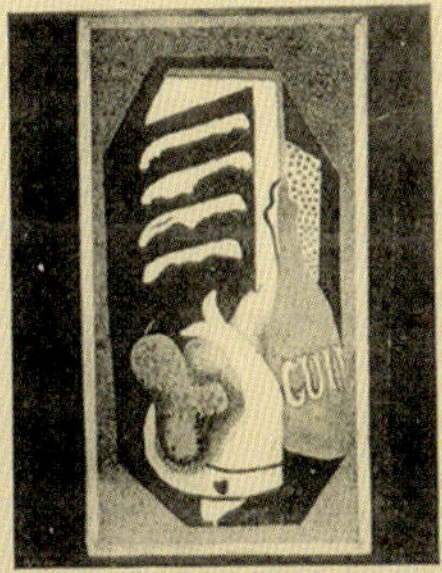

THE ORIGIN OF THE HOAX: An ingenious impressionistic study, called "The Bath Mat," painted on a cork bath-mat. It was the first picture ever painted by Mr. Howard, and suggested the original idea of holding a spoof exhibition

... at last I am in a position to give work to some of the unemployed." This is the title given to the above cartoon printed in the Russian newspaper, "Pravda," with the added comment, "In view of his special duties in connection with unemployment, Mr. Thomas will receive a salary of 50,000 roubles (£5000)."

Mystery of "Mr. Bruno Hat" Maintained by Mr. Bryan Guinness

The hoax which was perpetrated at a cocktail party given by Mr. and the Hon. Mrs. Bryan Guinness at their house in Buckingham-street, Westminster, yesterday, is still unsolved.

An exhibition of pictures was given by a "Mr. Bruno Hat," who was stated to be a German. Many art critics and connoisseurs were present, and were not aware that the identity of a fairly well-known artist was concealed under the false moustache and smoked spectacles of the pseudo "Mr. Hat."

Mr. Bryan Guinness told an "Evening Standard" representative to-day that the hoax was executed as "a good joke on our friends." He said:

"I am afraid that I cannot tell you who the Mr. Hat was, as to do so would spoil the whole thing. Many of my friends were impressed by the ultra-modern style of the art and went away unaware that Mr. Bruno Hat was only a name to cover the identity of an artist who is known to a number of people in London.

"He was spoken to in German by several of those present and, as he is naturalised, he quite deceived many of them because of his fluency in that language.

"I am afraid that I can neither deny nor affirm the statement that the pictures were painted by Mr. Brian Howard."

The Talk of London

By THE DRAGOMAN

... Lord and Lady ... dark and hand- ... Duchess of Rox- ... with diamonds, tall ... and Mr. Brian ...

... Roxburghe sat in the ... Howard, who is tall ... of the few people ... dress.

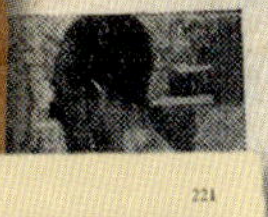

... Bruno Hat," whose initials and art are identical with those of Mr. Howard.

They even exhibited "Mr. Hat."

* * *

"MR. HAT" sat in a wheeled chair, a morose, taciturn figure, with a marked German accent, a moustache worthy of Harry Tate, and smoked glasses.

In one hand he held a thin cheroot, in the other a glass of iced coffee, and as he sipped and puffed he grumbled about the colour of the walls and about the publicity he was receiving.

He convinced quite a number of people, but not, I fancy, Mrs Sitwell, who was there with Lady Cynthia Mosley.

* * *

ADMIRING connoisseurs crowded about him.

"I *do* so admire your rope frames, Mr. Hat," said one.

"*Ja*," said Mr. Hat," it ees mine own idea."

And much admiration was excited by a picture painted on cork. This "canvas" was, so Mr. Guinness declared, a bath-mat from Mr. Hat's store.

* * *

MRS. CONVERSE, the American hostess and artist, stood in apparent rapture before some of the exhibits.

And an eminent art critic murmured his appreciation of the colour values.

But some of the pretty girls, including the Hon. Cecilia Keppel, Miss Marjorie Glasgow, Miss Penelope Chetwode, and Miss Rosalie Willoughby, who stood looking at Mr. Hat or drinking Mrs. Guinness' excellent cocktails, seemed, I thought, a little overwhelmed.

* * *

NOTHING, however, can overwhelm Mr. Maurice Bowra, who is an extremely brilliant and exuberant young Oxford don.

He approached Mr. Hat, and began talking volubly in German.

Mr. Hat made a gesture of distaste.

"Ach!" he said, "I am naturalised Englisch. I do not care to remember that I speak Cherman."

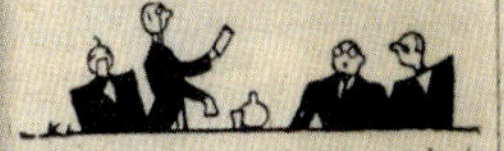

HISTORY, of a sort, was made in the House of Commons yesterday when a member of the dress reform league made his appearance.

He was Mr. Sandham, a new Liverpool Socialist member.

He did not wear shorts, but he favoured an open tennis shirt, and rose to move an amendment of importance without a tie and with his collar turned down so closely beneath his jacket that it looked cut away.

* * *

IT is rumoured in the lobbies, by the way, that a prize of an additional question on the order-paper is to be given to the first M.P. who succeeds in inducing Mr. William Adamson, the Scottish Secretary, to answer supplementary questions.

He is becoming a target for M.P.s who are not content with the official answer, but rise to heap fresh demands on a Minister.

"Wullie," however, is proof against them, for he simply sits still, studies the answer he has given, and is completely unmoved when ex-Ministers and even present Ministers jocularly urge him to answer. Mr. Thomas was so amused yesterday that he went red in the face and made much use of his handkerchief.

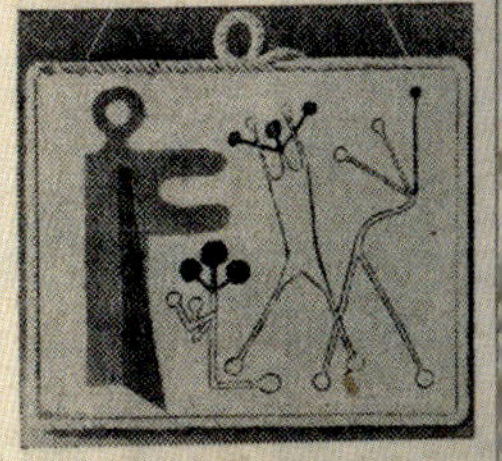

Any connoisseur of modern art will realise that this picture represents "The Adoration of the Magi." It is by "Mr. Bruno Hat." Note the rope frame.

* * *

ANOTHER Scotsman, and another Willie with some of the same mannerisms, is Mr. Graham, the President of the Board of Trade, who has an uncanny facility with figures and an inexhaustible command of fluent language.

He, on the contrary, will answer every question put to him with alacrity, but his questioner, when the rounded sentences are concluded, generally finds he has been worsted in this daily battle of wits.

Mr. Graham has a mannerism of beginning every statement with a loud "Sir"—referring no doubt to the Speaker—in which one can detect more r's than the spelling warrants.

AS THE WORLD GOES BY

The Masterpieces of Bruno Hat

If one wants to attract attention in contemporary art, one must do ridiculous work. The fake exhibition of the pictures by "Mr. Bruno Hat," which brought together a number of admiring "connoisseurs" and critics, is the joke of the studios.

Since the futurist stunt began miles of rubbish have been painted and oceans of ink have poured out in praise of worthless pictures. Society and art snobs, not to mention public galleries, have enjoyed the privilege of hanging works which could have been better done by idiots.

Modern art in all its branches is 75 per cent. leg-pulling.

The exhibition of "Mr. Bruno Hat" has proved how easy it is to mislead the public. These fake works, some of which are framed in rope, were quite as good in point of technique and subject as hundreds of pictures that I have seen offered for serious criticism and patronage in the shows.

The joke may have a salutary effect, but it is a pity that it did not go further.

A few highbrow criticisms, full of the redundant jargon which is part of the mumbo-jumbo of modern pictures and sculpture, would have added piquancy to this delightful fraud.

JOHN ENGLISH.

guests, art critics and journalists were invited to an 'at home' at Buckingham Gate to view an exhibition of 'Pictures and Sculptures by Bruno Hat'.

Lady Eleanor Smith who had been 'leaked' about the exhibition prior to it taking place was 'completely taken in' and wrote in the *Sunday Dispatch*, 'Bruno Hat is a painter of German extraction and his work is mainly of the abstract type seemingly derivative from Picasso and de Chirico. So good are the paintings that they are to be exhibited at Bryan Guinness's house in Westminster. I have seen one or two and they are surprisingly clever'.

The perpetrators managed to create an overnight sensation and the private view for the 'unknown' Bruno Hat was considered a huge success by all involved, particularly as some of the critics took it seriously. The concept was the idea of artist Brian Howard and was planned with scrupulous attention to detail, including a parody catalogue introduction, 'Approach to Hat', written by Waugh under the name A. R. de T. He referred to Hat as the 'First English Abstract Painter' and that he 'is the first signal of the coming world movement towards the creation of pure form'. Tom Mitford posed as Hat, 'the natural abstract discovery'. Initially the paintings were believed to be the work of Brian Howard (whose initials mirror those of Bruno Hat), though this rumour was probably an attempt at gaining the dilettante artist some recognition. In reality, his friend John Banting was the creator of the works, as the paintings exhibit the accomplishment and style of a more experienced artist and they bear many of Banting's trademark stylistic elements of the time, as well as the use of rope frames. The works were well received and Lytton Strachey bought a picture, the painting *The Adoration of the Magi*, now in the Sherwin Collection.

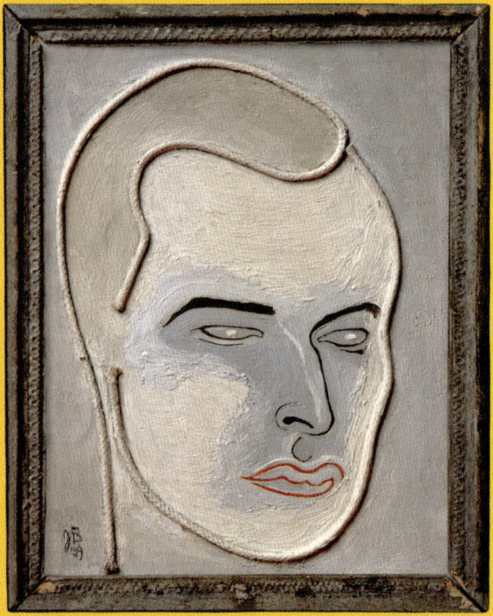

Self Portrait with String
John Banting, 1929

Why the rope frame? John Banting had been in Paris in 1923 and seen works by Picasso and Braque. A friend of Man Ray he had made a photogram in 1929 including chord in the work. Also he had outlined a sensitive self portrait with string – both executed in 1929 the same year as the hoax. As the rope is more like a fisherman's rope from a ships chandler, James Rawlin of Sotheby's has suggested that it is a back-handed reference to Ben Nicholson who had discovered a primitive painter, the fisherman Alfred Wallis, the previous year in St Ives and had boasted of his discovery.

If correct it would have been typical of Banting's humorous response and in keeping with the whole tongue in cheek approach of the exhibition.

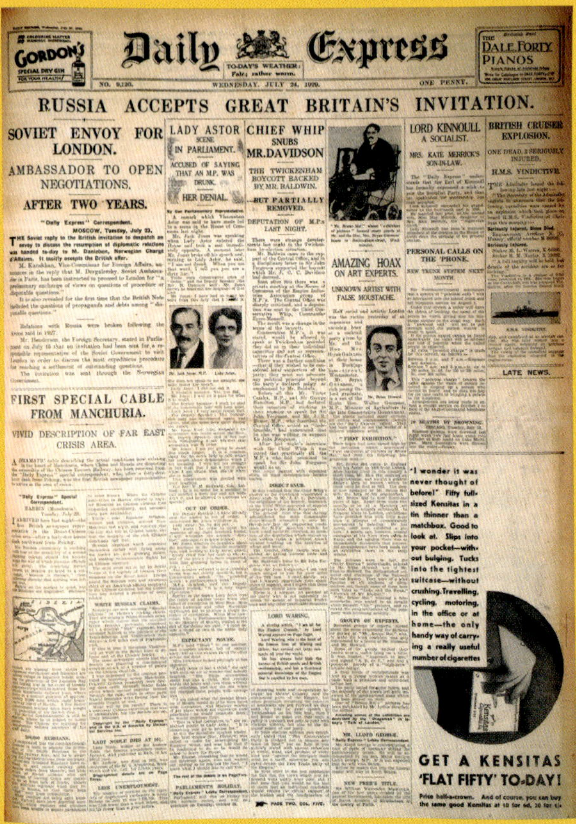

Daily Express

TO-DAY'S WEATHER: Fair; rather warm.

No. 9,120. WEDNESDAY, JULY 24, 1929. ONE PENNY.

GORDON'S SPECIAL DRY GIN

THE DALE FORTY PIANOS

RUSSIA ACCEPTS GREAT BRITAIN'S INVITATION.

SOVIET ENVOY FOR LONDON.

AMBASSADOR TO OPEN NEGOTIATIONS.

AFTER TWO YEARS.

"Daily Express" Correspondent. MOSCOW, Tuesday, July 23.

FIRST SPECIAL CABLE FROM MANCHURIA.

VIVID DESCRIPTION OF FAR EAST CRISIS AREA.

LADY ASTOR SCENE IN PARLIAMENT.

ACCUSED OF SAYING THAT AN M.P. WAS DRUNK.

HER DENIAL.

OUT OF ORDER.

EXPECTANT HOUSE.

LADY NOBLE DIES AT 101.

LESS UNEMPLOYMENT.

PARLIAMENT'S HOLIDAY.

CHIEF WHIP SNUBS MR. DAVIDSON

THE TWICKENHAM BOYCOTT BACKED BY MR. BALDWIN.

BUT PARTIALLY REMOVED.

DEPUTATION OF M.P.s LAST NIGHT.

DIRECT SNUB.

LORD WARING.

AMAZING HOAX ON ART EXPERTS.

UNKNOWN ARTIST WITH FALSE MOUSTACHE.

"FIRST EXHIBITION."

GROUPS OF EXPERTS.

MR. LLOYD GEORGE.

NEW PEER'S TITLE.

LORD KINNOULL A SOCIALIST.

MRS. KATE MERRICK'S SON-IN-LAW.

PERSONAL CALLS ON THE 'PHONE.

NEW TRUNK SYSTEM NEXT MONTH.

BRITISH CRUISER EXPLOSION.

ONE DEAD, 2 SERIOUSLY INJURED.

H.M.S. VINDICTIVE.

LATE NEWS.

"I wonder it was never thought of before!" Fifty full-sized Kensitas in a tin thinner than a matchbox. Good to look at. Slips into your pocket—without bulging. Tucks into the tightest suitcase—without crushing. Travelling, cycling, motoring, in the office or at home—the only handy way of carrying a really useful number of cigarettes

GET A KENSITAS 'FLAT FIFTY' TO-DAY!

Price half-a-crown. And of course, you can buy the same good Kensitas at 10 for 6d, 20 for 1/-

Front cover of the *Daily Express*, July 23 1929

Approach to Hat.

THIS is in no sense (except the Christian) a Charity Exhibition. In overcoming for the first time what the artist himself admits as his extraordinary shyness, and opening her house to those who wish to see the works of Bruno Hat, Mrs. Guinness is attempting to do a service less to him than to the artistic public.

Now everyone is aware that what has come to be termed "abstract" painting has only just begun to be "taken seriously" in England. Some years ago Mr. Roberts and Mr. Wyndham Lewis achieved a certain success in that direction, but the acknowledged masters, such as Picasso, Gris and, perhaps, Marcoussis, have only recently found a market in this country. Artistically, we are incurably unpunctual. Co-incidentally, however, with this awakening on the part of England towards the most important artistic discovery of our time—namely, the progression from "significant" to "pure" form, appears ***the first English abstract painter***. This rather startling phrase is not my own invention. (A naturalised Englishman, preferring to live in England, he wishes to be considered English, and was spoken of as such in Paris, when some examples of his work were taken there some weeks ago.) It was used of him by several of the French authorities to whom his work was submitted.

The painting of Bruno Hat presents a problem of very real importance. He is no Cezanne agonisedly tussling to reconcile the visual appearance of form with his own intuitional perception of it. Like Picasso, he creates it. Though the experienced eye can see at a glance that his work is entirely free from Picasso's influence, it is to that artist that we go so far as to compare him. Picasso is the greatest painter of our time for one reason: this reason is that he is the most inspired of all the creators of abstract pictures. Those experts who have seen Bruno Hat's work definitely accredit him with a similar power, developed, because of his youth only, to a less degree. The significance of this cannot be sufficiently stressed. It means, among other things, that Bruno Hat may lead the way in this century's European painting from Discovery to Tradition. Uninfluenced, virtually untaught, he is the first natural, lonely, spontaneous flower of the one considerable movement in painting to-day. Hitherto, good abstract painting has been the close preserve of its Hispano-Parisian discoverers. Bruno Hat is the first signal of the coming world movement towards the creation of Pure Form.

A. R. DE T.

Pages from the parody catalogue introduction entitled Approach to Hat, written by Evelyn Waugh

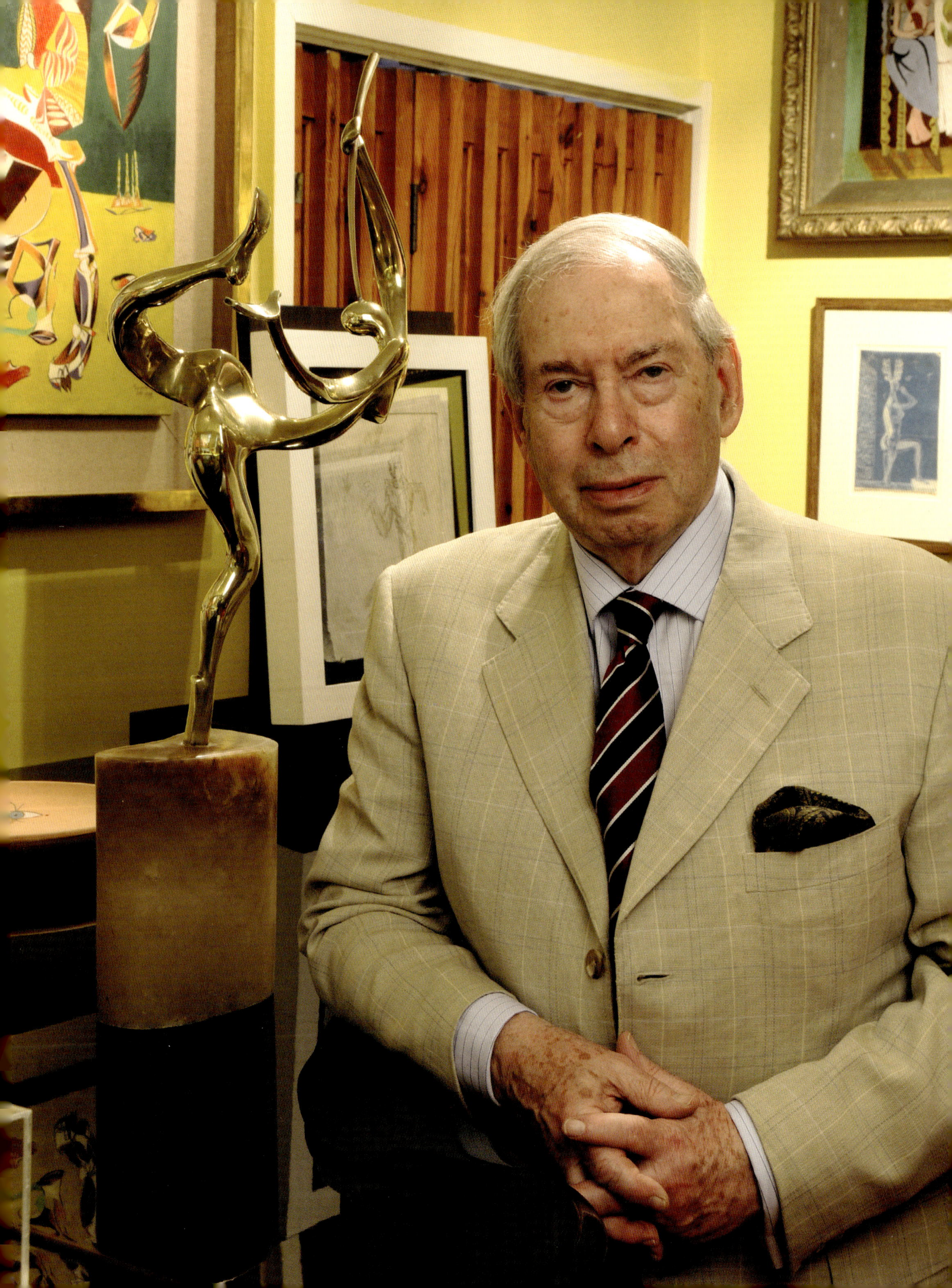

SO WHAT SORT OF A BLOKE WOULD COLLECT PICTURES LIKE THESE?

CONFESSIONS OF A COLLECTOR

JEFFREY SHERWIN

My personal interest in British surrealism began in 1986 with an exhibition curated by Leeds City Art Gallery with the title *Surrealism in Britain in the 30s*. Until that time I never knew that British surrealism existed. The exhibition not only stimulated my interest in the movement but also in the work of contemporaries and the politics of the time. For me, collecting had to be a little bit like joined up writing. Works have to compliment each other or build a contrast. The context is for me as important as the content.

I was lucky in coming into contact with the professional curators from Leeds Art Gallery, Terry Friedman, Alex Robertson and latterly Nigel Walsh, Jon Wood and of course Michel Remy, the art historian from Nice; also the surrealist artist Conroy Maddox. Hearing them talk about their subject, not only to me directly, but through lectures or seminars given to The Friends of the Art Gallery (The Leeds Art Collections Fund) was pivotally important. All opened my eyes to aspects of art that might otherwise have remained closed.

Do I find the process of collecting enjoyable? Frankly, I often do not. It is stressful, often disappointing, though occasionally it can be very satisfying. As a GP, finance was always the limiting factor. I hate auctions and the competition. I only bid on the phone and feel sick until the phone rings and I am paranoid that the auction house will forget to telephone. I like buying directly from artists, but the problem is that many artists see price as an indication of status. Eduardo Paolozzi, for example, never stopped telling me about the famous people who had bought works from him and the high prices they paid. Dealers are more amenable. They not only have to make a living, but often offer works that will not see the auction room, will negotiate a price and then let you pay it off over a couple of years.

In 1951 my parents took me to London to visit The Festival of Britain on the South Bank. I remember the Skylon and Dome of Discovery. I was taken to Battersea Park to see the open air Henry Moore exhibition, with no idea that one day I would be responsible for creating the Moore Sculpture Gallery in Leeds. The Festival brimmed with imagination and excitement. It opened up

Jeffrey Sherwin at home

a gateway to a bright new future that only those who had gone through the deprivations and austerity of the Second World War could appreciate.

While at Leeds Medical School I read in the *Yorkshire Evening Post* that Lord Harewood and Jack Lyons had rescued Jacob Epstein's colossal sculpture *Adam*. It is now in the entrance hall of Harewood House. Despite being a student I felt I should stick up for my city and wrote a letter to the paper, asking why such a great sculpture should go to Harewood House and not Leeds Art Gallery. The Gallery did not respond. Years later, as chairman of Leeds Leisure Services, I was able to support Terry Friedman in his successful attempt to bring Epstein's great stone sculpture *Maternity* to Leeds Art Gallery where it is now on show.

My time at Leeds Medical School was not without incident. Shortlisted for the First Year Prize, I had written a poem on the value of medical statistics on my statistics paper, rather than answering any of the questions. At the interview this was read back to me. The other chap got the prize. No sense of humour! I also appeared on the boards of the now demolished Leeds Empire in the Rag Review alongside Barry Cryer and Wole Solynka, Nigeria's future Nobel Prize winner. Deciding that University in one's home town could prove a little restrictive I applied to Balliol College Oxford.

I first started collecting paintings when I was in digs in Oxford. My bed-cum-settee was pushed against the wall. I decided that if I had some pictures behind the settee it might encourage my girlfriends to crawl on to it to have a closer look. I went up to London and bought some pictures from Hyde Park railings and hung them on the wall. When I look back at that time I am really rather embarrassed; not at the subterfuge but at the poor quality of the paintings.

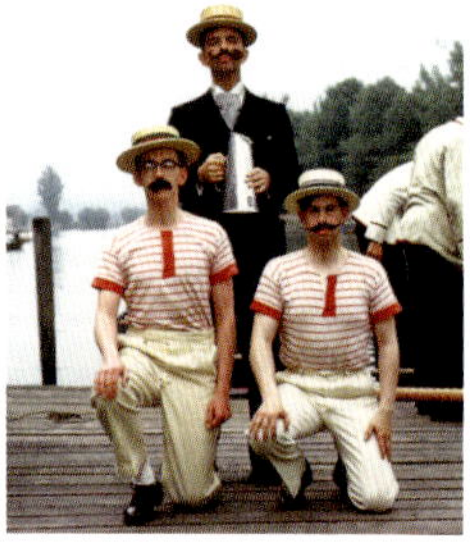

Balliol Victorian Society on the river, Jeffrey Sherwin with friends

The first time I bought a canvas from a well-known artist was from John Bratby. I had seen the film *The Horse's Mouth* by Joyce Cary in which John Bratby had painted large aggressive, expressionist works to represent the paintings of the irreverent feisty artist Gulley Jimson played by Alec Guinness. I had also seen John Bratby's works in the Royal Academy Summer Show. I drove down from Oxford, where I studied at the time, to his rambling house in Blackheath where he pulled out his 'Kitchen Sink' works for which he was widely recognised – except by me. I thought he was trying to palm me off with works that hadn't sold. Stupidly, I insisted on buying three of his recent paintings. I have since sold two, but kept one to remind me that enthusiasm, which is always the driving force of collecting, also needs to be tempered with both humility and knowledge. For the latter I have to thank Leeds City Art Gallery and its curators.

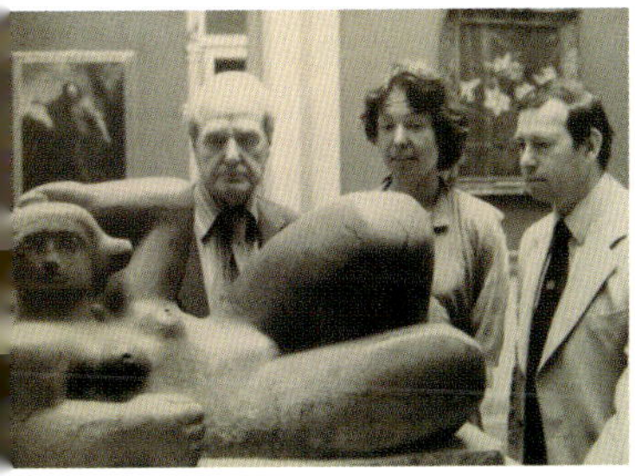

Henry Moore, Mary Moore and Jeffrey Sherwin at Leeds City Art Gallery

In 1977, as deputy chairman of Leisure in Leeds with responsibility for the Arts I invited Henry Moore and his daughter Mary to visit Leeds Art Gallery, arranging a lunch with the then Lord Mayor. Although Henry Moore had been born in Castleford and had attended Leeds College of Art, he had never been invited back to Leeds. It was a formal occasion as we sat round the luncheon table in the Blue Room of the Civic Hall, not knowing how to approach the world's most famous sculptor. It was my Chairman, Jack Binks, a joiner and undertaker from Morley, with a sense of humour, who broke the ice. Nudging the sculptor gently in the ribs he said 'Eh Henry, how can a little fellow like you knock those holes in those big women?' There was a sudden silence! Then Henry Moore laughed – 'It's great to be back in Yorkshire' – and everyone relaxed. Then Jack added 'By the way do you do memorials? – if so I can put a bit of work your way'.

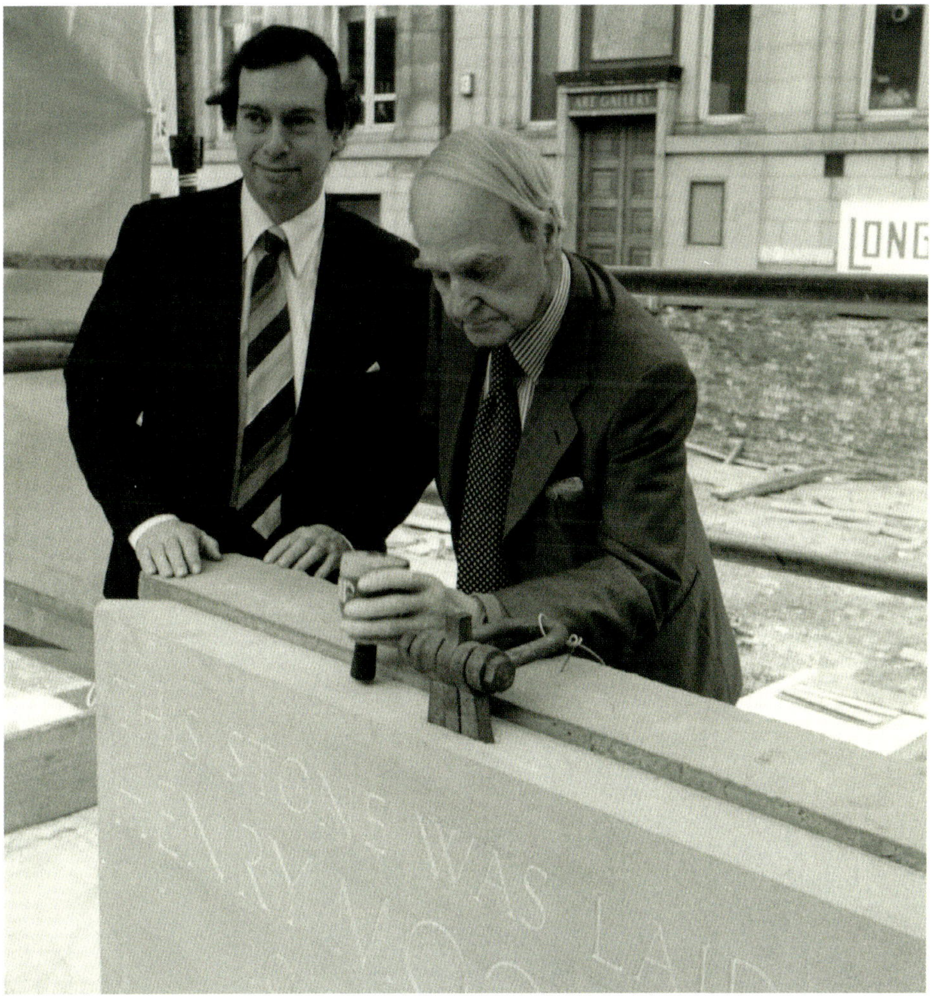

Henry Moore laying the Foundation Stone of the Henry Moore Extension, work started in 1980

Robert Rowe, then director of Leeds City Art Gallery, and I used to drive regularly to see Henry Moore at his home, Hoglands at Perry Green in Hertfordshire. I often got lost driving down the high hedged twisty lanes from Much Haddam. The road took us through a ford, until eventually we saw the village's single red telephone box and turned right up a drive to park in front of a white painted house to be greeted by Mrs Tinsley, Henry Moore's secretary. After our first visit, I remember excitedly telling my wife, Ruth, that this was the first time I had seen original Henry Moore's hanging in a toilet! At that time a lot of the sculptor's work took place in the adjacent garage, though soon there was to be the large garden-cum-park that swept down from the house to accommodate all his studios. Henry Moore would say 'why don't you go down to see my latest pieces in the Maquette Studio? You will find the key as usual hanging behind the ivy'. Security is very different now.

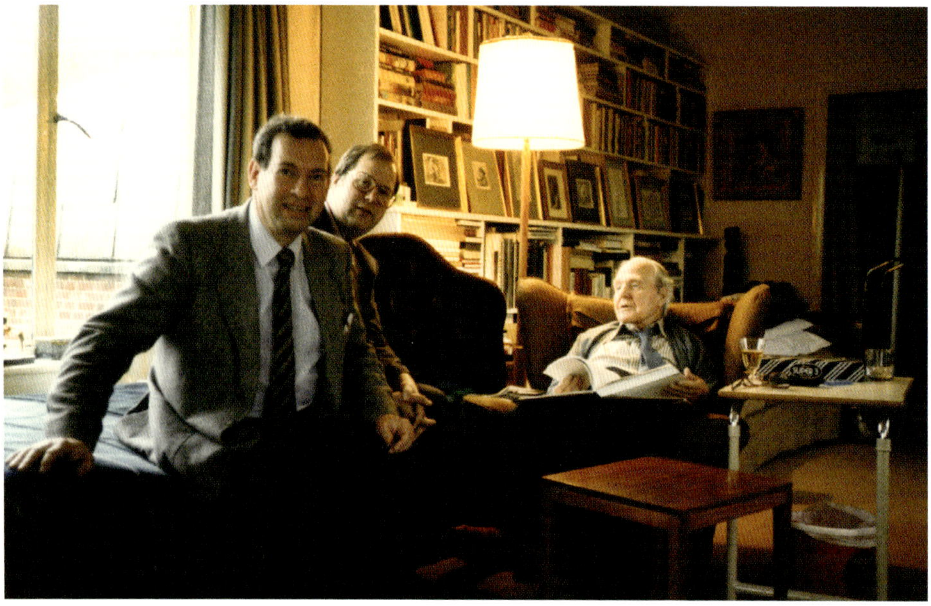

Henry Moore, Terry Friedman, and Jeffrey Sherwin at Hoglands, Perry Green

During afternoon tea, Henry Moore would express his views on art and also on the tax system, on which he had some fairly strong views. In his opinion, it unfairly targeted the successful – and he was very successful. He indicated his strong support for Margaret Thatcher – he approved of those who pulled themselves up by their own boot straps as he felt he had done. It is an interesting reflection on the perceived political views of artists that they are always presumed to be left wing. Perhaps that is why, whenever I have suggested to art historians or curators that Henry Moore was a Margaret Thatcher supporter, they didn't wish to know. In fact one replied 'that is only because she has one of his works in the front hall of 10 Downing Street!'

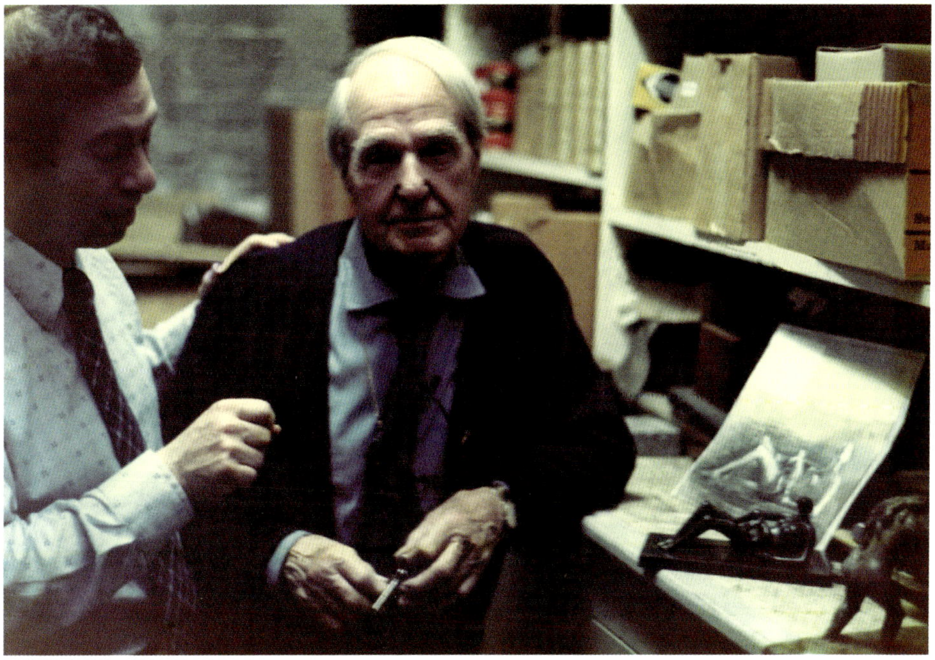

Henry Moore and Jeffrey Sherwin with drawing and maquette, both in the Sherwin Collection

I recall that Margaret Thatcher's speech at the opening of *The Henry Moore Retrospective* at the Royal Academy, was the best speech of the evening. There was warmth in her words that cannot have been completely ghosted.

One day while we were having tea with Henry Moore his secretary, Mrs Tinsley, came in and said: 'Mr Moore, there is Lauren Bacall on the phone.' 'Oh not her again' he answered in a slightly irritated tone, 'tell her I have my friends from Leeds with me. I will ring her back later.' To put us poor mortals from Leeds before Lauren Bacall – now that was something! The icing on the cake came later the same afternoon when, noticing the interest expressed by our young curator, Terry Friedman, in a forthcoming Moore exhibition in Madrid, the sculptor turned round to Terry and said 'would you like to come to the opening – we will pay all your expenses'. Terry beamed his acceptance.

Mary Moore and her husband, Raymond Dunowsky, lived just down the road from Hoglands and were very supportive of Leeds. I had always wanted to buy a piece of sculpture, but thought that asking might prejudice the relationship with Leeds Art Gallery. Eventually, I mentioned this and was told not to be silly – selling was part of the business and I then bought my first two pieces, a small bronze reclining figure and a preliminary drawing.

In 1972, on the basis of doing rather than talking, I opened a small art gallery in a converted cottage, Boundary Cottage in Chapel Allerton. I called it Northern Artist Gallery with the intention of promoting artists from the north.

In reality though, it lost money every year, and even when I moved the gallery to Harrogate it continued to haemorrhage cash for the ten years of its existence. At one point, I had an exhibition of works by Henry Moore and, although I was on the local TV and the artist himself allowed me to sell his works for less than his London dealers, nobody bought a piece – but I had a lot of visitors. The treadmill of regular exhibitions, printing and sending invitations, VAT, staff and the fact that I only took 20% on sales became a burden, both financially and mentally. When I finally closed the gallery it was a weight lifted from my shoulders. I could again concentrate on being a GP without too many distractions. Though, I have to admit, my wife Ruth benefited when I put on jewellery exhibitions. I used to give her, as birthday presents, some of the pieces that hadn't sold!

An amusing story from my gallery days is as follows. I had always admired the painter William Roberts and having him exhibiting works in my gallery would have been a highlight. Unfortunately, I invited the wrong William Roberts. The one that came was a painter known in Wales but not in Leeds! I hadn't had the heart to cancel him and, when none of his paintings sold, I bought the best and most expensive painting. For a couple of years, it hung on the wall of our lounge before it was relegated to a cupboard. A chance conversation with a curator from the National Gallery of Wales revealed that they were looking for a good early William Roberts. The painting is now in the Derek Williams Trust Collection, on loan to the National Museum Wales.

As mentioned before, in 1986 Leeds Art Gallery mounted a major exhibition to commemorate the fiftieth anniversary of the *International Surrealist Exhibition*, originally held at the New Burlington Galleries, London in 1936. The show made a huge impression on me and triggered my interest in British surrealism. The exhibition was curated by Terry Friedman and Alex Robertson.

On the strength of the show Ruth and I decided to buy a British surrealist work. We were advised to visit the Mayor Gallery in London. With a mixture of both anticipation and unease we walked down Cork Street, lined with a succession of well-known galleries. We had been told that if we entered a London gallery we had better count our fingers afterwards. To our surprise, the gallery owner, Andrew Murray, turned out to be most helpful and we bought an etching by Merlyn Evans titled *The Chess Players*.

Shortly afterwards I met Conroy Maddox, who was England's leading surrealist artist at that time. He lived with his girlfriend Des in the top half of a large house in Lambole Road, Belsize Park, in London. One climbed an outside metal staircase to his glass front door which had his visiting card stuck on it with the words Conroy Maddox. A small, neat, dapper man with a moustache and a great sense of humour greeted us. The walls were dotted with paintings, collages and constructions. He was a writer on surrealism as well as an artist. He had written a book on Dali and visited Paris in the 1930s. I suppose I became his honorary GP. Conroy, Des, Ruth and I used to visit the surrealist conferences at West Dean, near Brighton, where he was always the guest of honour. I arranged a number of visits to Leeds and an exhibition at Harrogate's Mercer Gallery. Along with John Welson, Conroy wrote the *Hinge of History* and arranged an exhibition at the Camden Arts Centre as a response to the Hayward show *Dada and Surrealism Reviewed* which, he felt, didn't cover the English aspect of surrealism sufficiently. A vegetarian in principle he nevertheless enjoyed Chinese duck pancakes. 'Conroy' I said 'you can't be a vegetarian and eat duck'. The response was: 'No problem – ducks are vegetarian'.

Maddox was fond of recounting the time during the Second World War when the British Surrealist Group used to meet at the Barcelona restaurant in Beak Street, off Regent Street, under the leadership of E.L.T. Mesens.

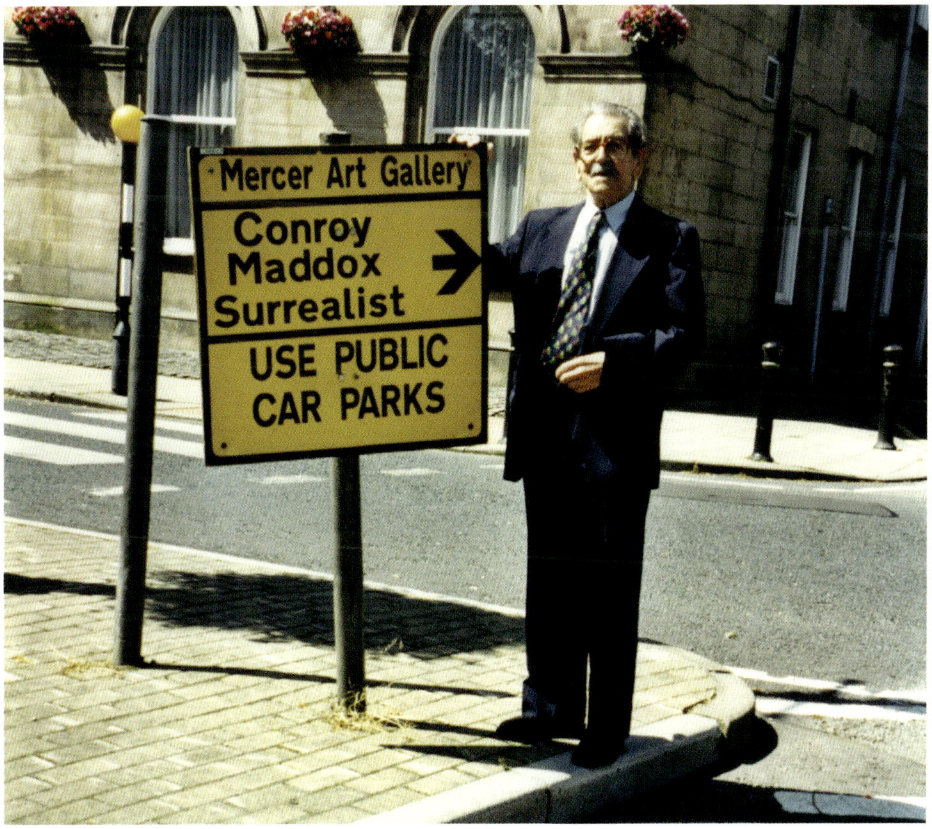

Conroy Maddox in Harrogate

George Melly used to call in when on leave from the Navy and, wearing his seaman's uniform, used to approach old ladies saying 'would you like to see a picture of my dear mother?' What a nice young man they thought, before George would pull out some 'naughty' nude postcards from Paris and grin mischievously at their shocked expressions. At the end of the evening he would recite a poem finishing with the line 'it is raining knives and forks' and with that he would pick up the cutlery tray and throw the contents in the air. Afterwards, the group was asked to leave – but was always allowed back.

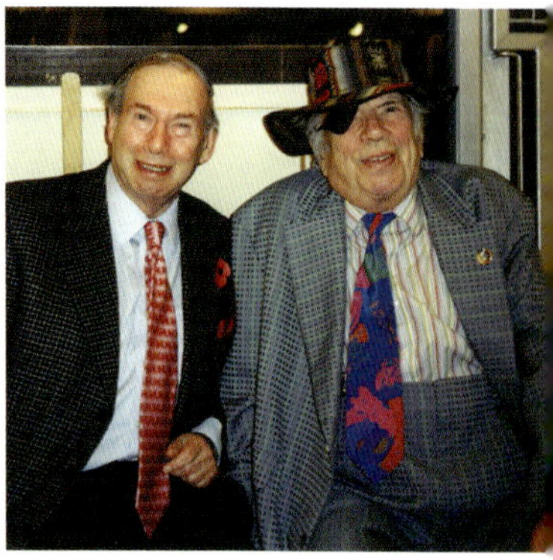

Jeffrey Sherwin and George Melly

Another surrealist artist I met was Eileen Agar in her later years. She was a link with the beginnings of the British surrealism movement. Luckily, I have one of her most important works, the collaged plaster head *The Angel of Mercy* which is often exhibited. A great deal has been written about Eileen Agar and a number of exhibitions of her work organised. What had never been noticed was that in the magazine *Arson*, produced by Toni del Renzio in 1942, there was a photograph of *The Angel of Mercy*. In the photograph the sculpture is collaged with fur and titled *The Politician*.

F.E. McWilliam was a sculptor from Northern Ireland who lived in Holland Park. When we first visited him I asked if I could buy *The Long Arm*. This was a 6ft 6in white arm made of apple wood and ending with a clenched fist.

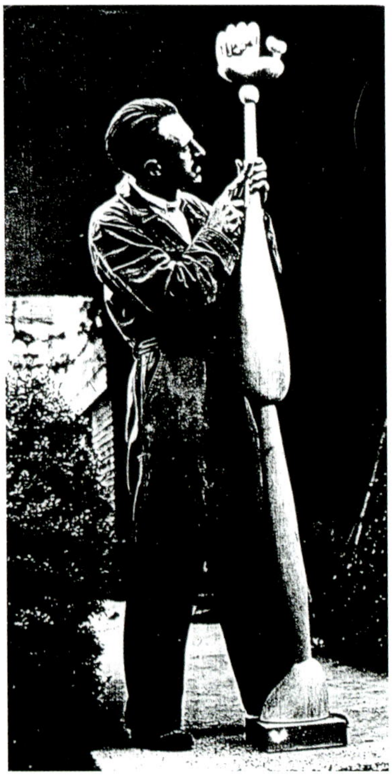

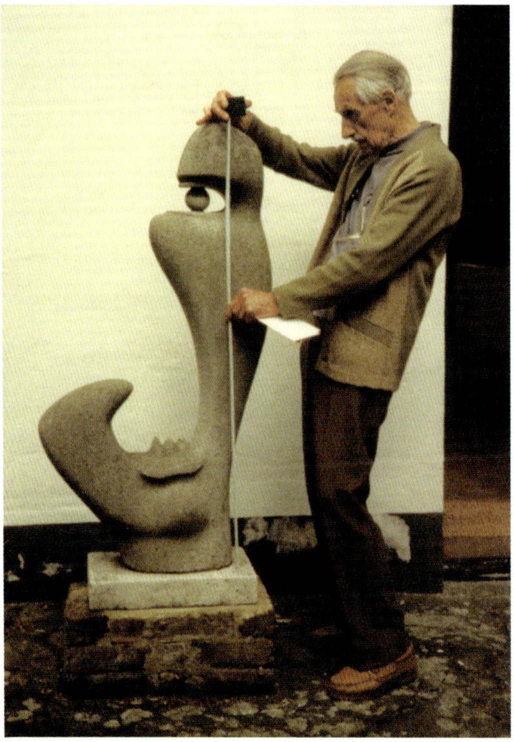

F.E. McWilliam as young artist with *The Long Arm*

F.E. McWilliam with the *Spanish Head*

'It is the Spanish Republicans' salute. They shall not pass', Mac added. To get it home I dropped down the back seat of my old Renault 16, propping up the sculpture with some old towels and a few books, oblivious of the proper way of packing a valuable work. Thankfully, it didn't fracture. On another visit to Mac, I noticed that the large Hoptonwood stone piece, *Spanish Head,* standing in the garden, was being damaged by the rain. Is it for sale? I asked. 'It belonged to my late wife, he replied, but as you were the only person who ever asked to buy *The Long Arm* I will sell you the sculpture'. This time I didn't bring it back in my car. I got a professional remover from Harrogate. Unfortunately, they were not specialist art shippers. It seems they had used a wheel barrow to move it from the garden to the van. Once again the gods were smiling on me – I now have a case for its transport. When Andrew Murray from the Mayor Gallery heard that I had bought *The Spanish Head* I am told he turned to a friend and said 'That bloody Sherwin – he comes with a van and takes the best piece.' Said in jest, I am sure.

Toni del Renzio was another fascinating character with whom I became friends. Born a Romanov he left Russia for Italy, where as an equestrian, he was called up by Mussolini to fight in Abyssinia. Hearing that Italian prisoners were castrated, he fled to Spain, where he fought for the Republicans, and then to Paris.

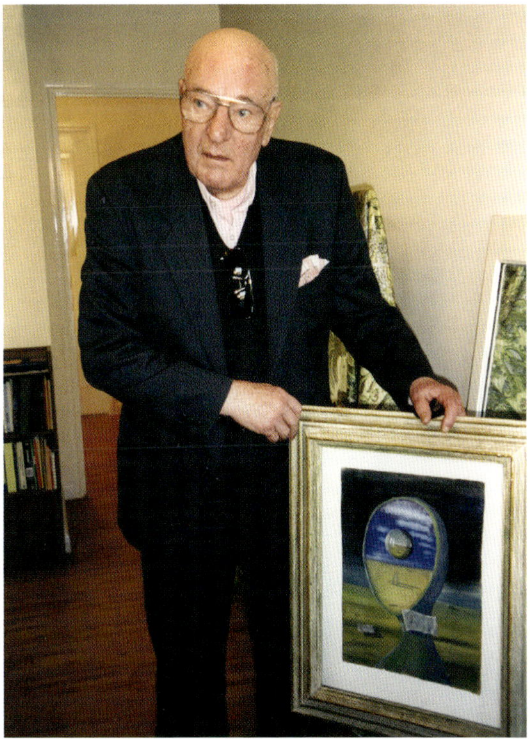

Toni del Renzio holding *Paranoiac Regression*, now in the Sherwin Collection

Del Renzio tried to stir the British surrealists into action. On the occasion that he and his surrealist artist wife Ithell Colquhoun (later known as the witch of Cornwall) held a public poetry reading in 1944 they were pelted with vegetables by a belligerent group, led by his rival E.L.T. Mesens. This event so traumatized del Renzio that he virtually stopped painting for the rest of his life. It was Silvano Levy, the writer, academic and biographer of Conroy Maddox, who suggested that we should reactivate del Renzio's creative spirit by offering to buy any work he produced, good or bad. As Toni was a bit hard up at the time it seemed to work. Toni's last act was to write an illustrated manifesto called *Alter Ego & Doppelgänger* – which I financed. Luckily, he had the satisfaction of reading the printed publication just before he died; however Silvano must take the credit for all the ground work that made it happen.

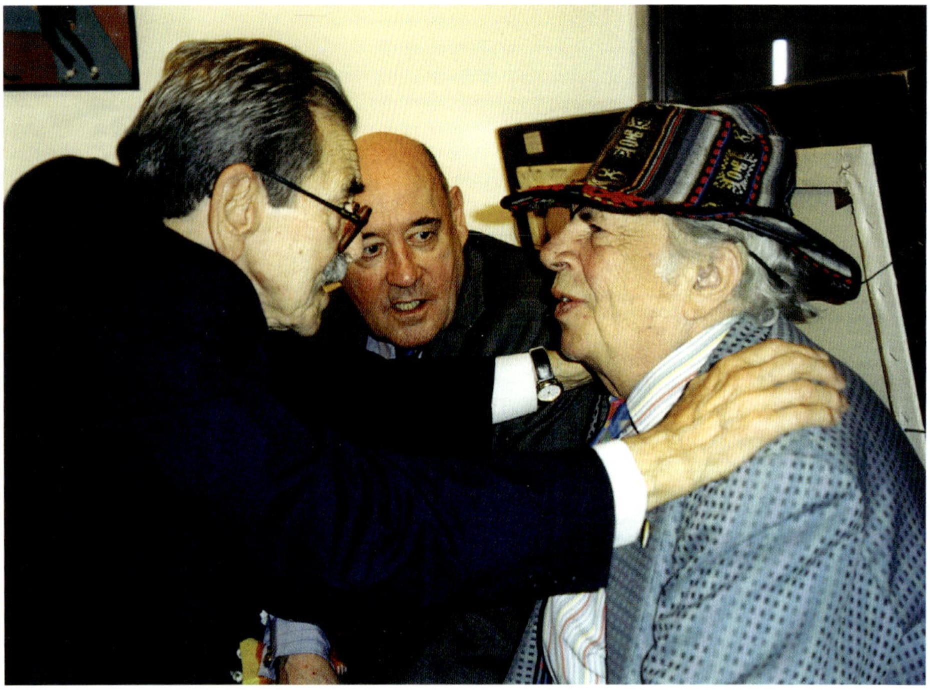

Conroy Maddox, Desmond Morris and George Melly

George Melly and Conroy Maddox were great friends. George was always happy to praise Conroy and his immutable surrealist roots. A Conroy Maddox exhibition opened by George was always a memorable occasion and was packed with the friends of the surrealist movement, who seemed to surface solely for these occasions.

Tony Earnshaw was a surrealist and anarchist from Leeds. He painted, illustrated, constructed visual witty boxes and transcribed his own acerbic view of life onto paper in *Flick Knives and Forks*. He taught at Leeds College

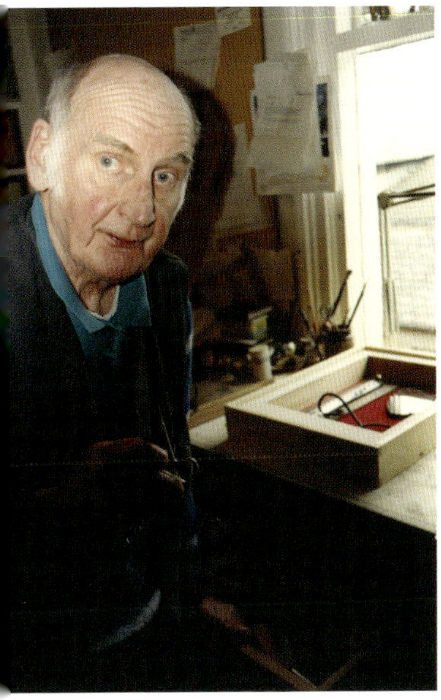

Tony Earnshaw in his studio

of Art. I first met him when he lived in Northbrook Street in Chapel Allerton, Leeds, and had just finished his book *Musrum*. After my heart attack and quadruple by-pass, I commissioned him in 2000 to construct two boxes using objects from my surgery. He came up with the endearing titles *The Glamorous Heart Attack* and *Make Mine a Quadruple*.

Tony was never well and spent the last part of his life in Saltburn-by-the-Sea with his wife and former student Gail. When he died Gail kindly asked me to join George Melly and Patrick Hughes to participate in his funeral oration. It was, of course, an anarchist funeral and took place in his favourite pub. The coffin was cardboard and all those who wished to do so signed it with comments and brought mementoes. His body was laid to rest to the sound of his favourite jazz musician, Bix Beiderbecke. Anthony Earnshaw's prodigious talent deserves to be better known.

Other Leeds College of Art alumni who are still 'in business' include Paul Hammond who moved to Barcelona. He gave up painting to become a writer and surreal film critic as well as translator. Ruth and I went to visit him. Following sherry stops at various tapas bars, we ended up at one of Barcelona's most popular restaurants, with the spits of food sending flames crackling high into the chimney, but also with a big queue of waiting diners. As it was cold and I am rather short of hair, I wore my deer stalker. Ruth said I looked bloody stupid. 'No one wears a hat like that in Barcelona' she said. The owner of the restaurant apologised, but there would be a long delay. However, on seeing my hat he said 'ah but for Sherlock Holmes we have a table'.

On another Spanish occasion, I loaned a painting by Gordon Onslow Ford to the Grenell Foundation in Santiago de Compostella in Spain for an exhibition. The Foundation was named after Eugenio Grenell, a surrealist and Republican, who had to flee from Spain during the Civil War. The Foundation was run by his daughter, Natalia Fernandez. A visit to a restaurant after the show along with Marie Louise Boras, the academic, suddenly changed its character as they and fellow guests began to sing the old Republican revolutionary songs. The stone walls of the restaurant reverberated with the sounds of history and we were back in the 1930s. Clearly the politics and bitterness of the past are not yet forgotten.

Patrick Hughes, another Leeds College artist and lecturer, now lives in London. He is very successful in making 3D visually disturbing images. His original surrealist roots were, however, in Leeds where he taught at the college. His pupils included Glen Baxter, the successful author and cartoonist, and Paul Hammond. Although not a student, Tony Pusey, who now lives in Sweden, was responsible for the first edition of the Leeds surrealist magazine *Melmoth* in 1980.

A few words about John Welson and Desmond Morris: both are talented surrealist artists who have had other careers. John, who worked with Conroy Maddox on a *Hinge of History*, is a fluent Welsh speaker, a one time civil servant for the Welsh Office and acted as an advisor to William Hague. He now has his main success with European galleries and keeps in touch with all the European surrealist movements, as well as carrying on farming in 'deepest' Wales.

Desmond Morris, the author of the *Naked Ape* and an anthropologist, is a most talented surrealist painter and object-maker. He was also for a while the director of the ICA. His interest in surrealism stems from his time in Birmingham and his meetings with Conroy Maddox, who lived in the same city. Desmond continues to plough a productive and very successful surrealist furrow and has also recently produced a personal manifesto.

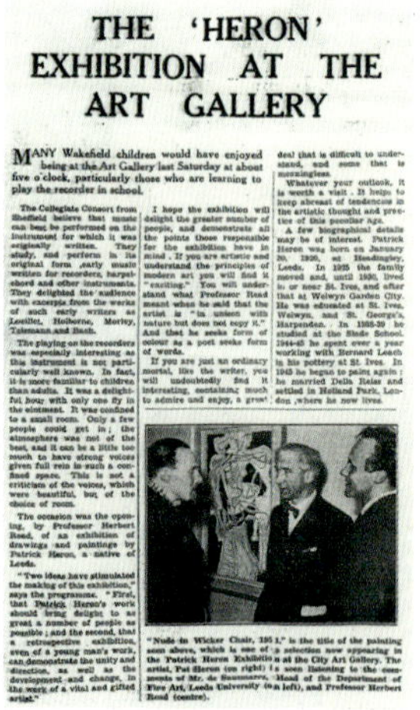
THE 'HERON' EXHIBITION AT THE ART GALLERY

MANY Wakefield children would have enjoyed being at the Art Gallery last Saturday at about five o'clock, particularly those who are learning to play the recorder in school.

The Collegiate Consort from Sheffield believe that music can best be performed on the instrument for which it was originally written. They study, and perform in its original form, early music written for recorders, harpsichord and other instruments. They delighted the audience with excerpts from the works of such early writers as Loeillet, Holborne, Morley, Telemann and Bach.

The playing on the recorders was especially interesting as this instrument is not particularly well known. In fact, it is more familiar to children than adults. It was a delightful hour with only one fly in the ointment. It was confined to a small room. Only a few people could get in; the atmosphere was not of the best, and it can be a little too much to have strong voices given full rein in such a confined space. This is not a criticism of the voices, which were beautiful, but of the choice of room.

The occasion was the opening, by Professor Herbert Read, of an exhibition of drawings and paintings by Patrick Heron, a native of Leeds.

"Two ideas have stimulated the making of this exhibition," says the programme. "First, that Patrick Heron's work should bring delight to as great a number of people as possible; and the second, that a retrospective exhibition, even of a young man's work, can demonstrate the unity and direction, as well as the development and change, in the work of a vital and gifted artist."

I hope the exhibition will delight the greater number of people, and demonstrate all the points those responsible for the exhibition have in mind. If you are artistic and understand the principles of modern art you will find it "exciting." You will understand what Professor Read meant when he said that the artist is "in unison with nature but does not copy it." And that he seeks form of colour as a poet seeks form of words.

If you are just an ordinary mortal, like the writer, you will undoubtedly find it interesting, containing much to admire and enjoy, a great deal that is difficult to understand, and some that is meaningless.

Whatever your outlook, it is worth a visit. It helps to keep abreast of tendencies in the artistic thought and practice of this peculiar age.

A few biographical details may be of interest. Patrick Heron was born on January 30, 1920, at Headingley, Leeds. In 1925 the family moved and, until 1930, lived in or near St. Ives, and after that at Welwyn Garden City. He was educated at St. Ives, Welwyn, and St. George's, Harpenden. In 1937-39 he studied at the Slade School. 1944-45 he spent over a year working with Bernard Leach in his pottery at St. Ives. In 1945 he began to paint again; he married Delia Reiss and settled in Holland Park, London, where he now lives.

"Nude in Wicker Chair, 1951," is the title of the painting seen above, which is one of a selection now appearing in the Patrick Heron Exhibition at the City Art Gallery. The artist, Pat Heron (on right) is seen listening to the comments of Mr. de Sausmarez, Head of the Department of Fine Art, Leeds University (on left), and Professor Herbert Read (centre).

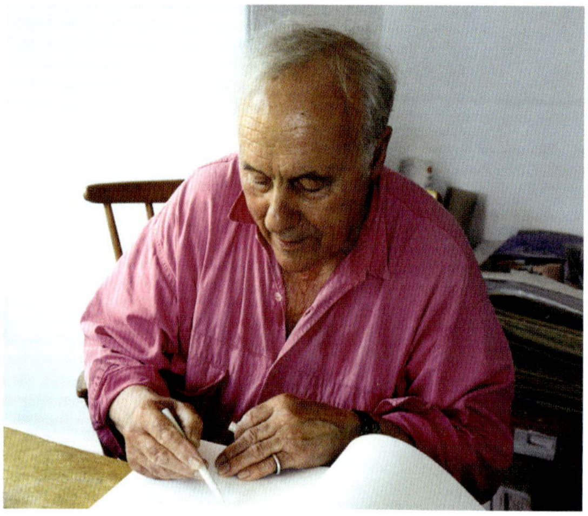

Patrick Heron exhibition at Wakefield Art Gallery: Patrick Heron (right) is seen listening to Mr de Sauzmarez, Head of the Department of Fine Art, Leeds University (left) and Professor Herbert Read (centre)

Patrick Heron signing his book at Eagles Nest

Patrick Heron was a lovely man. He was born in Leeds and his father, a member of the Leeds Arts Club, founded the Cresta Silks factory. Ruth and I visited Patrick at his home, Eagles Nest in Zennor, Cornwall, overlooking the sea. All the rooms were painted white and covered with his paintings. No other art work was on show, with the exception of a tall pot by Sam Haile. He was genuinely enthusiastic about everything, his house, his paintings, his plants and even his kitchen. One of the bedrooms at Eagles Nest was a picture store. It was there that we found the painting *Nude in a Wicker Chair* which, as I discovered later, had first been exhibited at Wakefield Art Gallery.

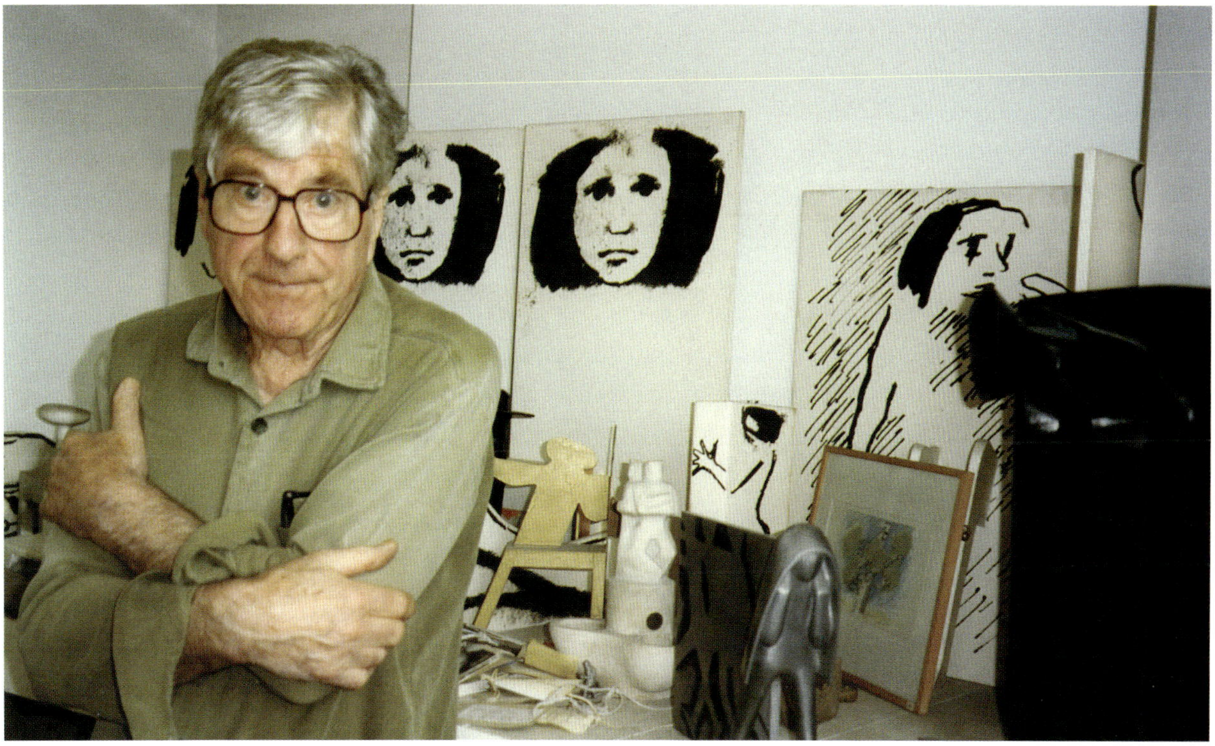

Kenneth Armitage in his studio

Kenneth Armitage was another Leeds born artist. I first met him in a room over the Victoria pub behind the Town Hall when he came to lecture at a hoped for, but unrealised, resurrection of the historic Leeds Arts Club. At his home in Kensington his studio was down steep steps with only a thick rope as a hand rail. He was very price conscious and kept on referring to a little book with all the latest prices of his work in it. It was Armitage who told me that my work *Family Going for a Walk*, which had always been considered as a terracotta sculpture, was in fact made from dental plaster. He found it was a harder material.

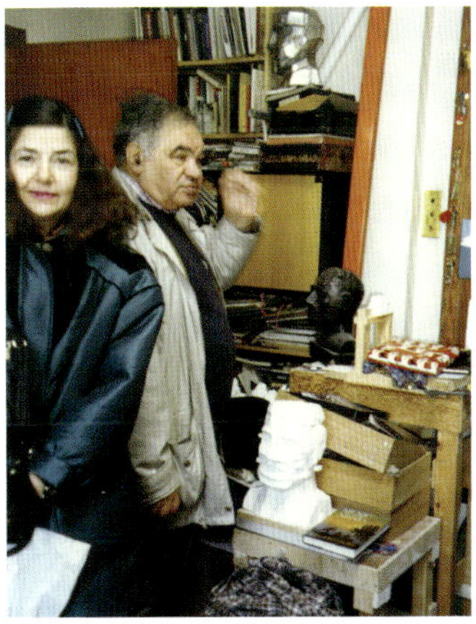

Eduardo Paolozzi with Ruth Sherwin in his studio

We also met Eduardo Paolozzi on a visit he made to Leeds to coincide with an exhibition of his work at the Gallery. Eduardo Paolozzi lived in two converted garages in Chelsea. His bed was on a balcony overlooking a vast jumble of plaster casts, bronzes and bits of paper that he might use for collages. Despite his reputation for being difficult, I found him generous, though he could also appear oblivious to the feelings of others. Physically strong, the first thing one noticed was his enormous hands. He took us to meet his students at the Royal College. 'Who wants some sandwiches for lunch?' he asked generously. On the way out he bent down to pick up a colourful carton which someone had dropped on the pavement, 'this will do for something' – and then added, 'oh yes sandwiches – Jeffrey can you lend me fifteen quid?'

Ruth and I also went to see David Mach, now a Royal Academician, in November 1995. He lived south of the river Thames. I had always wanted a match stick head and David made one for me. The *Head with Crossbow Arrows* had an immediate appeal. When finished he told me that, as it was such a time-consuming business, he got his father to put the match sticks in the mould. David wanted to set fire to the mask on Leeds Art Gallery steps as he had done with other masks. However, I liked the colour and the flames would have played havoc with the feathers of the arrows.

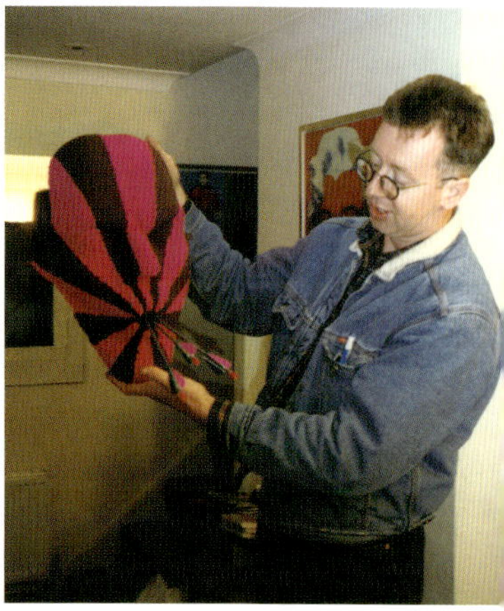

David Mach holding the *Head with Crossbow Arrows*, 1995

Laurie Burt, now aged eighty-four, is another voice from the past. This sprightly man still works in his York studio at the bottom of his garden, producing sculpture and collages. Following war-time service he took a job as a technician at Leeds College of Art. He progressed through night school, to become a lecturer at Leeds and later at Leicester. He was Principal Lecturer at Cardiff College of Art and had exhibitions at the Drian and Grabowski Galleries in London. His works are in the Tate, the Arts Council Collection and Leeds Art Gallery, among others. His sculptures are often provocative with surrealist overtones. In one you pull a lever and a foetus drops out. The works which I have bought are a little gentler.

I bought a small painting by Peter Blake, after I had recovered from my by-pass, as a small thank-you to my wife Ruth for looking after me. It was called *Baby Ruth*. How often do you find a painting with your wife's name on it? A visit to Peter Blake's fascinating studio is dominated by the life-size figure of the black boxer Sonny Liston. The visit resulted in the acquisition of a group of four somewhat surrealist prints with the title *Madonna in Naples*.

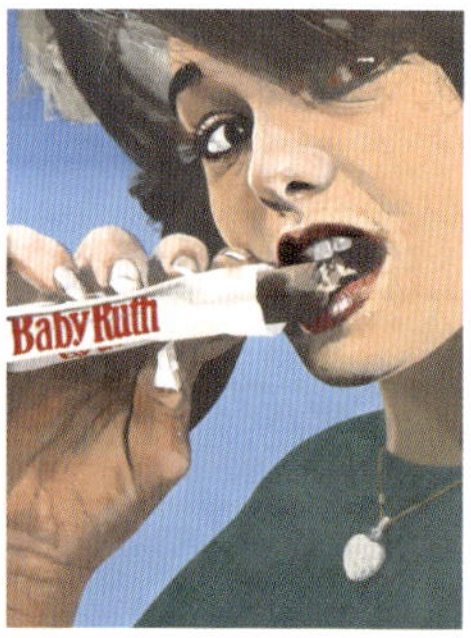

Baby Ruth
Peter Blake, 1972 and 1989

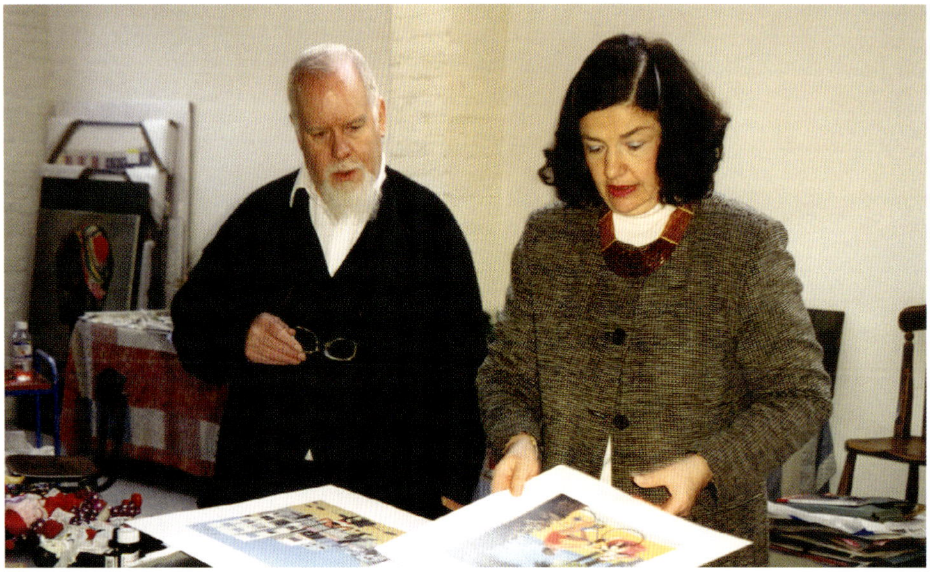

Peter Blake with Ruth Sherwin in his studio

Marking family occasions with a picture is probably just an excuse on my part to add to the family collection. When my sons Jonathan and Adam got into Cambridge I gave them works by Andy Goldsworthy and Richard Hamilton respectively.

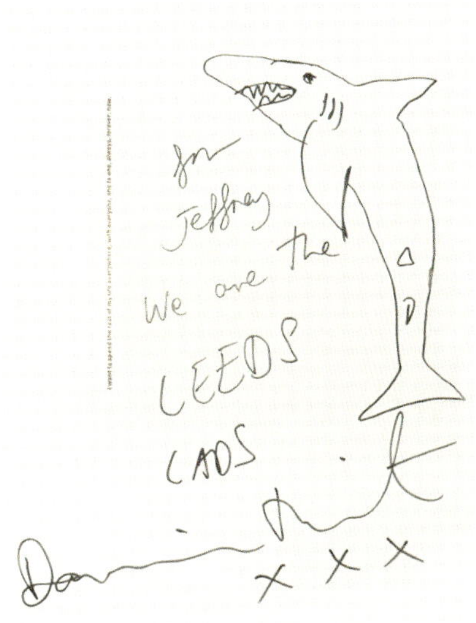

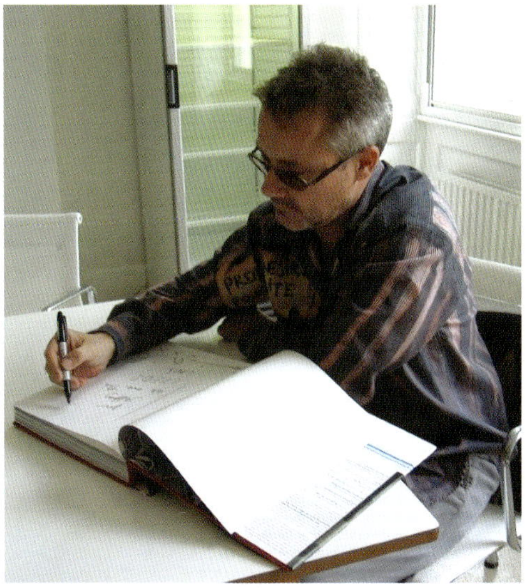

Damien Hirst is drawing a shark with the dedication 'we are the Leeds Lads'

As with Henry Moore, no one at the Civic Hall had thought of officially inviting Damien Hirst to Leeds, despite the fact that he had not only been brought up in Leeds, but also attended Leeds College of Art and always presented himself as a Leeds lad. Because I had an early collage by him, I used it as an excuse for contacting Damien and, with the agreement of the Lord Mayor, handed over a personal invitation. He came up with his adviser, Frank Dunphy, whose Irish sense of humour, coupled with Damien's puckish Yorkshire 'down to earth' approach, made for a relaxed and very enjoyable lunch. This was carried over into the afternoon when Damien, on a tour of Leeds Art Gallery, pushed his way into the staff room and saw someone had already done a 'Damien Hirst' on the notice board. Instead of being offended, he just laughed and added his own signature.

Meeting artists is the plus side of collecting. However, for me, a bigger plus is giving others the opportunity to enjoy my collection.

TECHNIQUES

FROTTAGE

Frottage, the French word for rubbing, is a surrealist automatist technique developed by Max Ernst in drawings which he made from 1925 onwards. He was inspired by an ancient wooden floor where the grain of the planks had been accentuated by many years of scrubbing. The patterns of the graining suggested strange images to Ernst. He captured these by laying sheets of paper on the floor and then rubbing over them with a soft pencil. The results suggest mysterious forests peopled with bird-like creatures. In 1926 Ernst published a collection of these drawings titled Histoire Naturelle (natural history). He went on to use a wide range of textured surfaces and quickly adapted the technique to oil painting, calling it grattage (scraping). In grattage the canvas is prepared with a layer or more of paint then laid over the textured object which is then scraped over.

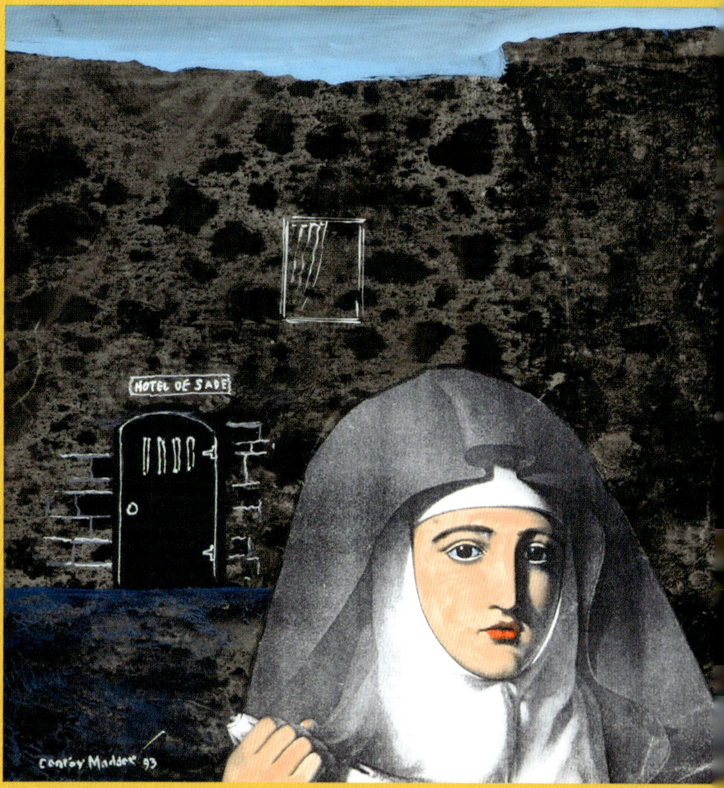

The Marquis de Sade and the Nun
Conroy Maddox, 1993

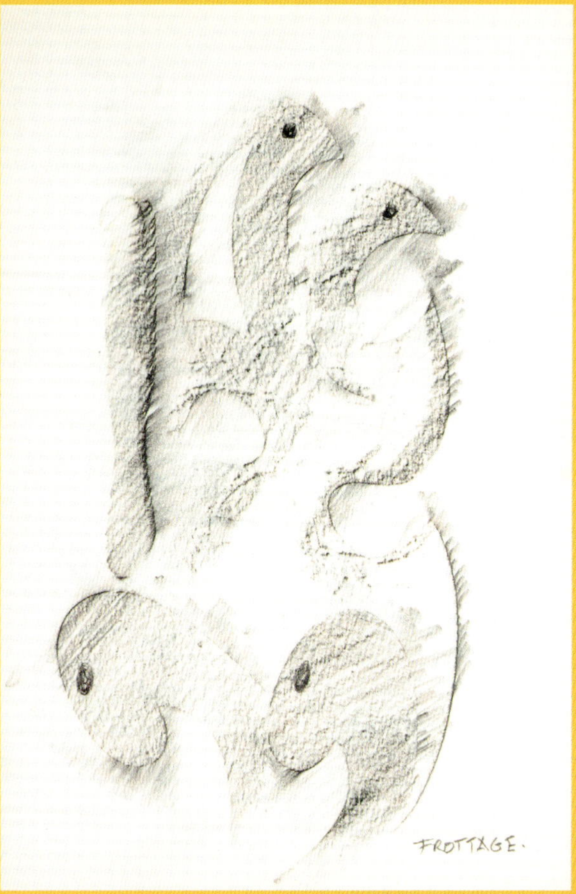

Frottage
Conroy Maddox, c.1999

DECALCOMANIA

Decalcomania is a process of spreading thick paint upon a canvas then – while it is still wet – covering it with further material such as paper or aluminum foil. This covering is then removed (again before the paint dries), and the resultant paint pattern becomes the basis of the finished painting. The technique was much employed by artists such as Max Ernst and Conroy Maddox.

FUMAGE

Fumage is a surrealist technique invented by Wolfgang Paalen in which impressions or evocative patterns are made by the smoke or soot of a lit candle or kerosene lamp on a piece of paper or canvas. He created the technique in the course of his association with the surrealists and their attempts to transform automatic writing into drawing and painting. Between 1936 and 1937 Paalen developed with these visionary-ephemeral forms on canvas, which he then mostly painted over in oil. The technique was later employed by Salvador Dali who called it 'sfumato'. Both Paalen and Dali used the technique as a basis for their oil paintings. Paalen's elongated surreal landscapes and Dali's elongated, wavy treatment of animals and objects reveal the influence of the technique on their imagery. It is a technique also explored by Conroy Maddox.

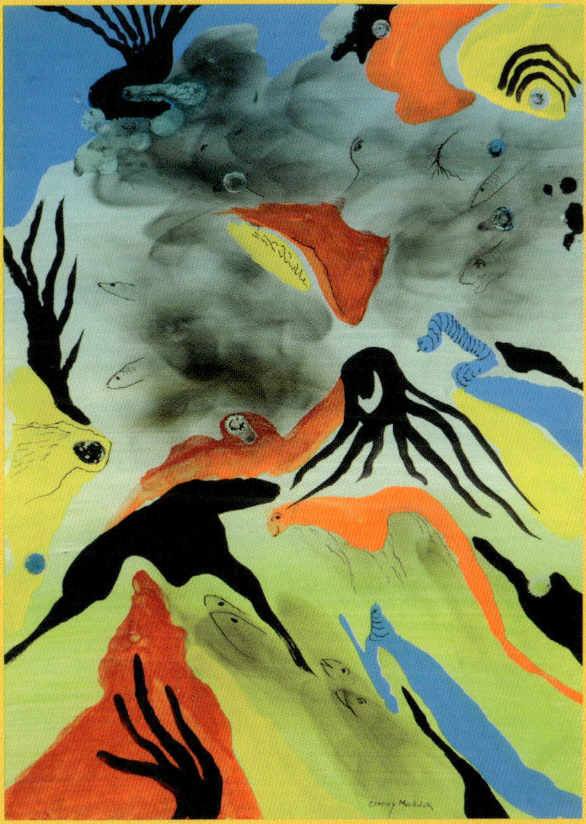

The Battle of the Sea
Conroy Maddox

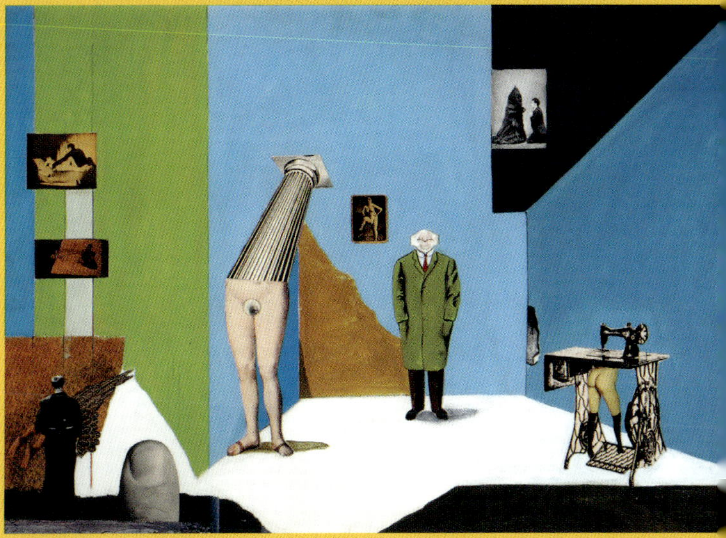

Reflections on Prince Vibescu
Conroy Maddox, 1996

COLLAGE

Collage, from the French word coller – to glue, is a term used to describe both the technique and the resulting work of art in which pieces of paper, photographs, fabric, ephemera or found objects are arranged and glued to a supporting surface. Collage can also include other media such as painting and drawing as well as three dimensional elements. The term collage derives from the French words papiers collés or découpage, used to describe techniques of pasting paper cut-outs onto various surfaces. It was first used as an artists' technique in the 20th century, including by Conroy Maddox.

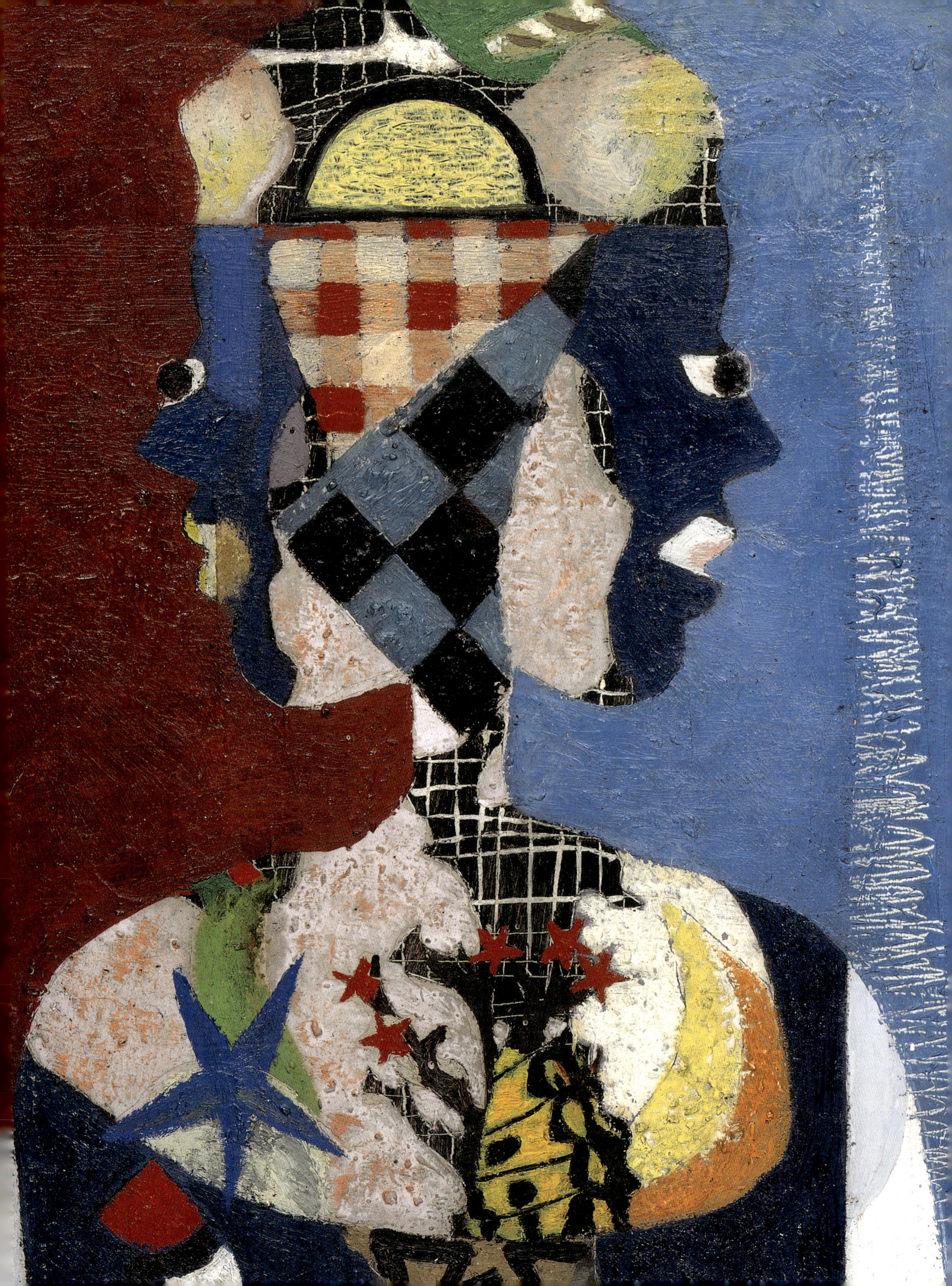

EILEEN AGAR (1899–1991)

Agar occupies a unique position in the history of British surrealism. She was the first female artist to join the group and the only professional woman painter to represent Britain in the great International Surrealist Exhibition of 1936. As a result she exhibited with the surrealists in Paris and New York. For Agar, as with many involved with the surrealist movement, especially women, surrealism offered a unique opportunity for experimentation and self-expression.

Oscar Wilde
1929
Pen and ink
49 x 33 cm
Provenance: Redfern Gallery, London

Exhibited: *Eileen Agar: A Retrospective*, Birch & Conran, London, 1987

Angel of Mercy
1934
Plaster with collage and watercolour
Signed and dated inside: 1934
44.5 cm high
Provenance: Christie's, London, 22 June 1993

Exhibited: *Eileen Agar: A Retrospective*, Birch & Conran, London, 8 July–7 August 1987, no. 8, illustration; *The Surrealist Spirit in Britain*, London, Whitford and Hughes, 1988; *British and European Surrealism*, Wolverhampton Art Gallery, Wolverhampton, 1995; *Europe in the 30s*, Paris, Musée d'Art Moderne, 1997; *Eileen Agar 1899–1991*, Scottish National Gallery of Modern Art, Edinburgh, 1999, no. 26; *Blast to Frieze, British Art in the 20th Century*, Kunstmuseum Wolfsburg, 2002; *British Surrealism & Other Realities: The Sherwin Collection*, Museum of Modern Art (Mima), Middlesbrough, 23 May–17 August 2008; *Eileen Agar, An Eye for Collage*, Pallant House, Chichester, 25 October 2008–15 March 2009

Literature: Louisa Buck, *The Surrealist Spirit in Britain*, London, Whitford and Hughes, 1988, no. 1, colour illustration; *Blast to Frieze, British Art in the 20th Century*, exhibition catalogue, Kunstmuseum Wolfsburg/Hatje Cantz, 2002, plate 51, colour illustration; *Eileen Agar: 1899–1991;* exhibition catalogue, Scottish National Gallery of Modern Art, 1999, by Ann Simpson *et.al*, cat. no. 26, colour illustration no. 6; *Eileen Agar, An Eye for Collage*, Pallant House, Chichester, no. 10, colour illustration

Angel of Mercy is the first of three plaster heads that Agar decorated between 1934 and 1940 and is a rare early piece. It was initially a cast of a portrait head modelled by Agar of her husband Joseph Bard, a classicist, who deepened her knowledge on mythology and the ancient civilisations of ancient Greece and Rome. The sculpture's painted design combines the fluid biomorphic line of natural forms with strong illusions of classical antiquity.

Happy Breakfast (left)
1937
Oil on canvas
30 x 19.5 cm
Provenance: Lord Croft; Christie's, London, 4 June 1999

Exhibited: *Eileen Agar*, Retrospective exhibition, Commonwealth Art Gallery, London, 29 September–24 October 1971, no. 12; *Eileen Agar 1899–1991*, A centenary exhibition, Scottish National Gallery of Modern Art, Edinburgh, 1 December 1999–27 February 2000; Leeds Art Gallery, Leeds, 9 March–30 April 2000; *British Surrealism & Other Realities: The Sherwin Collection*, Museum of Modern Art (Mima), Middlesbrough, 23 May–17 August 2008

Literature: *Eileen Agar: 1899–1991*, A centenary exhibition, exhibition catalogue, Scottish National Gallery of Modern Art, 1999, by Ann Simpson *et.al*, cat. no. 42

This tiny painting was likely painted in Mougins, France, where Agar stayed along with Picasso and friends in 1937. It is painted to look like a collage, in particular the red and white chequered tablecloths and French bread, which employs the use of scrafito, a popular technique of the time. Agar achieved the collage-like texture in this painting by scratching through the various paint layers with the end of her paintbrush.

Collage Letter (overleaf)
c.1939–40
Eileen Agar to E.L.T. Mesens
Paper butterfly, postage stamp, cloth poppy, gauze etc.
Mirror writing thanking Mesens for the 'Esquisse',
Signed: Eileen
Provenance: Belgium

The letter is written in French and can be translated: 'My dear Edward, a thousand thanks and three kisses for Esquisse'

Foot in Hand
1939
Collage
Postcards published by The English Surrealist Group (Roland Penrose) in the 1940s
Provenance: Estate of E.L.T. Mesens

Exhibited: *British Surrealism & Other Realities: The Sherwin Collection*, Museum of Modern Art (Mima), Middlesbrough, 23 May–17 August 2008,

Collage has always been of central interest to Agar, giving her endless avenues to explore and materials to exploit. She used magazines, children's plastic toys, and numerous relics of the beach and hedgerow to trigger and stimulate the imagination. After her career came to a standstill during the war, she re-kindled it in the 1950s. Until her death in 1991, she continued to paint and make collages and objects with undiminished vigour and originality.

Cadavre Exquis (Exquisite Corpse) (below)
c.1939
With John Banting, Roland Penrose and (Antonio Pedro) da Costa
Ink on paper
22 x 9 cm

Exhibited: *British Surrealism & Other Realities: The Sherwin Collection*, Museum of Modern Art (Mima), Middlesbrough, 23 May–17 August 2008,

Invented in 1925 in Paris by the surrealists Yves Tanquy, Jacques Prévert, André Breton and Marcel Duchamp, Cadavre Exquis is similar to the old parlour game Consequences, in which the players write in turn on a sheet of paper, fold to conceal part of the writing and pass it on to the next player. The surrealists adapted the game by drawing parts of the body. The name *Cadavre Exquis* was derived from a phrase that resulted when they first played the game 'Le cadaver/exquis/boira/le vin/nouveau (The exquisite corpse will drink the new wine)'.

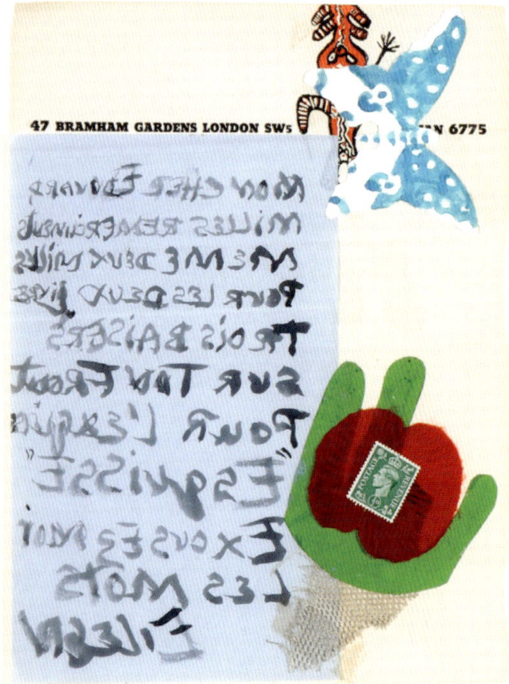

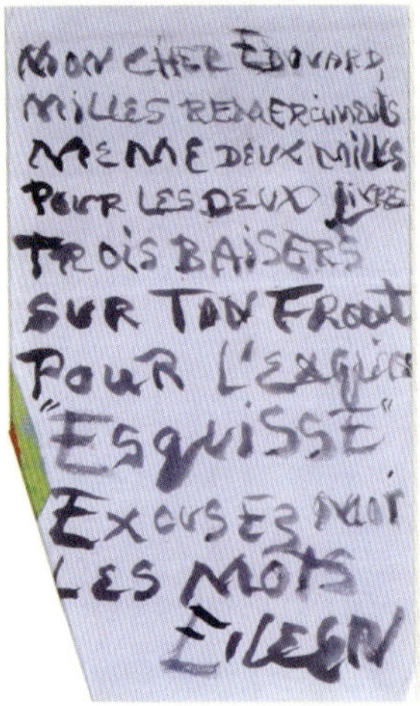

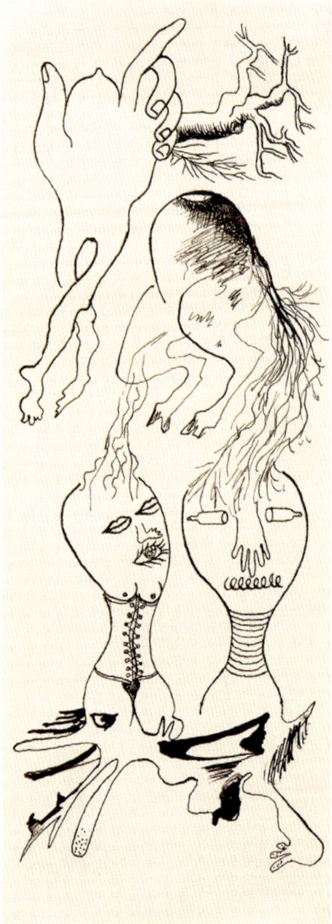

EDWARD ALLINGTON (born 1951)

Allington's work often reflects an interest in the cultural legacy of the classical world. However, in his preference for broken forms, salvaged motifs and fragments of text, his sculpture challenges the meanings of our cultural perceptions. He gives a form to the timeless question about the ideals of beauty, truth, relevance and sublimity.

Myron's Discobolus Diminished
1987
Resin casts and painted wood
102 x 45 x 29.5 cm
Provenance: Diane Brown Gallery, New York 1987; Lisson Gallery, London

Exhibited: *Exhibition of Sculpture and Drawings by Edward Allington*, Diane Brown Gallery, New York, 1987; *British Surrealism & Other Realities: The Sherwin Collection*, Museum of Modern Art (Mima), Middlesbrough, 23 May–17 August 2008,

Literature: *Edward Allington: Exhibition of Sculpture and Drawings by Edward Allington*, catalogue 1987, b/w illus. p.11; Interview with Edward Allington by Shin-ichi Nakazawa, *Gallery FACE*, Tokyo, 1988, b/w illus., no page number

The Discobolus of Myron (discus thrower) is a famous Roman marble copy of a lost Greek bronze original, the latter of which was completed c.460–450 BC. A discus thrower is depicted about to release his throw and the moment captured in the sculpture is an example of rhythm, harmony and balance. Allington's work stands in three parts and is painted in the Italian colours: red, white and green.

Preliminary drawings for Myron's Discobolus Diminished
1987
Ink on paper
27 x 20.5 cm and 13 x 20.5 cm
Provenance: Gift from the artist, 2009

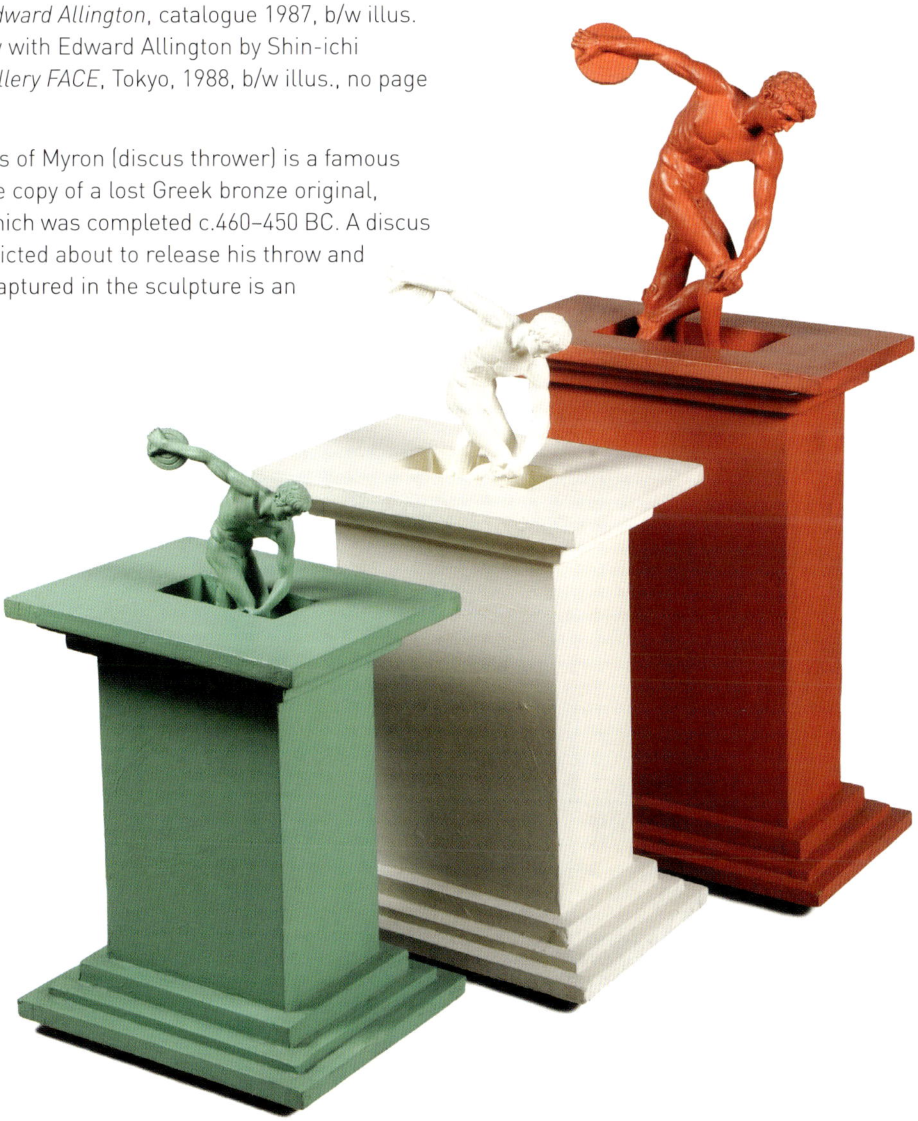

KENNETH ARMITAGE (1916–2002)

Armitage first attracted international attention as one of a group of young British sculptors, including Reg Butler, Lynn Chadwick, Eduardo Paolozzi and William Turnbull, who showed at the 26th Venice Biennale in 1952 and whose work signalled a new, anti-monumental, expressionist approach. His preoccupation was with the human figure, combined with an interest in vertical and horizontal structure. He created small-scale figures, full of droll humour, with broad, flattened bodies, pinheads and sprouting, stick-like limbs.

Family Going for a Walk
1951
Terracotta (dental plaster)
31 x 26 cm
Provenance: Purchased after Armitage's first one man show, 1952 at Gimpel Fils, London

Exhibited: *British Surrealism & Other Realities: The Sherwin Collection,* Museum of Modern Art (Mima), Middlesbrough, 23 May–17 August 2008

Family Going for a Walk, along with *People in the Wind* of 1950, is one of Armitage's best-known and most popular early sculptures. The present sculpture exists in a number of variants and sizes and thus attests to the ways in which the artist was exploring the theme of interlinked figure groups. It also combines both movement and humour. In the work, Armitage merges the tall attenuated forms and outstretched hands into a clear single unit, the thin central slab, which would be a feature of his group sculpture for the next five years. The stylised figures push forward together, clothes and limbs melding into one mass.

Family Going for a Walk
1951
Gouache on board
39 x 48 cm
Provenance: Sotheby's, London, 24 October 2005

Exhibited: *British Surrealism & Other Realities: The Sherwin Collection,* Museum of Modern Art (Mima), Middlesbrough, 23 May–17 August 2008

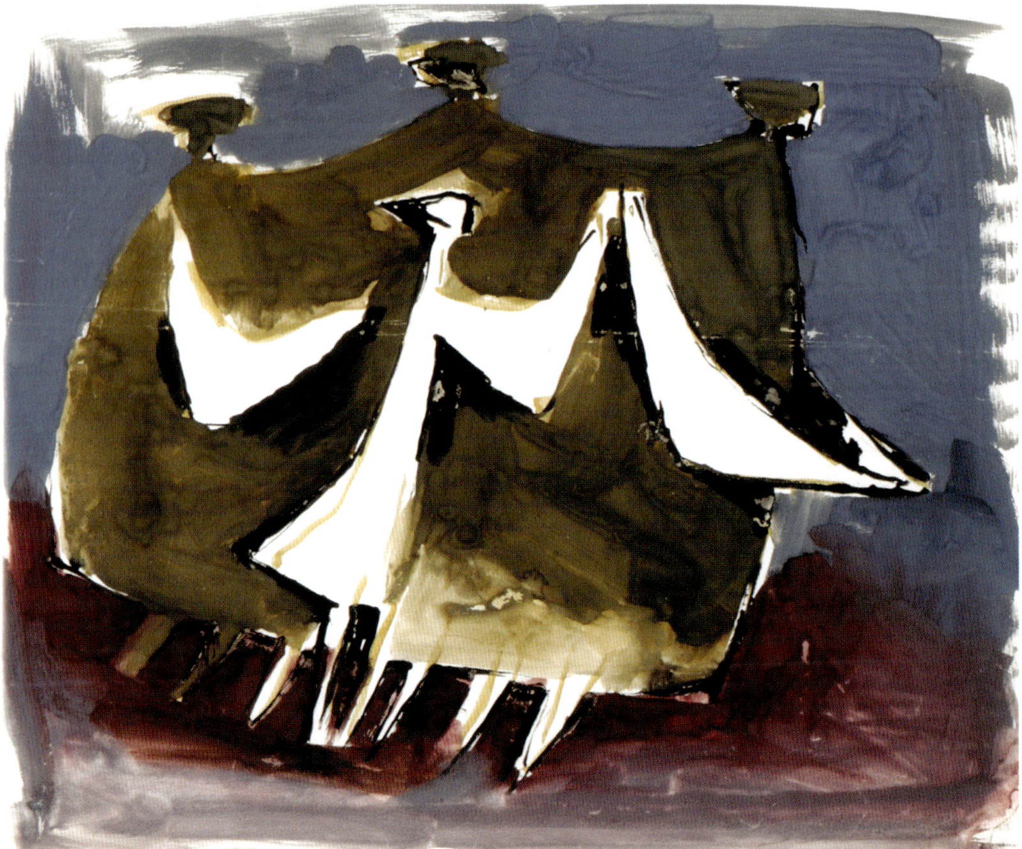

JOHN ARMSTRONG (1893–1973)

In 1933 Armstrong had joined the short-lived Unit One established by Paul Nash 'to express the truly contemporary spirit, for that thing which is recognised as peculiarly of today in painting, sculpture and architecture'. He fitted well into this loose association of eleven artists which included Nash, Edward Burra, Tristam Hillier, as well as Ben Nicholson, Henry Moore and Barbara Hepworth, all of whom were experimenting with abstraction and surrealism, often combined in the same work.

Unit One Composition
1933
Oil on canvas
74 x 61 cm
Signed initials: J.A.
Provenance: Mayor Gallery, London

Exhibited: *Blast to Frieze, British Art in the 20th Century*, Kunstmuseum Wolfsburg, 2002

Literature: *Blast to Frieze, British Art in the 20th Century*, exhibition catalogue, Kunstmuseum Wolfsburg/Hatje Cantz, 2002, plate 63, colour illustration; *British Surrealism & Other Realities: The Sherwin Collection*, Museum of Modern Art (Mima), Middlesbrough, 2008

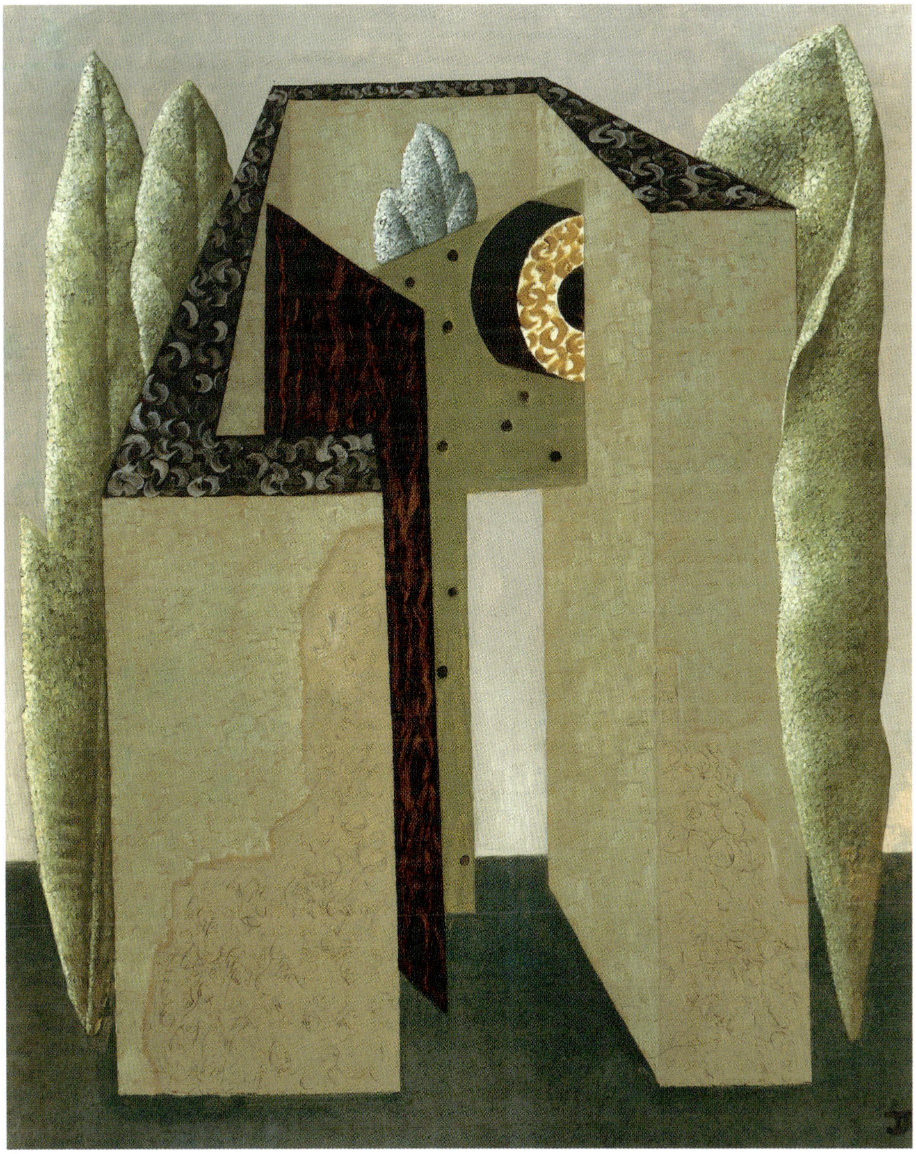

LAWRENCE ATKINSON (1873–1931)

Not much is known about Atkinson. He was not only an artist but also a musician and poet. He began by moving to Paris and studying musical composition, but moved back to London where he began to paint. Apparently influenced by Matisse and the Fauves, he executed mainly landscapes (almost all of these works are lost). However his style changed radically when he was introduced to the work of Wyndham Lewis and the vorticists.

Vorticist Composition
c.1914–15
Oil on canvas
106.5 x 85 cm
Provenance: The Hon David Bathurst, Mayor Gallery, London; Collection Sebastian Walker; Sotheby's, London, 20 November 1991 (after auction)

Exhibited: *Vorticist exhibition,* Dore Galleries, London, 1915; *Vorticism and its Allies,* The Hayward Gallery, London, 1974 (no. 386); *Blast: Vorticism 1914–1918,* Sprengel Museum, Hannover, 18 August–3 November 1996; *Haus der Kunst,* Munich, 1996–1997 illustration p.155; *Blast to Frieze, British Art in the 20th Century,* Kunstmuseum Wolfsburg, 2002, plate 8, colour illustration; *Blasting the Future: Vorticism and the Avant-Garde in Britain 1910–20,* Estorick Collection, London, 4 February–18 April 2004; Whitworth Art Gallery, Manchester, 7 May–25 July 2004; *British Surrealism & Other Realities: The Sherwin Collection,* Museum of Modern Art (Mima), Middlesbrough, 23 May–17 August 2008

Literature: *Blast to Frieze, British Art in the 20th Century,* exhibition catalogue, Kunstmuseum Wolfsburg/Hatje Cantz, 2002, plate 8, colour illustration

Atkinson appears to have used two picture easels bent to mimic human positions, the easels standing on his studio rug. This interpretation differs from Richard Cork in his two-volume book on vorticism, who likens the image to a man striding out of the painting.

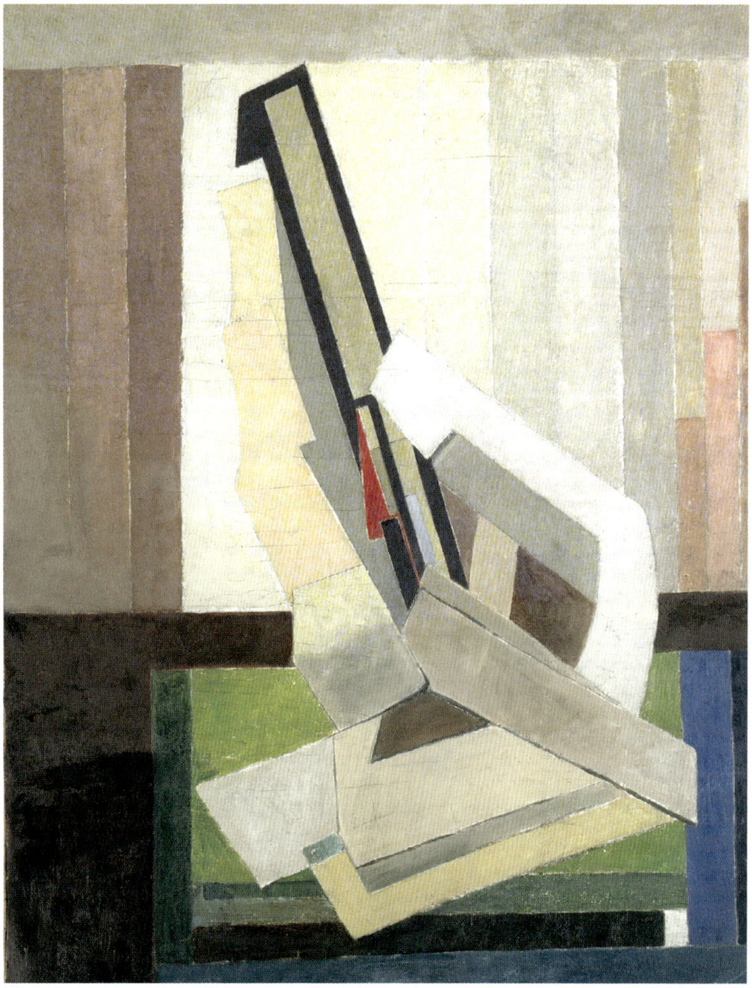

JOHN BANTING (1902–1972)

Banting's unconventional style of 'painting pictures' together with an idiosyncratic vocabulary of images set him at the forefront of British surrealism. He was one of the few artists who stayed with the British Surrealists Group from its inception at the 1936 exhibition until the closure of the London Gallery, the main venue for surrealist exhibitions, in 1951.

Self Portrait with String
1929
Oil and string on board
24.2 x 5.1 cm
Artist's monogram, dated and signed on verso

Exhibited: *British Surrealism & Other Realities: The Sherwin Collection*, Museum of Modern Art (Mima), Middlesbrough, 23 May–17 August 2008

The Adoration of the Magi
1929
Oil on canvas in original rope frame
50 x 57.8 cm
Inscribed lower left verso *'Bruno July 1929'*
Provenance: Lytton Strachey, purchased from the house of Bryan and Diana Guiness, 23 July 1929; Offer Waterman & Co, London

Exhibited: *British Surrealism & Other Realities: The Sherwin Collection*, Museum of Modern Art (Mima), Middlesbrough, 23 May–17 August 2008

In the summer of 1929, a sophisticated hoax was played upon the world of modern art. Evelyn Waugh, Brian Howard, John Banting and a handful of Mitfords successfully held an exhibition in the London house of Bryan Guinness. They claimed to have discovered the brilliant new talent of artist Bruno Hat, working in obscurity in a village near Clymping.

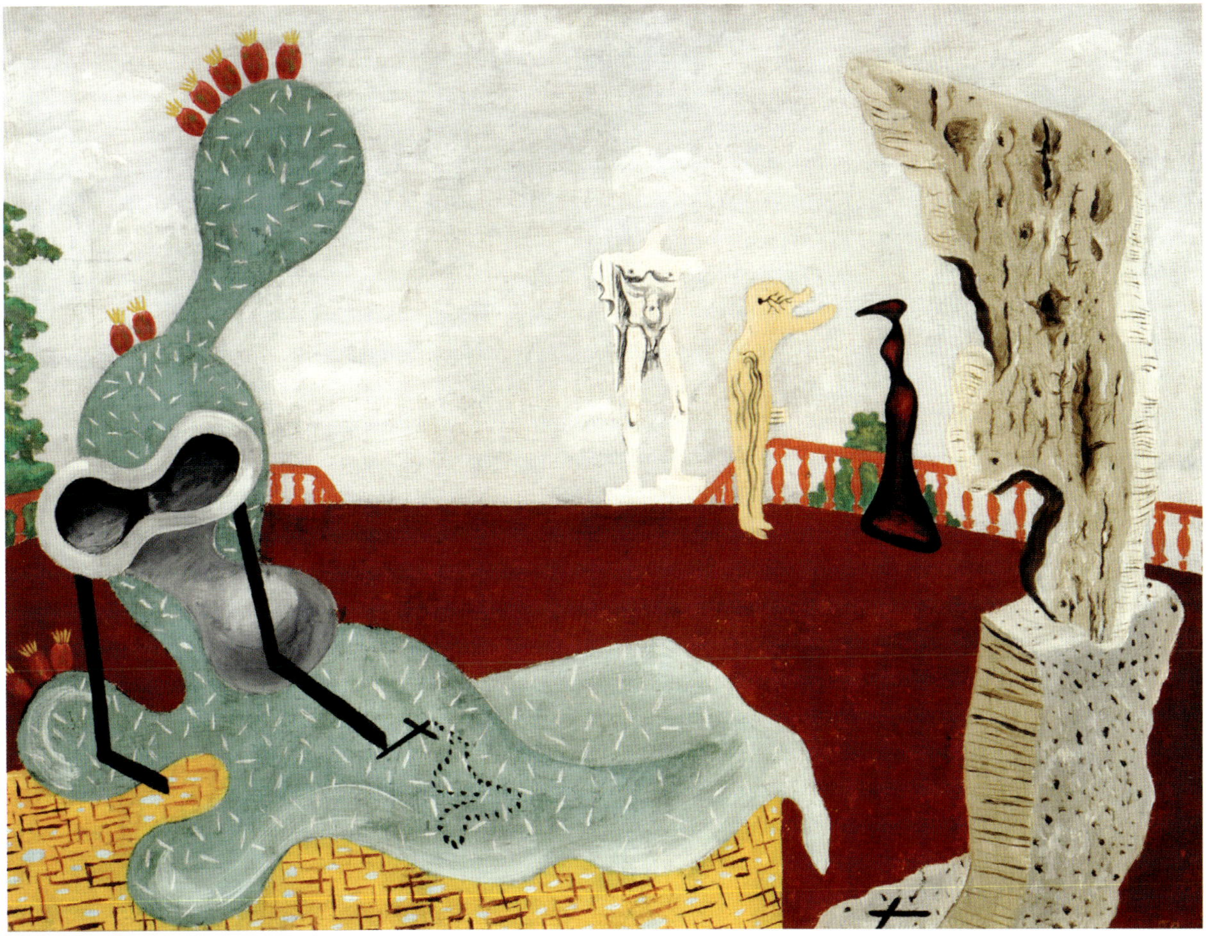

Ta Gueule
c.1929
Gouache
Provenance: United States

Exhibited: *British Surrealism & Other Realities: The Sherwin Collection*, Museum of Modern Art (Mima), Middlesbrough, 23 May–17 August 2008

Rayograph
c.1929
(Photogram)
35.5 x 43.2 cm
Provenance: Sotheby's, London, 13 May 1994; Phillips de Pury, London, 17 May 2008

Exhibited: *British Surrealism & Other Realities: The Sherwin Collection*, Museum of Modern Art (Mima), Middlesbrough, 23 May–17 August 2008

The Secret Visit
1931
Blueprint
23 x 16 cm
Also the published Blue Prints book sent to E.L.T. Mesens by John Banting with a personal dedication.
Provenance: Phillips, London, 25 September 2001

Exhibited: *British Surrealism & Other Realities: The Sherwin Collection*, Museum of Modern Art (Mima), Middlesbrough, 23 May–17 August 2008

The Couple (overleaf)
c.1932–33
Oil on board
29 x 39 cm
Signed initials: J.B.
Provenance: William Edmiston (or Humphrey Spender) who was a partner with Humphrey Spender in his photographic business. Humphrey Spender was a very close friend of John Banting.

Exhibited: John Banting, Oliver Bradbury and James Birch Fine Art, London, 1983; *A Salute to British Surrealism 1930–1950*, The Minories, Colchester, 6 April–5 May 1985; Blond Fine Art, London, 22 May–22 June 1985; Ferens Art Gallery, Hull, 6 July–4 August 1985; *Messages from Nowhere, The Figurative Avant-Garde and the Influence of Surrealism in Britain 1930-1951*, Austin Desmond, London, 8 November–5 December 1991, London; *Blast to Frieze, British Art in the 20th Century*, Kunstmuseum Wolfsburg, 2002; *British Surrealism & Other Realities: The Sherwin Collection*, Museum of Modern Art (Mima), Middlesbrough, 23 May–17 August 2008

Literature: *A Salute to British Surrealism 1930–1950*, Colchester, The Minories, 1985, no. 13 (untitled) illustration on back cover; *Blast to Frieze, British Art in the 20th Century*, exhibition catalogue, Kunstmuseum Wolfsburg/Hatje Cantz, 2002, plate 54, colour illustration

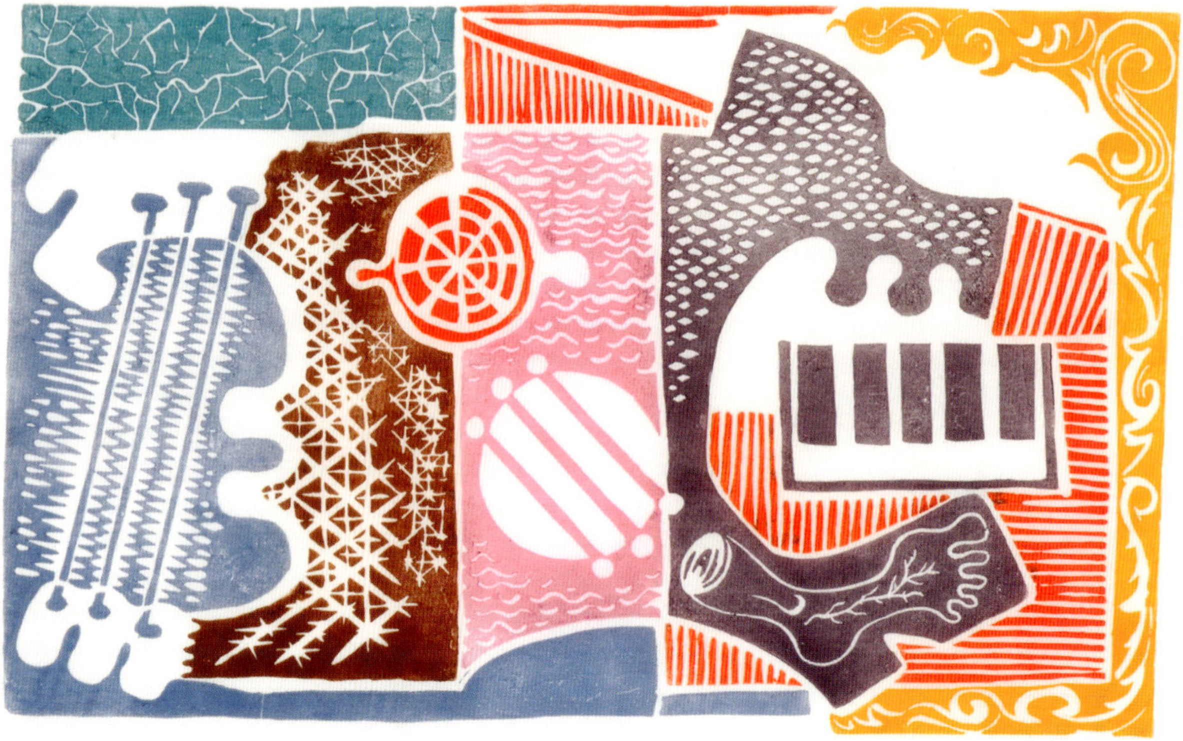

Battle of the Jaw Bones
1929
Oil on board
32.5 x 25.5 cm
Signed and dated by artist on verso
Provenance: Christie's, London, October 1996

Exhibited: *British Surrealism & Other Realities: The Sherwin Collection,* Museum of Modern Art (Mima), Middlesbrough, 23 May–17 August 2008

The Accordion Player (right)
c.1933
Gouache, wax crayon, scratching, collage on paper
38.5 x 52 cm
Provenance: Hanover Gallery, London

Exhibited: *British Surrealism & Other Realities: The Sherwin Collection,* Museum of Modern Art (Mima), Middlesbrough, 23 May–17 August 2008

Print (left)
1934
Exhibited: *British Surrealism & Other Realities: The Sherwin Collection,* Museum of Modern Art (Mima), Middlesbrough, 23 May–17 August 2008

Untitled (Photogram) 1925–28
Drawing on verso
Noted, numbered
43.1 x 35.4 cm
Provenance: Galerie Kicken, Berlin

Aries
1935
Oil on canvas
43 x 53.5 cm
Provenance: Austin Desmond, London

Exhibited: Brussels, 1935; *International Surrealist Exhibition,* Burlington Galleries, London, 1936; *Blast to Frieze, British Art in the 20th Century,* Kunstmuseum Wolfsburg, 2002; *British Surrealism & Other Realities: The Sherwin Collection,* Museum of Modern Art (Mima), Middlesbrough, 23 May–17 August 2008

Literature: *Blast to Frieze, British Art in the 20th Century,* exhibition catalogue, Kunstmuseum Wolfsburg/Hatje Cantz, 2002, plate 62, colour illustration

The title of the work *Aries* has many references to Aries, as a skull, as Aries the Greek God of war and Aries the ram, a sign of zodiac. The ram's head is part of a giant pawn and chess is the game of war. Aries was also Hitler's birth sign. The subject of the painting is a warning of impending war, storm clouds gathering overhead whilst the small figure takes no notice.

Woman Boxer
1934
Charcoal on paper
Provenance: Jonathan Blond Fine Art, London

Exhibited: *British Surrealism & Other Realities: The Sherwin Collection,* Museum of Modern Art (Mima), Middlesbrough, 23 May–17 August 2008

Twilight Symphony
1954
Oil on board
33 x 41 cm
Provenance: Sotheby's, London

Exhibited: *British Surrealism & Other Realities: The Sherwin Collection,* Museum of Modern Art (Mima), Middlesbrough, 23 May–17 August 2008

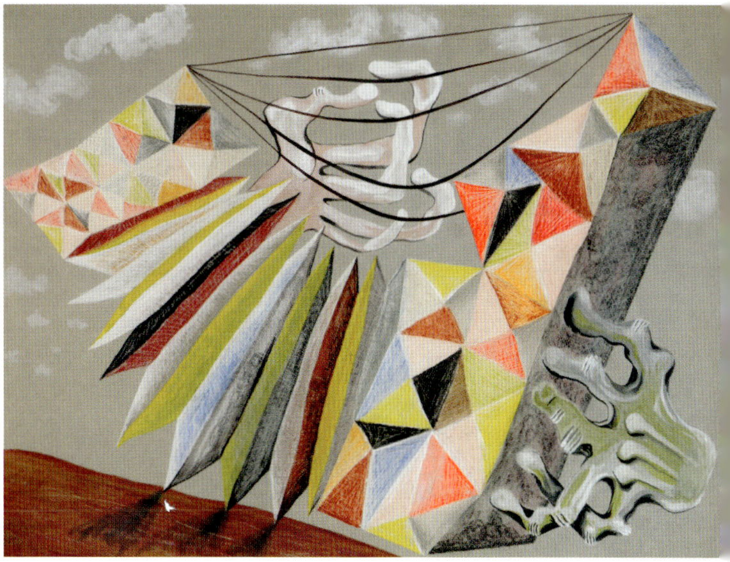

GLENN BAXTER (born 1944)

Born in Leeds in 1944, Baxter was trained at Leeds College of Art. His images, and their corresponding captions, fuse art and language inspired by pulp fiction and adventure comics, with intellectual jokes and references. Baxter's art has been collected in numerous books, and his work has appeared in *The New Yorker*, *Vanity Fair* and *The Independent on Sunday*. His simple line-drawings often feature cowboys, gangsters, explorers and school children, who utter incongruous intellectual statements regarding art and philosophy.

He Took Her in His Arms and Gently Squeezed Her Goatee
1979
Crayon
40 x 30 cm
Provenance: the artist

Exhibited: *British Surrealism & Other Realities: The Sherwin Collection*, Museum of Modern Art (Mima), Middlesbrough, 23 May–17 August 2008

The Wonder Book of Sex How To Do It
Crayon
76 x 56 cm
Provenance: the artist

Exhibited: *British Surrealism & Other Realities: The Sherwin Collection*, Museum of Modern Art (Mima), Middlesbrough, 23 May–17 August 2008

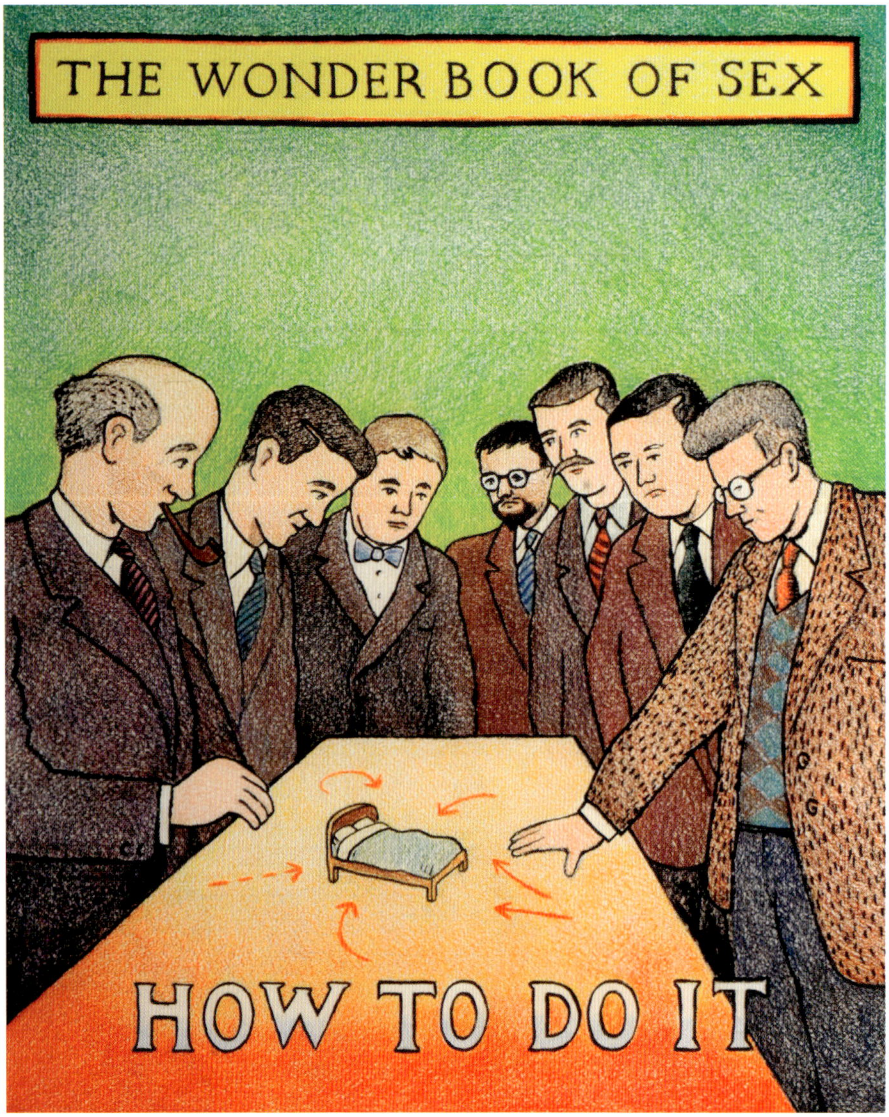

GILBERT BAYES (1872–1953)

Over his long and prolific career, Bayes drew on a wide range of images and styles to develop a distinctive manner of his own. The diversity of his subject matter and his versatile use of materials, which included concrete and cement, make him a significant sculptor of his generation. His fine art work was often inspired by the classics and Wagner's operas, but his architectural and public sculpture was more conventional in subject and style.

Mask of Woman/Head
1925
Doulton stoneware
43 cm with ceramic empire style base
Provenance: Fine Art Society, London

Literature: Illustrated in *The Builder*, 1927; *Modelling for Sculpture*, 1930.

Exhibited: *Royal Academy exhibition*, 1927; *British Surrealism & Other Realities: The Sherwin Collection*, Museum of Modern Art (Mima), Middlesbrough, 23 May–17 August 2008

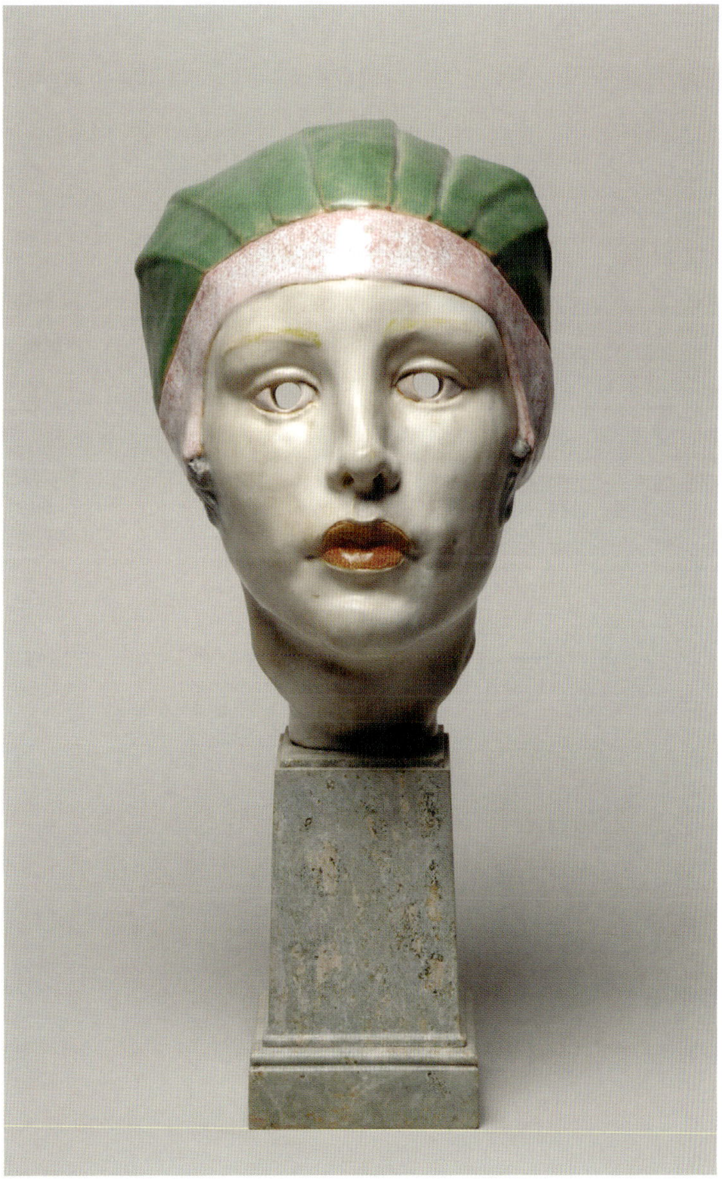

PEARL BINDER (1904–1990)

Lady Elwyn-Jones née Pearl Binder was a legendary character who had a lifelong fascination with the East End of London where she settled in the late 1920s. She visited Russia several times and due to the demand for graphic artists worked there for a while. In addition to a one man show at the Museum of Modern Western Art in Moscow, where she showed drawings and prints based on life in London's East End and another series entitled 'backstage', based on the working life of the theatre, she was asked to contribute to the satirical magazine *Krokodile*. In Britain she illustrated a number of books and articles about Russia, such as Bertha Malnick's *Everyday life in Russia* (1938).

The Meeting
c.1940
Charcoal on paper
44 x 38 cm
Provenance: Hartley's, Ilkley

Exhibited: *British Surrealism & Other Realities: The Sherwin Collection*, Museum of Modern Art (Mima), Middlesbrough, 23 May–17 August 2008

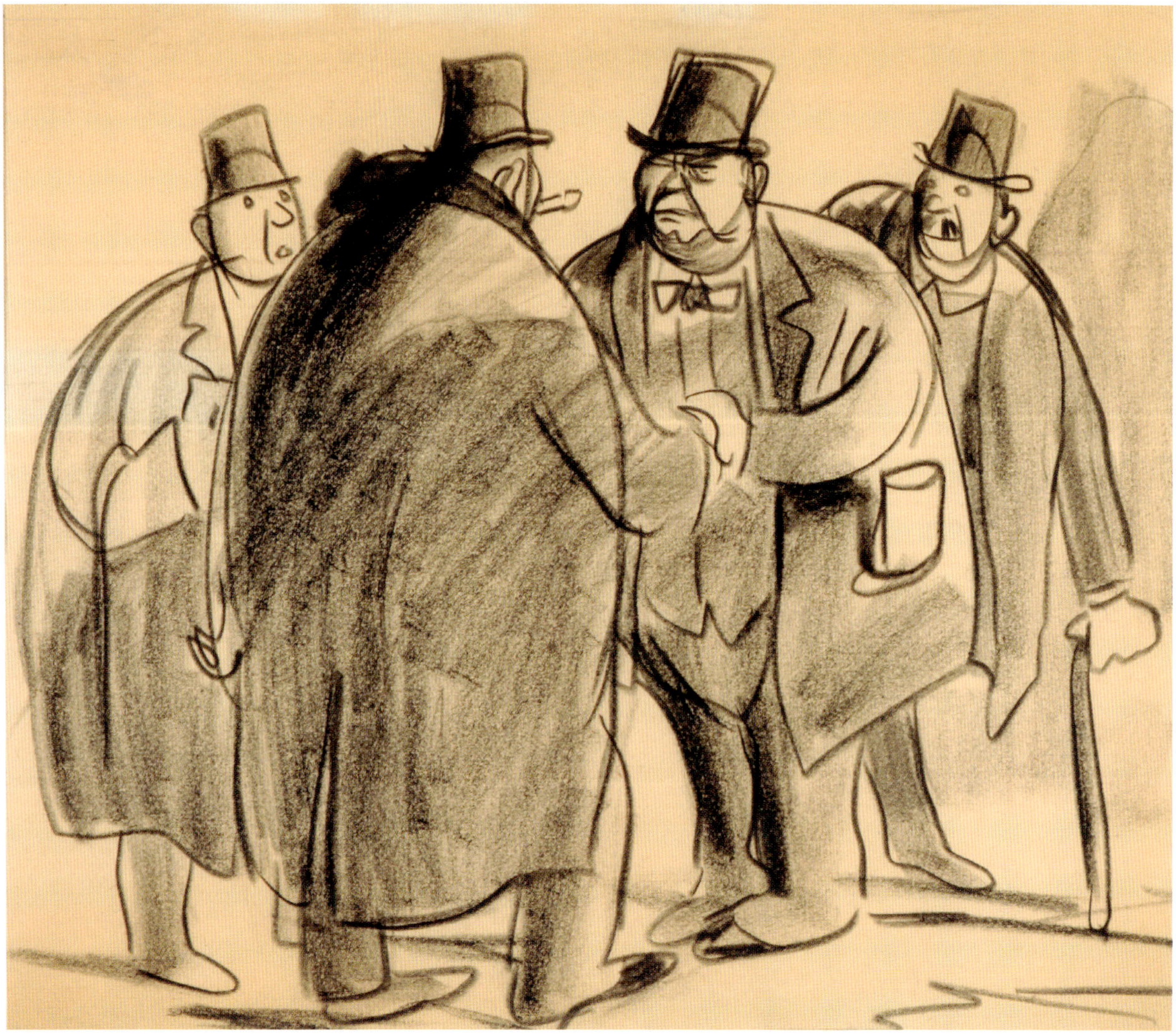

PETER BLAKE (born 1932)

During the late 1950s, Blake became one of the best known British pop artists. His paintings from this time included imagery from advertisements, music hall entertainment and wrestlers, often with collaged elements. It was with the *Young Contemporaries* exhibition of 1961, where he exhibited alongside David Hockney and R. B. Kitaj, that he was first identified with the emerging British Pop Art movement. Blake first came to wider public attention when, along with Pauline Boty, Derek Boshier and Peter Phillips, he featured in Ken Russell's film on pop art, *Pop Goes the Easel*, which was broadcast on BBC television in 1962.

Baby Ruth, Girl Eating, Candy/Bar
1972 and 1989
Oil on board
21 x 16 cm
Signed on the reverse
Provenance: Waddington Galleries, London; Christie's, London, 1997

Exhibited: *British Surrealism & Other Realities: The Sherwin Collection*, Museum of Modern Art (Mima), Middlesbrough, 23 May–17 August 2008

This work by Blake is a small picture with a full face of a girl eating a candy bar with the words 'Baby Ruth' on it. It's an American candy bar referring to the famous baseball player. Purchased in May 1997, following Dr. Sherwin's quadruple heart bypass operation as a 'thank you' to his wife Ruth, for looking after him.

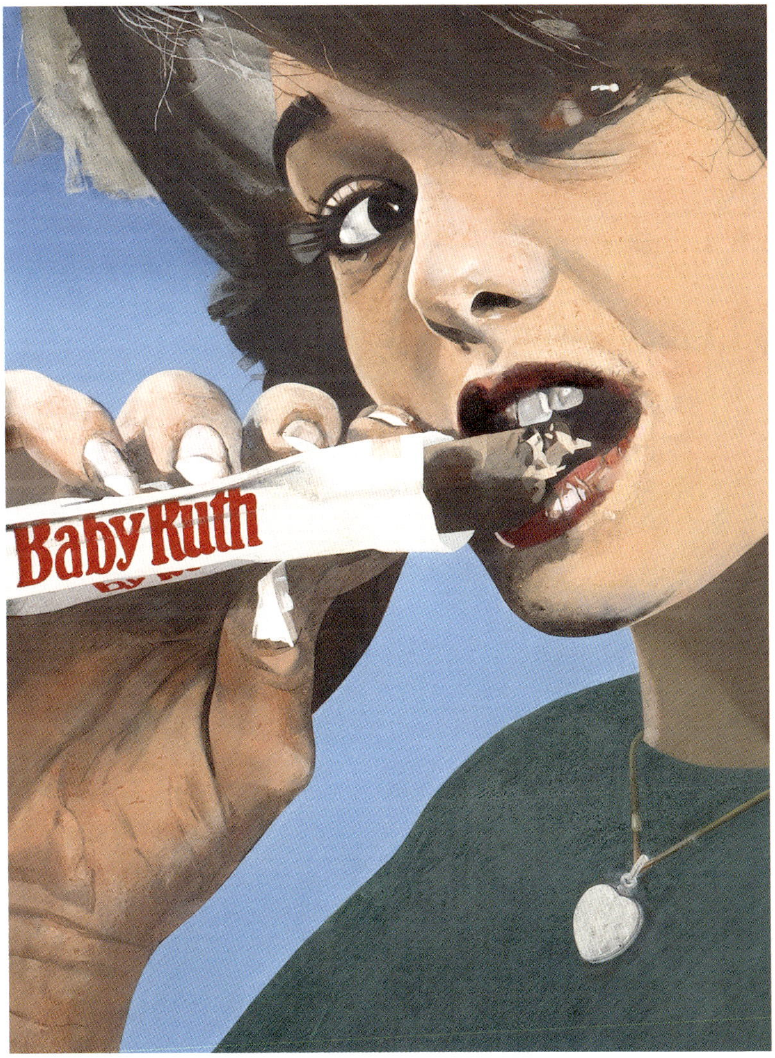

SIR JOHN AMHERST SELBY-BIGGE (1892–1973)

Selby-Bigge was born in Oxford and entered the Slade School of Fine Art only briefly in 1914 due to his military service in the war. After the war, unable to resume his art studies for financial reasons, he had to earn a living taking several unskilled jobs. His art, therefore, developed freely without the restrictions of art schools. His inclusion in the Unit One Group exemplifies the fresh and avant-garde path he led as a modern artist.

Tyrolean Dreams
1935
Oil on board
41.9 x 30.5 cm
Signed
Provenance: Sotheby's, London, 5 October 1995

Exhibited: *British Surrealism & Other Realities: The Sherwin Collection*, Museum of Modern Art (Mima), Middlesbrough, 23 May–17 August 2008

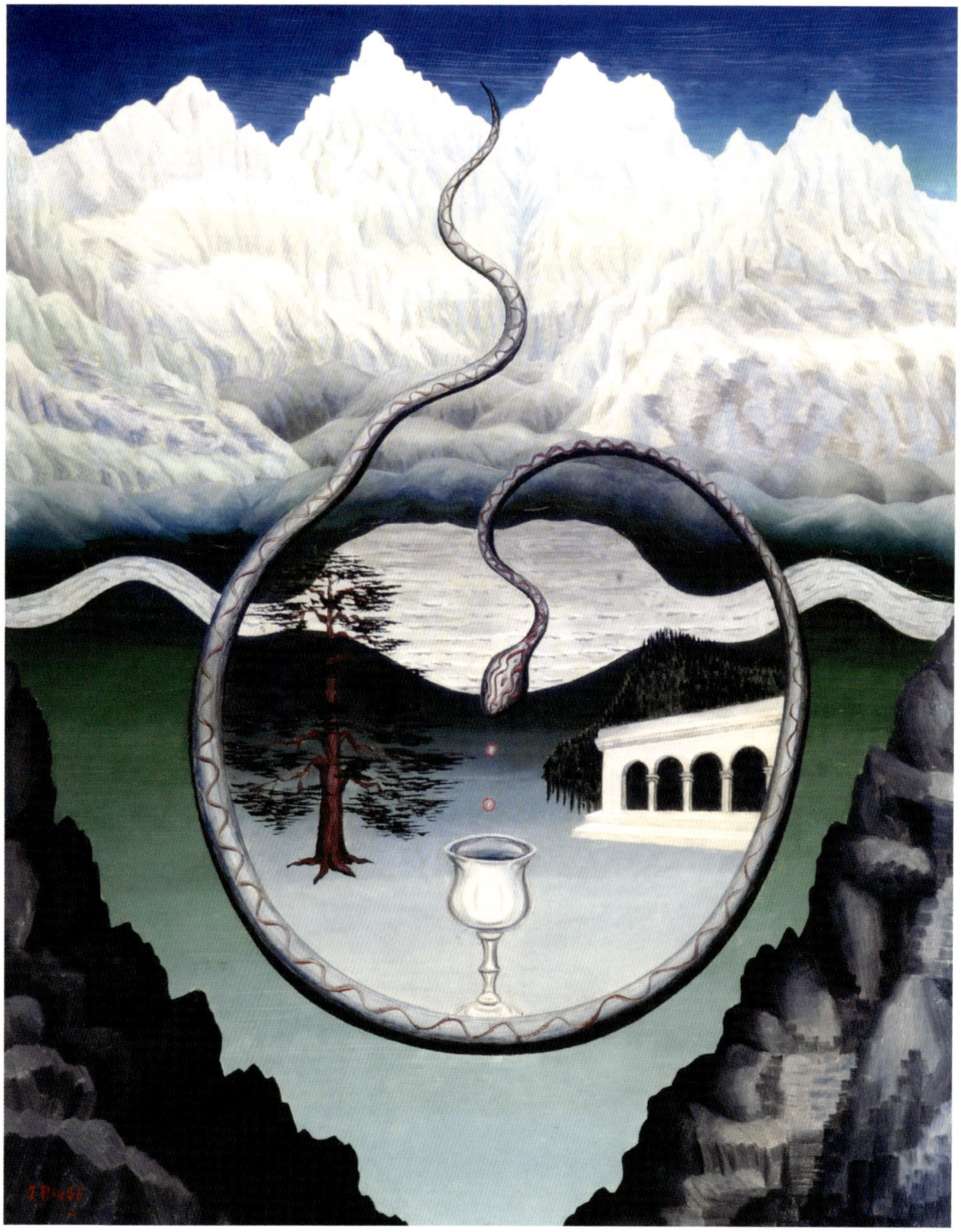

DAVID BOMBERG (1890–1957)

Bomberg was the most audacious painter of his generation at the Slade. His treatment of the human figure, in terms of angular, clear-cut forms charged with enormous energy, reveals his determination to bring about a drastic renewal in British painting. With the advent of World War I everything changed dramatically. By November 1915, Bomberg had enlisted in the Royal Engineers, and his harrowing experiences at the Front brought about a profound transformation in his outlook. Bomberg never again returned to this dogged and limiting idiom, but he did explore a radically different path during the 1920s. His disillusion with the destructive power of the machine at war led to a few years spent experimenting with ways of making his stark pre-war style more rounded and organic.

From the Players Series
1913–1919
Watercolour on Japanese paper
25.4 x 19.7 cm
Provenance: Lilian Bomberg; Christie's, London, 21 March 1996

Literature: Richard Cork, *David Bomberg,* New Haven and London, Yale University Press, 1987

Exhibited: J.P.L. Fine Arts, London, 1974; *David Bomberg,* Marlborough Fine Arts, London, 1967, no. 73; *David Bomberg 1890–1957,* Paintings and Drawings, Arts Council of Great Britain, 1967, no. 27, illustration; *David Bomberg,* Tate, London, 1988; *Blasting the Future: Vorticism and the Avant-Garde in Britain 1910–20,* Estorick Collection, London, 4 February–18 April 2004; Whitworth Art Gallery, Manchester, 7 May–25 July 2004; *British Surrealism & Other Realities: The Sherwin Collection,* Museum of Modern Art (Mima), Middlesbrough, 23 May–17 August 2008

The hats, seen in this picture, are traditionally worn by Polish Jews.

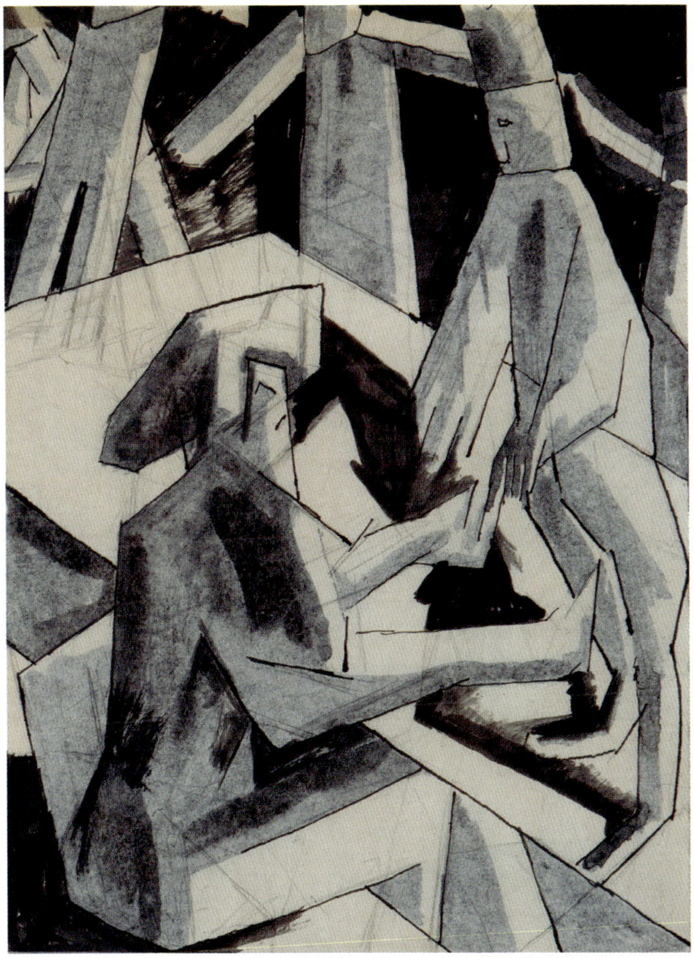

PAULINE BOTY (1938–1966)

Boty became a well-known personality in London during the 1960s, attracting attention for her striking looks and minor roles in television drama, as well as through her reputation as a painter. By 1963 she had evolved a pop vocabulary in her paintings using images of celebrities with a celebratory and humorous approach to female sexuality.

Collage of Church
c.1960
Collage
23.5 x 34.5
Provenance: Mayor Gallery, London

Exhibited: *British Surrealism & Other Realities: The Sherwin Collection*, Museum of Modern Art (Mima), Middlesbrough, 23 May–17 August 2008

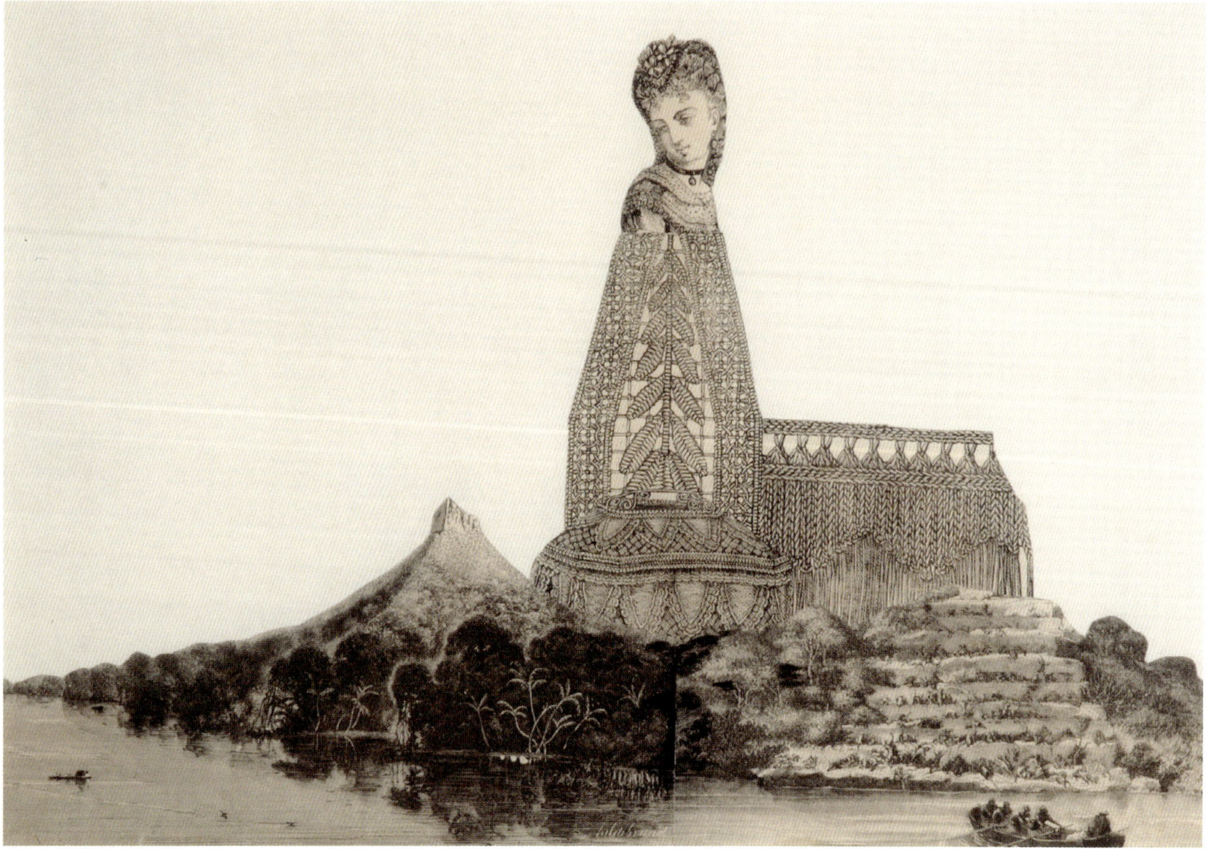

REG BUTLER (1913–1981)

Butler began to sculpt in 1944, without having had any formal training, and held his first one man show at the Hanover Gallery, London, in 1949. While working at the University of Leeds, he had time to mature as a sculptor, turning to modelling in clay, plaster or wax instead of welding and casting in a thin-shell bronze technique of his own. By the mid 1950s, he was considered one of the most promising British sculptors. In 1953, he won first prize in an international competition for a monument to the Unknown Political Prisoner, which culminated in a working model. It was never realized at its full envisaged height of 18 m. In the late 1950s Butler returned to a more directly figurative style, concentrating on bronze female figures, sometimes encased in a framework of metal bars, that contrasted with the softness and vulnerability of the figures.

Composition for 1945
Abstract watercolour signed and dated '45
21.6 x 19 cm
'A present to Ambrose and Ann.' on the reverse – Ambrose Appleby was Butler's solicitor
Provenance: Birch and Conran, London

Exhibited: *British Surrealism & Other Realities: The Sherwin Collection,* Museum of Modern Art (Mima), Middlesbrough, 23 May–17 August 2008

Study for a Sacrificial Figure
1951
Wire and bronze shell
27.9 cm
Provenance: Pierre Matisse Gallery, New York; Offer Waterman & Co, London

Exhibited: *British Surrealism & Other Realities: The Sherwin Collection,* Museum of Modern Art (Mima), Middlesbrough, 23 May–17 August 2008

Cold bronze shell produced in tandem by his wife, Rosemary Young, also a sculptor.

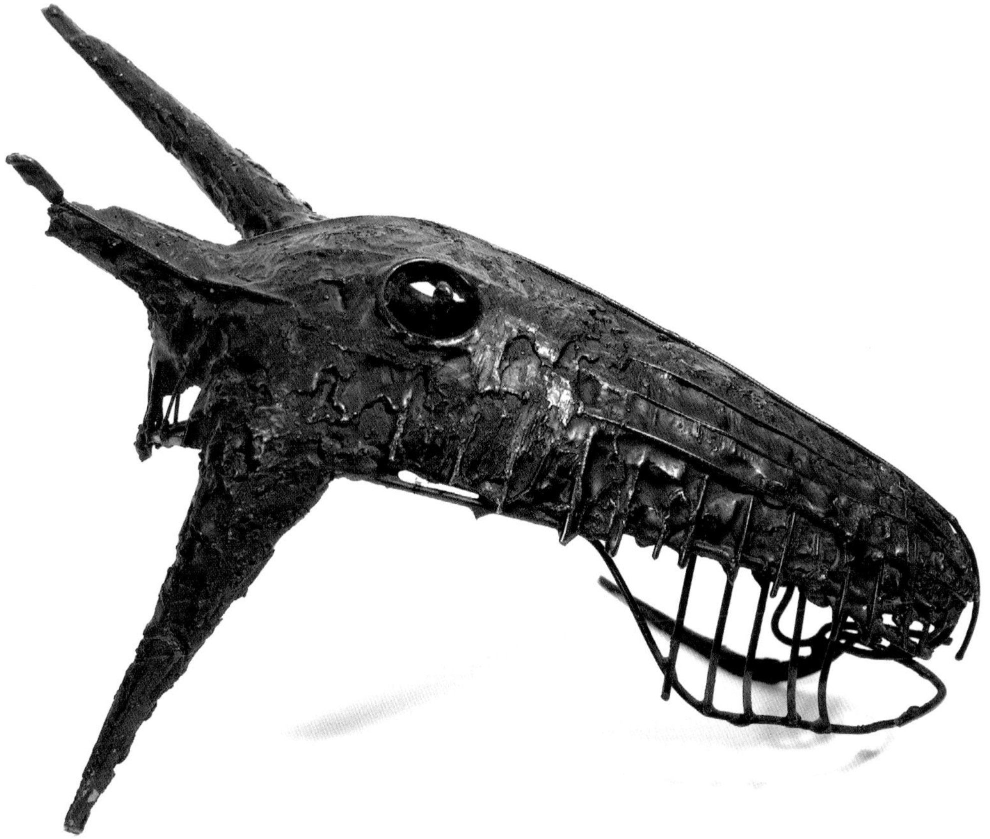

EMMY BRIDGWATER (1906–1999)

Bridgwater occupied a distinctive place in the history of surrealism in Britain as an 'Automatist', using a technique deployed by surrealists for liberating the imagination and stimulating the subconscious. She produced a small, but highly original output of paintings, drawings, collages and poetry. Her paintings show an ability to enter a personal dream world and transform the visions she experienced there into bold, unselfconscious, emotionally charged landscapes, which more often than not strike into the very depths of one's mind. Using a limited palette and painting thickly, she was able to bring together seemingly unrelated objects which she used to fill desolate landscapes, giving the paintings a narrative quality of her own making.

Brave Morning
c.1942
Oil on canvas
Signed
61 x 80 cm
Provenance: Jonathan Blond Fine Art

Exhibited: *Surrealism-Surrealism,* Retretti Art Centre, Finland, 1987, not numbered; *Real Surreal,* Wolverhampton Art Gallery, Wolverhampton, 1995; *British Surrealism & Other Realities: The Sherwin Collection,* Museum of Modern Art (Mima), Middlesbrough, 23 May–17 August 2008

Transplanted (right)
1947
Oil on paper
52 x 36 cm
Provenance: Jonathan Blond Fine Art, London

Literature: Front cover of soft-back *Surrealism in Britain* by Michel Remy, Ashgate, 1999, catalogue no. 146, colour illustration p.294

Exhibited: *Real Surreal,* Wolverhampton Art Gallery, Wolverhampton, 1995; *British Surrealism & Other Realities: The Sherwin Collection,* Museum of Modern Art (Mima), Middlesbrough, 23 May–17 August 2008

Necessary Bandages (far right)
c.1942
Oil on panel
35 x 29.2 cm
Signed: Emmy Bridgewater (lower right). There is a surrealist composition on the reverse
Provenance: Blond Fine Art, London; Peter Nahum, London

Exhibited: Probably, London, Blond Fine Art, *British Women Surrealists*, Eileen Agar, Emmy Bridgwater, Ithell Colquhoun, Grace Pailthorpe, Edith Rimmington: an exhibition arranged in conjunction with the publication by Thames & Hudson of *Women Artists and Surrealist Movement* by Whitney Chadwick, Oct–Nov 1985, no. 19 as *Search for a Fading Prospect*; London, Blond Fine Art, *British Surrealism*, June 1989, no. 8; Aldeburgh, Peter Pears Gallery, Festival Exhibition, June 2006; *British Surrealism & Other Realities: The Sherwin Collection,* Museum of Modern Art (Mima), Middlesbrough, 23 May–17 August 2008

Literature: *The Poetry of Crisis, The Peter Nahum Collection of British Surrealist and Avant-Garde Art 1930–1951,* Christie's, London, 15 November 2006; *British Surrealism,* London, Blond Fine Art, 1989, p.10 illustrated

Self portrait after Toni del Renzio broke off his affair with her and went on to marry Ithell Cologhoun. The profile in repilian green is thought by Jeffrey Sherwin to be of her former lover.

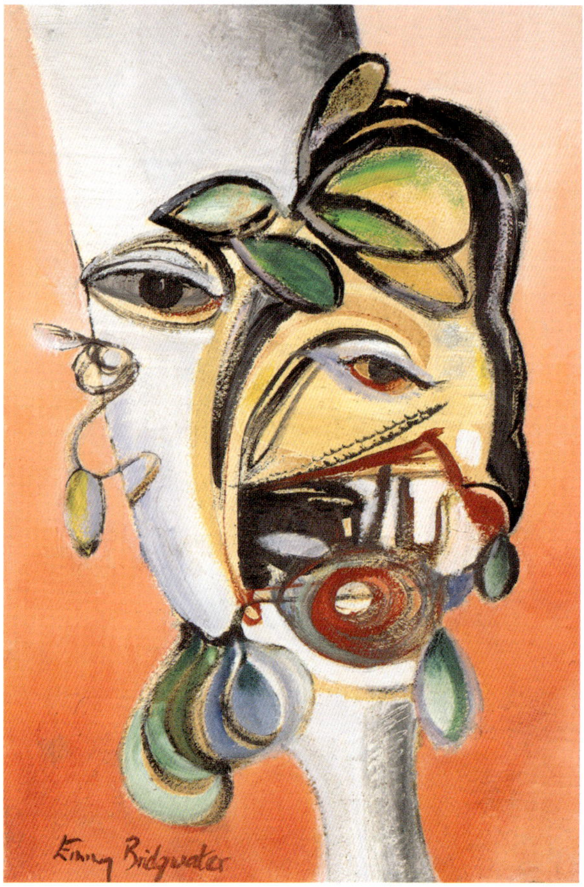

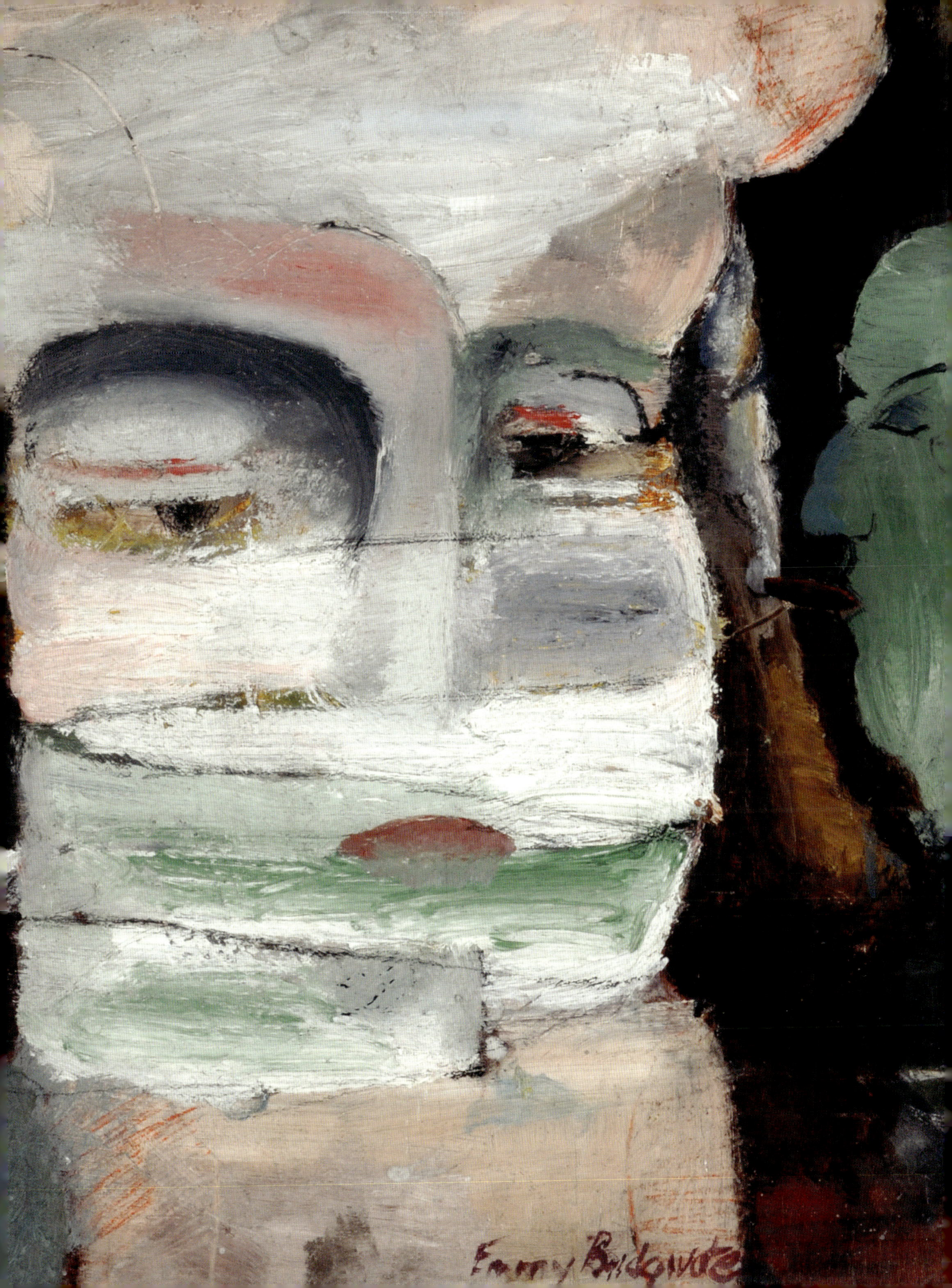

HORACE BRODZKY (1885–1969)

Brodzky was a student at the School of the National Gallery of Victoria in Melbourne, but spent most of his creative life in London. He was one of the earliest Australian artists to embrace the modern style of the 20th century.

Portrait of Epstein
1938
Gouache and ink on paper
26 x 23 cm
Provenance: Woolsey Fine Art, London

Exhibited: *British Surrealism & Other Realities: The Sherwin Collection*, Museum of Modern Art (Mima), Middlesbrough, 23 May–17 August 2008

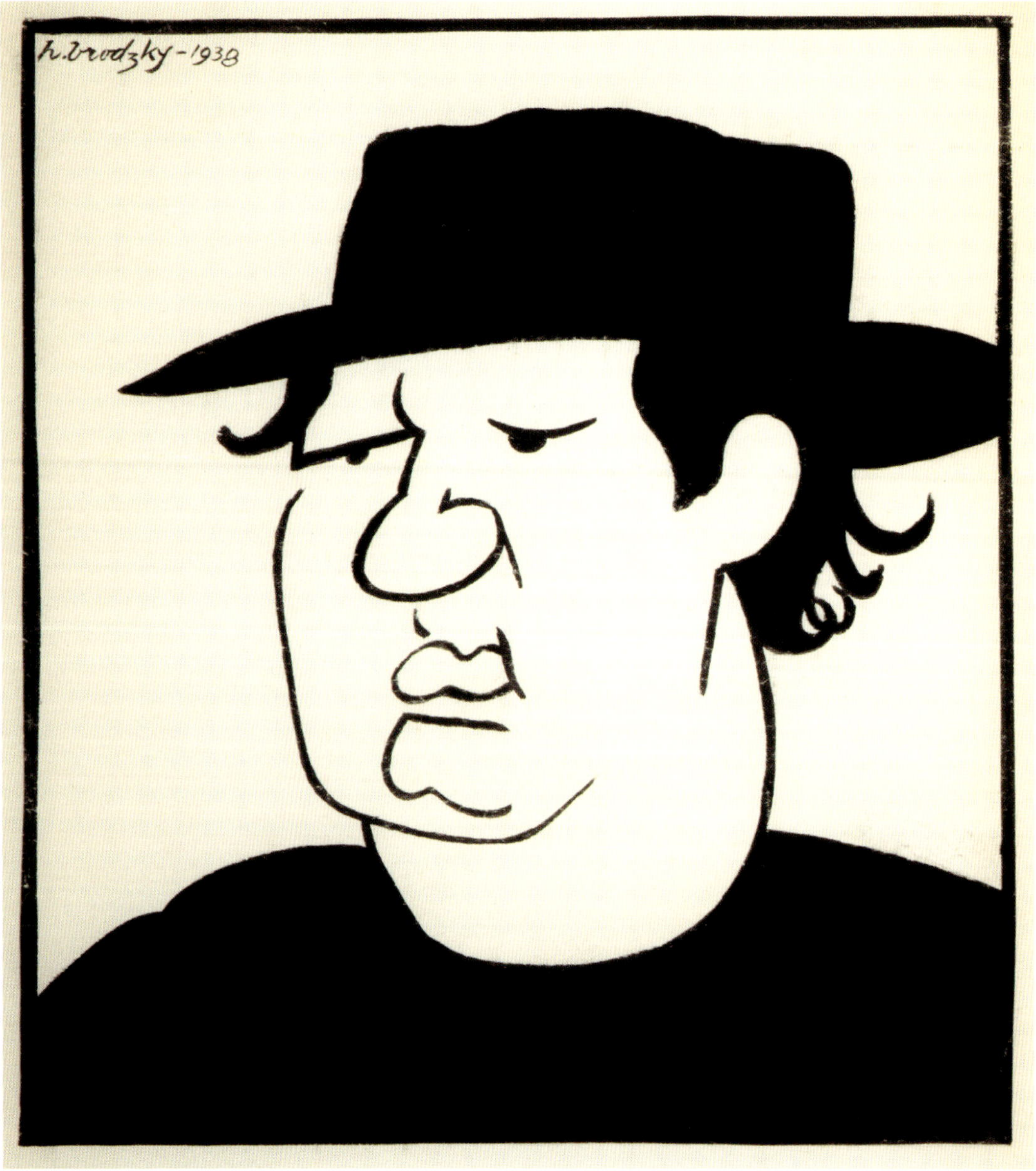

JOHN BUCKLAND WRIGHT (1897–1954)

Buckland Wright established himself as an international engraver, unusual in that he was equally proficient in the techniques of wood and copper engraving, intaglio and etching processes. Having learnt to engrave in wood, he began the same task in copper in 1929. It is in dry point that he initially achieved the greatest freedom of expression and the influence of Picasso can be seen in many of his wood and copper engravings. By 1933, he had achieved complete mastery of both wood and copper engraving and a few years later he joined William Hayter's Atelier 17. Here he met and worked with artists such as Brancusi, Miró, Picasso and Matisse.

Fraternité
1939
Copper engraving
Provenance: Bloomsbury Auctions, London

Exhibited: *British Surrealism & Other Realities: The Sherwin Collection,* Museum of Modern Art (Mima), Middlesbrough, 23 May–17 August 2008

There is an illustration for *Fraternity* by Stephen Spender, translated by Louis Aragon of Spanish Civil War 1939. The portfolio was printed and sold in Paris to raise cash for the Spanish Republican Children's Fund. The image shows a weeping woman with a bombed townscape with a Liber(ty) wall poster.

Sibling
1940
Postcard with wood cut
Various colours printed by the English Surrealist Group in 1940–41
Provenance: Bloomsbury Auctions, London

Exhibited: *British Surrealism & Other Realities: The Sherwin Collection,* Museum of Modern Art (Mima), Middlesbrough, 23 May–17 August 2008

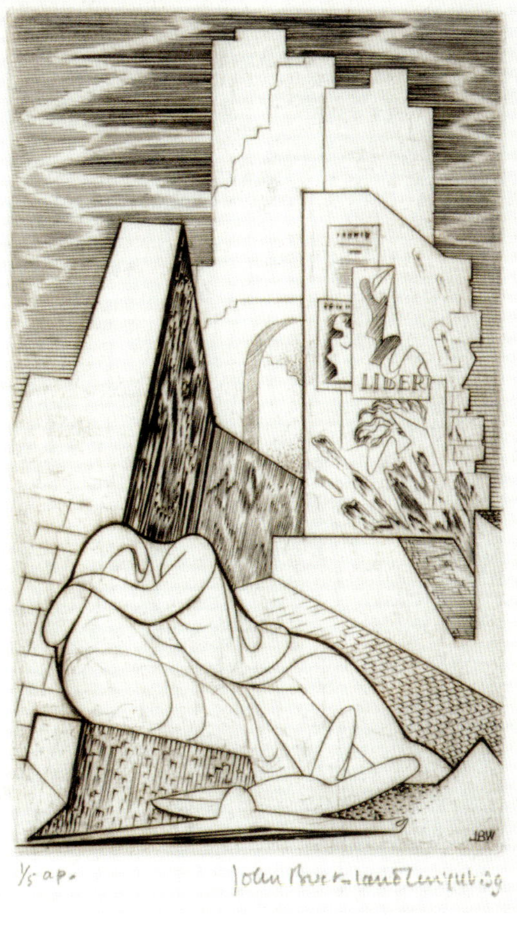

LAWRENCE BURT (born 1925)

Burt has practised and lectured in art for over fifty years, specialising in sculpture. Beginning as a studio assistant in Leeds College of Art, he has exhibited professionally since 1957 and taught Fine Art at various colleges, becoming principal lecturer at Cardiff College of Art in 1964.

Shall we – Shall we not
1986
Wood, iron, plastic putty, found object, acrylic
Height: 40 cm
Provenance: the artist, 2009

RIP the Bourgeois
1999
Wood, iron, aluminium and acrylic
Height: 40 cm
Provenance: the artist, 2009

Out of Reach 3500BC/AD1980
1980
Wood, iron, silver-solder, brass and acrylic paint
Height: 40 cm
Provenance: the artist, 2009

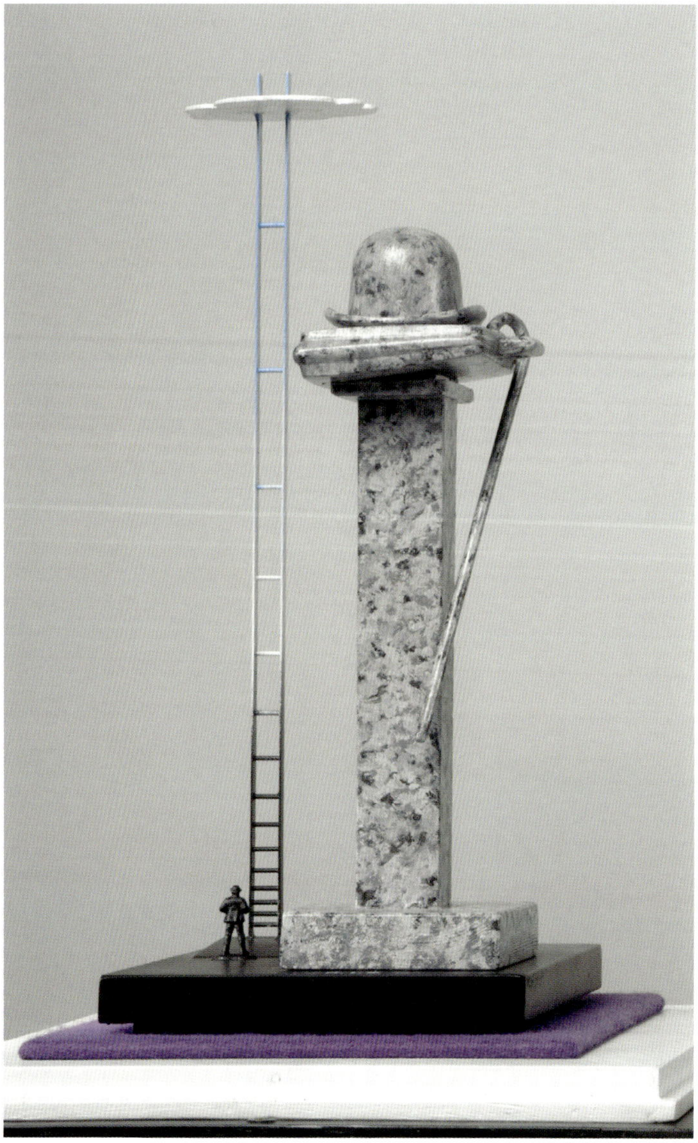

FRANCIS BUTTERFIELD (1905–1968)

Francis attended evening classes with Henry Butler at the Bradford School of Art, while working in wool-stapling. By the late 1920s, he was painting full-time and it was around this time that he developed a distinctive abstract style, encouraged by prominent collectors such as Sir Michael Sadler. He became a member of the Seven and Five Society, whose members included Henry Moore, Paul Nash and John Piper, and exhibited with them in 1935, showing abstract works. In 1937, after spending time in a studio on the Left Bank in Paris, he settled in London.

Whiskey Bottle
1934
Oil and pencil on board
39 x 27 cm
Provenance: Michael Sadler; Zwemmer Gallery, London; Offer Waterman & Co., London

Exhibited: *British Surrealism & Other Realities: The Sherwin Collection*, Museum of Modern Art (Mima), Middlesbrough, 23 May–17 August 2008

Reclining Nudes
c.1939
Collage
40.5 x 51 cm

Exhibited: Zwemmer Gallery, London, 1934; *British Surrealism & Other Realities: The Sherwin Collection*, Museum of Modern Art (Mima), Middlesbrough, 23 May–17 August 2008

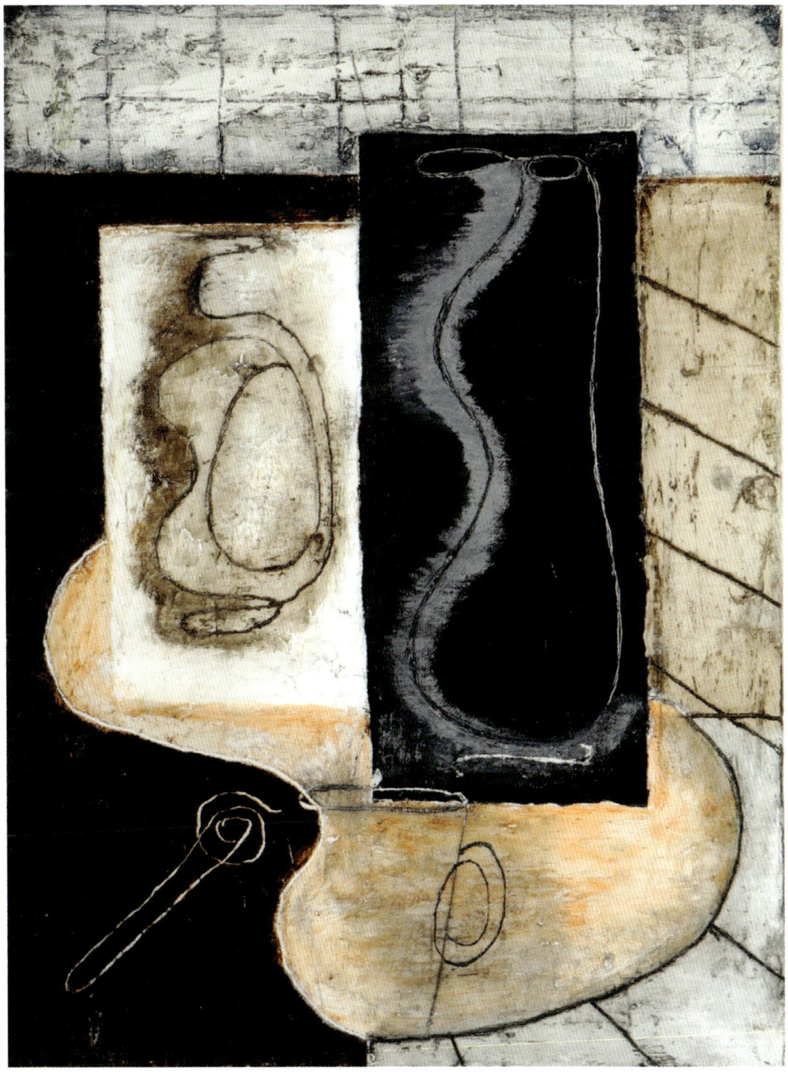

LEONORA CARRINGTON (born 1917)

During the years of World War II, Carrington suffered enormously due to her lover Max Ernst's imprisonment in an internment camp. In fact, she had several mental breakdowns. On one occasion she was institutionalized (by the intervention of her family in England) and given cardiazol, a powerful shock inducing drug. This drug was administered to many female patients for what doctors diagnosed as, or rather coined the term of, 'hysteria'. In an article she wrote in 1944, published in *Down Below*, Carrington describes her experiences of having a mental breakdown and the rupture of the world around her. This could be one of several drawings made by Carrington of her psychiatrist, Dr. Morales, who treated her in Santander Mental Asylum, Spain during 1940–43.

Head
c.1940
Pencil, ink and watercolour on paper
36 x 23 cm
Provenance: Christie's, London, 27 February 2008

Exhibited: *British Surrealism & Other Realities: The Sherwin Collection,* Museum of Modern Art (Mima), Middlesbrough, 23 May–17 August 2008

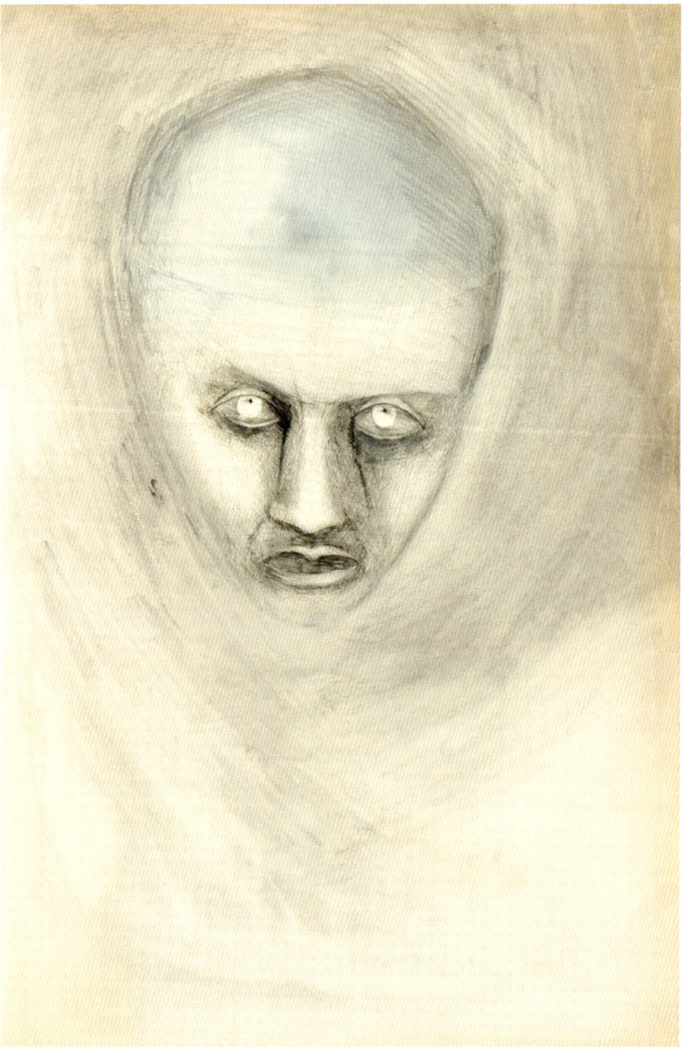

Leonora Carrington with her pychiatrist Dr Morales

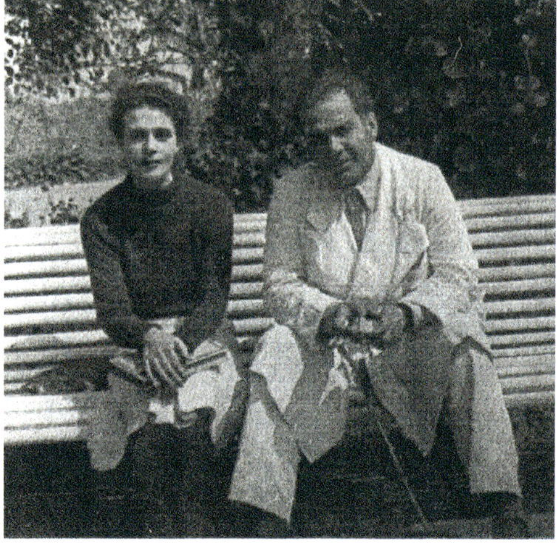

GEOFFREY CLARKE (born 1924)

Clarke is a sculptor in metal, an etcher and a designer of stained glass, but became famous as sculptor in iron in the 1950s. Herbert Read referred to the iron sculptural trend as expressive of the 'geometry of fear'. It still seems appropriate for the darkened, troubled works produced in the first decade of the post-war era, such as the painfully vulnerable *Head*. For Clarke, however, the same body of work represents liberation rather than fear.

Head
1951
Welded iron
29.4 x 11.8 x 5.1 cm
Provenance: the artist

Exhibited: *Geoffrey Clarke R.A.: Sculpture and Works on Paper,* Wakefield, Yorkshire Sculpture Park, 1994; *British Surrealism & Other Realities: The Sherwin Collection,* Museum of Modern Art (Mima), Middlesbrough, 23 May–17 August 2008

Literature: Geoffrey Clarke *'Early Engraved Work and Iron Sculpture'*, Taranman, London, 1976, no. 6 illustrated b/w, no page number

Maquette for The Unknown Political Prisoner (overleaf)
1952
Iron
44 x 16.5 x 13 cm
Provenance: the artist

Exhibited: New Burlington Galleries, 1953; *Geoffrey Clarke: 'Symbols for Man – Sculpture and Graphic Work 1949–94'*, Ipswich Borough Council Museums and Galleries and London, Lund Humphries, 1994; *British Surrealism & Other Realities: The Sherwin Collection,* Museum of Modern Art (Mima), Middlesbrough, 23 May–17 August 2008

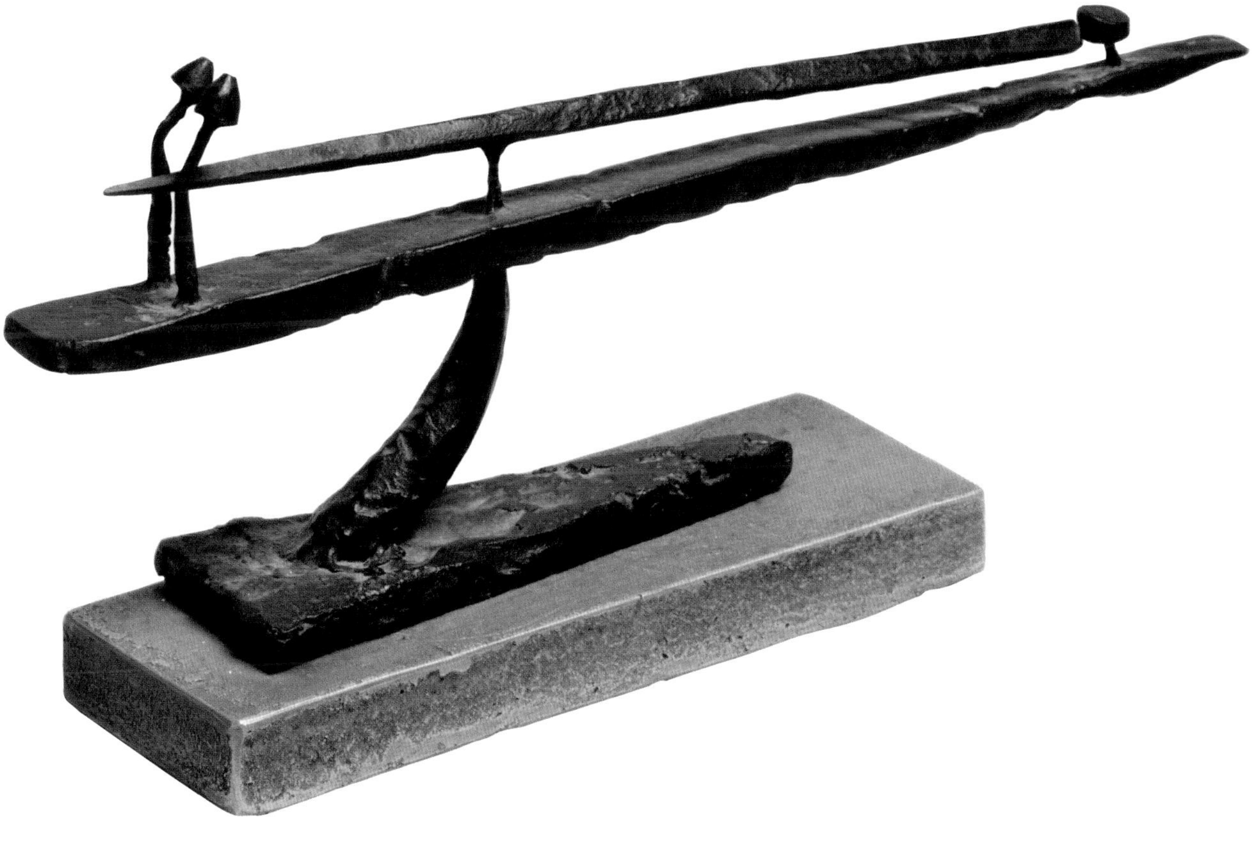

Literature: *Geoffrey Clarke: 'Symbols for Man – Sculpture and Graphic Work 1949–94'*, Ipswich Borough Council Museums and Galleries and London, Lund Humphries, 1994, by Peter Black, no. 34 colour illustration, p.40

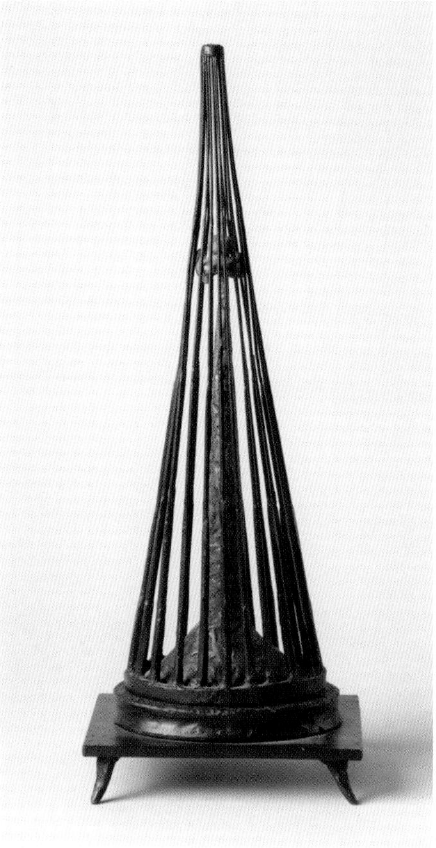

Geoffrey Clarke was one of the forty-five finalists in the International Sculpture Competition, *The Unknown Political Prisoner,* which was won by Reg Butler. This maquette was included in the exhibition at the New Burlington Galleries in 1953. Clarke made three other maquettes and many monotype designs. In this maquette, the rod structure forms a cage supported on a table, whilst the prisoner, represented by a clover-leaf, or cruciform bloom of freedom, is stunted by the restrictions of the prison cage as it narrows to the top.

Monoprint
1924

Exhibited: *British Surrealism & Other Realities: The Sherwin Collection*, Museum of Modern Art (Mima), Middlesbrough, 23 May–17 August 2008

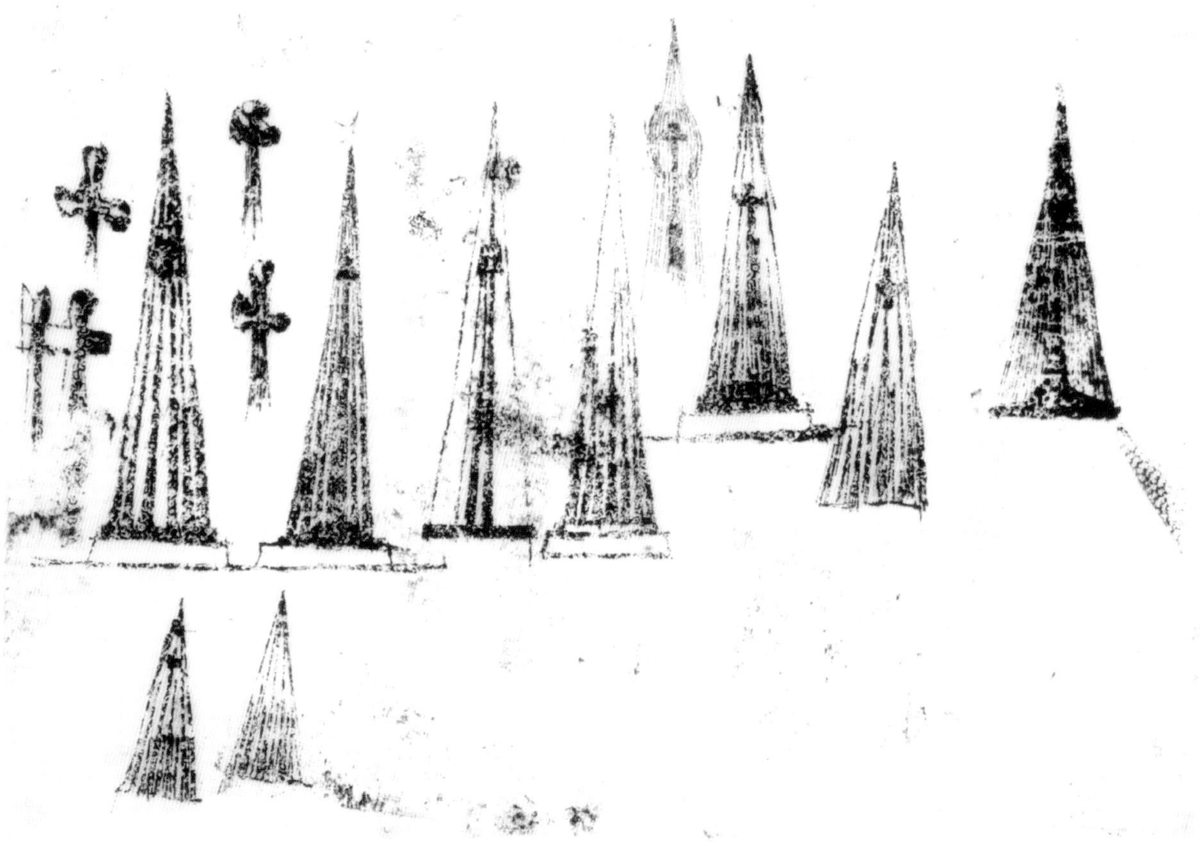

CECIL COLLINS (1908–1989)

Collins was born in Plymouth. He drew and painted from an early age, and after working briefly as an engineer, he enrolled at Plymouth School of Art. He later studied at the Royal College of Art, London, from 1927 to 1931. Collins painted visionary subjects, inspired by nature and by the writings of William Blake. He was associated briefly with the surrealist group, exhibiting with them in the 1936 International Surrealist Exhibition in London. However, Collins broke away from the surrealists after 1938 to pursue his own artistic agenda.

Obsequies of Time
1933
Charcoal, pen, brush, black ink and gum arabic on paper
38 x 55.8 cm
Signed and dated lower right, inscribed *Obsequies of Time*, Cecil Collins 1933
Provenance: Julian Trevelyan R.A.; Christie's, London, 30 May 1997

Exhibited: *Blast to Frieze, British Art in the 20th Century*, Kunstmuseum Wolfsburg/Hatje Cantz, 2002; *British Surrealism & Other Realities: The Sherwin Collection*, Museum of Modern Art (Mima), Middlesbrough, 23 May–17 August 2008

Literature: William Anderson, *The Quest for Happiness*. London 1988, p.47; Jeremy Lewison, *Going Modern And Being British, The Challenge of the 1930s*, in: *Blast to Frieze, British Art in the 20th Century*, Kunstmuseum Wolfsburg/Hatje Cantz, 2002, pp.66–72, illustration p.70

Obsequies means 'Death' and the painting, which is like a parchment or the corner illustration of an old sailing chart, is really a celebration of life forces arising from a primordial soup. *Obsequies of Time* is a typical surrealist device of reversing reality. Collins severed links with the surrealists the day after the International Surrealist Exhibition closed in 1936. Trevelyan wrote 'Collins, whom I knew well, had far too much of a personal religious mysticism to make a good surrealist'.

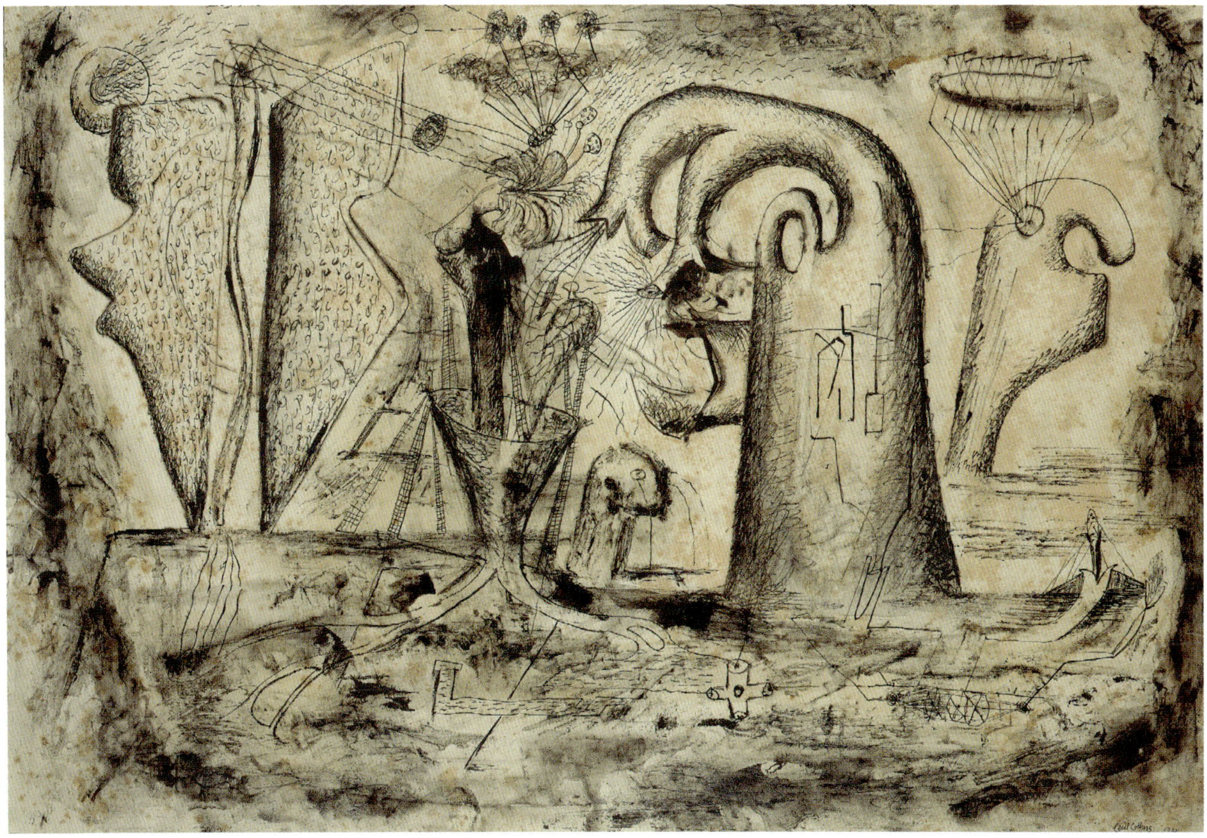

ITHELL COLQUHOUN (1906–1988)

Although she only joined the British Surrealist Group for a short period, Colquhoun was one of the most flamboyant and innovative members. Unique among the female surrealists, she mercilessly parodied the male dominant surrealist obsession with sexual imagery and notions of eroticism. By doing so she alienated herself from the surrealist idol of the female muse, whose role was inspiration and decoration.

The Dance of the Nine Opals (below)
1942
Oil on canvas
Signed
54.5 x 68.5 cm
Provenance: Christie's, London, 22 May 1996

Exhibited: London Museum, London, 1942, no. 3 dated 1941; Derby Art Gallery, Derby, 1945; Leva Gallery, 1974, no. 15 Newlyn Orion Gallery, 1976, no. 12; Blond Fine Art, London, 1985, no. 41; The Herbert Read Gallery, 1986, no. 80, colour illustration; *Surrealism-Surrealism*, Retretti Art Centre, Finland, 1987, not numbered; *Blast to Frieze, British Art in the 20th Century,* Kunstmuseum Wolfsburg, 2002;

Literature: *Blast to Frieze, British Art in the 20th Century,* exhibition catalogue, Kunstmuseum Wolfsburg/Hatje Cantz, 2002, plate 88, colour illustration; *British Surrealism & Other Realities: The Sherwin Collection,* Museum of Modern Art (Mima), Middlesbrough, 2008

In *Dance of the Nine Opals*, the artist has established an imaginary link between the 'Merry Maidens' – a magic circle of nineteen standing stones, a site of energy and Celtic lore near Penzance, which she often visited. From the centre of the circle a light issues forth, coming from the centre of the earth to secretly illuminate the stones and link them together – rearranged as nine opals: nine is the symbol of birth and opal is Colquhoun's birth stone. The device of connecting key points of the composition by lines of force was a common one for Colquhoun at this period. Writing of an (unidentified) painting of a standing naked man that he had seen in her studio in the early 1940s, Derek Stanford wrote: 'From every high point and opening of the figure radiated out in circling curves a line of circling astral force completely surrounding the man. The colouring was rainbow bright, and the effect of the picture as a whole was both extremely sensuous and ethereal' (*Inside the Forties*, 1977).

Tree Anatomy (far right)
1942
Oil on wood panel
57 x 29 cm
Provenance: Bradford City Art Gallery; Christie's, London, May 1996; Jane England

Exhibited: The Leicester Galleries, London, 1942; Cartwright Hall, Bradford, 1943; City of Exeter Art Gallery, Exeter, 1972, no. 42; Leva Gallery, London, 1974; Newlyn Orion Gallery, Penzance, 1976, no.10; Parkin Gallery, London, 1977, no. 23; Blond Fine Art, 1985, no. 40; The Herbert Read Gallery, 1986, no. 79, colour illustration; *Surrealism-Surrealism,* Retretti Art Centre, Finland, 1987, not numbered; *Blast to Frieze, British Art in the 20th Century,* Kunstmuseum Wolfsburg, 2002

Literature: *Blast to Frieze, British Art in the 20th Century,* exhibition catalogue, Kunstmuseum Wolfsburg/Hatje Cantz, 2002; *British Surrealism & Other Realities: The Sherwin Collection,* Museum of Modern Art (Mima), Middlesbrough, 2008

Sex is never far away in Colqhoun's work. Sometimes it is present in the sense of what we might nowadays call sexual politics. Sometimes it is present as a natural generative force, in particular a celebration of the female aspect. The fusion of the body with the landscape is a theme that occurs elsewhere in her work, not only in her paintings, but also, perhaps more commonly, in her poetry. *Tree Anatomy* can be seen as an aspect of this. It can be related to myths concerning vegetation deities, dealt with in the *Golden Bough* – the work by James Fraser – with which she was familiar. (Richard Shillitoe)

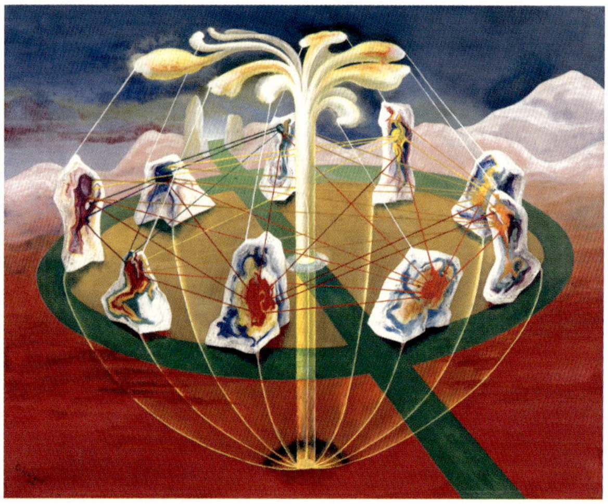

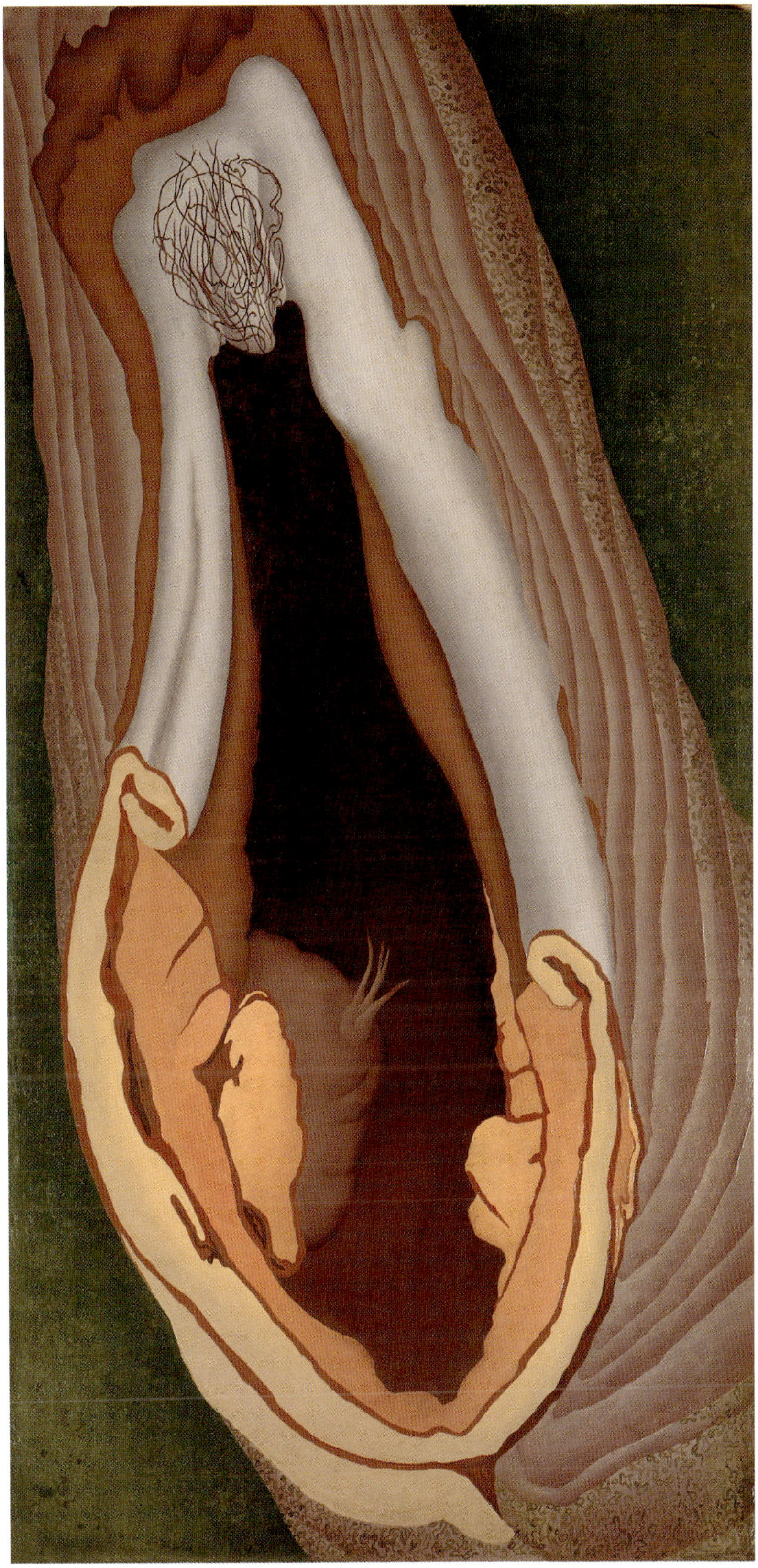

HUBERT DALWOOD (1914–1976)

After working as an engineer in the Royal Navy during the Second World War, Dalwood studied at Bath Academy of Art and was then awarded the Gregory Fellowship at Leeds University. Sensitive and distinctive, his work was chosen for display at the 1962 Venice Biennale and he was soon in league with the leading post-war British sculptors of his time. His work of 1959, *Large Object*, won the John Moore's Prize in 1959. He shifted from figurative subjects early on in his career and turned to abstract forms that are always surprising in scale, surface and composition.

Shield Screen
1959–60
Aluminium
190.5 x 239 cm
Provenance: Commissioned by Tom Hancock, The Ionian Bank; Christie's, London, 8 March 1991 (purchased after the sale)

Literature: *Connoisseur Magazine*, vol. 155, April 1964, p.213

Exhibited: London, Arts Council of Great Britain, Hayward Gallery, *Hubert Dalwood Sculptures And Reliefs*, 1979 no. 24; *British Surrealism & Other Realities: The Sherwin Collection*, Museum of Modern Art (Mima), Middlesbrough, 23 May–17 August 2008

Shield Screen was designed for Ionian Securities Ltd (formerly The Ionian Bank Ltd) to act as a room divider in the main dining room in their offices at St. Martins Place. The shield forms allude to the bank's Greek associations.

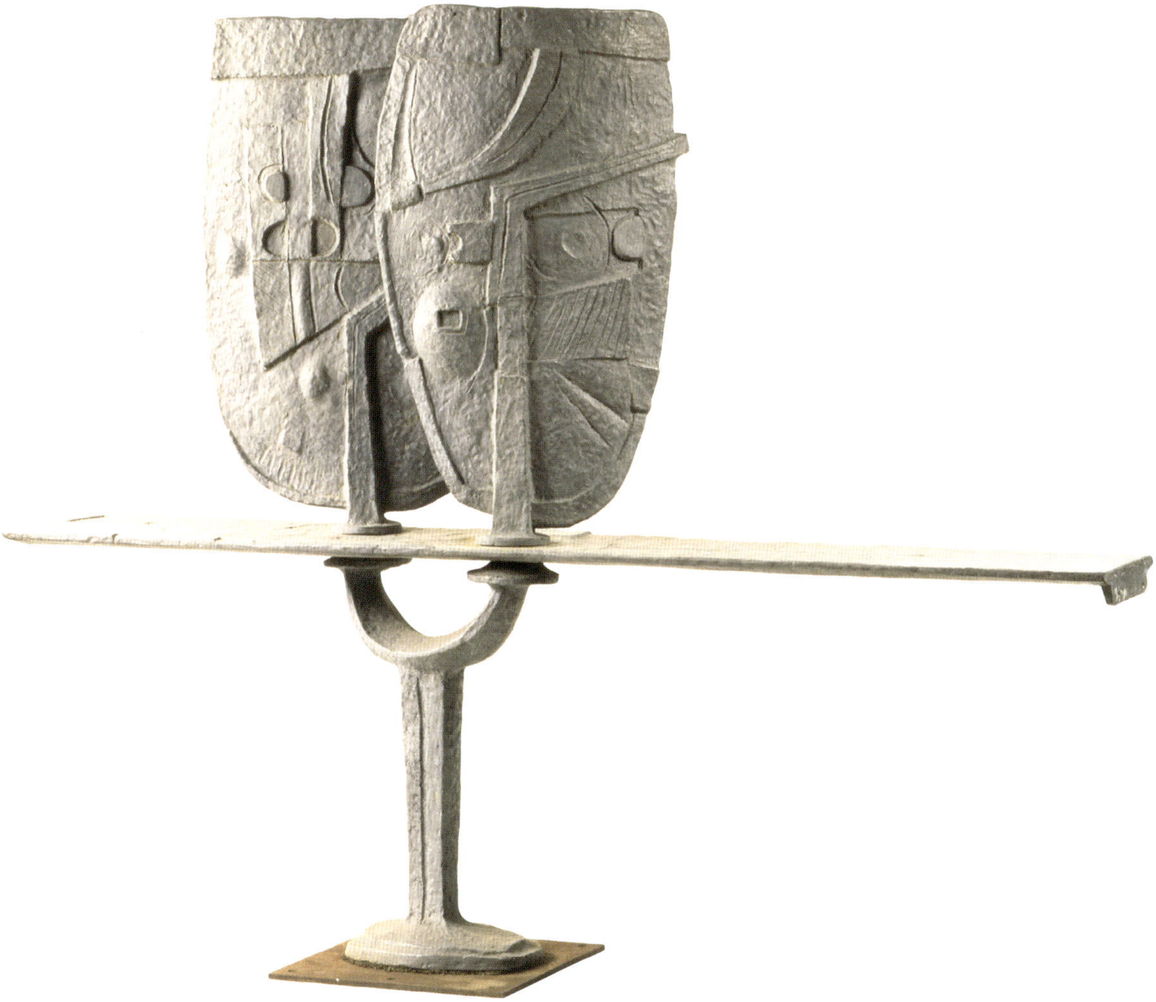

JOHN DAVIES (born 1946)

Born in Cheshire, Davies studied sculpture at the Slade School of Fine Art in London, under Reg Butler, from 1967 to 1969. In the late 1960s, Davies began making body and head casts in plaster, incorporating glass eyes and clothing the figures in real clothes. He became particularly well-known for his life-size figures with deathly-grey faces, which were exhibited both individually and in groups. The groups of figures were posed in such a way as to make the exhibition space into a theatre, with numerous combinations of figures possible, suggesting a number of different relationships.

William Jeffrey with Device
1972
Painted polyester resin, fibreglass, wire, beads and steel
30.5 x 20.3 x 39.4 cm
Provenance: Christie's, London, 25 May 1995

Exhibited: Whitechapel Art Gallery, John Davies: June–July 1972, no. 19, illustrated; *Whitechapel* cat. 1975, illustrated book cover; *British Surrealism & Other Realities: The Sherwin Collection,* Museum of Modern Art (Mima), Middlesbrough, 23 May–17 August 2008

Literature: *John Davies: Sculptures and Drawings since 1968,* Museo de Bellas Artes Bilbao, 2004, illustrated p 112

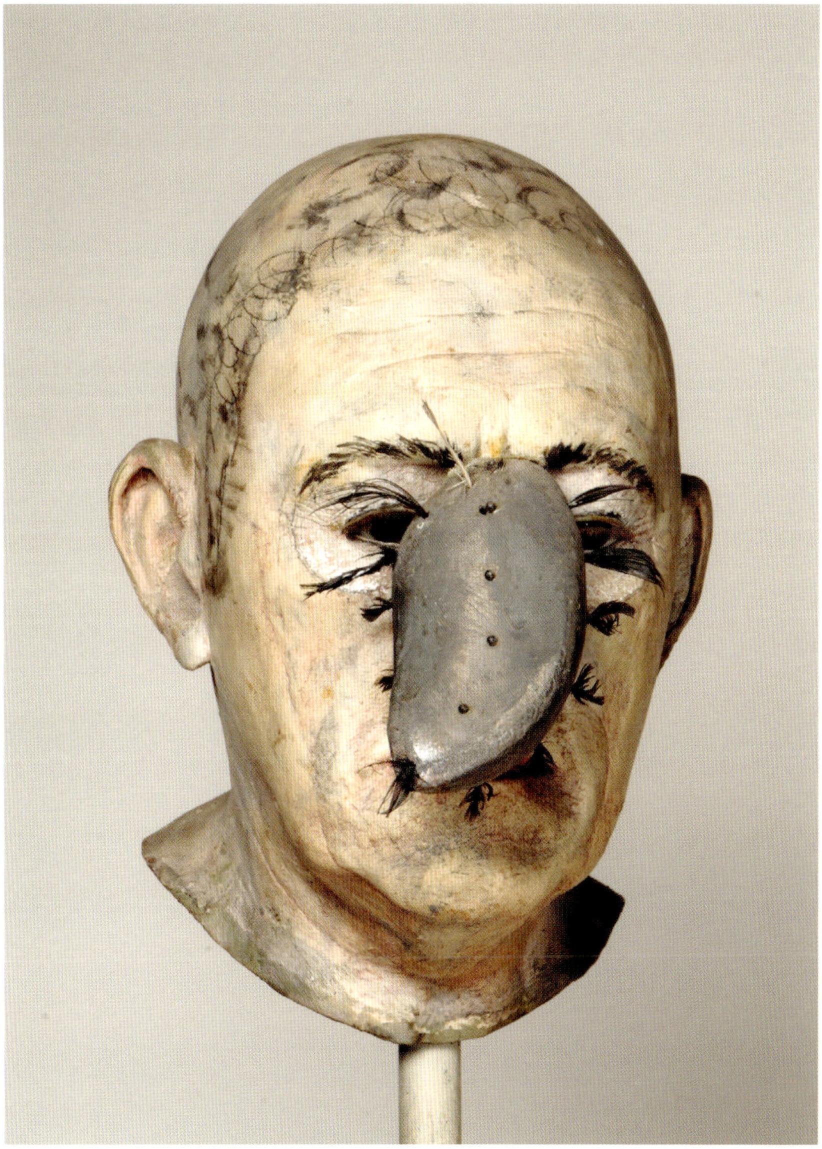

ANTHONY EARNSHAW (1924–2001)

Earnshaw was an expert in box assemblage. Although he discovered surrealism through an interest in literature and poetry in the early 1940s, he did not use the box as a preferred means of expression until the mid 1970s. He never had any formal art training, but he got a fellowship at Leeds Polytechnic in 1972. He adopted what were already well-tried surrealist strategies for provoking unease and revelation: locating familiar things (toys, ornaments, kitchen utensils, bones and jumble sale stuff) in unexpected settings and disturbing juxtapositions.

Homage to Jason (right)
1985
Mixed media
36 x 20 x 26 cm
Provenance: Flowers East, London

Exhibited: *British Surrealism & Other Realities: The Sherwin Collection*, Museum of Modern Art (Mima), Middlesbrough, 23 May–17 August 2008

Literature: *Surrealism in Britain*, Michel Remy, 1999, b/w illustration 170, p.333; *A View From Back O'Town*, Anthony Earnshaw: Work 1945–1987 exhibition catalogue, Leeds City Art Gallery 1987, b/w illustration, no page number

This assemblage pays tribute to the simplest materials: paper and a ball of string. The paper has been used to make a simple boat sat on a white plate attached to white string; the ball of string has been fixed to a stand and made to look like the globe of the earth. This homage to Jason the Argonaut makes fun of the hero's obsession with finding the Golden Fleece, which is here reduced to a ball of string.

The Glamorous Heart Attack
2000
Boxed assemblage
52 x 40 cm

Provenance: commissioned by Dr. Sherwin to celebrate the new millennium. The work also commemorates Dr. Sherwin's heart attack and subsequent quadruple heart bypass. The artist used equipment from Dr. Sherwin's surgery.

Exhibited: *British Surrealism & Other Realities:* The Sherwin Collection, Museum of Modern Art (Mima), Middlesbrough, 23 May–17 August 2008

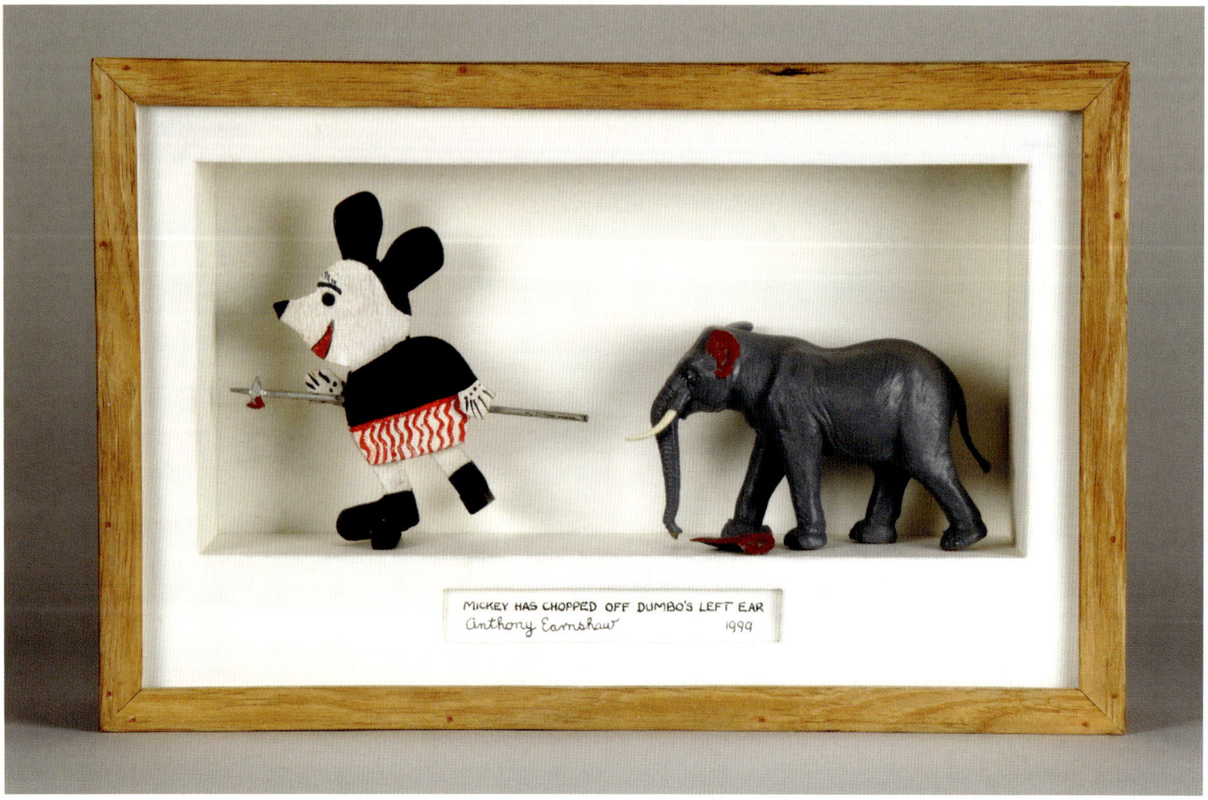

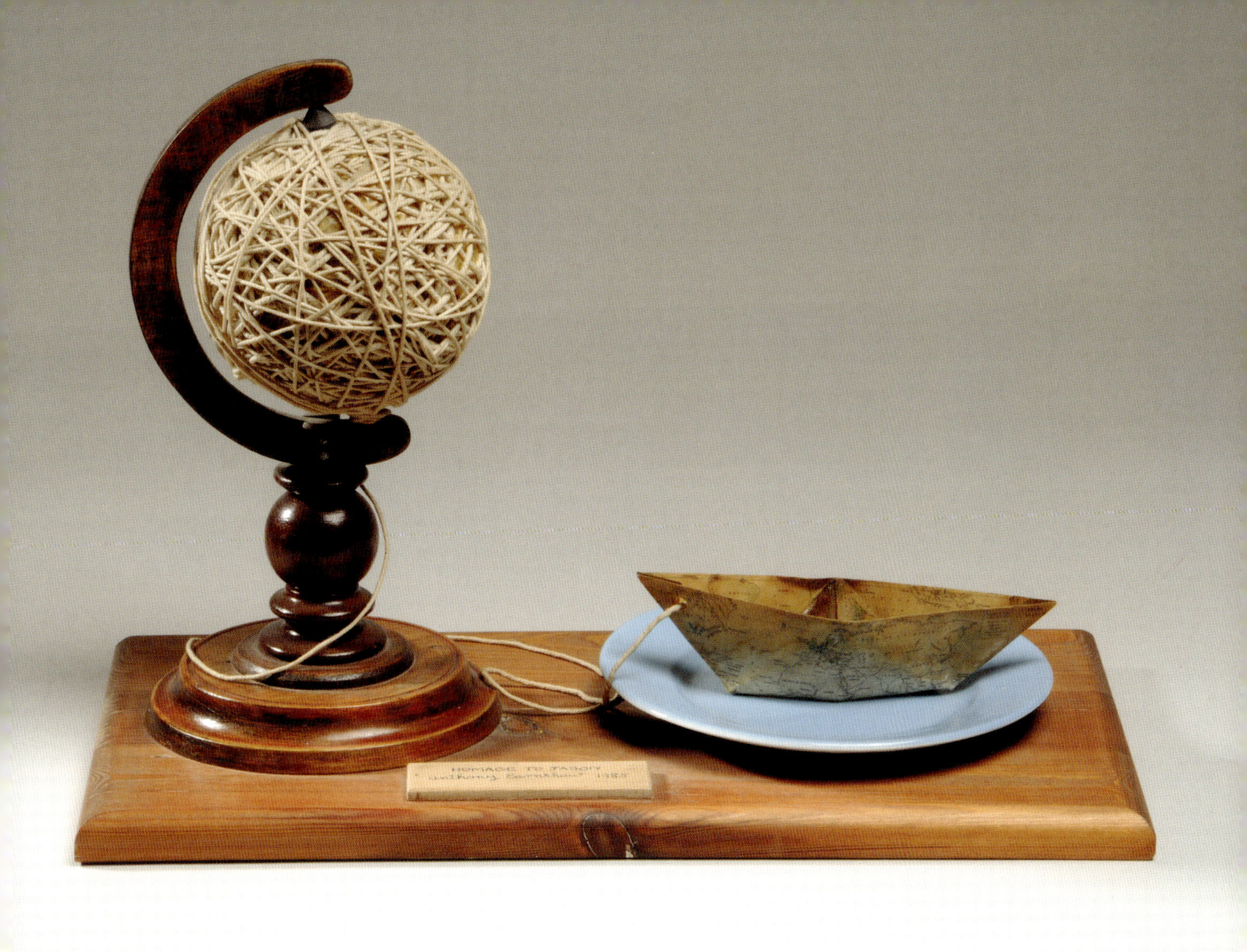

Make Mine a Quadruple
2000
Boxed assemblage
53.2 x 55.5 cm
Provenance: commissioned by Dr. Sherwin to celebrate the new millennium. The work also commemorates Dr. Sherwin's heart attack and subsequent quadruple heart bypass. The artist used equipment from Dr. Sherwin's surgery.

Exhibited: *British Surrealism & Other Realities: The Sherwin Collection*, Museum of Modern Art (Mima), Middlesbrough, 23 May–17 August 2008

Mickey Has Cut Off Dumbo's Left Ear (left)
1999
Boxed assemblage
28 x 40.6 x 10 cm
Provenance: the artist's estate
Exhibited: *British Surrealism & Other Realities: The Sherwin Collection*, Museum of Modern Art (Mima), Middlesbrough, 23 May–17 August 2008

Alphabet
1971
Print
56 x 54 cm
Provenance: the artist's estate

Exhibited: *British Surrealism & Other Realities: The Sherwin Collection*, Museum of Modern Art (Mima), Middlesbrough, 23 May–17 August 2008

Alphabet
1976
Print
56 x 54 cm
Provenance: the artist's estate

Exhibited: *British Surrealism & Other Realities: The Sherwin Collection*, Museum of Modern Art (Mima), Middlesbrough, 23 May–17 August 2008

THE LEEDS SURREALIST GROUP

Anthony Earnshaw became interested in surrealism at the age of twenty and, with his lifelong friend Eric Thacker devised surreal activities such as boarding and alighting from trains at random. By the early 1960s, he had met Patrick Hughes, then teaching art in Leeds. Also in the group, drawn to the philosophy and practice of the almost moribund surrealist movement, were the artists Ian Breakwell and Glen Baxter. It was Hughes who persuaded Earnshaw to hold a retrospective exhibition at the Leeds Institute in 1966, which was followed by an exhibition in Exeter *The Enchanted Domain* in 1967, organized by John Lyle.

The general political bias of the group was anarchist, but, with the exception of the outrageous Jeff Nuttall, not especially militant. Earnshaw hated capitalism, bullies, exploiters and rule-makers, but described himself, typically, as 'an armchair anarchist'. His subversion was through his work.

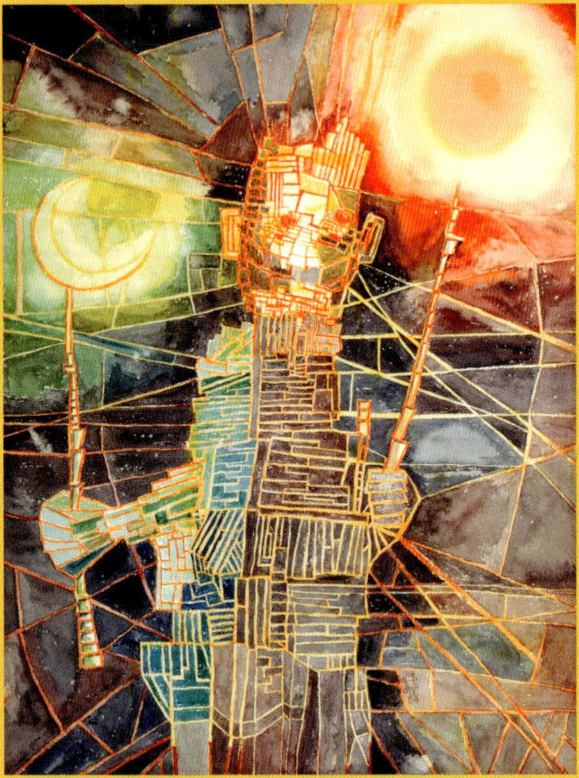

Man With Sun Moon
Anthony Earnshaw

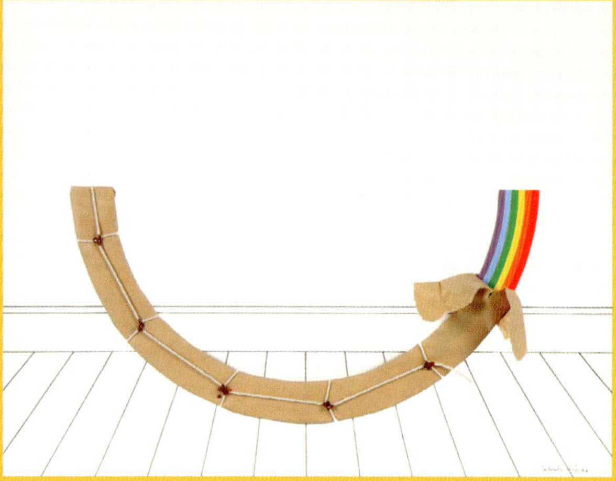

Rainbow Present
Patrick Hughes, c.1960

In time, his companions moved south, where some achieved great success. But Earnshaw's stay in Leeds meant comparative obscurity. He did, however, collaborate with Eric Thacker on two illustrated books, *Musrum* (1968), about a rather Maldoror-like hero at war with the Weed King – which although not particularly successful commercially became a cult classic – and *Wintersol* (1971), a revelation of the criminal nature of Father Christmas. Both books were praised for their elegant writing, wit and wordplay, and especially sheer invention.

Over the past decade there has been something of a resurgence of organized surrealist activity in Britain. March 1994 saw the formation of the Leeds Surrealist Group, who in the autumn of that year organized a major season of films at the National Museum of Photography, Film & Television in Bradford. This was the first significant attempt at establishing a collective surrealist presence in Britain since the group around the magazine *Melmoth*, which broke up in 1981. The Leeds Group was formed after an invitation from the Stockholm Surrealist Group to participate in their game, *The New Man*, which involved the exploration of urban spaces in search of poetic evidence of utopian vision.

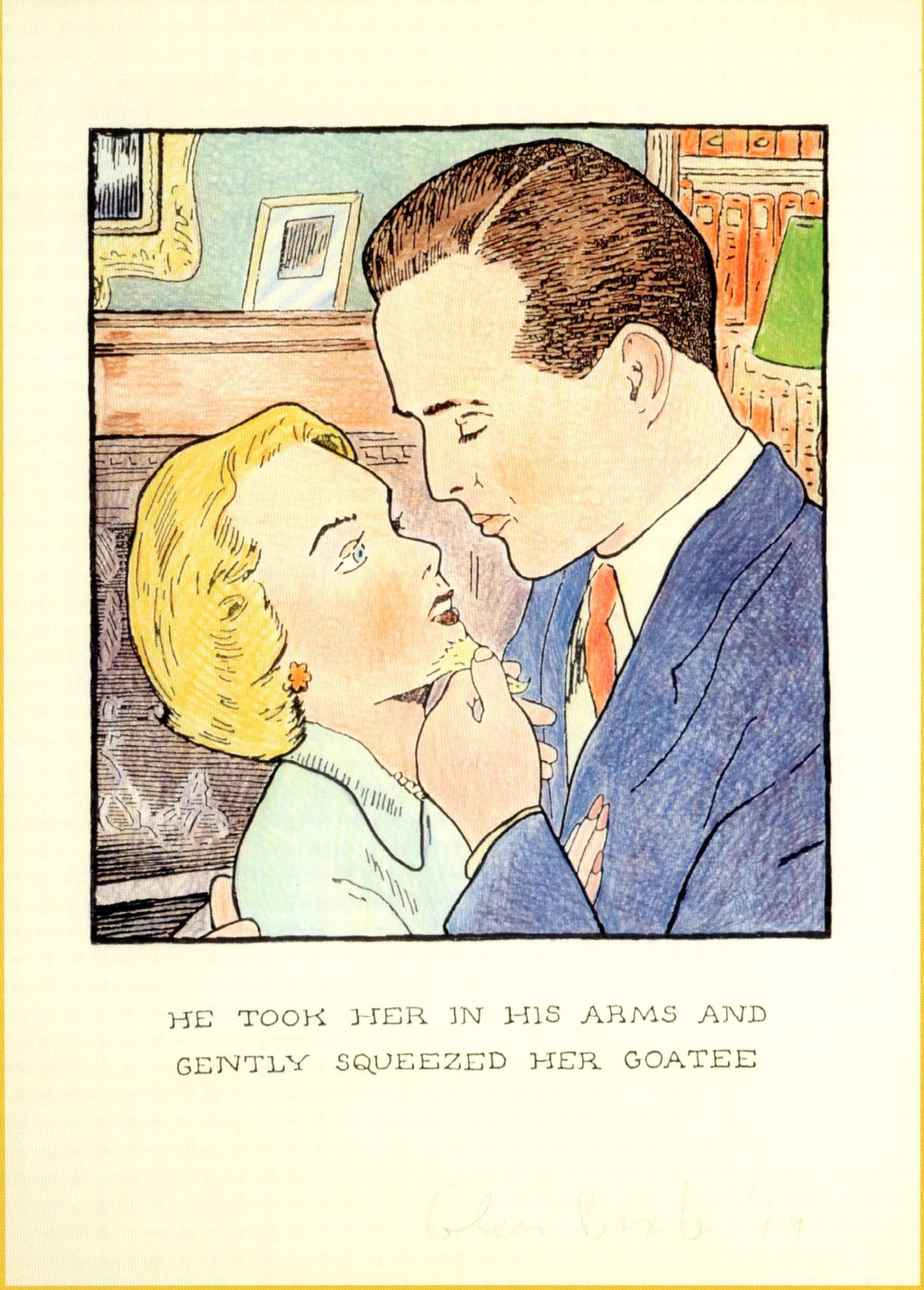

He Took Her in His Arms and Gently Squeezed Her Goatee
Glenn Baxter, 1979

SIR JACOB EPSTEIN (1880–1959)

American-born Epstein studied art in Paris, then settled in England in 1905. He was one of the first sculptors to take an interest in (so-called) primitive and ancient sculpture and had an outstanding collection of his own. By 1920, he had become probably the most notorious modern artist working in Britain, condemned for the stylized treatment of form in some works and for the brazen nudity in others. Like Moore, Hepworth and many other early 20th century sculptors, Epstein wanted his carvings to reflect the individual qualities and form of the original block of stone. This tendency is often referred to as being 'true to the materials'.

Evening Twilight
1938
Pencil, signed 1939, 2
55.9 x 43.2 cm
Provenance: Brighton

Exhibited: *British Surrealism & Other Realities: The Sherwin Collection*, Museum of Modern Art (Mima), Middlesbrough, 23 May–17 August 2008

Literature: *From Baudelaire Fleur du Mal* Limited Edition Club printed by Fanfare Press, 1940; Illustrated in the *Flowers of Evil* book

Mournful Madrigal
1938
Pencil on paper
55.9 x 43.2 cm
Provenance: Brighton

Exhibited: Tooth's Gallery, 1938 (original frame and mount from the exhibition at Tooth's Gallery, 1938); *British Surrealism & Other Realities: The Sherwin Collection*, Museum of Modern Art (Mima), Middlesbrough, 23 May–17 August 2008

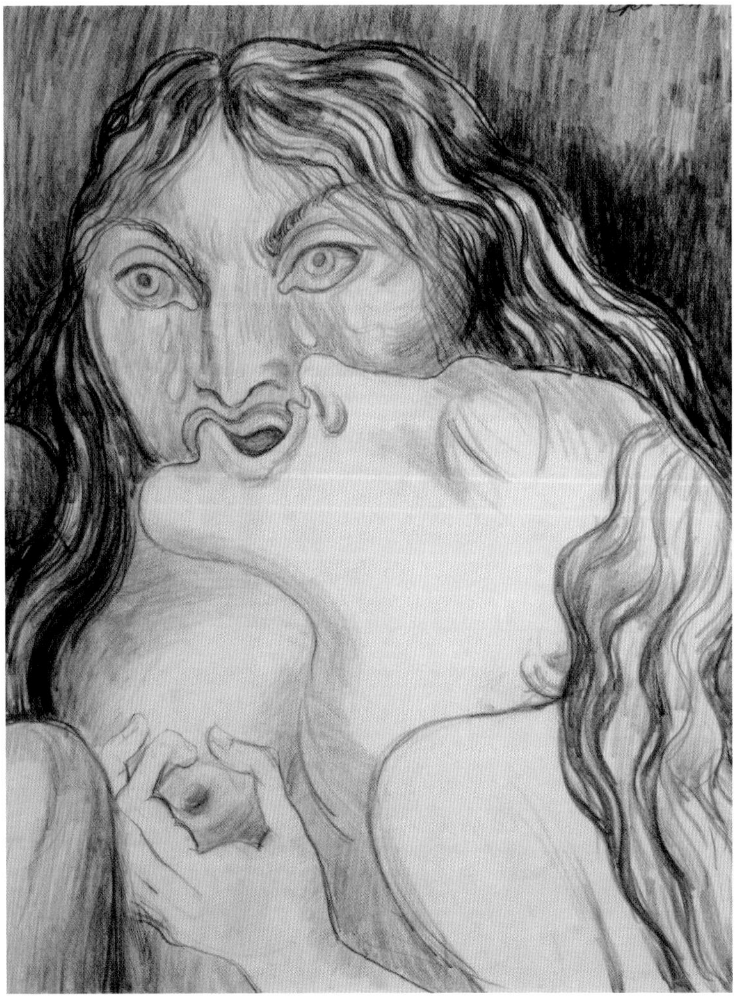

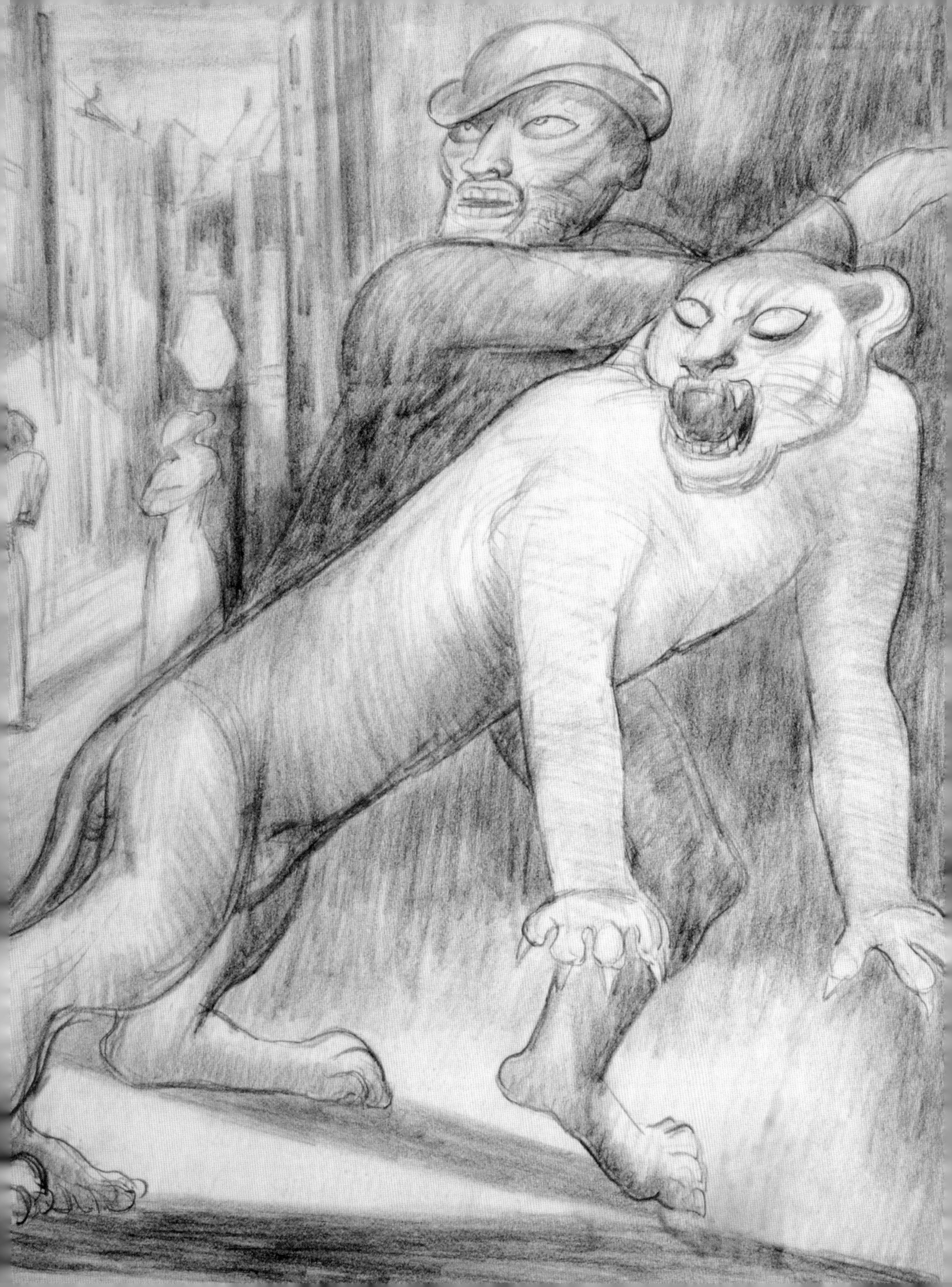

MAX ERNST (1891–1976)

Ernst was born near Cologne in Germany. After studying philosophy at university, he turned his attention to art, and became the leader of the Cologne Dada Group in 1919. He moved to Paris in 1922 to work with the surrealists, adapting the techniques of collage and photomontage for use by the group. He worked in a range of media throughout his artistic career, producing work that was irregular, experimental and highly imaginative.

Facile

Frottage
1925
Pencil frottage on paper
20.6 x 16 cm
Signed, titled and dated 1925 on the artist's mount
Provenance: Paul Eluard, Paris; Rene Gaffe, Brussels; Berggruen et Cie Paris; Waddington Galleries; Galerie Motte, Geneva; Sotheby's, London, 22 October 1997

Exhibited: *British Surrealism & Other Realities: The Sherwin Collection,* Museum of Modern Art (Mima), Middlesbrough, 23 May–17 August 2008

Literature: M.E. Histoire, *Naturelle,* Galerie Der Spiegel, Cologne, 1964, illustrated; Patrick Waldberg *Der Surrealismus,* Cologne, 1956, Ill; Herta Wescher, *Die Collage etc,* Cologne, 1956, Ill; Werner Spies, *M.E. Frottagen,* Stuttgart, 1968, Ill; Maurice Henry, *Antologia Grafica etc.* Milan, 1972, Ill; Werner Spies, *M.E. Werke 1925–1929,* Ill

This work was owned by Paul Eluard, who had written the famous poem entitled *Facile*. 1925 was the year that Max Ernst discovered frottage for his work.

Poster for the International Surrealist Exhibition

1936
86 x 61 cm
Image block by Max Ernst

Exhibited: *British Surrealism & Other Realities: The Sherwin Collection,* Museum of Modern Art (Mima), Middlesbrough, 23 May–17 August 2008

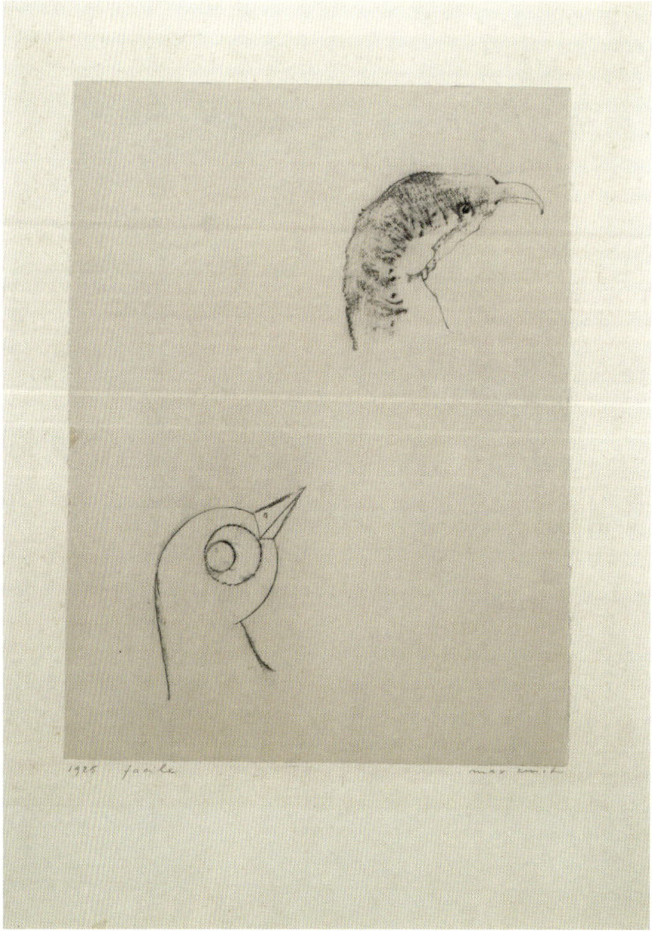

MERLYN EVANS (1910–1973)

A travelling scholarship from the Royal College in 1931 had enabled Evans to tour Scandinavia, France and Germany, where he was especially impressed by Kandinsky, Klee and Feininger. During his brief involvement with the British Surrealist Group, he attended many meetings at Roland Penrose's house and participated in the *Surrealist Objects and Poems* exhibition at the end of 1937. However, he refused to be implicated politically. He shortly afterwards left for South Africa and, on his return to Britain, he had confirmed a distrust of group allegiances and remained outside any artistic associations.

Tyrannopolis (right)
1939
Oil on canvas
Signed: Evans
76 x 91.5 cm
Provenance: Mayor Gallery, London; Austin Desmond, London

Exhibited: *Works by Merlyn Evans,* Durban Art Gallery, 1939; *The Political Paintings by Merlyn Evans,* Tate, London, 1985, no. 12, illustration; *Messages From Nowhere, The Figurative Avant-Garde and the Influence of Surrealism in Britain 1930–1951,* Austin Desmond, London, 1991; Musée d'Art Moderne, Paris, 1997; *El Surrealismo y la Guerra Civil Espanola,* Museum of Teruel, Teruel, Spain, 30 October–13 December 1998; Mayor Gallery, London, 1998, illustration; *Real Surreal,* Wolverhampton Art Gallery, Wolverhampton, 1995; *British Surrealism & Other Realities: The Sherwin Collection*, Museum of Modern Art (Mima), Middlesbrough, 23 May–17 August 2008; 23 May–17 August 2008; *Thirties,* Arts Council of Great Britain, London, cat. no. 22

Literature: Michel Remy, *Surrealism in Britain,* Ashgate, 1999, p.84, no. 28, illustration; Jeremy Lewison, *Going Modern And Being British, The Challenge of the 1930s,* in: *Blast to Frieze, British Art in the 20th Century,* Kunstmuseum Wolfsburg/Hatje Cantz, 2002, pp.66–72, illustration p.70, and plate 66, colour illustration

Also known as *The Protesters* this was one of the first paintings completed after the artist moved to South Africa. The painting, finished in July 1939, at which time war had not been officially declared between England and Germany, suggests a battle and triumph of the human spirit against the dehumanised and evil oppressive power of the state. Above, strange flying machines hover and attack, perhaps referencing *Guernica*, by Picasso, and the horror experienced on the realisation that aeroplanes, when strategically used in warfare, could cause great suffering to a civilian population, as was demonstrated only too graphically in the Spanish Civil War.

The Chess Players
1948
Etching
1st. state 1/6
Signed in pencil
40.6 x 40.6 cm
Provenance: Mayor Gallery, London

Exhibited: *Real Surreal,* Wolverhampton Art Gallery, Wolverhampton, 1995; *British Surrealism & Other Realities: The Sherwin Collection*, Museum of Modern Art (Mima), Middlesbrough, 23 May–17 August 2008

This is the first surrealist work bought by Dr Sherwin. In this painting we see Molotov and Ribbentrop playing chess for Europe. The two leaders signed a non-aggression pact between Germany and Russia in August 1939. Hitler broke the pact and invaded Russia on June 22nd 1941. In 1942 Merlyn Evans enlisted in the South African Army and his artistic career was interrupted by the war.

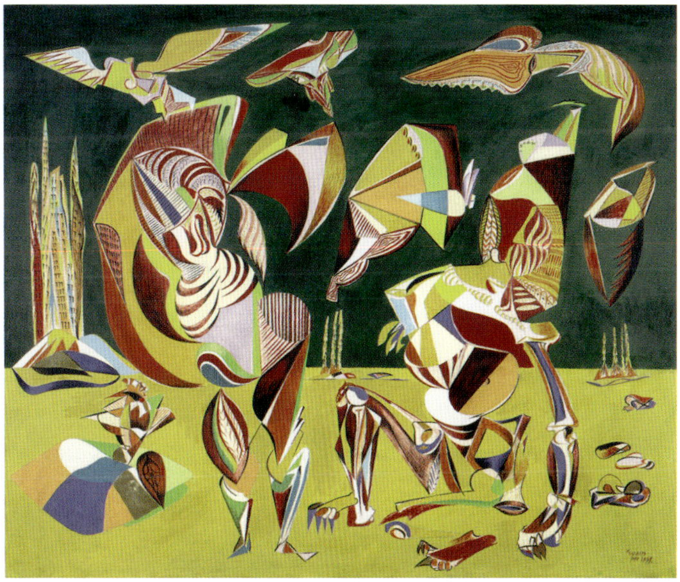

GORDON ONSLOW FORD (1912–2003)

Born in England in 1912 to a family of artists, Onslow Ford began painting at an early age. In 1938, he joined the surrealist group in Paris and attended their meetings in Café Deux Magots; besides Matta he became friends with Pierre Mabille, André Breton, Yves Tanguy and Victor Brauner, among others. His love of painting also led him to collect paintings and he made frequent visits to the studios of Picasso, Miró, de Chirico and André Masson. As a surrealist, Onslow Ford was initially interested in dreams; recording and making sketches of his own dream experiences. Early on, however, it became apparent to him that it was impossible to paint dreams and that the rendering of the dream image was merely a copy of a past event. Unlike many surrealists who were interested in Freud's theory of dreams, he gravitated towards Carl Jung's idea of the Collective Unconscious and Ouspenski's theory of the Fourth Dimension. His artistic passion aimed toward expressing what lies beyond the personal in dreams.

Checkmate
1940
Oil on canvas
Signed and dated
76 x 102 cm
Provenance: given by the artist to Robert Mellville; Phillips, London, 11 November 1991

Exhibited: *Onslow Ford Retrospective*, Granel Foundation, Santiago de Compostella, 1998; *British Surrealism & Other Realities: The Sherwin Collection*, Museum of Modern Art (Mima), Middlesbrough, 23 May–17 August 2008

In a letter to Dr. Sherwin, the artist wrote that 'this painting is in transition from the symbolic worlds of dreams to the spaces in the mind beyond. It deals with the interconnectedness of all forms of life… I was more guided by spontaneous intuition than preconceived ideas – though I built on what had already been discovered.' It was painted in 1940, during his one year in England between living in France and sailing to America.

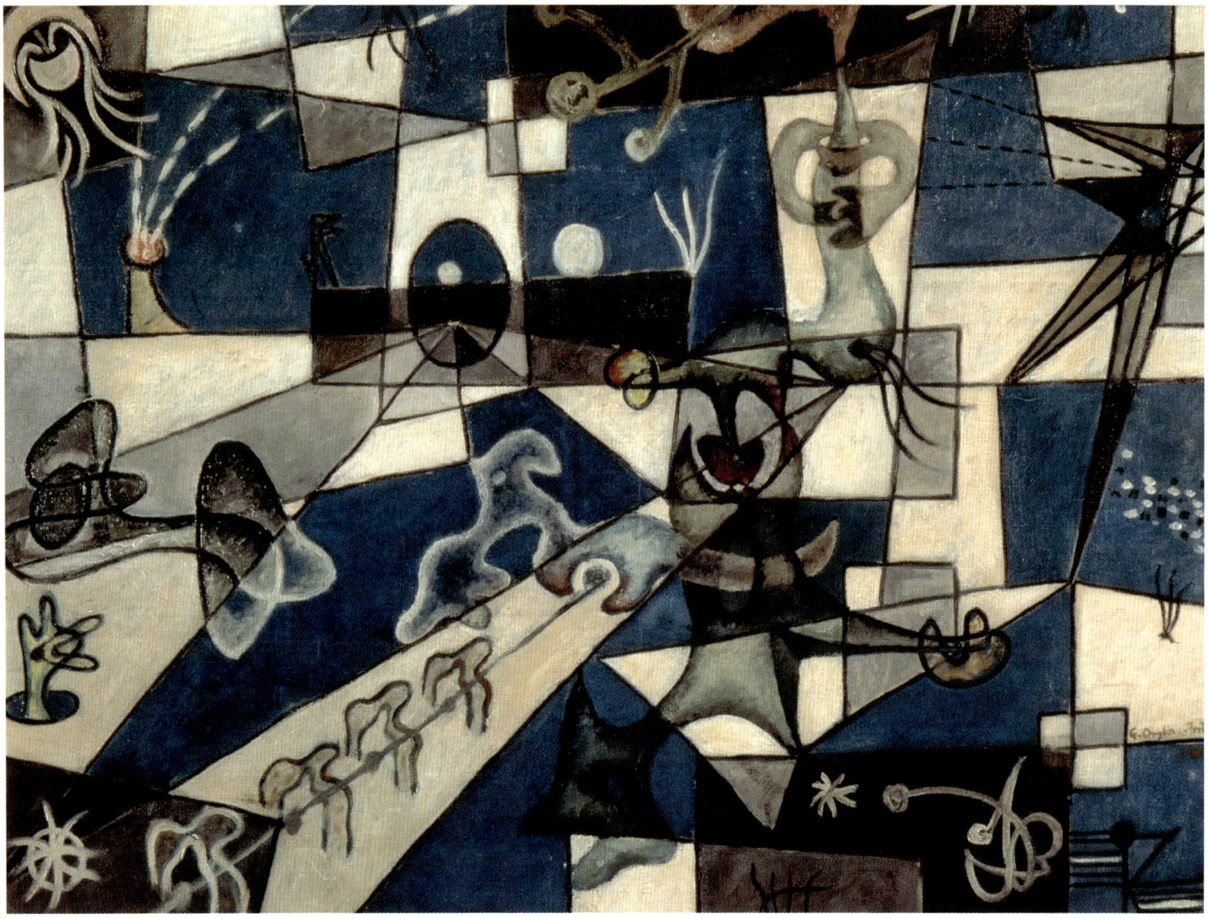

TERRY FROST (1915–2003)

Frost was born in Leamington Spa. He began painting while he was a prisoner of war in Germany during the Second World War and moved to Cornwall in 1946, studying at art school in St. Ives. From 1947 to 1950 he studied in London. He returned to St. Ives in 1950 and worked as an assistant to Barbara Hepworth in 1951.

Frost's abstract paintings are based on the observation of nature. The harbour at St. Ives was one of his favourite subjects. Frost taught at Bath Academy and Leeds and Reading Universities, holding the prestigious Gregory Fellowship in Leeds.

Regatta
1995
Oil and collage on paper
33 x 23 cm
Provenance: the artist

Exhibited: *British Surrealism & Other Realities: The Sherwin Collection*, Museum of Modern Art (Mima), Middlesbrough, 23 May–17 August 2008

Red and Black
1995
Oil and collage on paper
33 x 74 cm
Provenance: the artist

Exhibited: *British Surrealism & Other Realities: The Sherwin Collection*, Museum of Modern Art (Mima), Middlesbrough, 23 May–17 August 2008

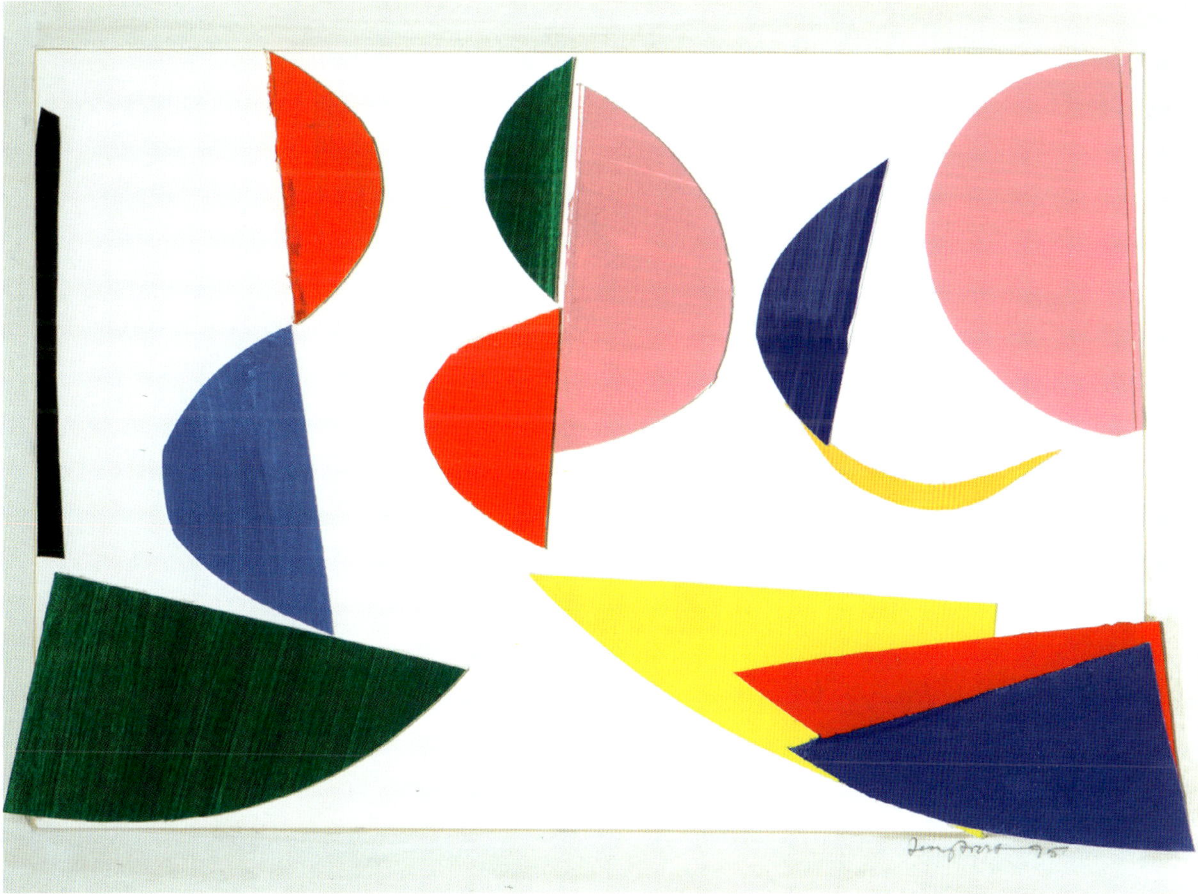

HENRI GAUDIER-BRZESKA (1891–1915)

Born in France, Gaudier-Brzeska received a scholarship to study English in Bristol. After a period of study in Germany in 1909, he returned to England in 1911 and settled in London, where he quickly became one of the leaders of the avant-garde. From 1913 to 1914, he was affiliated with the Omega Workshops. Although Gaudier-Brzeska worked primarily as a sculptor, he briefly experimented with etching and dry-point and made a single linocut, *Wrestlers*, in the studio of Horace Brodzky, an experienced printmaker and close friend.

Wrestlers
1913 (cast in 1965)
Herculite Relief
Edition of nine
72 x 91 cm
Provenance: H.S. Ede, Colnaghi, Browse & Darby for Gillian Jason

Exhibited: Musée d'Orleon and Musée d'Art Moderne, Toulouse, 1993, p.117; Sprengel Museum, Hannover and Haus der Kunst, Munich, 1996/1997; *Blast to Frieze, British Art in the 20th Century,* Kunstmuseum Wolfsburg, 2002; *British Surrealism & Other Realities: The Sherwin Collection,* Museum of Modern Art (Mima), Middlesbrough, 23 May–17 August 2008

Literature: *Blast to Frieze, British Art in the 20th Century,* exhibition catalogue, Kunstmuseum Wolfsburg/Hatje Cantz, 2002

The relief was a culmination of a large body of drawings on this subject, which gradually became more simplified. In this two-dimensional relief, the artist has established a rhythmic interrelation of shapes. The proportion and natural physical organisation of the figure has been abandoned in favour of direct expression and the flat treatment of the hands serves to accentuate the flow of lines in the two figures.

Wrestlers
c.1913
Pencil on paper
26 x 38 cm
Provenance: H.S. Ede, Colnaghi, Browse & Darby for Gillian Jason

Exhibited: *British Surrealism & Other Realities: The Sherwin Collection,* Museum of Modern Art (Mima), Middlesbrough, 23 May–17 August 2008

Wrestlers
c.1914
Linocut, printed posthumously by Horace Brodzky
6/50
23 x 27 cm
Edition: from a projected posthumous edition of 50
Provenance: Anthony d'Offay, London; Sotheby's, London; Christie's, London, 20 June 1996

Exhibited: *British Surrealism & Other Realities: The Sherwin Collection,* Museum of Modern Art (Mima), Middlesbrough, 23 May–17 August 2008

Drawing for a Decorated Cupboard
1913
Pencil on paper
26 x 38 cm
Provenance: H.S. Ede

Exhibited: *British Surrealism & Other Realities: The Sherwin Collection,* Museum of Modern Art (Mima), Middlesbrough, 23 May–17 August 2008

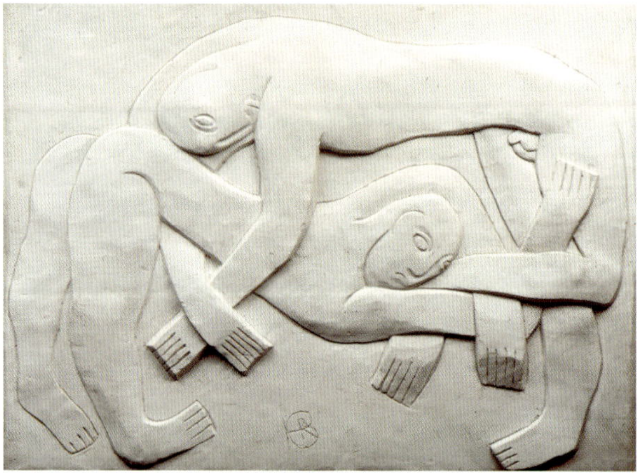

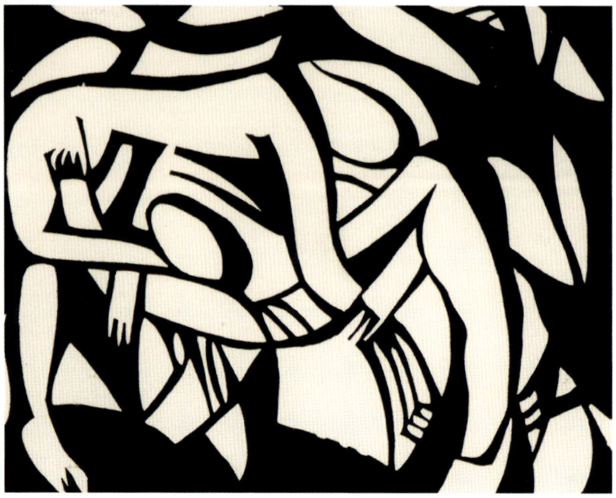

WILLIAM GEAR (1915–1997)

Gear was born in Methil, Fife, and attended Edinburgh College of Art. In 1937, he studied briefly under Fernand Léger in Paris. After the war, Gear worked in Germany, mounting exhibitions for the allies. From 1948 to 1950 he lived in Paris, where be became affiliated to the COBRA movement. The COBRA artists (the initials stand for Copenhagen, Brussels and Amsterdam, the home cities of many of the group's members), advocated a gestural, near abstract style of painting, influenced by primitivism and the art of children.

Dancing Landscape
c.1938
Oil on panel
27 x 53 cm
Provenance: Bonham's, London

Exhibited: *British Surrealism & Other Realities: The Sherwin Collection*, Museum of Modern Art (Mima), Middlesbrough, 23 May–17 August 2008

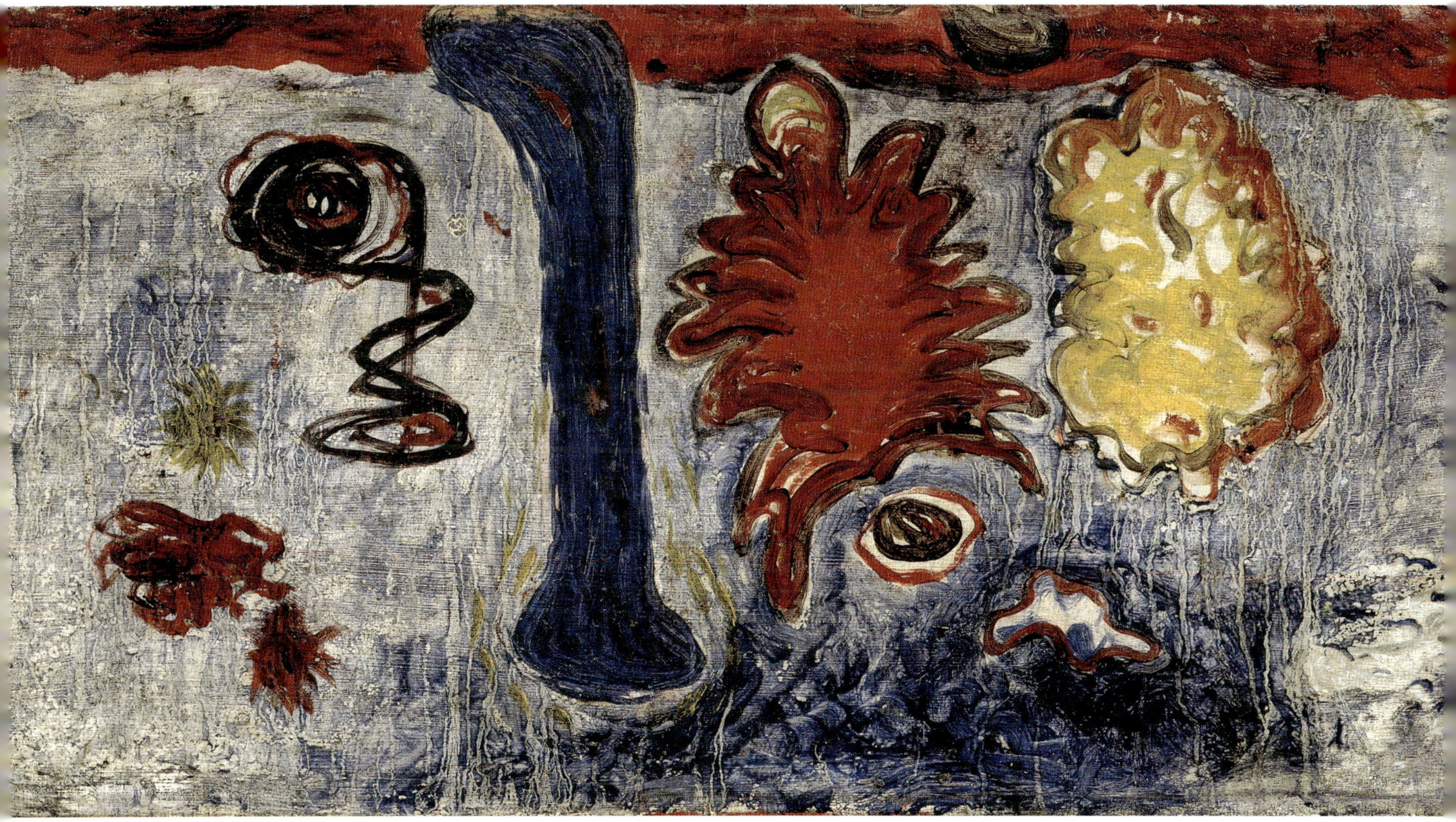

THOMAS SAMUEL HAILE (1909–1948)

Sam Haile was born in London. After working in a shipping firm and taking art evening classes, he trained at the Royal College of Art. He originally studied painting, but moved to the pottery department under William Staite Murray. From 1936, Haile taught briefly at Hammersmith and Kingston art schools and shared a studio in Raynes Park, Wimbledon with Margaret Rey. Here he produced slipware and stoneware, having his first solo exhibition in 1937.

Shop Windows in Trinidad (right)
1938
Oil on canvas
Signed and dated
90 x 71 cm
Provenance: The Moire Art Collection Society, Christie's, London, 25 May 1994

Exhibited: Empire Society Exhibition; *Real Surreal*, Wolverhampton Art Gallery, Wolverhampton, 1995; *British Surrealism & Other Realities:* The Sherwin Collection, Museum of Modern Art (Mima), Middlesbrough, 23 May–17 August 2008

The mysterious nature of this painting is emphasised by the half white, half black hairdresser, gloves and stockings, the sexless cat-like female staring out at the viewer. The hairdresser stands in contrast to the decaying malevolence of the three witches; the ghostly-staring, upturned chemise and the fork-like tree with hands, its roots in the soil of Trinidad attacking the onlooker. Who can doubt Sam Haile's anti-colonial soul?

Exhibited: Empire Society Exhibition; *Real Surreal*, Wolverhampton Art Gallery, Wolverhampton, 1995; *British Surrealism & Other Realities:* The Sherwin Collection, Museum of Modern Art (Mima), Middlesbrough, 23 May–17 August 2008

Brain Operation
1939
Oil on canvas
61 x 51 cm
Provenance: Austin Desmond, London

Exhibited: *British Surrealism & Other Realities:* The Sherwin Collection, Museum of Modern Art (Mima), Middlesbrough, 23 May–17 August 2008

Literature: *Surrealism in Britain,* Michael Remy, 1999, colour illustration no. 79, p.175

Tea Pot
1946
Solt glaze, brown and cream glaze decorated with abstract figures front and rear
17.8 x 30 cm
Provenance: bought from the artist's widow

Exhibited: *British Surrealism & Other Realities: The Sherwin Collection,* Museum of Modern Art (Mima), Middlesbrough, 23 May–17 August 2008

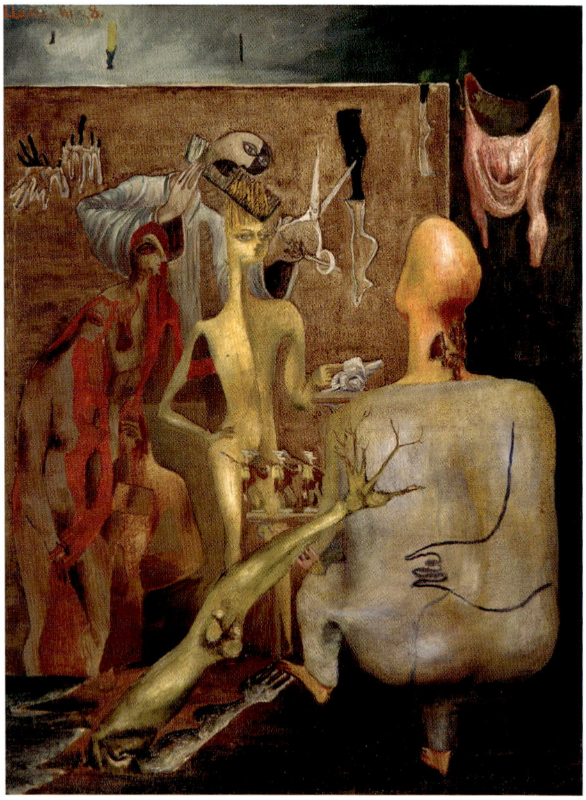

PAUL HAMMOND (born 1947)

Hammond was a student at Leeds College of Art in the 1960s and his works were included into British surrealist exhibitions. More recently however, he has worked as a writer, editor and translator. Among others, he edited and translated *The Shadow and Its Shadow: Surrealist Writings on the Cinema* and is the author of *Constellations of Miró, Breton*. Hammond lives in Barcelona.

High Jinks
1971 (–1985)
Acrylic on board
44 x 56 cm
Provenance: the artist

Exhibited: *British Surrealism & Other Realities: The Sherwin Collection*, Museum of Modern Art (Mima), Middlesbrough, 23 May–17 August 2008

High Jinks depicts a roundelay of avatars, the kind of 'low' beings – or non-beings – who rarely find their way into fine art: a ghost, a snowman, a scarecrow, the Invisible Man. Hammond was interested in the primitive cinema of George Melly and the 'coming to life' of such figures is a common theme to be found in his work.

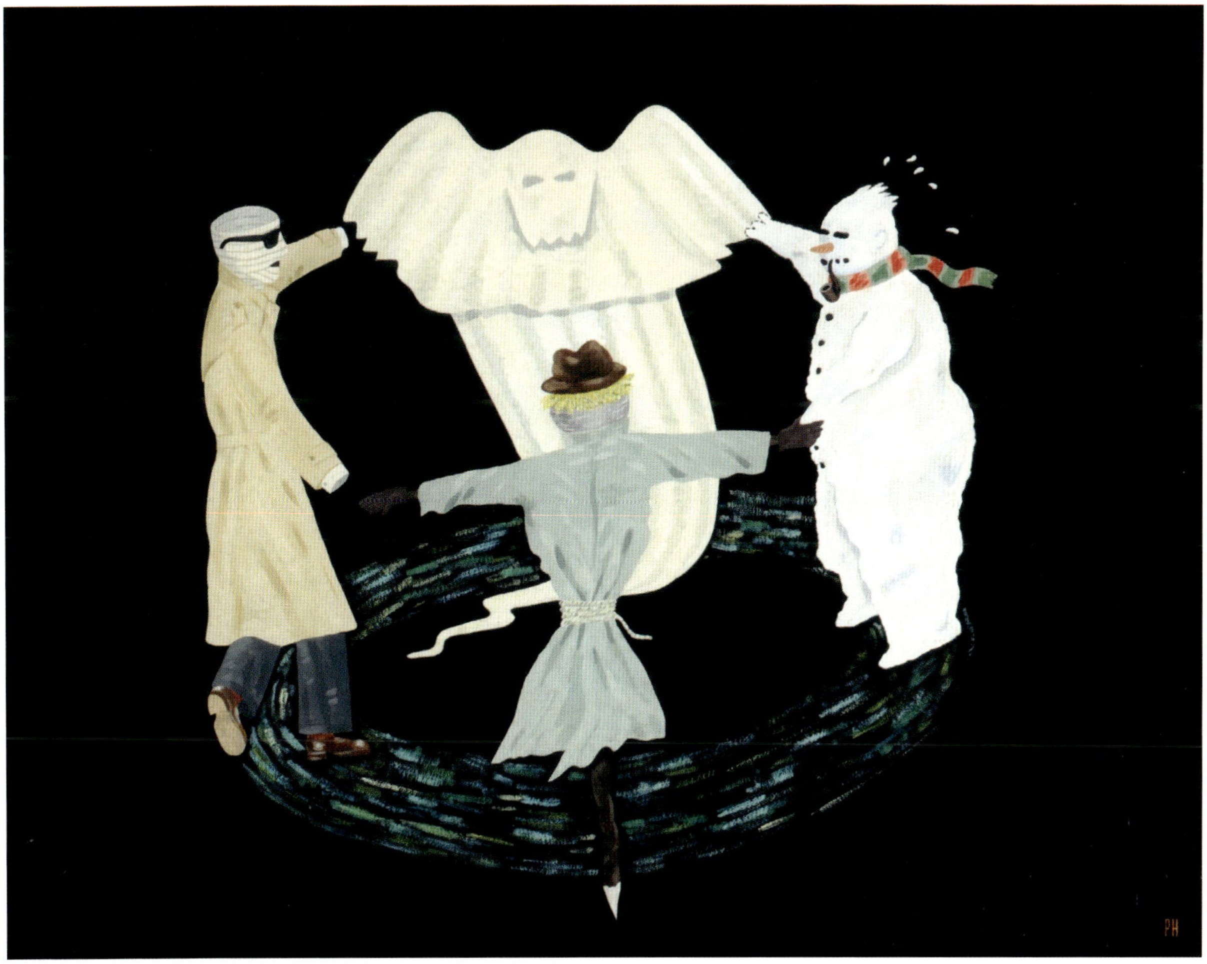

STANLEY WILLIAM HAYTER (1901–1988)

Hayter spent most of his life in Paris, where in 1927 he founded an experimental workshop for the graphic arts, Atelier 17, that played a central role in the 20th century revival of print as an independent art form. Hayter was a chemist by training and had an unrivalled knowledge of the technicalities of printmaking, on which he wrote two major books. His prints are varied in technique and style, but most characteristically are influenced by the abstract vein of surrealism and are notable for their experiments with texture and colour.

Reflections
1928
Oil on canvas
Signed: Hayter with 28 faintly Rt.
74 x 60 cm
Provenance: Jonathan Clarke Fine Art, London

Exhibited: *British Surrealism & Other Realities: The Sherwin Collection,* Museum of Modern Art (Mima), Middlesbrough, 23 May–17 August 2008

In *Reflections*, the half-face is not a self-portrait, but that of Anthony Gross, the painter and engraver who was a close friend of Hayter. Stylistically the painting reflects the popular genre of that period, a still-life composition inside a room with a balcony overlooking the sea. Using a mirror, the image has been painted in reverse: the balcony facing the viewer is really behind the artist with the light coming from over his shoulder onto the objects on the table.

The Runner
1939
33 x 25 cm
Print on plaster
Provenance: Sylvan Cole Collection, Swann Galleries, 6 March 2006, Lot 136

Exhibited: *British Surrealism & Other Realities: The Sherwin Collection,* Museum of Modern Art (Mima), Middlesbrough, 23 May–17 August 2008

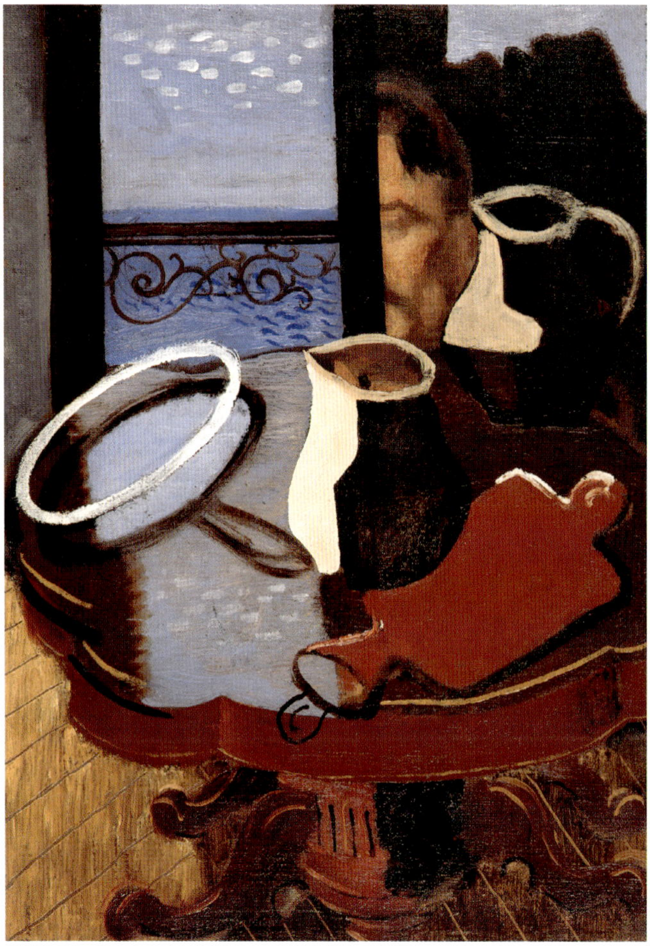

NIGEL HENDERSON (1917–1985)

Nigel Henderson was one of the founding members of the Independent Group. He was a documentary and experimental photographer and artist. Henderson's images of the human head have been seen as the culmination of what he referred to as his 'stressed' photographs. These are full of destruction, atrophy and decay. They have been related to his traumatic experiences during the Second World War (1939–45) and have been seen to be suited to an age of nuclear anxiety.

Japanese Head
1956
Mixed media on photographic paper
38 x 29 cm
Initialled and dated '56 lower right
Provenance: Mayor Gallery, London

Exhibited: *This is Tomorrow,* Whitechapel Gallery, London, 1956; *British Surrealism & Other Realities: The Sherwin Collection,* Museum of Modern Art (Mima), Middlesbrough, 23 May–17 August 2008

In 1954, the world witnessed the first U.S. detonation of the hydrogen bomb and the totally devastating effect of this impacted the entire world. Henderson was included in the group exhibition *This is Tomorrow* at the Whitechapel Art Gallery, London, where the selected artists were invited to present imagined future environments.

The Best Days of Your Life
1975
Photo collage and paint
22.5 x 29.5cm
Provenance: Austin Desmond, London

Exhibited: *British Surrealism & Other Realities: The Sherwin Collection,* Museum of Modern Art (Mima), Middlesbrough, 23 May–17 August 2008

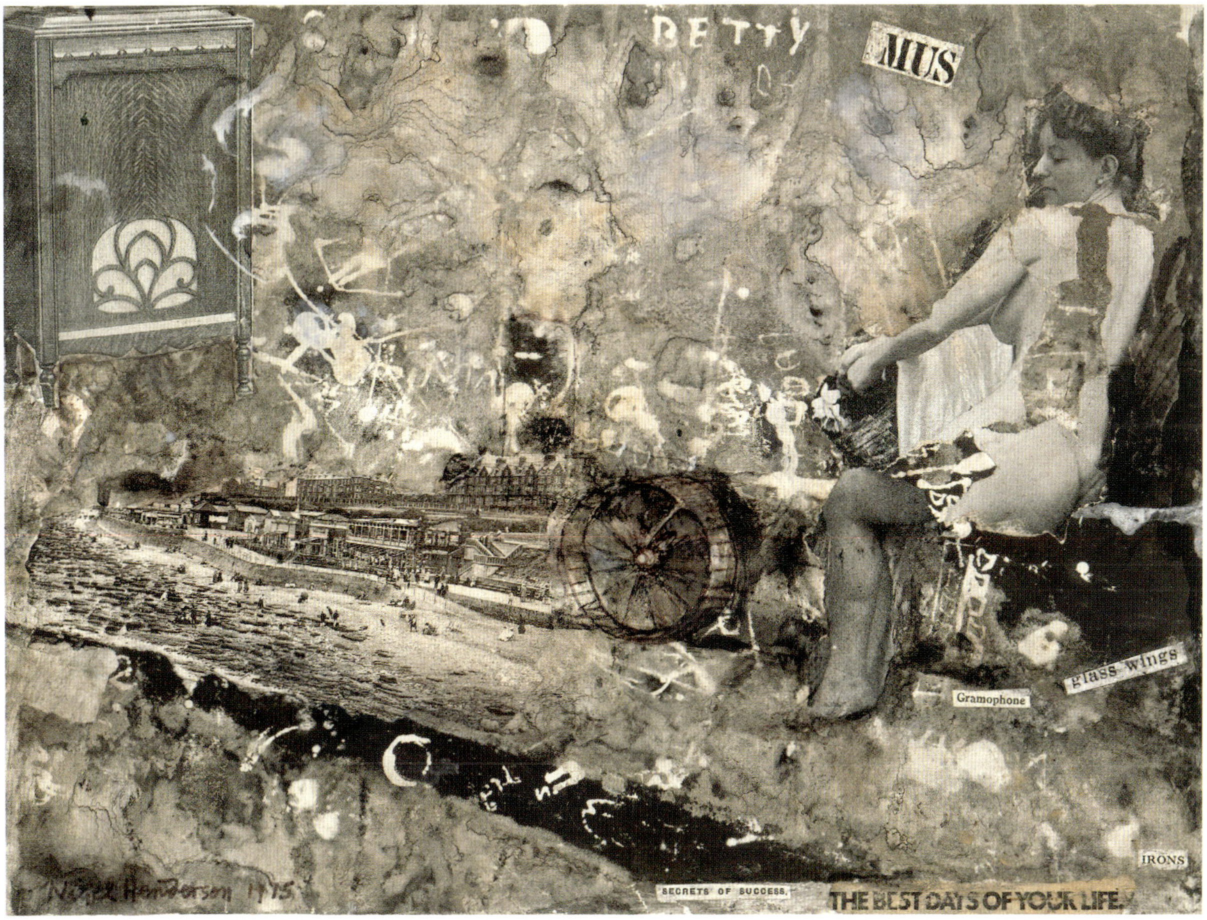

ARTHUR JACKSON HEPWORTH (1911–2003)

For long overlooked by the art world, Arthur Jackson Hepworth made a unique contribution to the modern movement in painting and architecture in the 1930s. Because of his early association with such luminaries as his cousin, Dame Barbara Hepworth, J.L. (later Sir Leslie) Martin, Henry Moore, Ben and Winifred Nicholson and John and Myfanwy Piper, he became in old age a valuable source of information for researchers.

From the mid 1960s, his pre-war pictures began to appear in survey exhibitions, specialist biographies and catalogues. Scholars were helped, when they contacted him, because of his methodical numbering system. Part of his important photographic record found its way into the Tate archive.

From the outset of his exhibiting career, at Barbara Hepworth's suggestion, he adopted the painting surname Jackson, his mother's maiden name, and his middle name, 'to avoid inevitable confusion and comparison'.

Drawing
1937
26 x 36 cm
Gouache on paper

Exhibited: *British Surrealism & Other Realities: The Sherwin Collection*, Museum of Modern Art (Mima), Middlesbrough, 23 May–17 August 2008

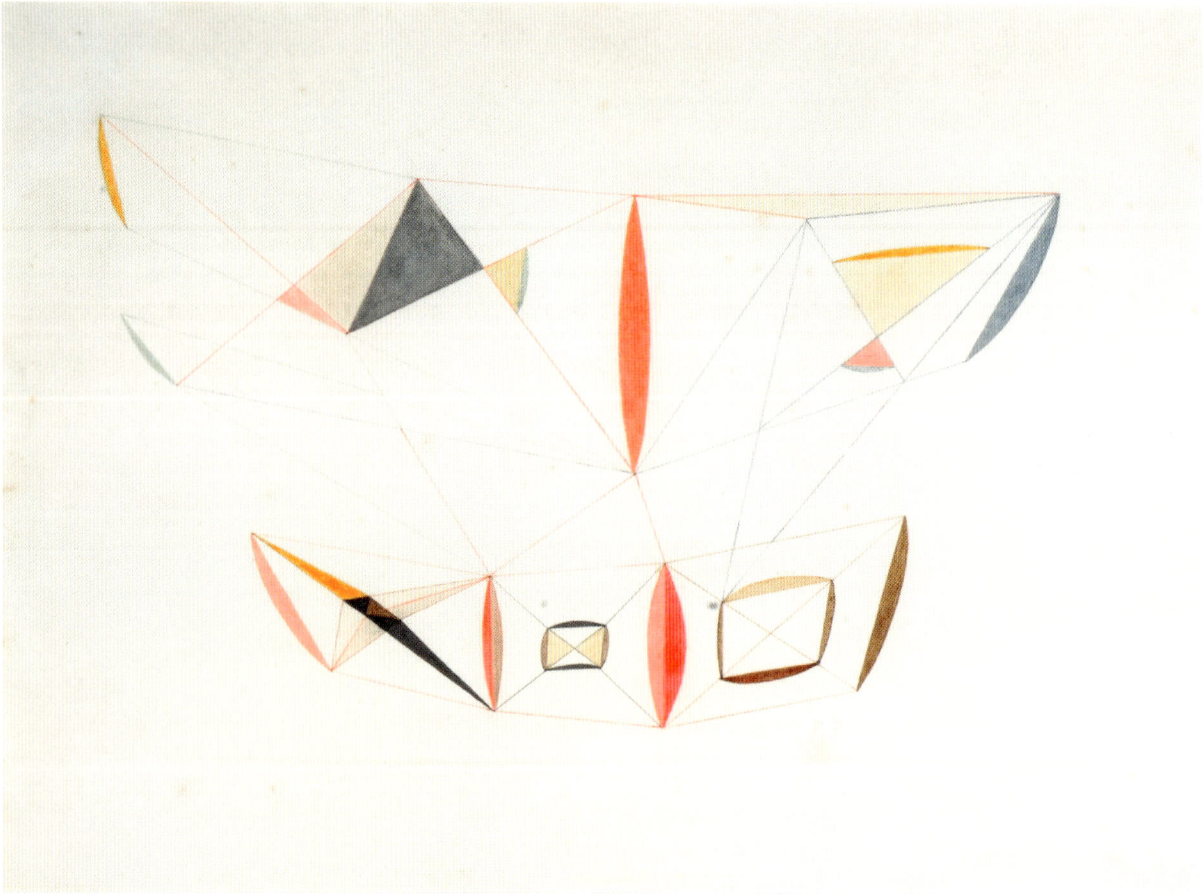

GERTRUDE HERMES (1901–1983)

Hermes attended Beckenham School of Art from 1919 to 1920, and between 1919 and 1921 became acquainted with the work of Rodin and Lehmbruck. From 1921 to 1925, she attended Leon Underwood's School of Painting and Sculpture, where contemporaries included Moore, Coxon and Pitchforth. Hermes was devoted to the idea of transformation. Duality and fecundity became consistent themes. Many of her subjects in sculpture and prints are animals and children, and her work was influenced by Brancusi and Gaudier-Brzeska. All her work is elegant and concentrated, expressing the essential rhythms and detail of the natural world with economy.

Swallow Door Knocker
Circa 1929
Brass
Length: 26 cm
Provenance: Michael Parkin Fine Art, London

Exhibited: *Royal Academy Exhibition*, London 1981, no. 9; *British Surrealism & Other Realities: The Sherwin Collection*, Museum of Modern Art (Mima), Middlesbrough, 23 May–17 August 2008

Two Frogs (Copulating)
Bronze
14 x 14 x 24 cm
Provenance: Michael Parkin Fine Art, London

Exhibited: *British Surrealism & Other Realities: The Sherwin Collection*, Museum of Modern Art (Mima), Middlesbrough, 23 May–17 August 2008

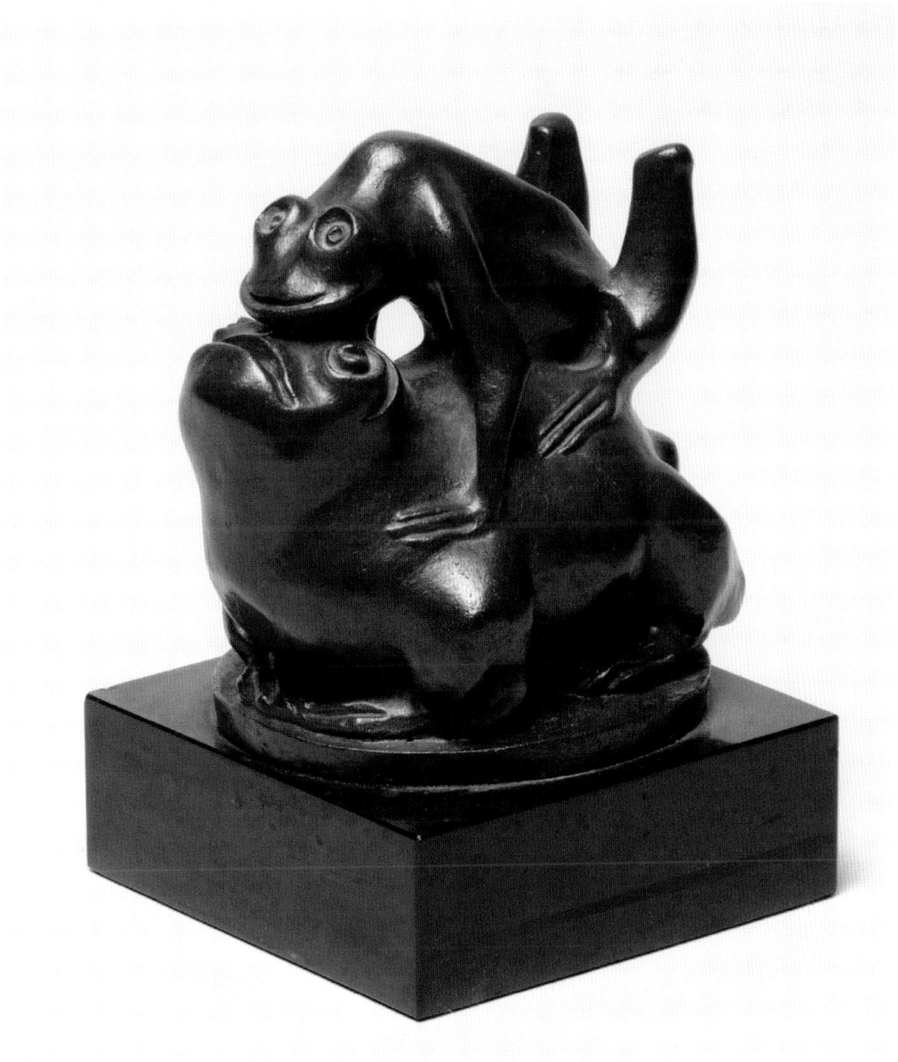

PATRICK HERON (1920–1999)

Patrick Heron was born in Leeds and settled in Cornwall with his family in 1925. He studied at the Slade School of Art in London from 1937 to 1939. As a conscientious objector during the Second World War, Heron worked on a farm before becoming an assistant to the potter Bernard Leach in St. Ives. He also worked as an art critic for *The New Statesman* magazine and as a teacher. From the mid 1950s, Heron produced abstract paintings, featuring distinctive 'lozenges' of bright, vibrant colour.

Nude in Wicker Chair
1951
Oil on canvas,
61 x 102 cm
Signed: P. Heron 51 on the face
Provenance: bought from the artist's daughter, Katherine

Exhibited: *Patrick Heron,* Redfern Gallery, London, 1951; *Patrick Heron, Retrospective,* Wakefield Art Gallery, 1952; *Ten Contemporary British Painters,* touring exhibition, Sweden, 1953-54; *Abstract, Cubist, Formalist, Surrealist,* Redfern Gallery, London, 1954; *Contemporary British Art,* Norwich Castle Museum, Norwich, 1954-55; *British Surrealism & Other Realities: The Sherwin Collection,* Museum of Modern Art (Mima), Middlesbrough, 23 May–17 August 2008

Literature: press cutting, April 10 1952, *The Wakefield Times*, photograph of the painting behind the young Patrick Heron with Professor Herbert Read and Maurice de Sauzmarez

October XI
1973
Gouache
55 x 80 cm
Provenance: Waddington and Tooth Galleries, London; The Continental Bank, Christie's, London, 11 June 1992

Exhibited: *British Surrealism & Other Realities: The Sherwin Collection,* Museum of Modern Art (Mima), Middlesbrough, 23 May–17 August 2008

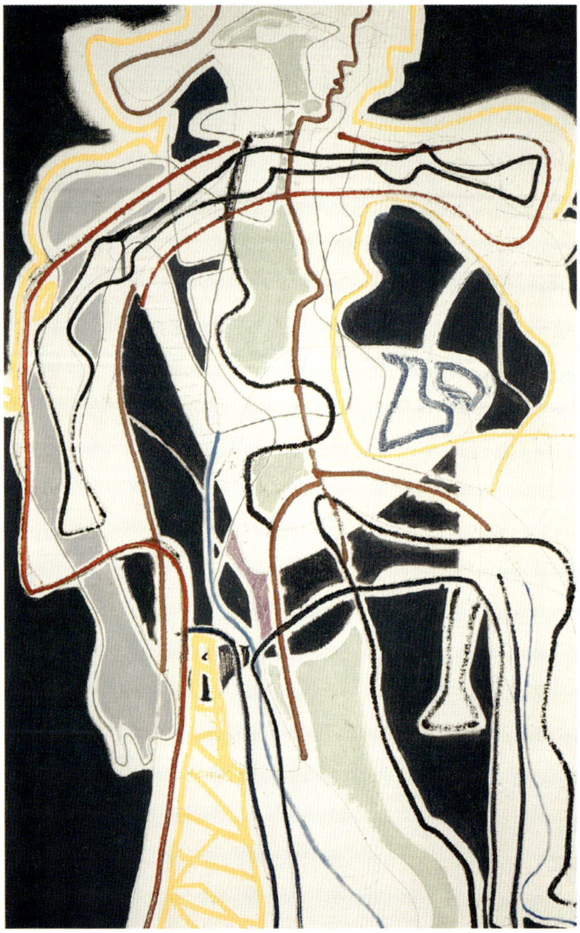

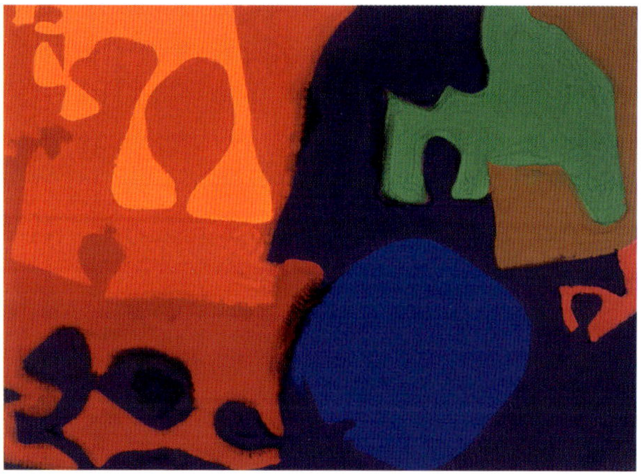

ROGER HILTON (1911–1975)

Hilton was born in Middlesex. He studied at the Slade School of Fine Art, London and also enjoyed a bohemian lifestyle in Paris during the 1930s. Hilton joined the army in 1939 and spent the years of 1942 to 1945 as a prisoner of war. He began painting in an abstract style in the early 1950s. From 1957, Hilton spent an increasing proportion of his time in St. Ives in Cornwall, settling there in 1965. During this period he moved away from abstraction and began to incorporate landscape and figurative motifs into his work.

June, Sept. 53
1953
Oil on canvas
33 x 44 cm
Provenance: Bonham's, London, 12 March 2002,
Lot 110

Exhibited: *Blast to Frieze, British Art in the 20th Century,* Kunstmuseum Wolfsburg, 2002

Literature: *Blast to Frieze, British Art in the 20th Century,* exhibition catalogue, Kunstmuseum Wolfsburg/Hatje Cantz, 2002; *British Surrealism & Other Realities: The Sherwin Collection,* Museum of Modern Art (Mima), Middlesbrough, 2008

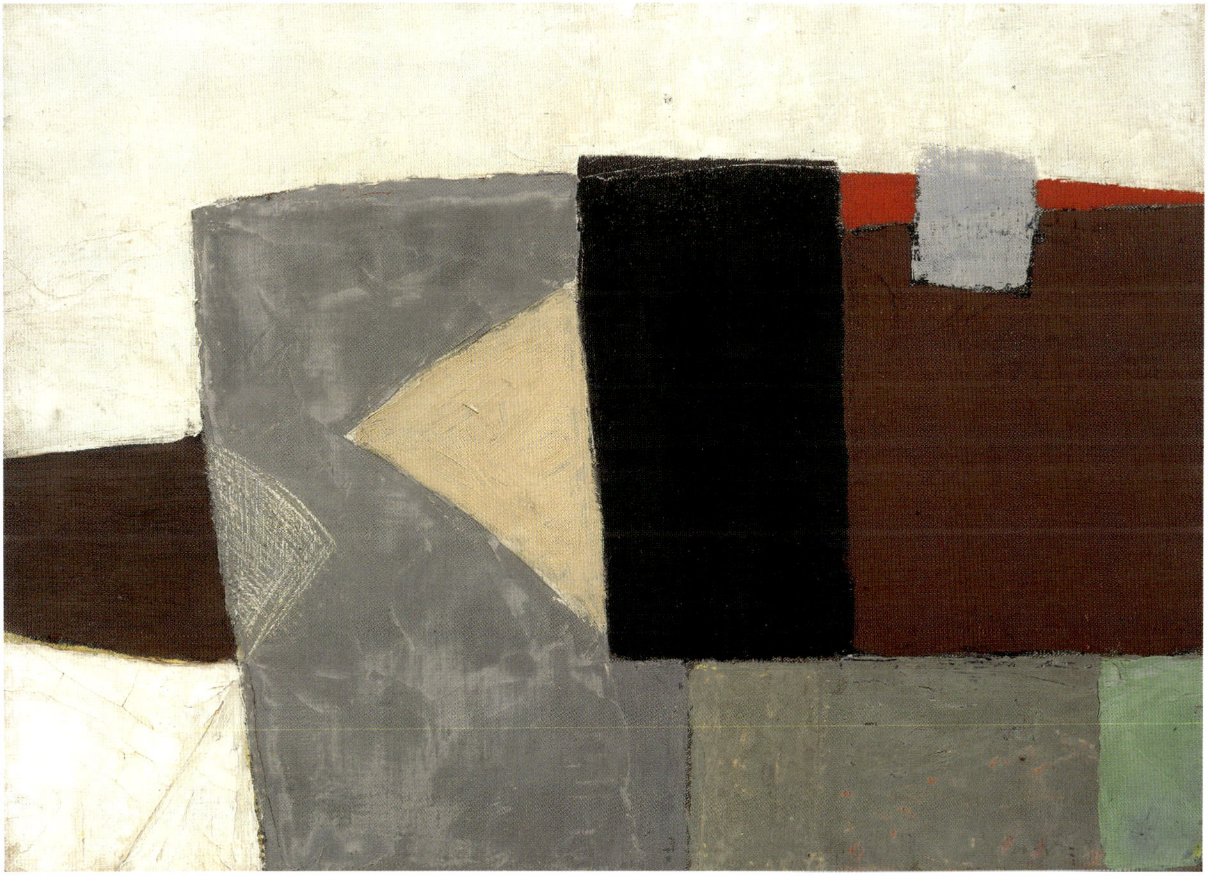

DAMIEN HIRST (born 1965)

Hirst was born in Bristol and grew up in Leeds, moving to London in 1986 to study at Goldsmith's College. While still a student, he organised the enormously successful *Freeze* exhibition, which featured his own work as well as that of fellow students. This brought him to the attention of the highly influential art collector Charles Saatchi, and is generally seen as the starting point for the 'Young British Artists' movement. The central theme of Hirst's work is mortality. He is best known for the 'Natural History' series of works, in which dead animals are preserved in tanks. He is also interested in medical paraphernalia and has produced series of spot paintings, spin paintings, and steel and glass cases.

On His Majesty's Service
1983–86
Collage
15 x 24.5 cm
Signed on edge of board
Provenance: the artist; 21st birthday present to James Rawlin; Phillips, London

Exhibited: *British Surrealism & Other Realities: The Sherwin Collection*, Museum of Modern Art (Mima), Middlesbrough, 23 May–17 August 2008

Statement from the vendor, via Phillips: 'This collage was given to me as a 21st birthday present back in '86. The paper used on it was taken from our next door neighbour's house, Mr Barnes. We had previously kicked his door in thinking, as he was an old man who hadn't been seen in weeks, he may be dead in there. Instead we stepped into another world, one of a deranged ex-policeman who'd stockpiled objects over 50 years. These pieces bleached (sic) in history gave Damien a lot of ideas and inspired a great body of work... His artist of the moment was Kurt Schwitters and his influence is clear. The frame I believe was stolen from the Royal Albert Hall, maybe from a skip, maybe off the wall.'

The Last Supper
Screen print
152.5 x 101.5 cm
43/150
Provenance: Phillips, London, 14 November 2008

Exhibited: *British Surrealism & Other Realities: The Sherwin Collection*, Museum of Modern Art (Mima), Middlesbrough, 23 May–17 August 2008

The *Last Supper* is a suite of 13 screenprints which mimic the graphic design of medicinal industry packaging, using colours reminiscent of Hirst's ongoing Spot Painting series and inspired by commercial drug firm product catalogues. Lisinopril was the tablet prescribed to Dr. Sherwin for his blood pressure. In addition to the product number and dosage information, each typographically individual print has the drug name substituted for pedestrian British foods such as Beans, Chips, Steak and Kidney, and Chicken and Dumpling.

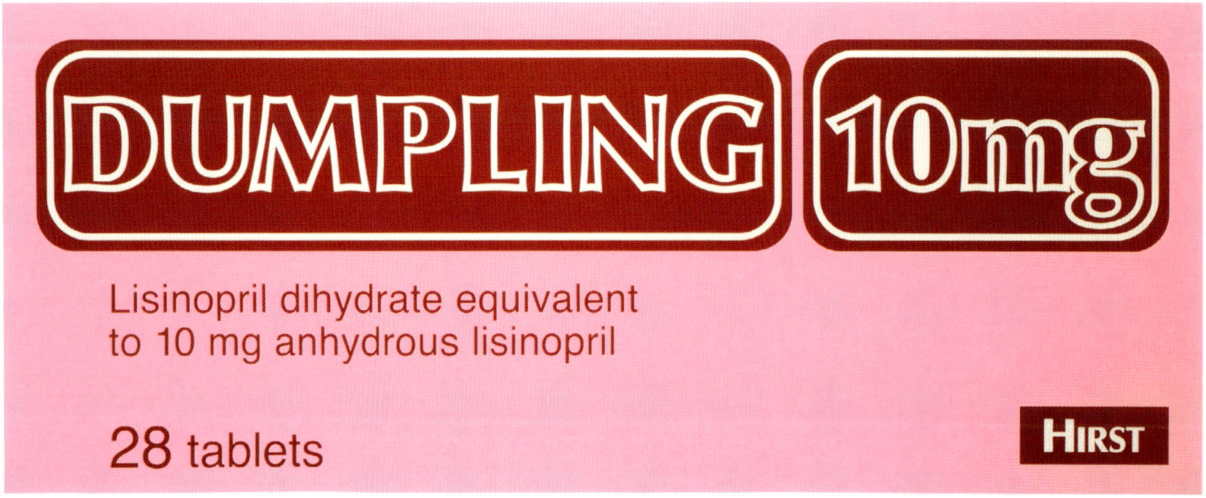

JOHN HOSKIN (1921–1990)

Hoskin trained as an architectural draughtsman, before starting to paint and sculpt in 1951. He soon realised that sculpture was the only way forward and, after a brief period working in Lynn Chadwick's studio, he found his own individual style. Most of his sculptures are unique and constructed out of welded mild steel. From the early 1950s to 1961, animals and figures were his preferred subjects.

Monolith
Welded steel
Height: 42 cm
Provenance: bought from the artist by Henry Cliffe in late 1950s–60 when both were teaching at the same college; Phillips, London, 25 March 1997

Exhibited: *British Surrealism & Other Realities: The Sherwin Collection*, Museum of Modern Art (Mima), Middlesbrough, 23 May–17 August 2008

Tripod
Welded steel
14 x 10 cm
Provenance: bought from the artist by Henry Cliffe in late 1950s–60 when both were teaching at the same college; Phillips, London

Exhibited: *British Surrealism & Other Realities: The Sherwin Collection*, Museum of Modern Art (Mima), Middlesbrough, 23 May–17 August 2008

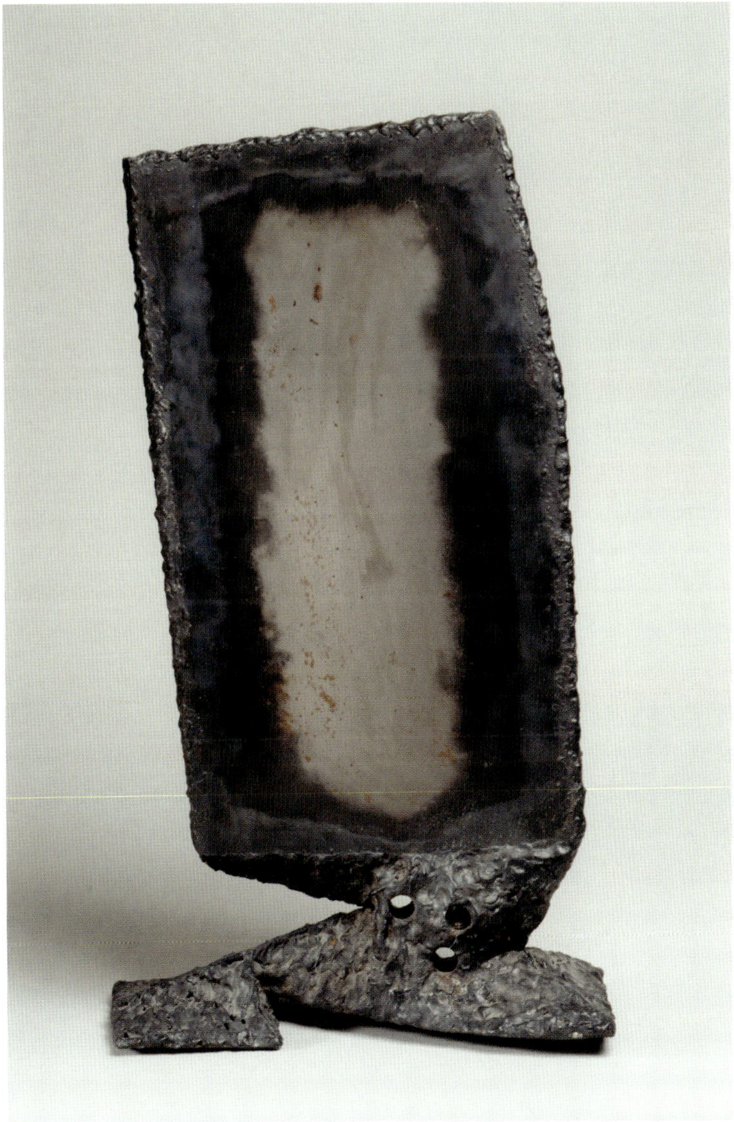

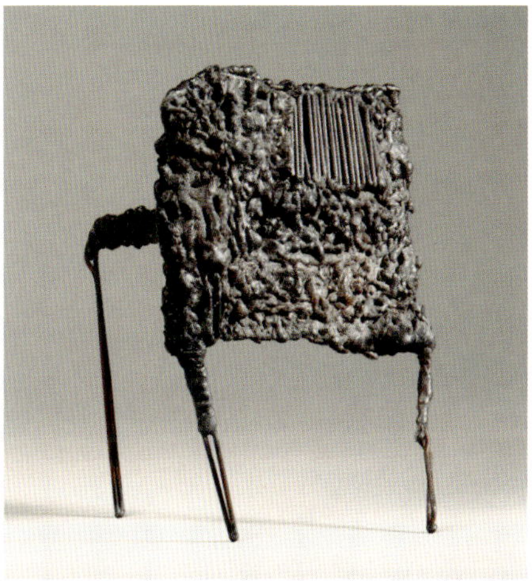

PATRICK HUGHES (born 1939)

Hughes was born in Birmingham in 1939. He trained to be a teacher in Leeds from 1959–61 and taught in schools and at Leeds College of Art. Like many young artists and poets of his generation, Hughes was inspired by the work of the European surrealists. The 1950s and early 1960s saw a revival of interest in surrealist art, film and literature, which became widely available for the first time. Hughes admired Paul Klee for his subversive wit, underlying geometry and experimental drawing, and also Rene Magritte, for his exploration of the pictorial paradox – his way of laying bare the process of perception. The famous rainbow is taken through a series of permutations that contradict its nature. The cipher of prismatic light becomes a solid, casts a shadow, appears at night, enters rooms, but its associations are so fixed that it retains its value as a signifier. Over one million of the rainbow cards were sold during the 1970s, integrating seamlessly into popular culture.

Rainbow Present
c.1960
Construction
50 x 62 cm

Exhibited: *British Surrealism & Other Realities: The Sherwin Collection*, Museum of Modern Art (Mima), Middlesbrough, 23 May–17 August 2008

Fear Itself (below)
c.1960
32 x 32 cm
Gouache on paper

Exhibited: *British Surrealism & Other Realities: The Sherwin Collection*, Museum of Modern Art (Mima), Middlesbrough, 23 May–17 August 2008

Weather Cock
1979
Screenprint
74 x 55 cm

Exhibited: *British Surrealism & Other Realities: The Sherwin Collection*, Museum of Modern Art (Mima), Middlesbrough, 23 May–17 August 2008

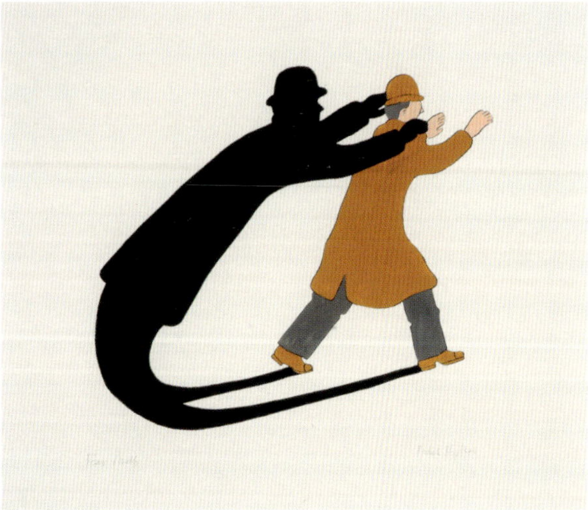

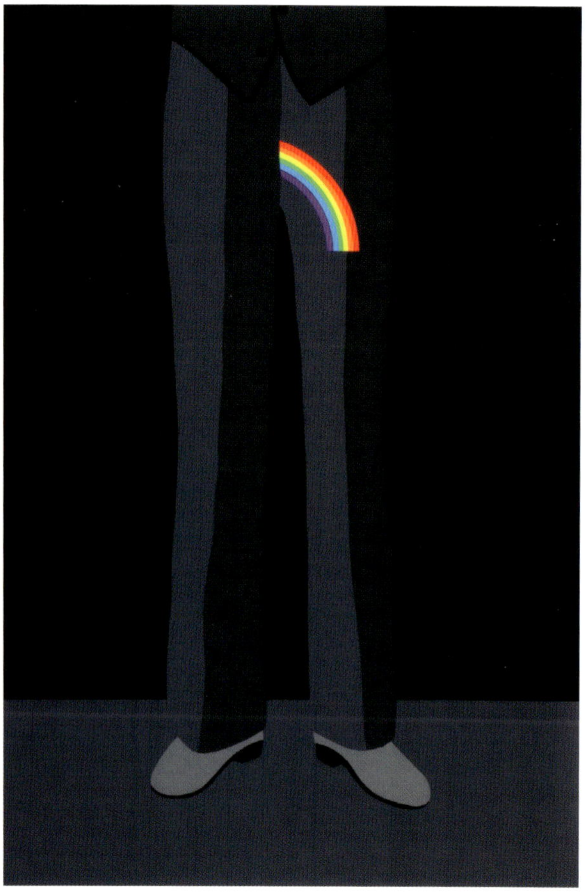

HUMPHREY JENNINGS (1907–1950)

Jennings became widely acclaimed as an imaginative filmmaker, but in the 1930s it was his paintings and writings that were important in establishing the early reputation of the British Surrealist Group. He admired Magritte and studied the techniques by Marcel Duchamp and Max Ernst. In 1936 he was a leading modernist and organised the International Surrealist Exhibition in London, along with Herbert Read, Roland Penrose and André Breton. Jennings was also involved in another kind of documentary project: the founding of Mass Observation in 1937–38 to study the anthropology of the British. Subjects ranged from the abdication crisis and the rise of Hitler, to the aspidistra cult and gestures of motorists. Humphrey Jennings, Julian Trevelyan and Humphrey Spender, among others, investigated the population of Bolton and London and recorded their findings in all media.

Commode with Swiss Roll
1936
Photograph with collage
21.5 x 25.5 cm
Provenance: Jonathan Blond Fine Art, London; Galerie 1900/2000, Paris

Exhibited: *Blast to Frieze, British Art in the 20th Century,* Kunstmuseum Wolfsburg, 2002

Literature: *Blast to Frieze, British Art in the 20th Century,* exhibition catalogue, Kunstmuseum Wolfsburg/Hatje Cantz, 2002, plate 59, colour illustration; *British Surrealism & Other Realities: The Sherwin Collection,* Museum of Modern Art (Mima), Middlesbrough, 2008

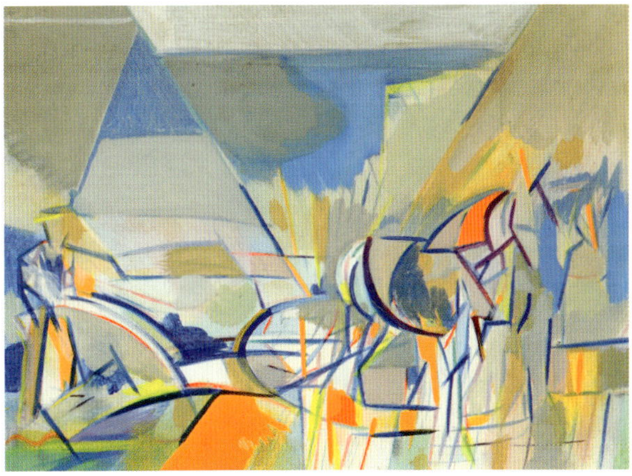

Trees with a Rainbow Stripe
c.1935
Photograph with collage
16 x 24 cm
Provenance: Jonathan Blond Fine Art, London; Galerie 1900/2000, Paris

Exhibited: *British Surrealism & Other Realities: The Sherwin Collection,* Museum of Modern Art (Mima), Middlesbrough, 23 May–17 August 2008

Hospice de La Bernina
With Etagere and Art Nouveau Pot
1935
Photograph and collage
19 x 25 cm
Provenance: Jonathan Blond Fine Art, London; Galerie 1900/2000, Paris

Exhibited: *British Surrealism & Other Realities: The Sherwin Collection,* Museum of Modern Art (Mima), Middlesbrough, 23 May–17 August 2008

Concealed House by the Water
1938
27.6 x 35.2 cm
Signed and dated
Provenance: Christie's, London

Exhibited: *British Surrealism & Other Realities: The Sherwin Collection,* Museum of Modern Art (Mima), Middlesbrough, 23 May–17 August 2008

Plough and Team
c.1948
Studio stamp
28 x 38 cm
Provenance: Christie's, London

Exhibited: *British Surrealism & Other Realities: The Sherwin Collection,* Museum of Modern Art (Mima), Middlesbrough, 23 May–17 August 2008

Smoke
c.1949
No. 2 Studio Stamp
35.6 x 45.7 cm
Provenance: Christie's, London

Exhibited: *British Surrealism & Other Realities: The Sherwin Collection,* Museum of Modern Art (Mima), Middlesbrough, 23 May–17 August 2008

MICHAEL KIDNER (born 1917)

A pioneer of Optical Art, Kidner has devoted much of his career to developing work of a constructive nature. After brushes with American Abstract Expressionism and Bauhaus ideas, he began to develop his own distinctive style. His interests in mathematics, science and the theories of chaos have informed an art that is at once rational and playful.

Red
1961
Perspex abstract
38 x 48 cm
Provenance: the artist

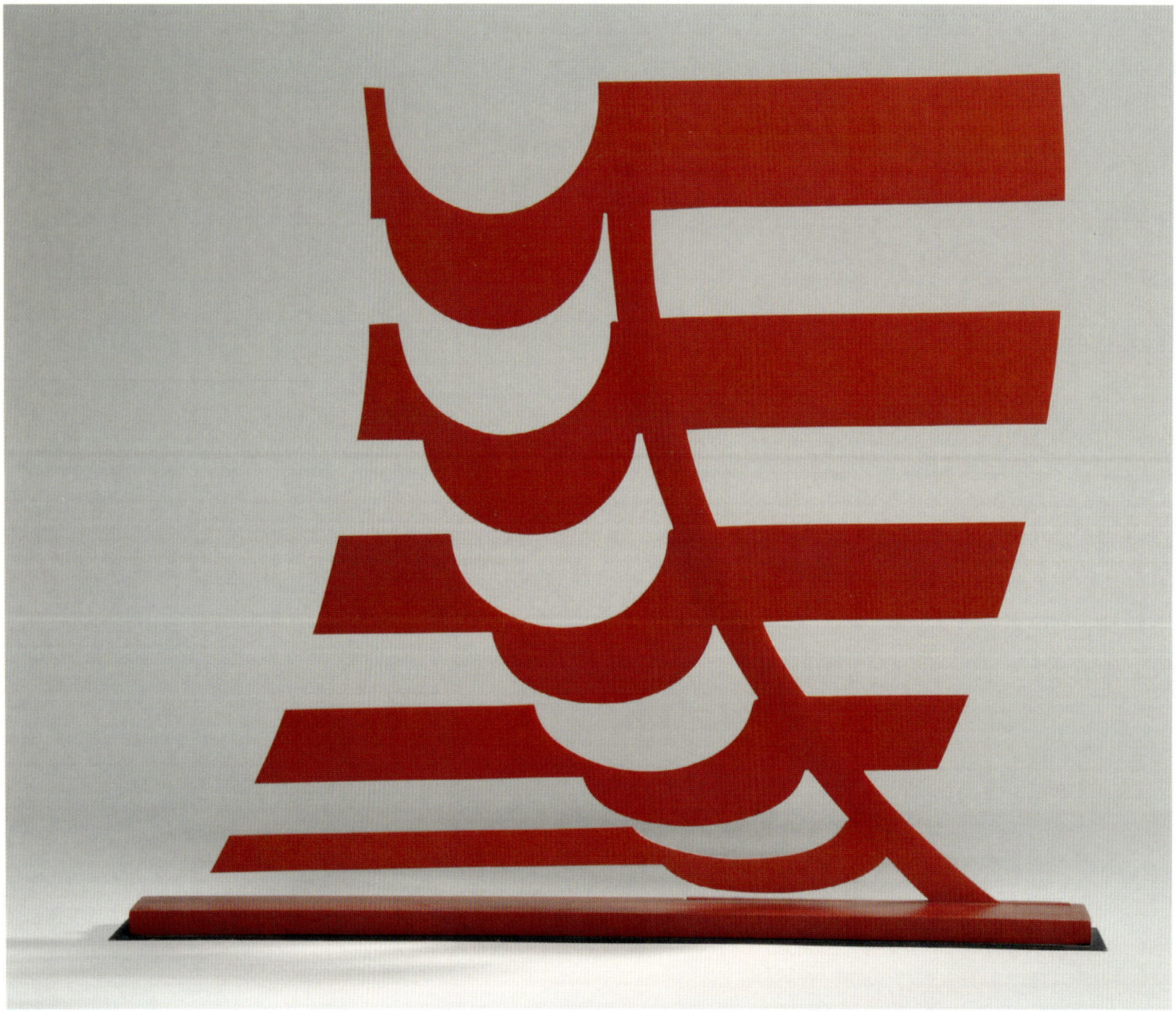

BRYAN KNEALE (born 1930)

In 1948, Kneale won the Rome Prize, and spent his time travelling in Italy where he was greatly influenced by the work of the Futurists and metaphysical painters. His early ambition was to be a painter, and on returning to London in 1951 he started to paint using palette knives as a method of 'constructing' with paint. In 1960, having learnt welding techniques, he turned to three dimensions and held his first exhibition of sculpture. An overriding characteristic in his work is an emphasis on linkages: the way in which separate forms are conjoined. Skeletons and joints of animals were explored through drawing and construction in metal. He prefers to work directly in metal rather than modelling in an intermediary material before casting.

Opposed Forms
1950s
Bronze, iron and slate
Height: 41 cm
Provenance: Sotheby's, London, 8 March 1995

Exhibited: Redfern Gallery, London, 1962

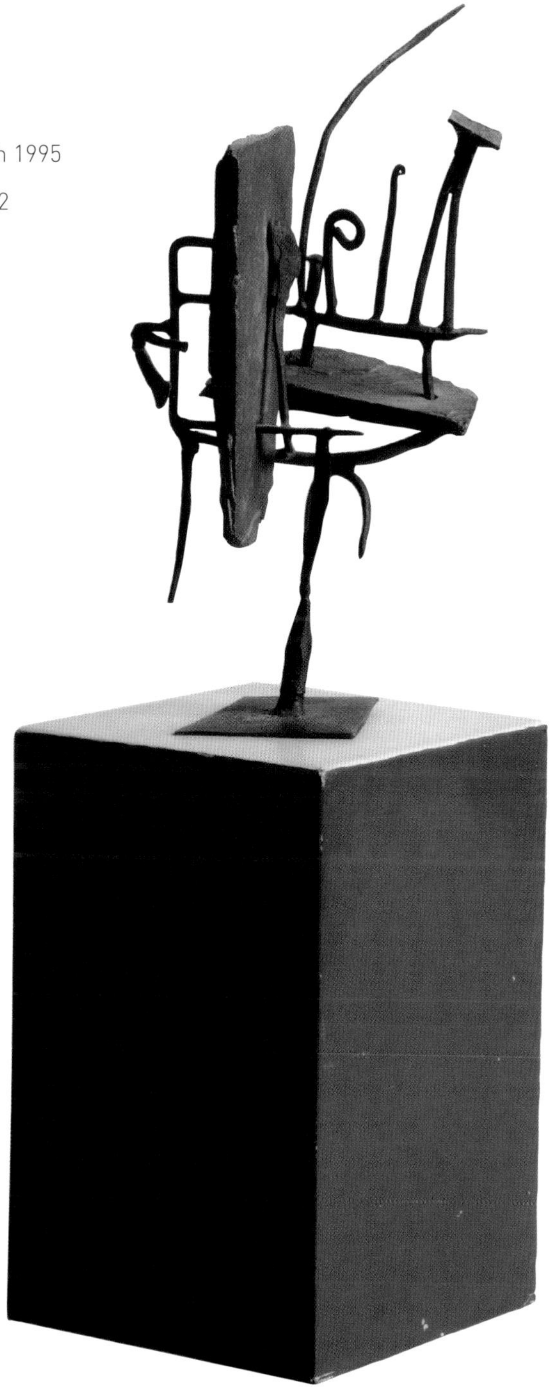

LEON KOSSOFF (born 1926)

For Kossoff, drawing is a necessary prelude to painting and all the drawings are working ideas, enabling him to move into the painting and bring the presence of the motif or subject into the studio. In the late 1980s, he began printmaking, bringing the plates to the National Gallery, and drawing on them directly in front of the paintings. During this time, he also drew and made prints at the exhibitions at the Royal Academy devoted to the art of Venice, Poussin, early Cézanne, and Goya.

The Lamentation Over the Dead Christ
(After Poussin)
Pencil on paper
45.7 x 57.2 cm
Provenance: Bonham's, London

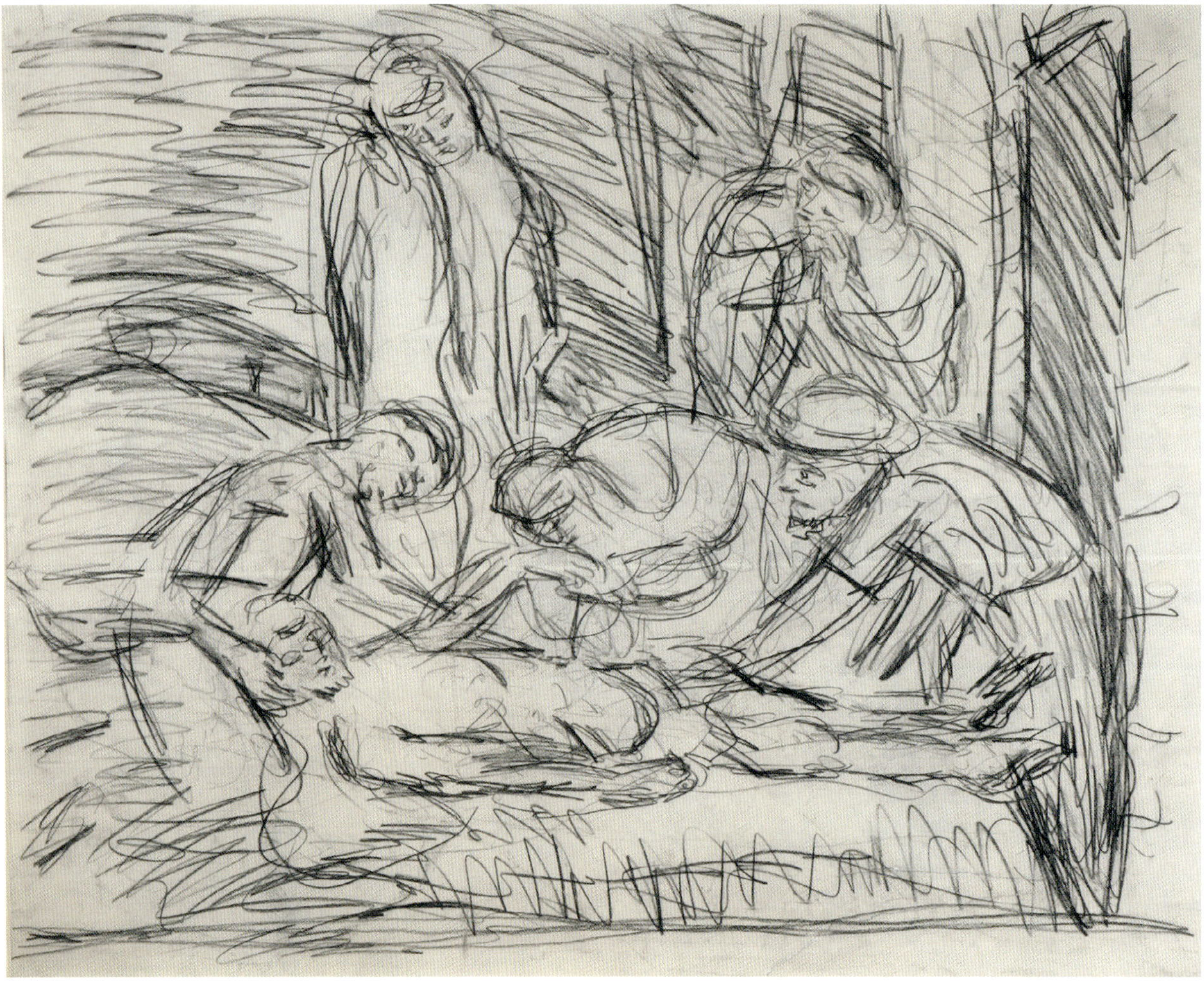

JACOB KRAMER (1892–1962)

Kramer's first formal art education was at Leeds School of Art, which he attended from 1907 until 1913. During this time he was also to become involved in the radical modernist organisation, The Leeds Art Club, which introduced him to the ideas of expressionist artists such as Wassily Kandinsky. Kramer stated that when he looked at an object he saw both its physical appearance and its spiritual manifestation. His struggle, he claimed, was to escape the physical appearance and only paint the spiritual form. Kramer was a friend of both David Bomberg and William Roberts.

The Philosopher
1922
Lithograph
46 x 31 cm
Provenance: Chester, Cheshire, 4 March 1999, Lot 580

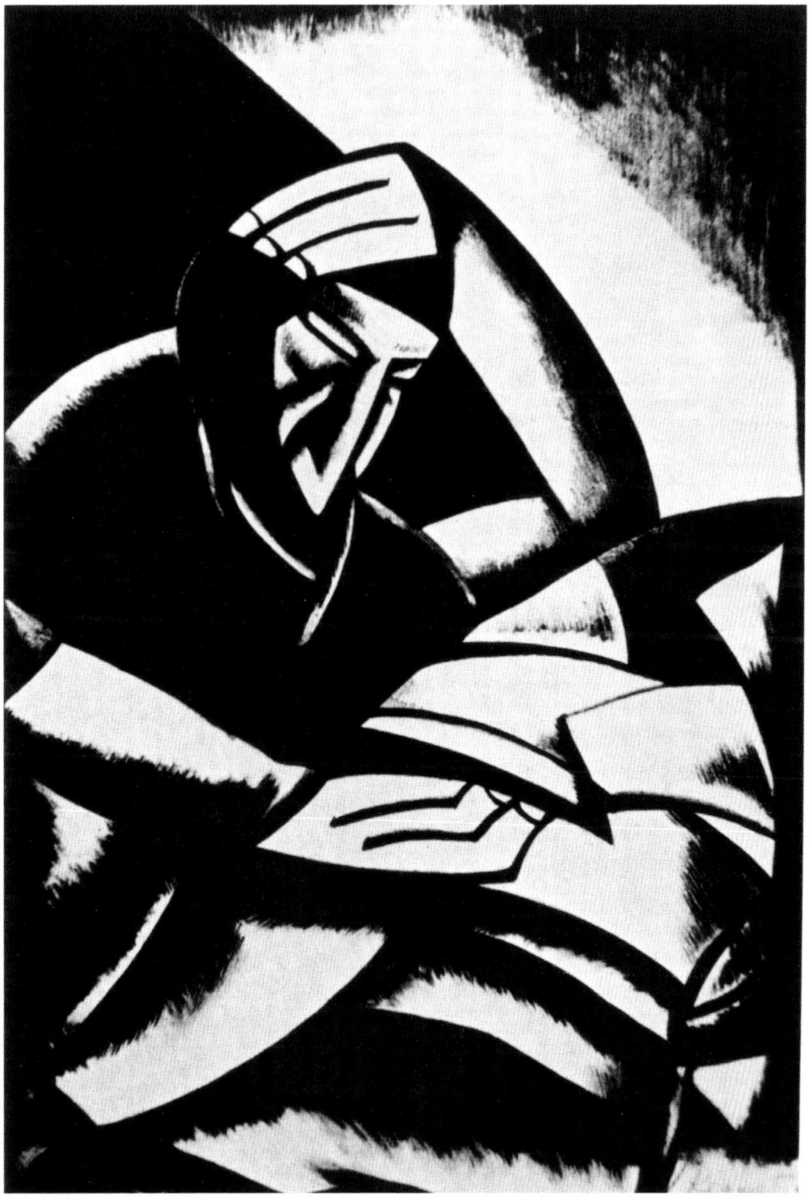

MAURICE LAMBERT (1901–1964)

Maurice Lambert's work is highly eclectic. He drew inspiration from the primitive, and the art of other cultures, experimented with materials and investigated form and movement. The dominant theme in his work is the human or animal form in motion. He pursues the potential of the family group as well as the single figure, thus enabling him to explore the range of tensions and harmonies in the relationship between forms.

Woman Lifting Child (also known as Woman with Child on her Shoulders)
c.1934
Terracotta with stone base
Height: 41 cm (excluding base)
Inscribed: ML
Provenance: Phillips, London, 2 March 1999, Lot 103

Exhibited: Maurice Lambert, Alex Reid and Lefevre Ltd, London, 1934

Literature: Maurice Lambert, exhibition catalogue, London, Alex Reid and Lefevre Ltd, 1934, no. 8; Vanessa Nicolson, *The Sculpture of Maurice Lambert,* The Henry Moore Foundation/Lund Humphries, 2002, plate 4 (cat. 126), illustration

Brother and Sister
c.1935
Bronze with marble base
Height: 63 cm (including base)
Provenance: Fine Art Society, London

Exhibited: *Sculpture in Britain between the Wars,* The Fine Art Society, London, 1986

Literature: *Sculpture in Britain between the Wars,* exhibition catalogue, London, The Fine Art Society, 1986, no. 69, illustration; Vanessa Nicolson, *The Sculpture of Maurice Lambert,* The Henry Moore Foundation/Lund Humphries, 2002, plate 5 (cat. 143), illustration

Kneeling Torso
1927
Alabaster
Height: 47.5 cm (56 cm including base)
Provenance: Sotheby's, London, 6 December 2000, Lot 111, illustration; Offer Waterman & Co., London

Exhibited: *Exhibition of Sculpture by Maurice Lambert,* The Claridge Gallery, London, 1927; Fine Art Society, London, 2000; *Shine: Sculpture and Surface in the 1920s and 1930s,* Leeds Art Gallery, Leeds, 2002

Literature: *Exhibition of Sculpture by Maurice Lambert,* The Claridge Gallery, London, 1927, no. 3; P.G. Konody, *The Art of Maurice Lambert,* Artwork, Vol. III, 1927, pp.190–193, p.191; London, Fine Art Society, 2000, no. 59, illustration; Vanessa Nicolson, *The Sculpture of Maurice Lambert,* The Henry Moore Foundation/Lund Humphries, 2002, cat. 29, p.47, illustration p.35 (plate 3); *Shine: Sculpture and Surface in the 1920s and 1930s,* in: *Henry Moore Institute, Essays on Sculpture,* no. 36, Leeds, Henry Moore Institute, 2002, p.15–16

Lambert's *Kneeling Torso* is a strange work. It is at the same time sexual and sexless, a female torso or a phallus. It is reminiscent of Brancusi's *Princesse X* of 1916, which can similarly be read as a phallus or as a female head, neck and breasts. Although the sexual ambivalence is visible in Lambert's work, the human form is dominant: the material evokes flesh, the legs remain strong and the torso seems to kneel. The sculpture in itself is complete, not fragmentary, and polished off to achieve a finished effect. The *Kneeling Torso* was mentioned by several newspapers, which reviewed his 1927 exhibition at the Claridge Gallery, London, in relation to the sculptor's use of material.

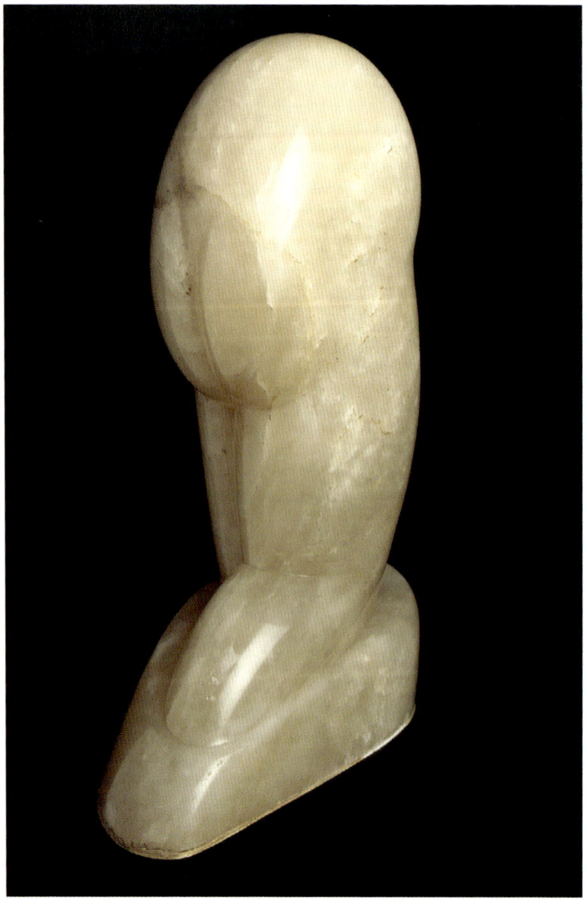

ROY LICHTENSTEIN (1923–1997)

Roy Lichtenstein was the master of the stereotype, and the most sophisticated of the major pop artists in terms of his analysis of visual convention and his ironic exploitation of past styles. His development as a mature painter was marked by his propensity for working in successive series or thematic groups. The later groups tended to be interpretations and to some extent parodies of earlier Modernist styles – cubism, futurism and surrealism.

Sky and Fish
1967
31 x 36 cm
Lithograph and 3D Plexiglas
Provenance: gift to Roland Penrose; Mayor Gallery, London

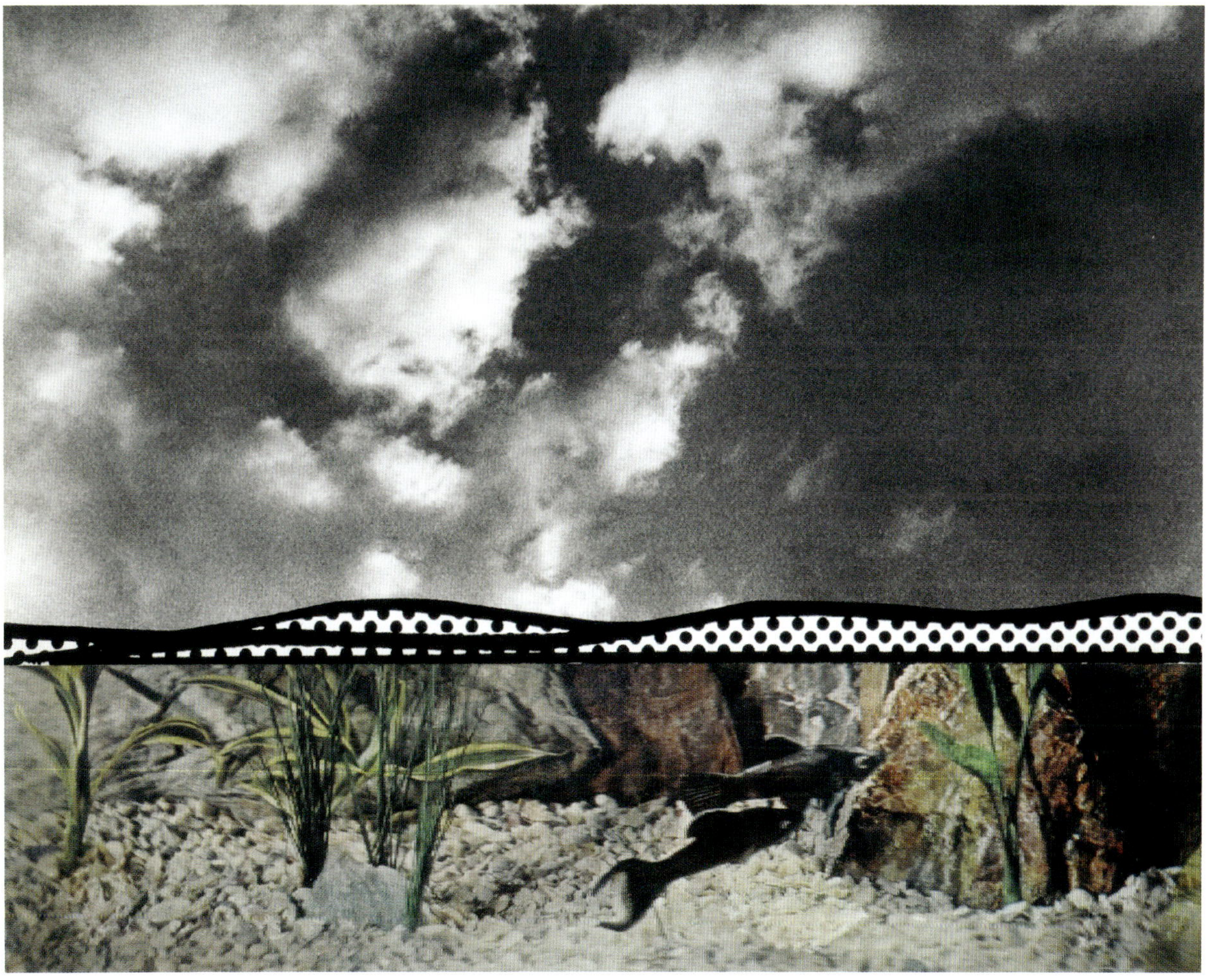

DAVID MACH (born 1956)

Mach made a dramatic debut into the world of public sculpture in 1983, when he constructed the submarine Polaris out of thousands of tyres on the South Bank of the Thames. Other projects include the *Big Heids* on the M8 motorway between Glasgow and Edinburgh. Mach's strikingly-original sculptures and collages are created from found materials – coat hangers, postcards, matches, among others.

Head with Crossbow Arrows
Matches
Height: 46 cm
Provenance: commissioned by Jeffrey Sherwin

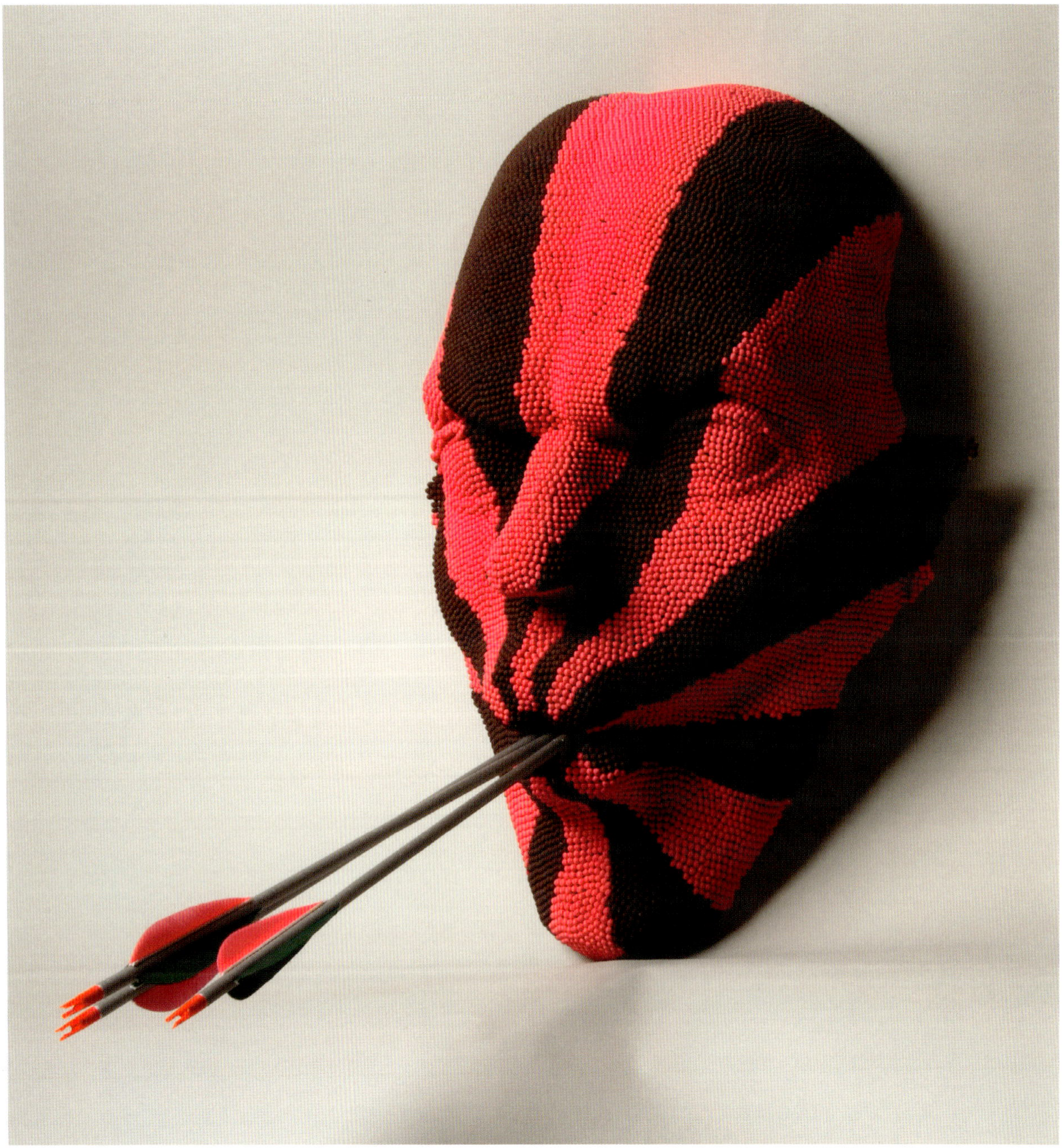

CONROY MADDOX (1912–2005)

Maddox, a member of the Birmingham Group, has been a consistent surrealist since the mid 1930s, producing paintings, objects and collages. In 1936, he refused an invitation to show work in the International Surrealist Exhibition in London, arguing that most of the artists chosen were, in fact, anti-surrealist. The following year he was introduced to the Paris Surrealist Group by Georges Hugnet. Maddox joined the short-lived English Surrealist Group in 1938. Much of his work is inspired by his antagonism towards religion. He employed a technique of deliberate misdating of some of his works, making them later or earlier than their date of production.

The Lesson
1938
Oil on canvas
80.5 x 70.2 cm
Signed
Provenance: Thomas Agnews and Sons, London

Exhibited: *La Peinture Surrealiste Anglaise 1930–1960, Les Enfants d'Alice,* Galerie 1900–2000, Paris, 14 May–30 June 1982; *Surrealism in Britain In The Thirties,* Leeds Art Gallery, 1986; *Conroy Maddox: Surreal Enigmas,* City Museum and Art Gallery, Stoke-on-Trent; Wolverhampton Art Gallery and Museum, Wolverhampton; Leeds City Art Gallery, Leeds, 1995; *Real Surreal, British and European Surrealism,* Wolverhampton Art Gallery and Museum, Wolverhampton, 17 June–19 August 1995; *Blast to Frieze, British Art in the 20th Century,* Kunstmuseum Wolfsburg, 2002

Literature: *Surrealism In Britain In The Thirties,* Leeds, Leeds Art Gallery, 1986, no. 94, illustration; Silvano Levi (ed.), *Conroy Maddox: Surreal Enigmas,* Keele University Press, 1995, p.66, colour illustration; *Blast to Frieze, British Art in the 20th Century,* exhibition catalogue, Kunstmuseum Wolfsburg/Hatje Cantz, 2002

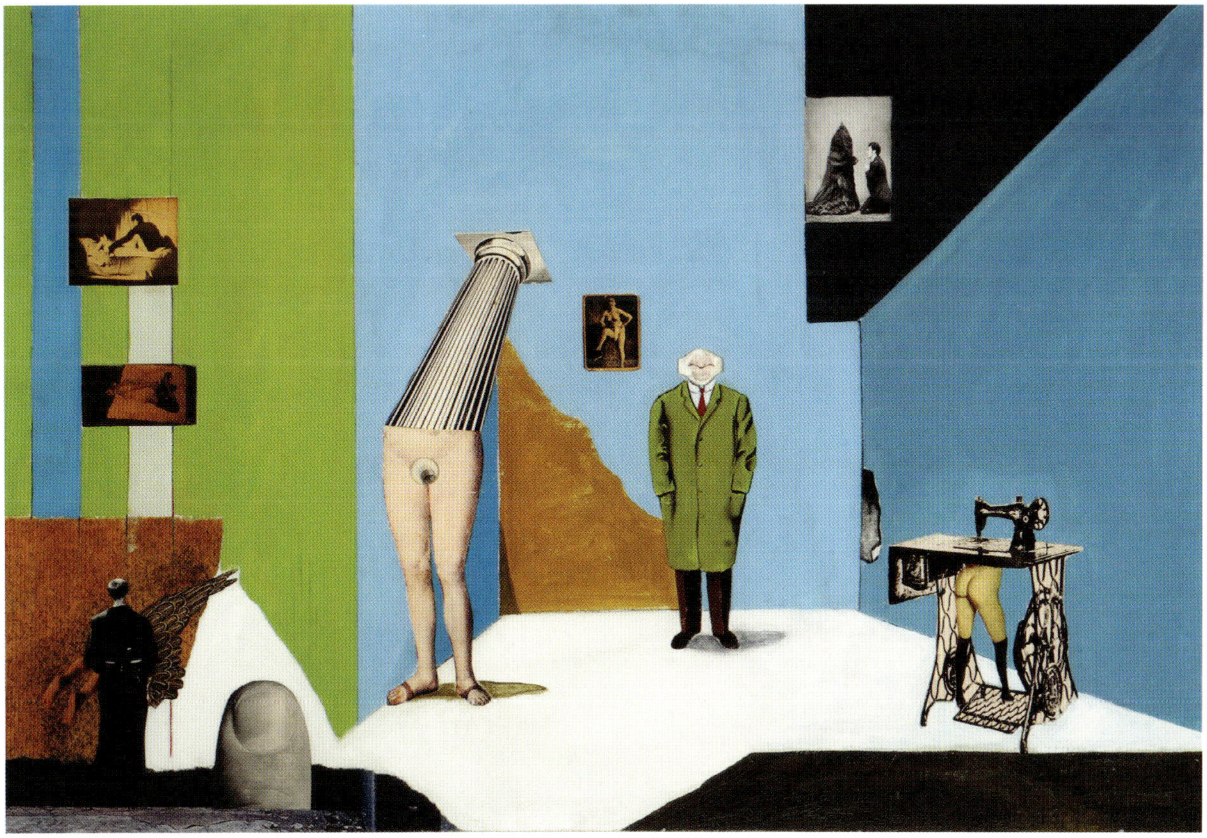

Landscape Of The Night
1939
Oil on canvas
51 x 76.5 cm
Provenance: the artist

Exhibited: *British Contribution to Surrealism,* Hamet Gallery, Leeds, 1986; *Conroy Maddox: Surreal Enigmas,* City Museum and Art Gallery, Stoke-on-Trent; Wolverhampton Art Gallery and Museum, Wolverhampton; Leeds City Art Gallery, Leeds, 1995; *El Surrealismo y la Guerra Civil Espanola,* Museum of Teruel, Teruel, Spain, 30 October–13 December 1998

Literature: Silvano Levi (ed.), *Conroy Maddox: Surreal Enigmas,* Keele University Press, 1995, p.64, illustration

The Night Watcher
1956
Collage and oil on board
30.5 x 44 cm
Provenance: the artist

Exhibited: *Conroy Maddox: Surreal Enigmas,* City Museum and Art Gallery, Stoke-on-Trent; Wolverhampton Art Gallery and Museum, Wolverhampton; Leeds City Art Gallery, Leeds, 1995

Literature: Silvano Levi (ed.), *Conroy Maddox: Surreal Enigmas,* Keele University Press, 1995, p.107, colour illustration

Reflections on Prince Vibescu (overleaf)
(from *The Debauched Hospodar* by Apollinaire, 1968)
1996
Oil with collage
53 x 81 cm
Provenance: Bonham's, London, 2 October 1994, Lot 101

Exhibited: *Conroy Maddox: Surreal Enigmas,* City Museum and Art Gallery, Stoke-on-Trent; Wolverhampton Art Gallery and Museum, Wolverhampton; Leeds City Art Gallery, Leeds, 1995

Literature: Silvano Levi (ed), *Conroy Maddox: Surreal Enigmas,* Keele University Press, 1995, p.119, colour illustration

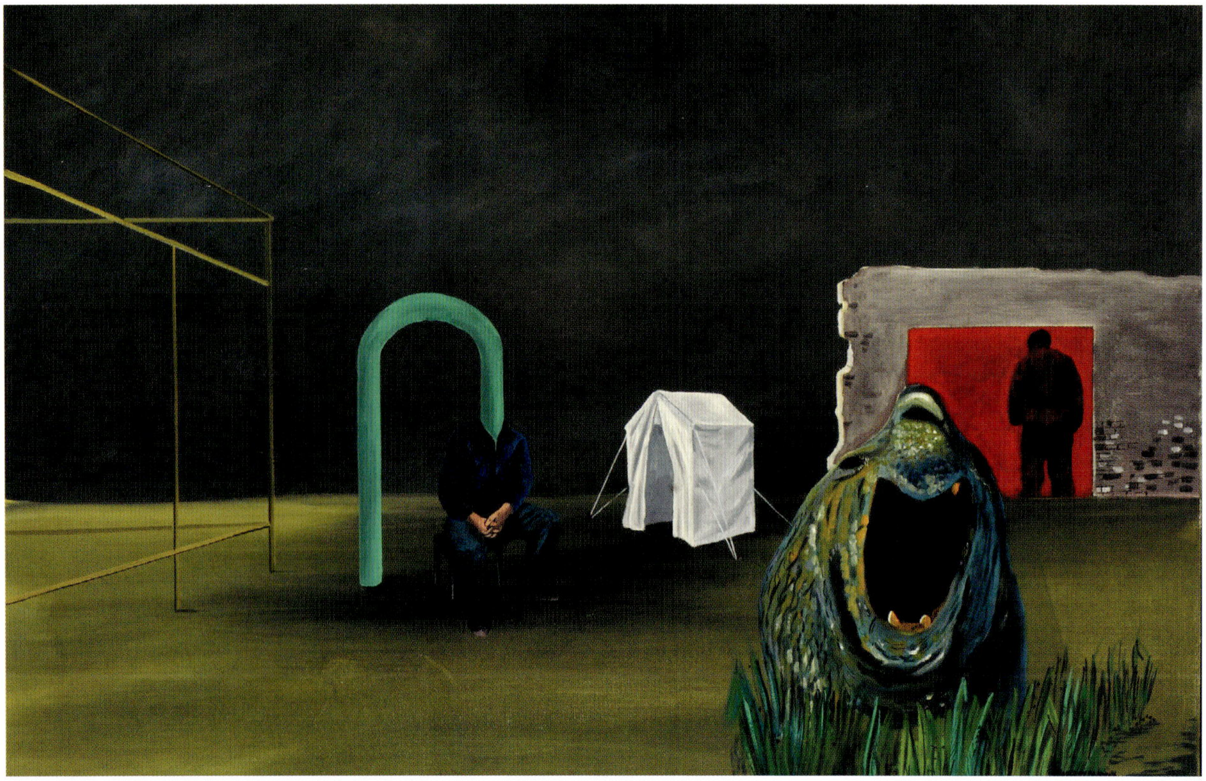

The Source (Male) (below right)
1968
Oil on board
24 x 16 cm

The Source (Female) (below left)
1971
Oil on canvas
61 x 45.75 cm
Provenance: the artist

Exhibited: *Conroy Maddox: Surreal Enigmas*, City Museum and Art Gallery, Stoke-on-Trent; Wolverhampton Art Gallery and Museum, Wolverhampton; Leeds City Art Gallery, Leeds, 1995

Literature: Silvano Levi (ed), *Conroy Maddox: Surreal Enigmas*, Keele University Press, 1995, p.74, colour illustration

You Are What You Eat (overleaf)
1981
Collage
27 x 30 cm
Provenance: the artist

Literature: Silvano Levi (ed.), *Conroy Maddox: Surreal Enigmas*, Keele University Press, 1995, p.107, colour illustration

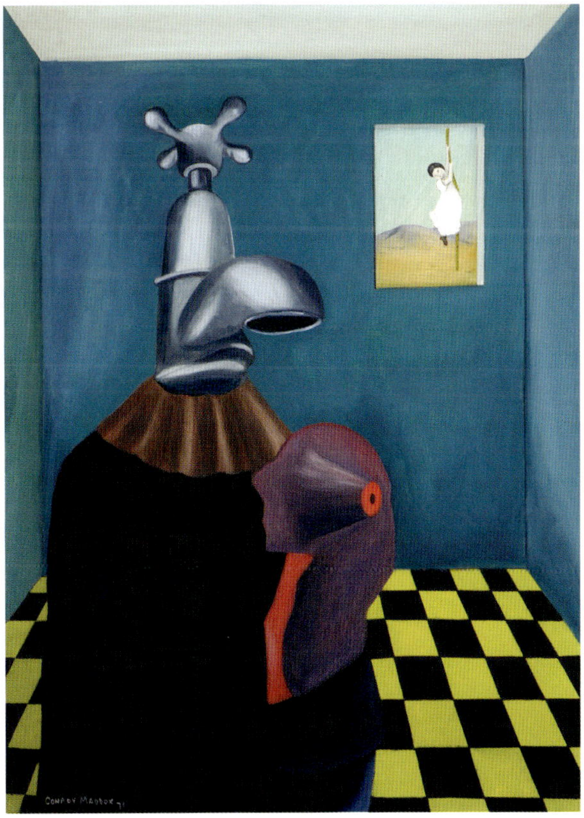

Gilles De Rais
1973
Collage
27 x 42 cm
Provenance: gift

Exhibited: *Conroy Maddox: Surreal Enigmas*, City Museum and Art Gallery, Stoke-on-Trent; Wolverhampton Art Gallery and Museum, Wolverhampton; Leeds City Art Gallery, Leeds, 1995

Literature: Silvano Levy (ed.), *Conroy Maddox: Surreal Enigmas*, Keele University Press, 1995, p.112, illustration

Gilles de Rais
1973
Pen and ink on paper
24 x 19 cm
Provenance: gift

Exhibited: *Conroy Maddox: Surreal Enigmas*, City Museum and Art Gallery, Stoke-on-Trent; Wolverhampton Art Gallery and Museum, Wolverhampton; Leeds City Art Gallery, Leeds, 1995

Literature: Silvano Levy (ed.), *Conroy Maddox: Surreal Enigmas*, Keele University Press, 1995, p.120, illustration

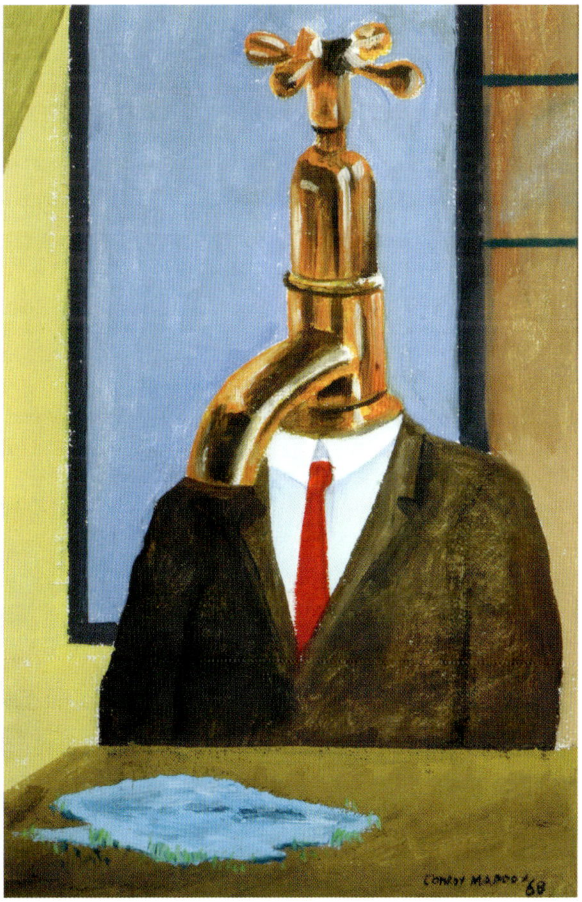

Denouément
1946
Object
6 x 33.5 x 24 cm (closed)
Inscribed: Conroy Maddox, titled on front edge of lid
Provenance: the artist

Exhibited: *A Salute to British Surrealism 1930–1950*, The Minories, Colchester, 6 April–5 May 1985; Blond Fine Art, London, 22 May–22 June 1985; Ferens Art Gallery, Hull, 6 July–4 August 1985; *Conroy Maddox: Surreal Enigmas*, City Museum and Art Gallery, Stoke-on-Trent; Wolverhampton Art Gallery and Museum, Wolverhampton; Leeds City Art Gallery, Leeds, 1995; Valencia

Literature: *A Salute to British Surrealism 1930–1950*, Colchester, The Minories, 1985, no. 44; Silvano Levy (ed.), *Conroy Maddox: Surreal Enigmas*, Keele University Press, 1995, p.128, illustration

A Secret Doll's House
1994
Object
23 x 47 x 17.5 cm
Provenance: the artist

Exhibited: *Conroy Maddox: Surreal Enigmas*, City Museum and Art Gallery, Stoke-on-Trent; Wolverhampton Art Gallery and Museum, Wolverhampton; Leeds City Art Gallery, Leeds, 1995

Literature: Silvano Levy (ed.), *Conroy Maddox: Surreal Enigmas*, Keele University Press, 1995, p.121, illustration

In The Shadow Of Fantomas
1990
Collage and oil on board
58 x 76 cm
Provenance: the artist

St. Lucy
1950
Object
20.5 x 20 x 7 cm
Provenance: the artist

Literature: Silvano Levi (ed.), *Conroy Maddox: Surreal Enigmas*, Keele University Press, 1995, p.25, illustration

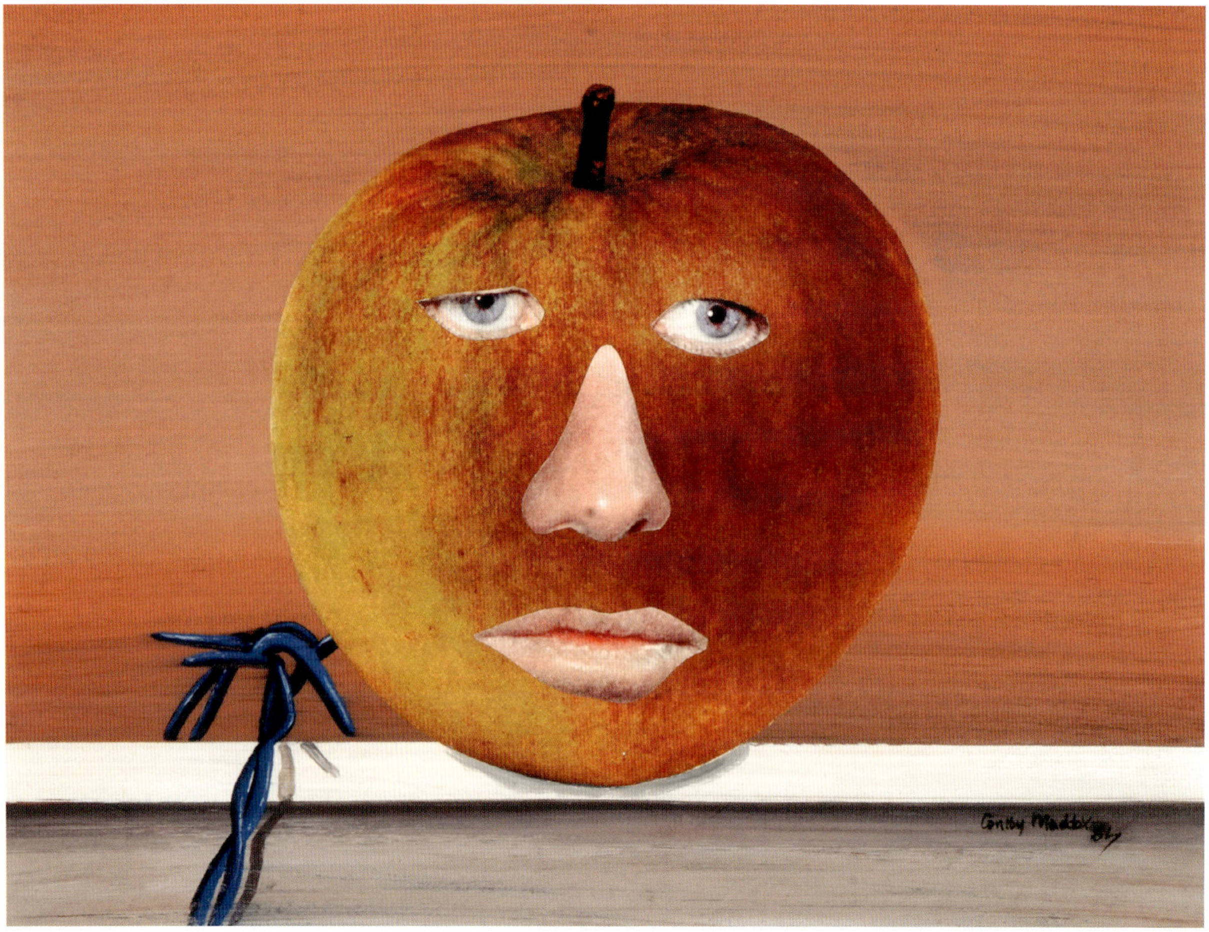

Guess Who?
1960
Object
38 x 26 x 9 cm
Provenance: the artist

Literature: Silvano Levi (ed.), *Conroy Maddox: Surreal Enigmas*, Keele University Press, 1995, p.103, colour illustration

The Playground of Saltpêtrière
1975
Oil on canvas
96.5 x 76 cm
Provenance: collection of Emscote Lawn School; Sotheby's, London, 27 November 2002, Lot 294

Literature: Silvano Levi (ed.), *Conroy Maddox: Surreal Enigmas*, Keele University Press, 1995, p.90 (collection of Emscote Lawn School)

More than any other subject of his works, the Saltpêtrière theme reveals the artist's inclination towards the disturbance of the spectator's state of mind. The work was inspired by the investigations into insanity carried out in the 19th century by Jean-Martin Charcot at the Parisian Saltpêtrière hospital. Charcot was responsible for novel ideas about mental illness and its treatment.

The Mischief Maker (below)
2000
Collage
38 x 48 cm

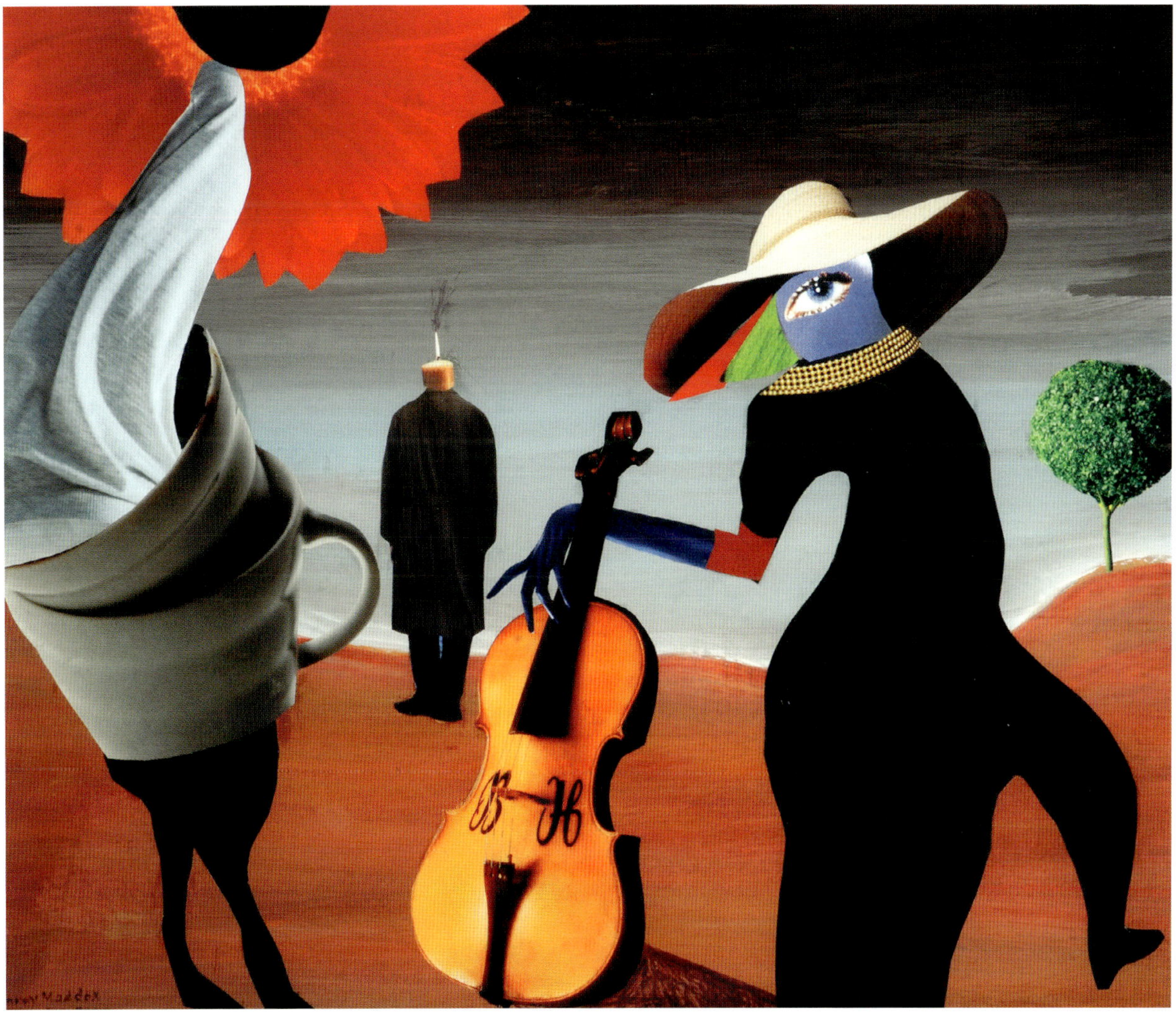

THE BIRMINGHAM SURREALISTS

The Birmingham Surrealists were an informal grouping of artists and intellectuals associated with the surrealist movement in art, based in Birmingham from the 1930s to the 1950s.The key figures were the artists Conroy Maddox and John Melville together with Melville's brother, Robert, an art critic. Other significant members included artists Emmy Bridgewater, Oscar Mellor and the young Desmond Morris.

In its early years the group distinguished itself from the London group and its vision-based vision of surrealism, epitomized by the English exhibitors at the *1936 London International Surrealist Exhibition*. The Birmingham group saw this approach as inauthentic or even anti-surrealist, preferring instead to build links directly with surrealism's French heartland.

As World War II approached, however, and the London-based British Surrealist Group fell under the influence of European exiles such as E.L.T. Mesens and Toni del Renzio, the ideological approaches of the two groups converged and they formed increasingly co-operative and overlapping parts of a wider international surrealist movement.

The major Birmingham surrealists were relatively unaffected by the onset of war: Maddox and the Melvilles all having reserved occupations in Birmingham's wartime industries, while Bridgewater escaped call-up as a woman. In contrast, surrealist activity in London virtually ceased with the closure of the London Gallery in 1939 and the *London Bulletin* in 1940, and the Birmingham group expended considerable energy in attempts to reinvigorate wider English surrealist activity.

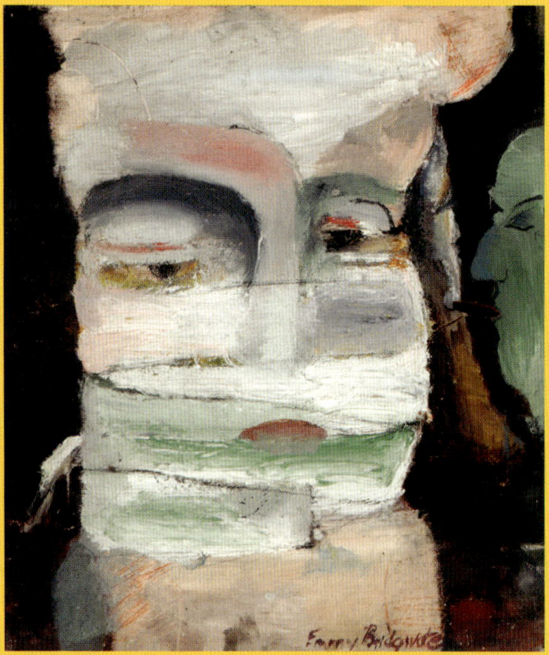

Necessary Bandages
Emmy Bridgewater, c.1942

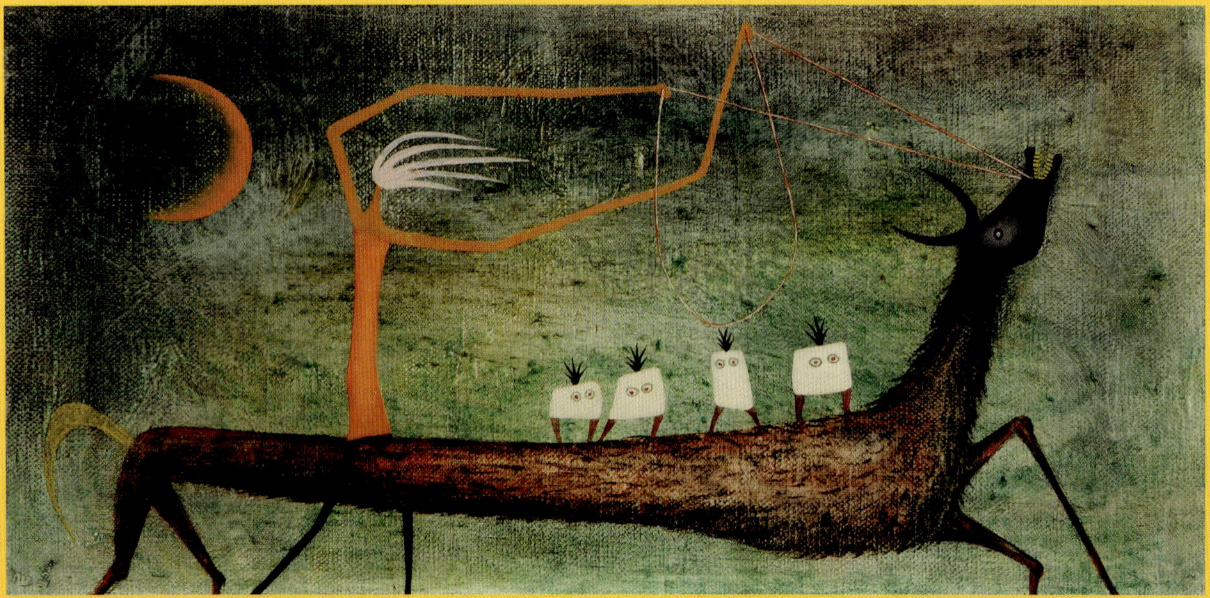

There's No Time Like the Future
Desmond Morris, 1957

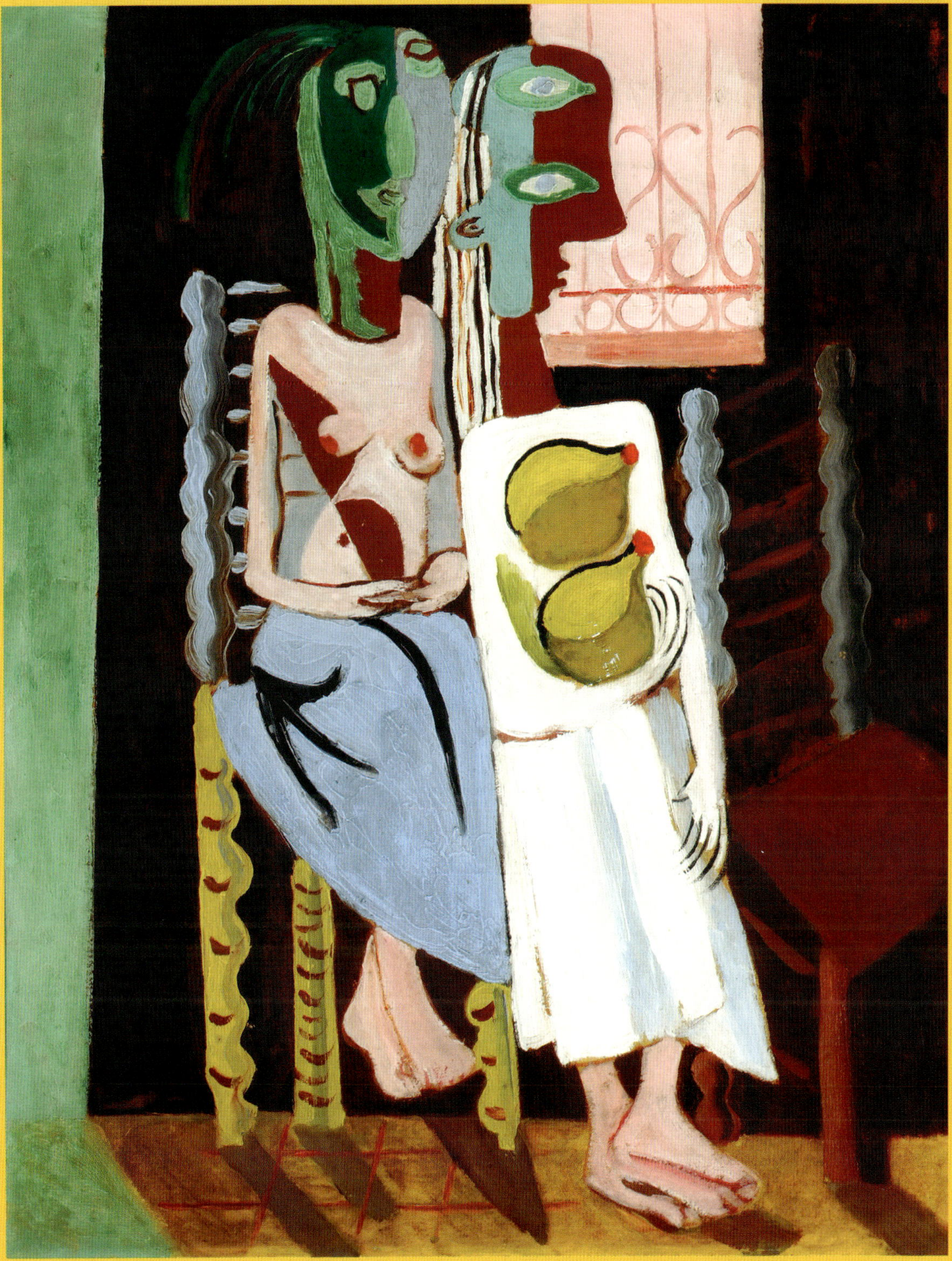

Chairs
John Melville, c.1934

RENE MAGRITTE (1898–1967)

Unlike many surrealists, Magritte did not subscribe to the view that the unconscious could be expressed through chance or 'automatic' techniques. Instead, he planned and executed his paintings with all the deliberation and skill of an academic painter. The results are surprisingly credible images of seemingly illogical scenes. Magritte would undermine logic by tampering with scale and by placing unrelated objects in unexpected settings. A constant theme running through his art is the relationship that exists between the painted image and the visible world, between fiction and reality.

Illustration For Vathek
1944
Gouache on paper
21 x 15.5 cm
Provenance: Christie's, London, 24 March 1992

Exhibited: *Real Surreal, British and European Surrealism,* Wolverhampton Art Gallery and Museum, Wolverhampton, 17 June–19 August 1995

Literature: *Catalogue Raisonné* by David Sylvester

In 1944, Magritte executed twelve drawings to illustrate the book *Vathek*, a Gothic novel written by William Thomas Beckford. The novel was composed in French in 1872 and then translated into English, in which form it was first published in 1786 (without Beckford's name) as An Arabian Tale, From an Unpublished Manuscript, claiming to be directly translated from Arabic.

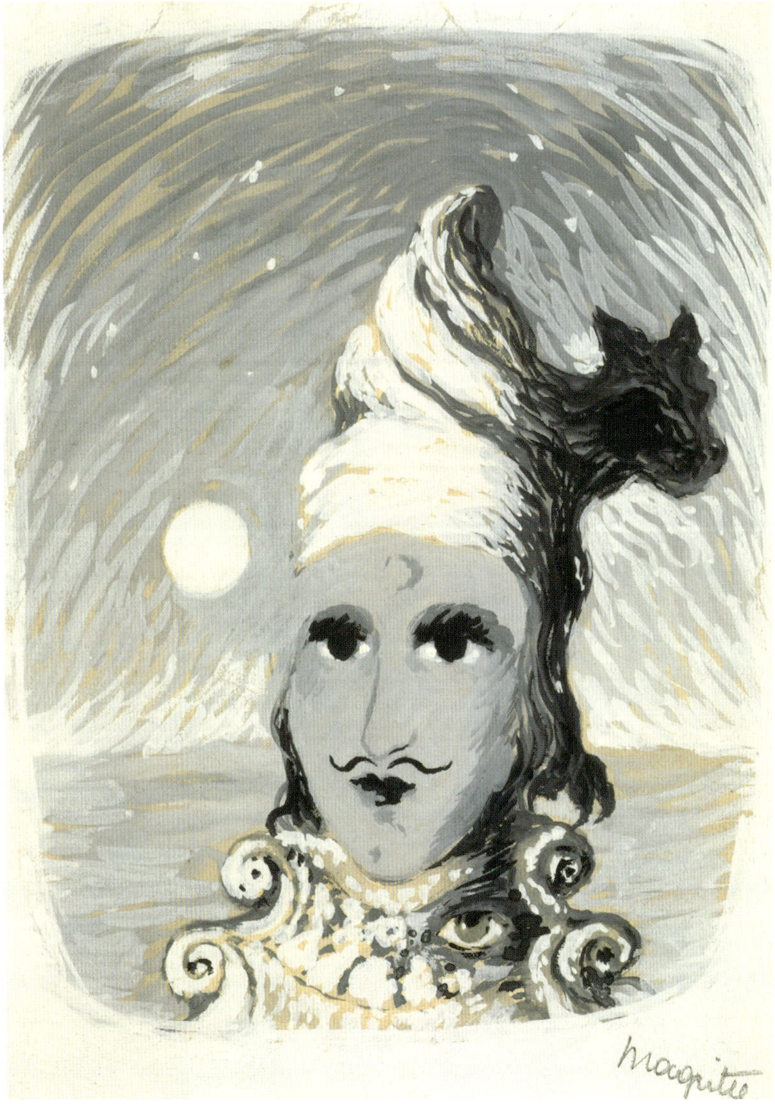

MARY MARTIN (1907–1999)

Mary Martin was an important member of the group of artists making constructed abstract art that formed around Victor Pasmore in 1951. She began as a painter, but her break into abstract art led her into real space, the constructed relief. Her use of modern sheet materials and proportional systems allied her work with modern architecture.

Expanding Form
1955
Perspex, stainless steel, wood, hardboard and asbestos
54.5 x 54.5 x 4.5 cm
Signed, dated and inscribed on reverse: Mary Martin *Expanding Form* 1955
Provenance: Adrian Flowers; Christie's, London

Exhibited: *Mary Martin – Kenneth Martin*, touring exhibition, Arts Council of Great Britain, London, 1970; *Mary Martin*, The Tate Gallery, London, 1984; *Mary Martin 1907–1969, The End is Always to Achieve Simplicity*, touring exhibition, Huddersfield Art Gallery, 16 October–18 December 2004; Kettle's Yard House and Art Gallery, Cambridge, 8 January–27 February 2005; Towner Art Gallery, Eastbourne, 12 March–8 May 2005; Russell-Cotes Art Gallery and Museum, Bournemouth, 25 June–11 September 2005

Literature: *Mary Martin – Kenneth Martin*, exhibition catalogue, London, Arts Council of Great Britain, 1970, no. 5; *Mary Martin*, exhibition catalogue, London, The Tate Gallery, 1984 (no. 10, illustration); *Mary Martin 1907–1969, The End is Always to Achieve Simplicity*, Huddersfield Art Gallery/Culture Company, 2004, p.54, colour illustration

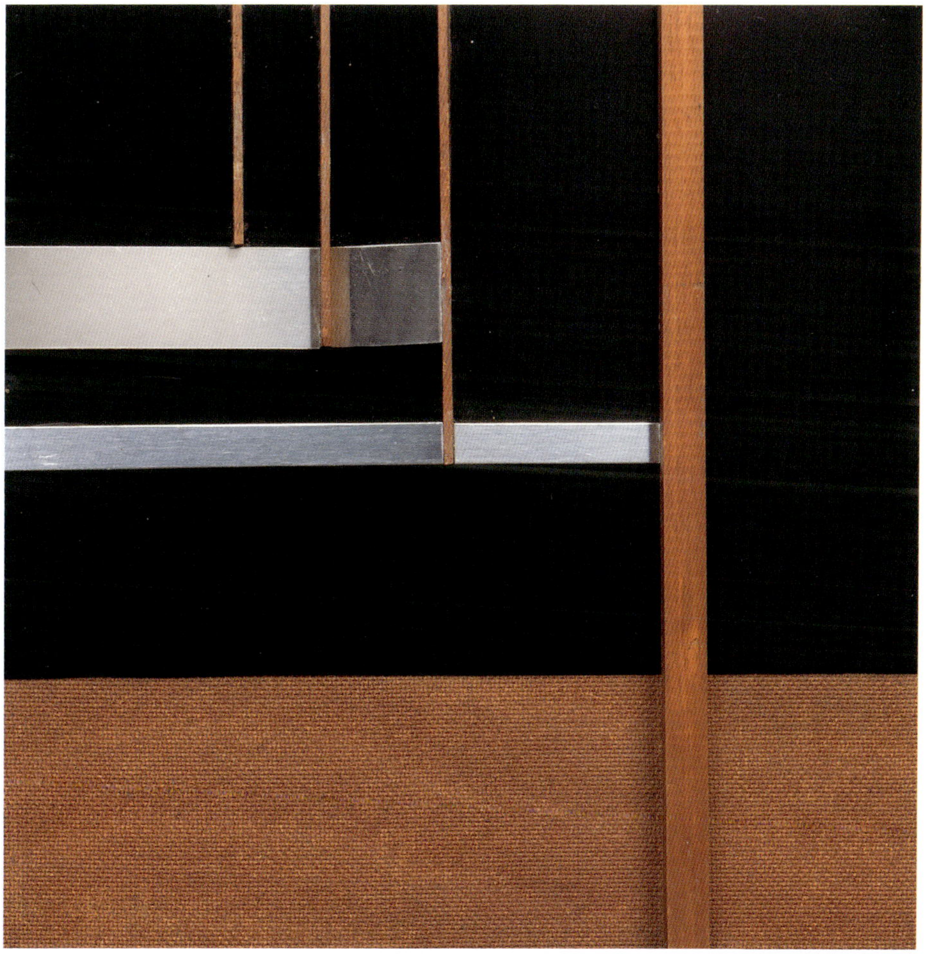

ANDRÉ MASSON (1896–1987)

Masson's early works display an interest in cubism, but he later became associated with surrealism. He was one of the most enthusiastic employers of automatic drawing, making a number of automatic works in pen and ink. He believed forcing himself into a reduced state of consciousness would help his art be free from rational control, and hence get closer to the workings of his subconscious mind. By the end of the 1920s, however, he was finding automatism rather restricting, and he left the surrealist movement and turned instead to a more structured style, often producing works with a violent or erotic theme, and making a number of paintings in reaction to the Spanish Civil War.

La Messe á Pampelone/Mass at Pamplona
1937
Black pen and ink on paper
50.8 x 64.8 cm
Inscribed: *La messe á Pampelone.* André Masson
Provenance: E.L.T. Mesens

Exhibited: Gallerie Simon, Paris, 1937; The London Gallery, London, 1947; *Real Surreal, British and European Surrealism,* Wolverhampton Art Gallery and Museum, Wolverhampton, 17 June–19 August 1995; *Europe in the 30s,* Musée d'Art Moderne, 1997; *El Surrealismo y la Guerra Civil Espanola,* Museum of Teruel, Teruel, Spain, 30 October–13 December 1998

Literature: *Now Magazine,* February/March 1947; Benedict Read and David Thistlewood (eds.), Herbert Read, *A British Vision of World Art,* Leeds Art Gallery, 1993, cat. no. 132, illustration no. 80

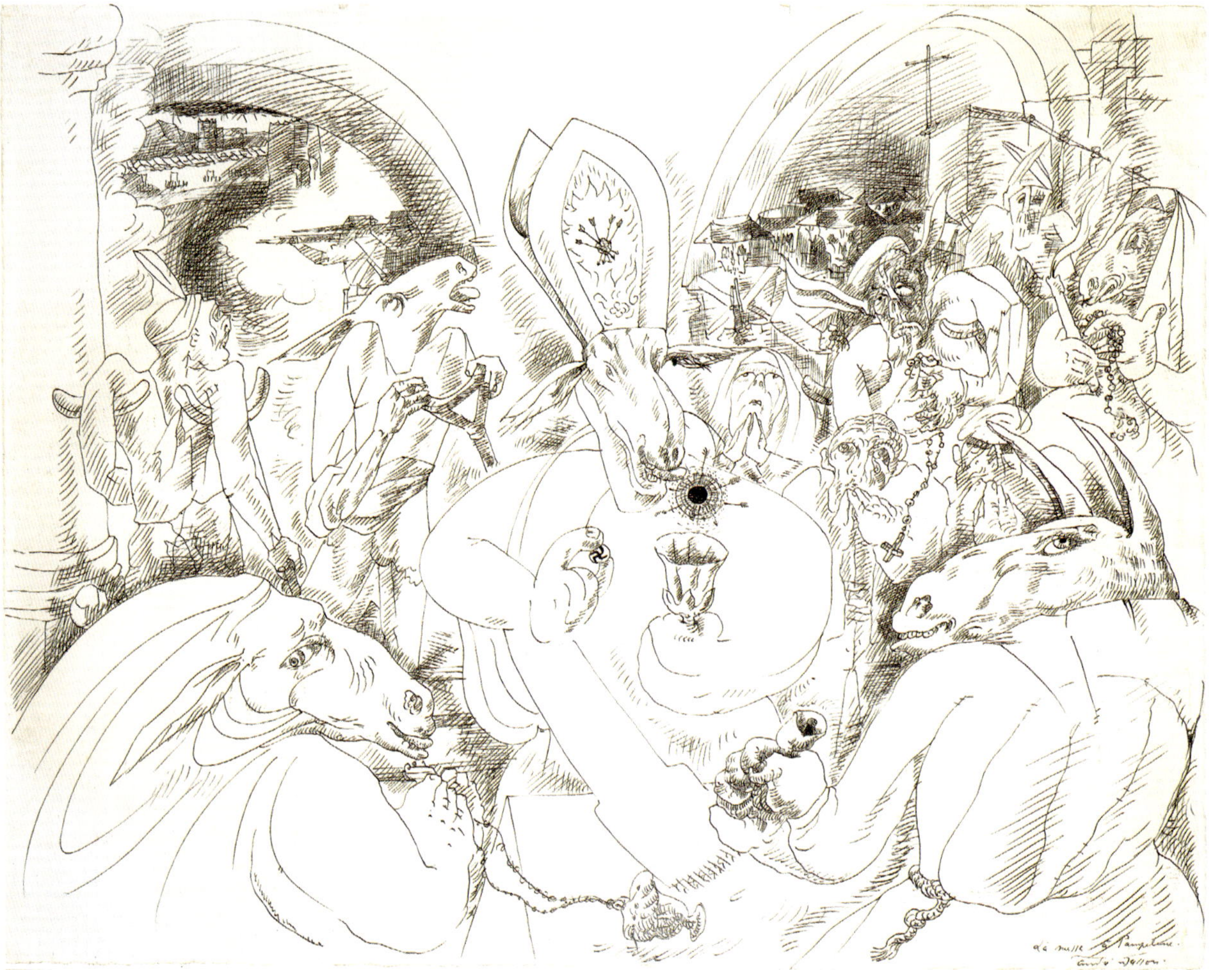

F.E. McWILLIAM (1909–1992)

Roland Penrose described McWilliam as an inventor of styles. He not only carved in a great variety of woods, limestone, cast stone and concrete, but his sculpture is also invested with qualities not often associated with the technique: wit, sexual humour and fantasy. His carvings are remarkable for their inventive variations on the theme of biomorphic abstraction. The fetish, the idol, and their combination in the surreal personage, are other themes he explored. Not surprisingly, his admirers were artists influenced by the spirit of surrealism: Henry Moore, Paul Nash, E.L.T. Mesens, Roland Penrose, Ceri Richards and Merlyn Evans.

Carving
1936 (renovated, 1984)
Walnut on marble base
Height 30 cm
Provenance: the artist

Exhibited: *F.E. McWilliam, Sculpture 1932–1989,* The Tate Gallery, London, 1989

Literature: Mel Gooding, *F.E. McWilliam, Sculpture 1932–1989,* London, The Tate Gallery, 1989, p.39, no. 11, illustration

McWilliam began in earnest to carve in wood upon his return from France in 1932. He was aware of the plastic vitality, emotive force and sculptural possibilities of primitive and archaic carving, but the use of these sources was more personal. McWilliam's carvings of this period are remarkable for their inventive variations on the theme of biomorphic abstraction.

Spanish Head, 1939
Hoptonwood stone
120 x 61 x 23 cm
Provenance: the artist

Exhibited: *Surrealism In Britain In The Thirties,* Leeds Art Gallery, 1986, no. 189 (Mrs Beth McWilliam); *F.E. McWilliam, Sculpture 1932–1989,* The Tate Gallery, London, 1989; *Europe in the 30s,* Musée d'Art Moderne, Paris, 1997

Literature: Illustrated in *The London Bulletin,* March 1939, No. 11, p.15, described 'PORTRAIT' (1938–39). In the front of the Bulletin described as Portrait 1938 Hoptonwood stone price 75 guineas; Illustrated in catalogue 1998 *Surrealism and the Spanish Civil War;* Mel Gooding, *F.E. McWilliam, Sculpture 1932–1989,* London, The Tate Gallery, 1989, p.45, no. 26, illustration

McWilliam ordered the stone from Hoptonwood Quarry on the occasion of his visit there with Henry Moore and Gerrard in 1937. Taking the idea of the complete fragment, which derived from Rodin and which had been developed by Brancusi and Arp, he made a major contribution to European surrealist sculpture. By fragmenting the head alone he introduced an element of dark humour and developed it here into one of his most devastating images, a head that almost seems to have been blown apart.

This piece was made in a time which saw the violence of the Spanish Civil War, the appeasement of Hitler and the approach to World War.

The Long Arm, 1939
(Fist raised in Republican Salute)
(re-worked 1945)
Lime wood
Height 185 cm
Provenance: the artist

Exhibited: *F.E. McWilliam, Sculpture 1932–1989,* London, The Tate Gallery, 1989; Musée d'Art Moderne, Paris, 1997; *Blast to Frieze, British Art in the 20th Century,* Kunstmuseum Wolfsburg, 2002

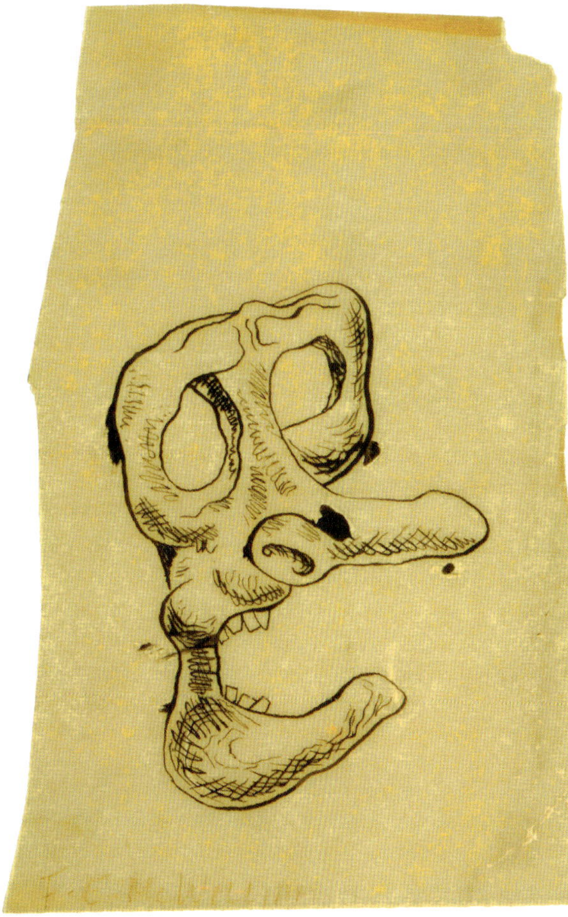

Literature: Mel Gooding, *F.E. McWilliam, Sculpture 1932–1989,* The Tate Gallery, London, 1989, p.41, no. 20, illustration; Jeremy Lewison, *Going Modern And Being British, The Challenge of the 1930s,* in: *Blast to Frieze, British Art in the 20th Century,* Kunstmuseum Wolfsburg/Hatje Cantz, 2002, pp.66–72, illustration p.70, and plate 44, colour illustration; Illustrated Arts Council cat. (Marle and Flannagan); *El Surrealismo y la Guerra Civil Espanola*, Museum of Teruel, Teruel, Spain, 30 October–13 December 1998

With *The Long Arm,* McWilliam carries to extremes an idea which is at odds with the formal tradition of sculpture, as body and mass with a centre of gravity: that of attenuation and balance upon a narrow base. Originally, the monumental Egyptian fragment arm in the British Museum (long since horizontal) inspired *The Long Arm*.

The Left-Handed Tea Drinker, 1981
Bronze
Height 47 cm
Provenance: the artist

Literature: Mel Gooding, *F.E. McWilliam, Sculpture 1932–1989,* The Tate Gallery, London, 1989, p.64, no. 68, illustration

The 'led' sculptures mark the return to a more playful imagery. They combine both the idea of the complete fragment and of the eliminated torso. The smaller of these works have an elegance and charm, while the larger pieces have a mysterious sculptural presence. The artist's ability to suggest character and movement with the most economic of means is visible.

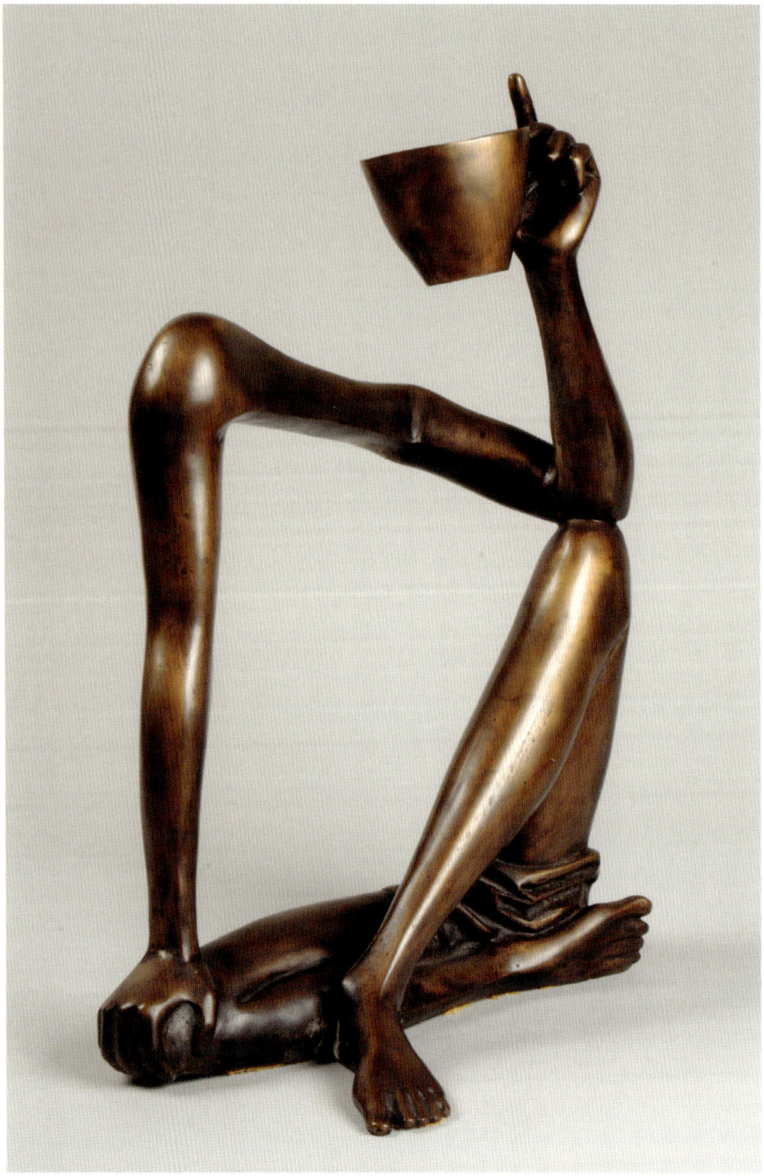

BERNARD MEADOWS (1915–2004)

Working with Henry Moore in the 1930s and 1940s brought Meadows in contact with the European avant-garde and introduced him to 'primitive art'. These experiences established his essentially surrealist approach to sculpture, which exploits the ambiguous meaning of forms. He first came to international prominence at the Venice Biennale of 1952, where he displayed his bronzes of predatory crabs and birds. The sculptures were not based on specific species, but intended to capture the essence of 'crabness'.

The Black Crab
1953
Bronze
Height: 42 cm
Provenance: Gimpel Fils, London

Exhibited: *Recent Sculpture by Bernard Meadows,* London, Gimpel Fils, 1959; *Bernard Meadows: Sculpture and Work on Paper: An 80th Birthday Survey,* Yorkshire Sculpture Park, Wakefield, 1995; *Blast to Frieze, British Art in the 20th Century,* Kunstmuseum Wolfsburg, 2002

Literature: Benedict Read and David Thistlewood (eds.), Herbert Read, *A British Vision of World Art,* Leeds Art Gallery, 1993, cat. no. 133, illustration no. 134; *Blast to Frieze, British Art in the 20th Century,* Kunstmuseum Wolfsburg/Hatje Cantz, 2002, plate 108, colour illustration

Study for Black Crab
1952
Gouache and pencil on paper
20 x 15 cm
Provenance: the artist

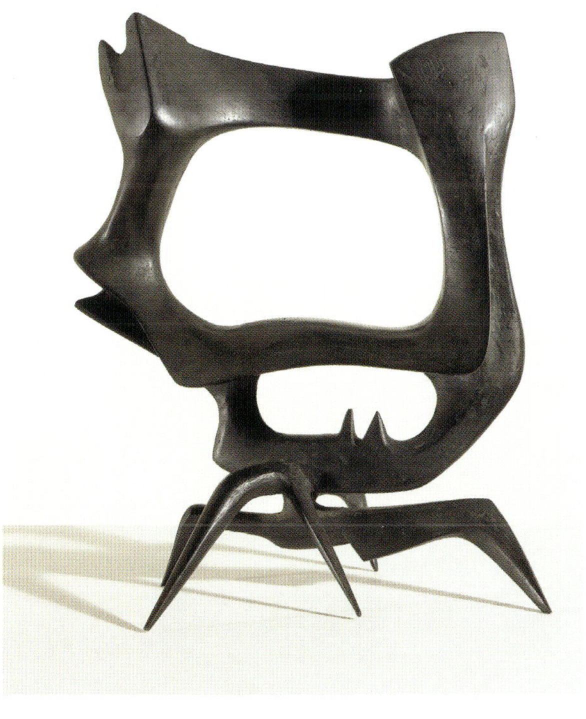

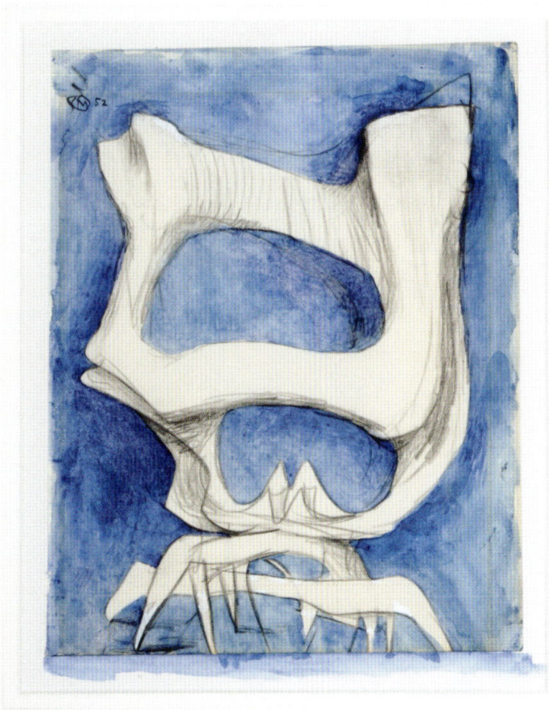

REUBEN MEDNIKOFF (1906–1972)

Mednikoff met Grace Pailthorpe (twenty-three years his senior) in 1935 and they became partners in experimenting to use art as a way of examining the unconscious and dealing with mental illness. Pailthorpe had trained as a surgeon, but was interested in the theories of Sigmund Freud, and produced paintings and drawings herself. She encouraged Mednikoff to paint, as she wanted him to bring his memories to a conscious level. They analysed each other's works, and in the 1930s were described by André Breton as 'the best and most truly surrealist' of any artists living in Britain. However, their scientific analysis of art went against the views of other members of the British Surrealist Group, and they were 'expelled' in 1940.

April 23 and 24, 1935
(Arboreal Bliss)
1935
Oil on canvas
60 x 49.4 cm
Signed: R. Mednikoff
Provenance: Mayor Gallery, London

Exhibited: *Surrealismi-Surrealism,* Retretti Art Centre, Finland, 1987, not numbered; *Blast to Frieze, British Art in the 20th Century,* Kunstmuseum Wolfsburg, 2002; *Sluice Gates of the Mind, The Collaborative Work of Pailthorpe and Mednikoff,* Leeds Art Gallery, Leeds, 15 January–8 March 1998

Literature: *Blast to Frieze, British Art in the 20th Century,* exhibition catalogue, Kunstmuseum Wolfsburg/Hatje Cantz, 2002, plate 52, colour illustration; *Sluice Gates of the Mind, The Collaborative Work of Pailthorpe and Mednikoff,* Leeds Art Gallery, 1998, cat. 48

October 2, 1938-2
1938
Watercolour on paper
28 x 39 cm
Provenance: private collection

Exhibited: *Surrealismi-Surrealism,* Retretti Art Centre, Finland, 1987, not numbered; *Blast to Frieze, British Art in the 20th Century,* Kunstmuseum Wolfsburg, 2002; *Sluice Gates of the Mind, The Collaborative Work of Pailthorpe and Mednikoff,* Leeds Art Gallery, Leeds, 15 January–8 March 1998

Literature: *Blast to Frieze, British Art in the 20th Century,* exhibition catalogue, Kunstmuseum Wolfsburg/Hatje Cantz, 2002, plate 52, colour illustration; *Sluice Gates of the Mind, The Collaborative Work of Pailthorpe and Mednikoff,* Leeds Art Gallery, 1998, cat. 48

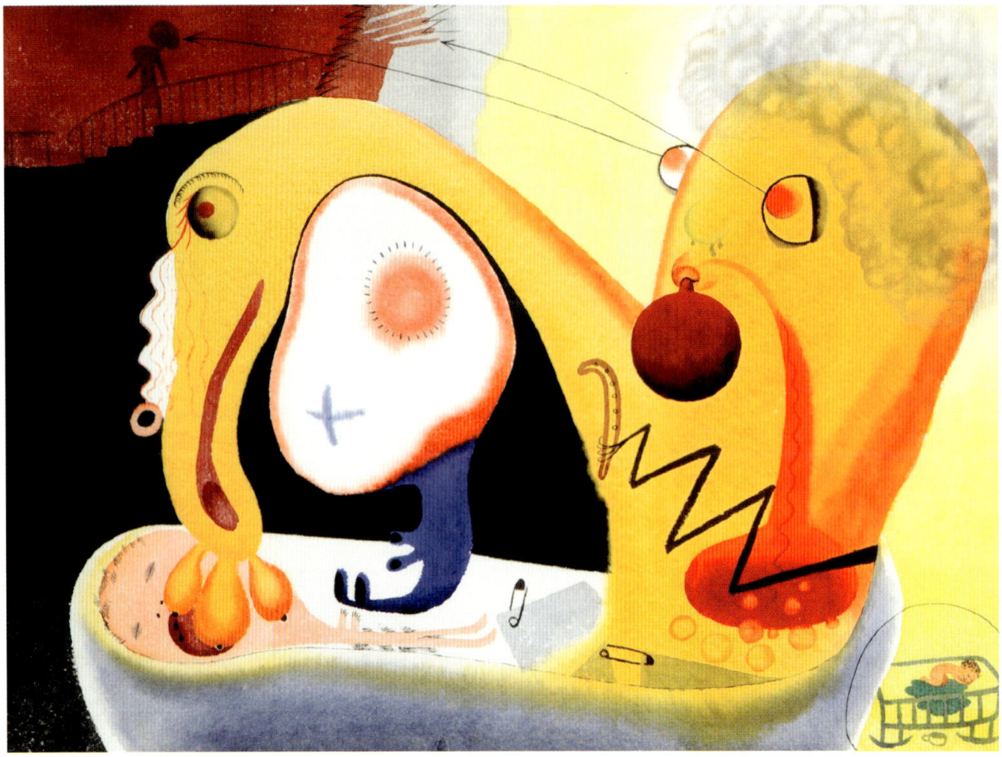

OSCAR MELLOR (1921–2005)

Although Mellor became best known as a publisher, he saw himself primarily as an artist whose business activities existed to support his painting. He studied art part-time at the Birmingham School of Art and the Ruskin School and became an associate of Conroy Maddox and the Birmingham Surrealists.

A Marriage of Convenience
1984
Canvas on board
33 x 71 cm

Double Portrait of Maureen, 1982
1982
Oil on canvas
66 x 82 cm
Provenance: Bonham's, London, 26 September 2006, Lot 213

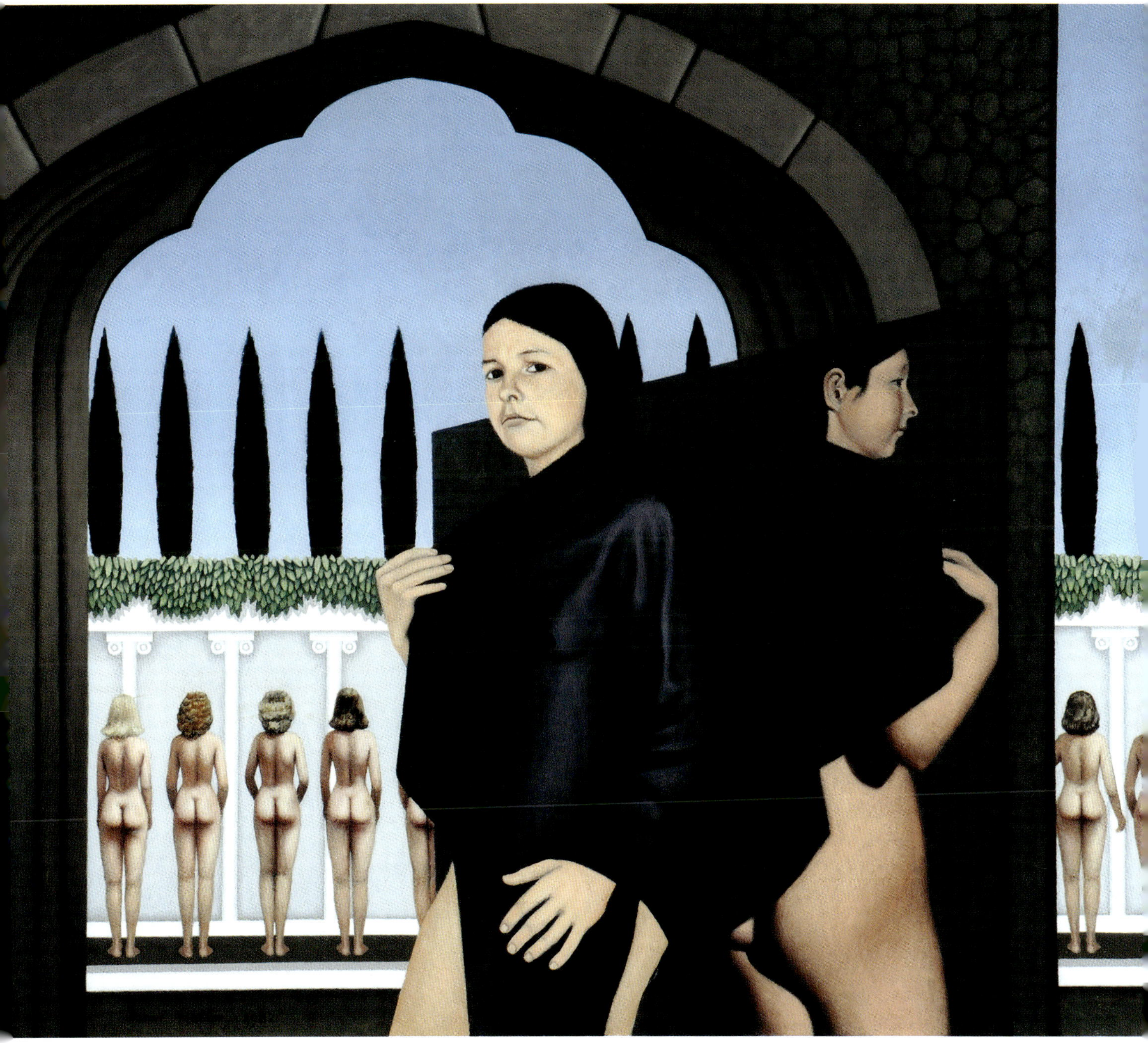

JOHN MELVILLE (1902–1986)

He was, along with his critic brother Robert Melville and the artist Conroy Maddox, a key member of the Birmingham Surrealists from the 1930s to the 1950s. He was a painter of figures, portraits, still-life and landscapes, in oil and watercolour. Self-taught, he was attracted to surrealism in 1930 and, as a member of the Birmingham Group, joined the Surrealist Group in 1938. He was a contributor to the *London Bulletin* in 1939 and to *Arson* in 1942.

Reclining Woman
1934
Oil and gouache on board
50 x 59 cm
Signed: John Melville
Provenance: Christie's, London, 8 June 1990, Lot 38

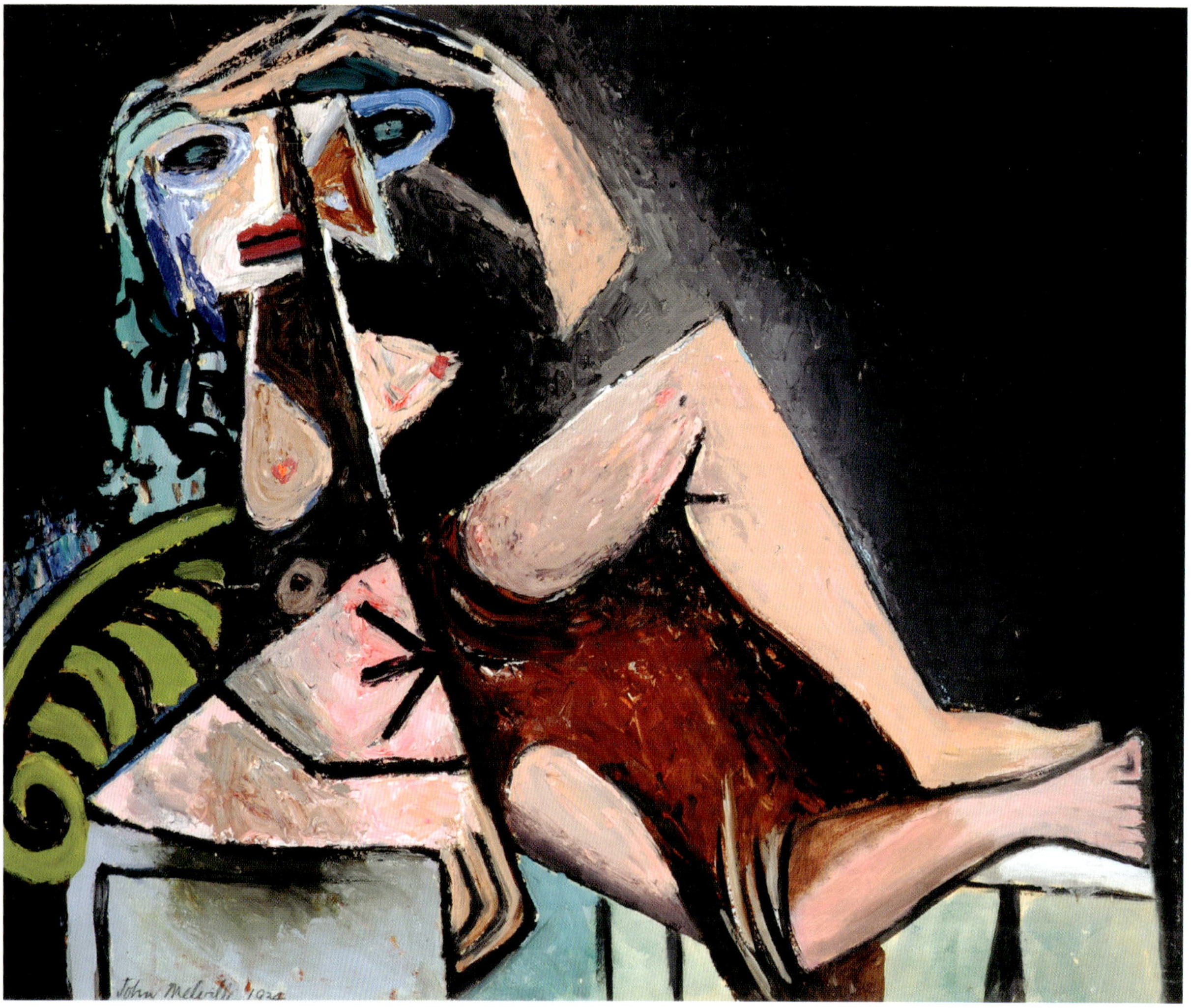

E.L.T. MESENS (1903–1971)

Mesens started his artistic career as a musician, but became increasingly interested in contemporary painting, especially dada and surrealism. He was a friend and champion of Magritte. His activity as one of the leaders of the surrealist movement in Belgium was eased by the fact that he was an owner of a gallery, where he organised the first surrealist exhibition in Belgium in 1934. As its organiser, he also went on to co-organise the London International Surrealist Exhibition, which made him settle down in London. There he became the director of the London Gallery (which he ran during the late 1930s and after the war with Roland Penrose) and the chief editor of the *London Bulletin* (1938–40) – one of the most important bulletins among the English language surrealist periodicals.

Simples VII
21/1970
Collage, crayon and gouache
21.5 x 28 cm
Signed and dated along the bottom of the collage
Provenance: Mayor Gallery, London, December 1997

Exhibited: Gallerie Isy Brachot, Bruxelles, 1989; Foire in Cologne, Guillame Campo Antwerp, 1975; Romney Van De Velde, Antwerp

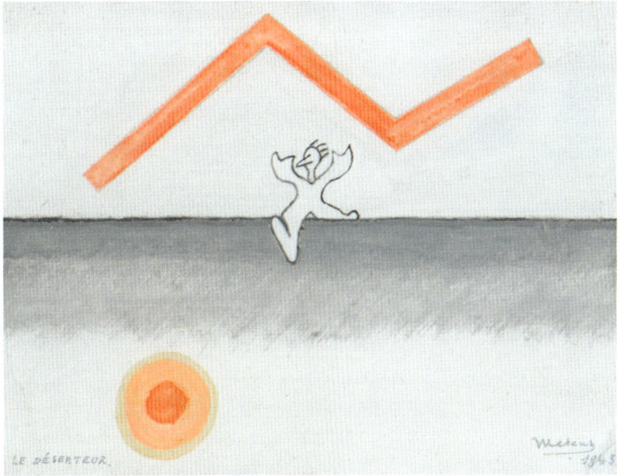

The Deserter (Le Deserteur)
1943
Gouache and Collage
18 x 25.5 cm
Provenance: George Melly

Exhibited: Musée de Marseille, 1986; *Surrealismi-Surrealism,* Retretti Art Centre, Finland, 1987, not numbered

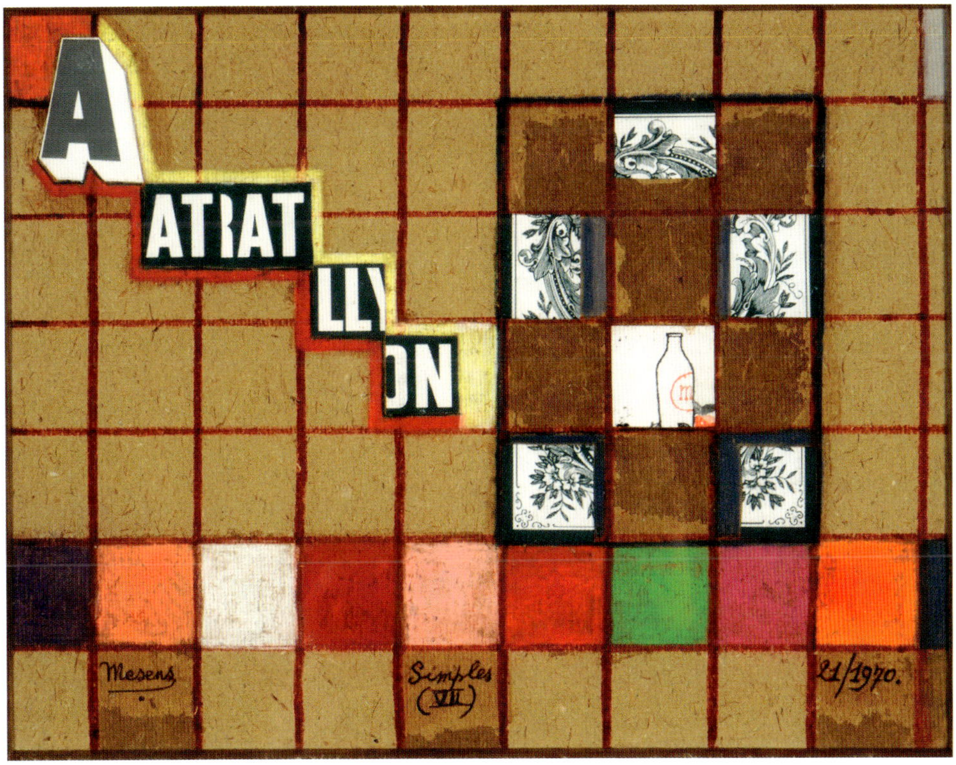

JUAN MIRÓ (1893–1983)

Miró was born in Barcelona and moved to Paris in 1920. His early work combined miniaturist detail with a cubist fragmentation of space. In Paris he abandoned this style and began to paint an imaginary world full of strange, insect-like figures and forms, which seemed to float in space. This fantastic sign language, which was partly inspired by images from the artist's unconscious mind, soon became a hallmark of surrealist art. Although he spent time away from Spain, Miró remained interested in Catalonian folklore throughout his career.

Aidez Espagne, Pochoir
1937
32 x 26 cm
Catalan Republican with Barcelona red beret and 'Shall Not Pass' clenched fist salute

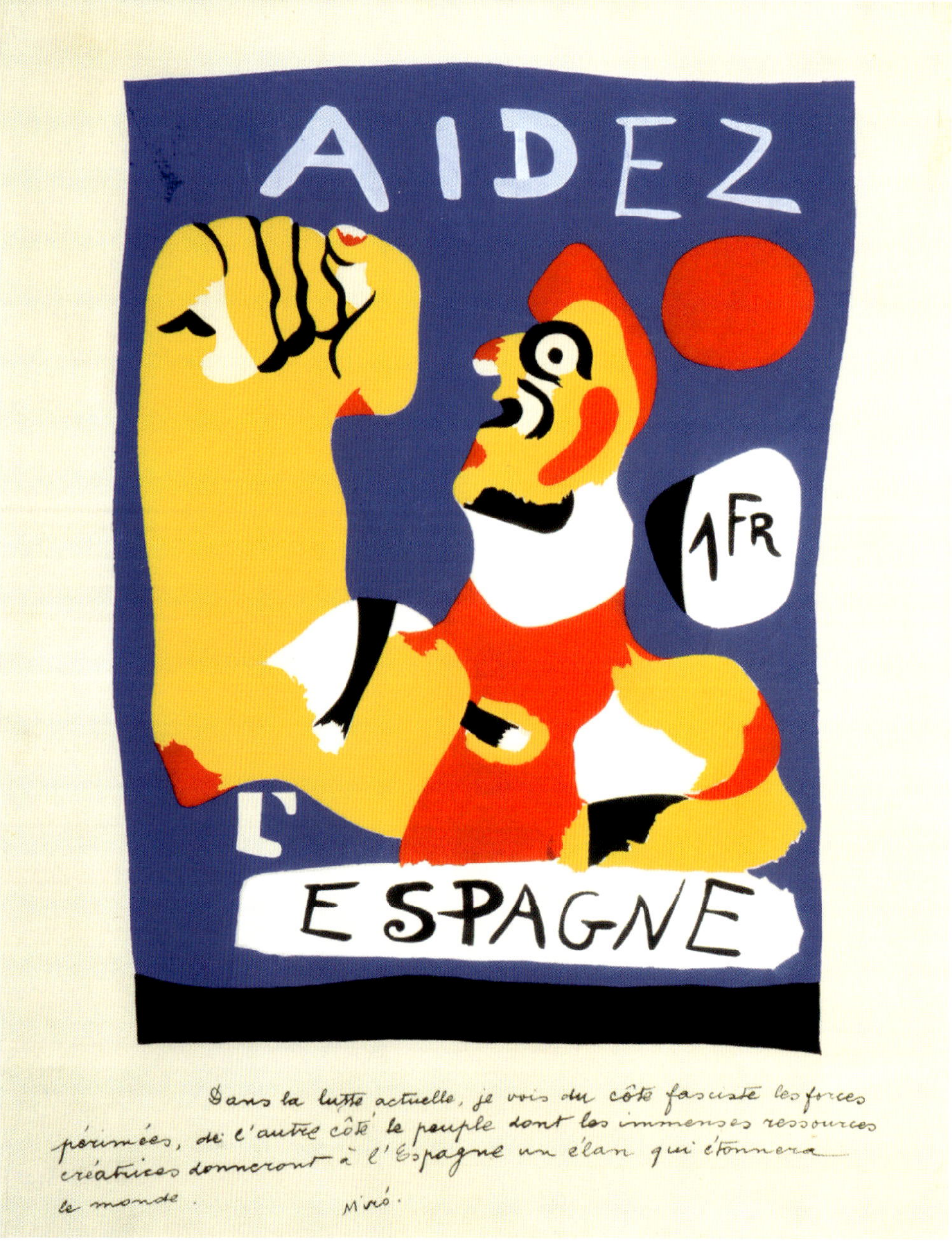

HENRY MOORE (1898–1986)

Born in Yorkshire, Moore worked briefly as a teacher before studying art at Leeds and the Royal College of Art in London. He served as an official war artist and saw his reputation growing through important public commissions. In 1948 he won the International Sculpture Prize at the 24th Venice Biennale.

Although Moore exhibited at the International Surrealist Exhibition in London in 1936, he never could be strictly classified as surrealist. Surrealism provides a useful tool in describing a specific period and a certain manner in his sculpture. Like the surrealists, Moore was interested in chance findings and such unprovoked visual inspirations influenced his art. It is as much a formal aspect of his work, as it is an emotional one.

Study for Reclining Mother and Child
1979
Crayon and white chalk on paper
8.75 x 10.25 in
Provenance: the artist

Exhibited: *Sculpture in the Making,* Cleveland Museum, 1984–85

Literature: *Drawing Before Bronze: David Mitchinson* (Henry Moore Foundation)

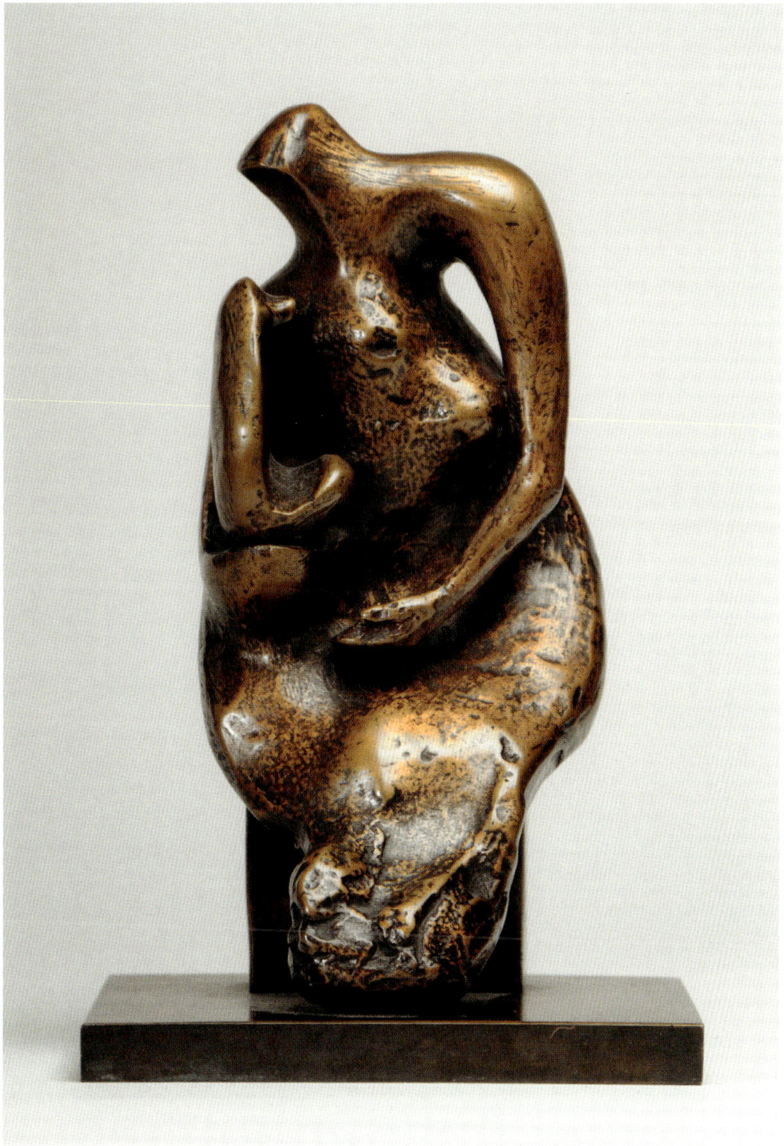

Reclining Mother and Child (overleaf)
1979
Bronze, green patina
Height: 20 cm
Provenance: the artist

Seated Figure: Thin Head
1984
Bronze, edition of 9
Height: 14.5 cm
Provenance: the artist

Marquette for Mother and Child on Block Seat
1981
Bronze, edition of 9
Height: 44.5 cm
Provenance: the artist

Helmet, Head and Shoulders
1952
Bronze, edition of 10
Height: 16.5 cm
Provenance: Sotheby's, London, Sale of Impressionist and Modern Art Part II, 6 February 2001, Lot 166

Literature: Alan Bowness (ed.), *Henry Moore, Volume 2, Complete Sculpture 1949–1954,* London, Lund Humphries, 1986 (1st edition 1955), no. 304, illustration

Two Henry Moore Scarfs
Zika Ascher came to England in 1939 and established his own production company and silk-screen printers in London. Moore was asked to collaborate in a printing project with the intention to revitalize the most important article of war-time style, the headscarf. Altogether, he filled three sketchbooks with design ideas and produced two headscarf designs. Other leading artists, among them Matisse, Derain, Piper, and Sutherland were commissioned, in addition to Moore. In 1946, they designed a collection of headscarves to brighten up the post-war British wardrobe.

Family Groups
c.1946
Serigraphy in five colours
Silk
91 x 86 cm
Printed by Ascher
Provenance: gift Dorin Shaundy

Bird
1945
Serigraphy in six colours
Crepe silk
96 x 93 cm
Printed by Ascher
Provenance: gift Dorin Shaundy

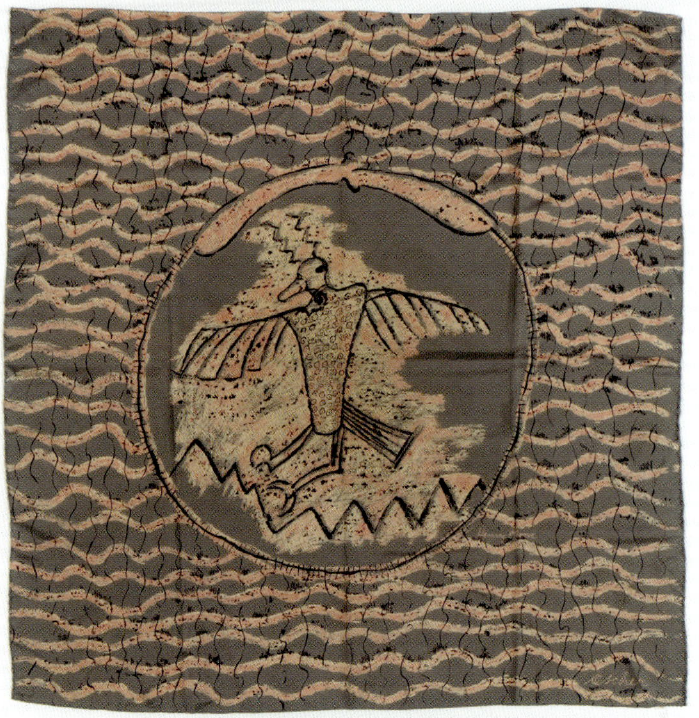

DESMOND MORRIS (born 1928)

In addition to his scientific pursuits, he is an artist in the surrealist tradition and was the director of ICA Gallery, London. Biomorphic figures inhabit Morris paintings. It is a personal world, full of ambiguous dramas and startling encounters of sexuality, humour, joy and violence. The biomorphic style of painting was to become the artist's lifelong preoccupation and the genesis of over a thousand works.

The Greeting Ceremony
1951
Oil on board
18 x 26 cm
Signed and dated
Provenance: Mayor Gallery, London

Exhibited: Retrospective Exhibition: *Fifty Years of Surrealism,* City Museum and Art Gallery, Stoke-on-Trent, 16 June–28 July 1996; Nottingham Natural History Museum, 14 September–17 November 1996; Solo exhibition at the Mayor Gallery to coincide with the publication of Silvano Levy's book: *Desmond Morris – Fifty Years of Surrealism,* 1997

Literature: *Desmond Morris, The Secret Surrealist, The Paintings of Desmond Morris,* Oxford, Phaidon, 1987, checklist, p.107, 1951, no. 6; Michel Remy, *The Surrealist World of Desmond Morris,* London, Jonathan Cape, 1991, colour illustration p.55; Silvano Levi, *Desmond Morris – Fifty Years of Surrealism,* London, Barrie and Jenkins, 1997, listed p.211, 1957, no. 6

The Serpent's Choice
January 11th, 1958
Oil on canvas
18 x 36 cm
Provenance: Mayor Gallery, London

Exhibited: Retrospective Exhibition: *Fifty Years of Surrealism,* City Museum and Art Gallery, Stoke-on-Trent, 16 June–28 July 1996; Nottingham Natural History Museum, 14 September–17 November 1996; Solo exhibition at the Mayor Gallery to coincide with the publication of Silvano Levy's book: *Desmond Morris – Fifty Years of Surrealism,* 1997

Literature: Desmond Morris, *The Secret Surrealist, The Paintings of Desmond Morris,* Oxford, Phaidon, 1987, checklist, p.108, 1958, no. 3; Michel Remy, *The Surrealist World of Desmond Morris,* London, Jonathan Cape, 1991, colour illustration p.64; Silvano Levi, *Desmond Morris – Fifty Years of Surrealism,* London, Barrie and Jenkins, 1997, colour illustration p.78 and listed p.212, 1958, no. 3; Silvano Levi, *Catalogue Raisonné,* Desmond Morris, *Analytical Catalogue Raisonné 1944–2000,* Pandora, Antwerp, 2001

In *The Serpent's Choice*, a small, defenceless group of birds is surprised by a snake. In a moment it will attack and kill one of the five creatures. Even in a painting that focuses on danger and conflict, Morris manages to introduce a humorous tone. The pink coloured serpent, the starry eyes of the young and the bearded face of the adult, create a comic element.

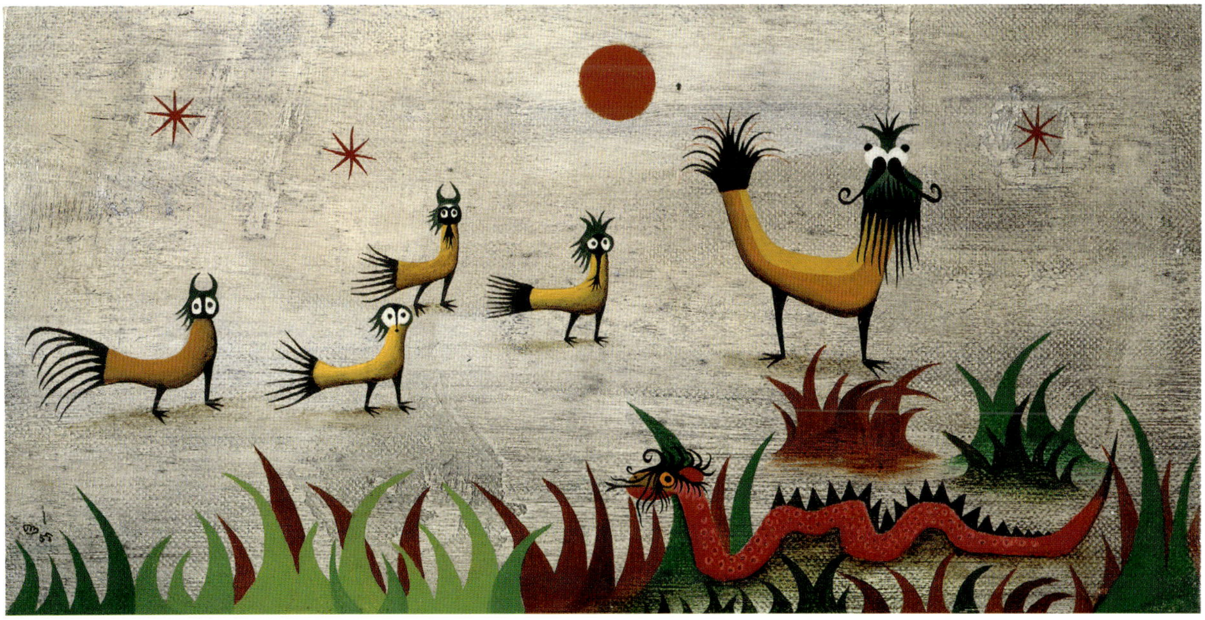

There's No Time Like The Future
November 23, 1957
Oil on canvas
18 x 36 cm
Signed with initials: D.M.
Provenance: collection Mrs Majorie Morris, Oxford; Mayor Gallery, London

Literature: Desmond Morris, *The Secret Surrealist, The Paintings of Desmond Morris,* Oxford, Phaidon, 1987, checklist, p.108, 1957, no. 12; Michel Remy, *The Surrealist World of Desmond Morris,* London, Jonathan Cape, 1991, colour illustration p.70; Silvano Levi, *Desmond Morris – Fifty Years of Surrealism,* London, Barrie and Jenkins, 1997, listed p.212, 1957, no.12; Silvano Levi, *Catalogue Raisonné,* Desmond Morris, *Analytical Catalogue Raisonné 1944–2000,* Pandora, Antwerp, 2001

Family Group,
September 1, 1960
Oil on canvas
56 x 63.5 cm

Literature: Desmond Morris, *The Secret Surrealist, The Paintings of Desmond Morris,* Oxford, Phaidon, 1987, checklist, p.108, 1960, no.14; Silvano Levi, *Desmond Morris – Fifty Years of Surrealism,* London, Barrie and Jenkins, 1997, p.213, 1960, no. 14; Silvano Levi, *Catalogue Raisonné,* Desmond Morris, *Analytical Catalogue Raisonné 1944–2000,* Pandora, Antwerp, 2001

The Attendant
May–June 2001
Gouache, pen and ink on paper
29 x 21 cm

Bone Idol
August 1999
Jaw bone with marble eyes and painted plastic lips
Height: 25 cm
Literature: Silvano Levi, *Catalogue Raisonné,* Desmond Morris, *Analytical Catalogue Raisonné 1944–2000,* Pandora, Antwerp, 2001

Good Morning Miss Smith
1969
Skull and plastic lips
Length: 22 cm
Provenance: Mayor Gallery, London

Exhibited: Retrospective Exhibition: *Fifty Years of Surrealism,* City Museum and Art Gallery, Stoke-on-Trent, 16 June–28 July 1996; Nottingham Natural History Museum, 14 September–17 November 1996

Literature: Silvano Levi, *Desmond Morris – Fifty Years of Surrealism,* London, Barrie and Jenkins, 1997, colour illustration p.82 and listed p.215, 1969, no. 18; Silvano Levi, *Catalogue Raisonné,* Desmond Morris, *Analytical Catalogue Raisonné 1944–2000,* Pandora, Antwerp, 2001

In *Good Morning Miss Smith* an antelope skull is garnished with a pair of red plastic lips. By doing so the artist combines the morbidity of the skull with a playful, almost frivolous, adornment. Playfulness is a persistent theme in Morris work and extends to his plastic creations. Silvano Levi explains that the origin of this object lies in the Morris tendency to perceive living humans in anatomical terms. (Levi: 1997, p.82)

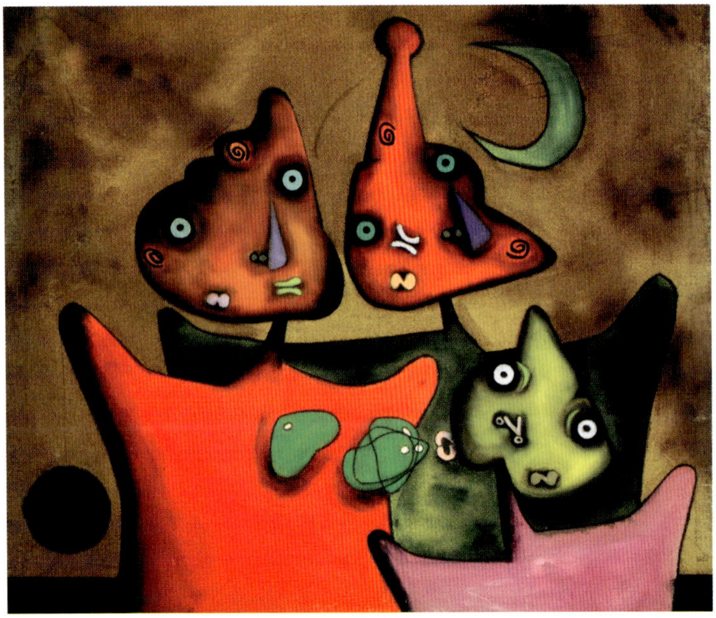

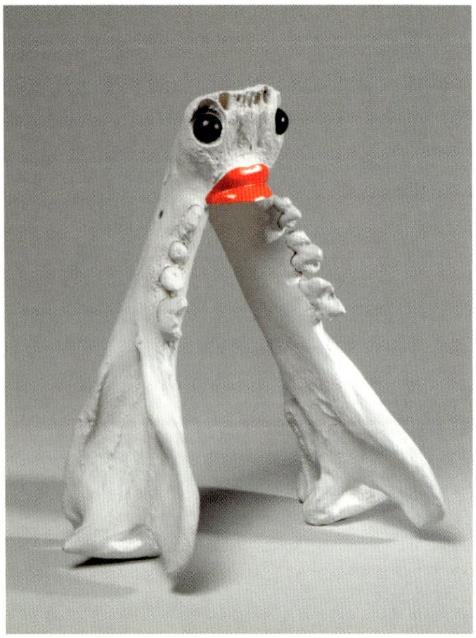

ALASTAIR MORTON (1910–1953)

In 1928, James Morton (the artist's father) founded the Edinburgh Weavers, as a research unit to discover how textiles could be produced in keeping with developments in contemporary architecture. In 1932, Alistair Morton was appointed artistic director and launched the Constructivist Fabrics range, with designs by Ben Nicholson, Barbara Hepworth and others. While his work as avant-garde textile producer is well documented, only little is known of Morton as an artist. Though Ben Nicolson and Barbara Hepworth were important influences, the use of form and colour show that – as an abstract constructivist – he was unique.

Irregular Shapes On Black
c.1941
Oil on canvas
15 x 30 cm
Provenance: Austin Desmond, London

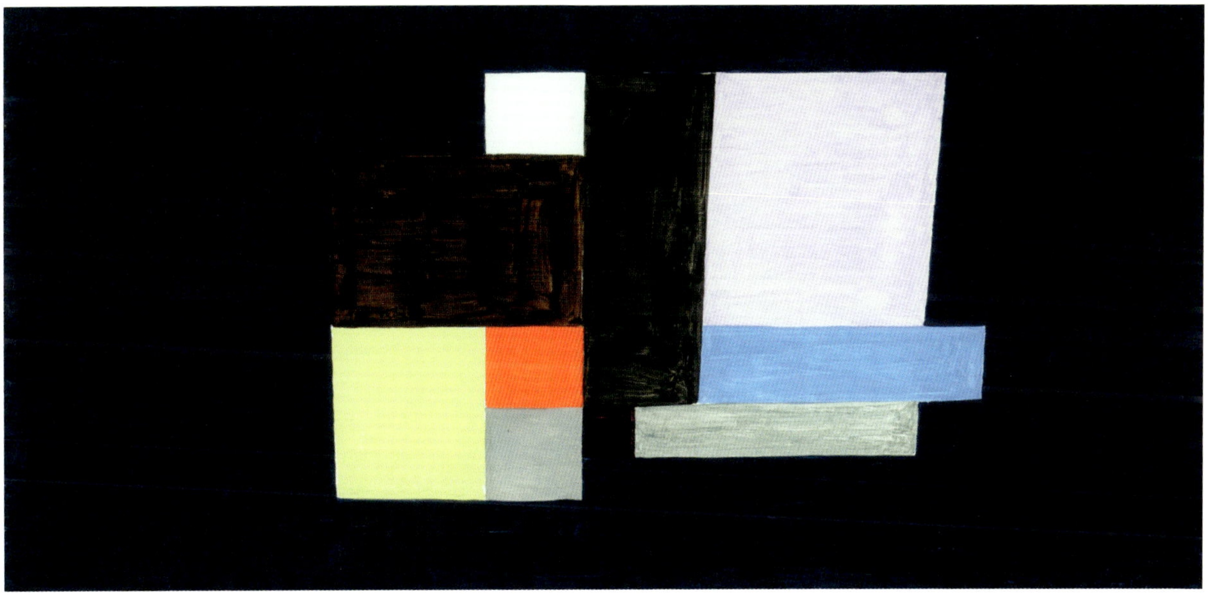

RICHARD NIMAN (born 1932)

Niman frequently works with dolls, mannequins, shop window installations and other ready-mades. As he has always regarded such objects in their original state as aesthetically dead, he administered some sort of surprise or shock to the viewer by trying to bring the dolls to life. He achieved this by transforming – by decontextualising, by stripping them of certain things and bringing in other parts of other objects that don't normally fit with them.

Head in the Clouds
1974/c.1998
59 x 41 cm
Object
Provenance: the artist

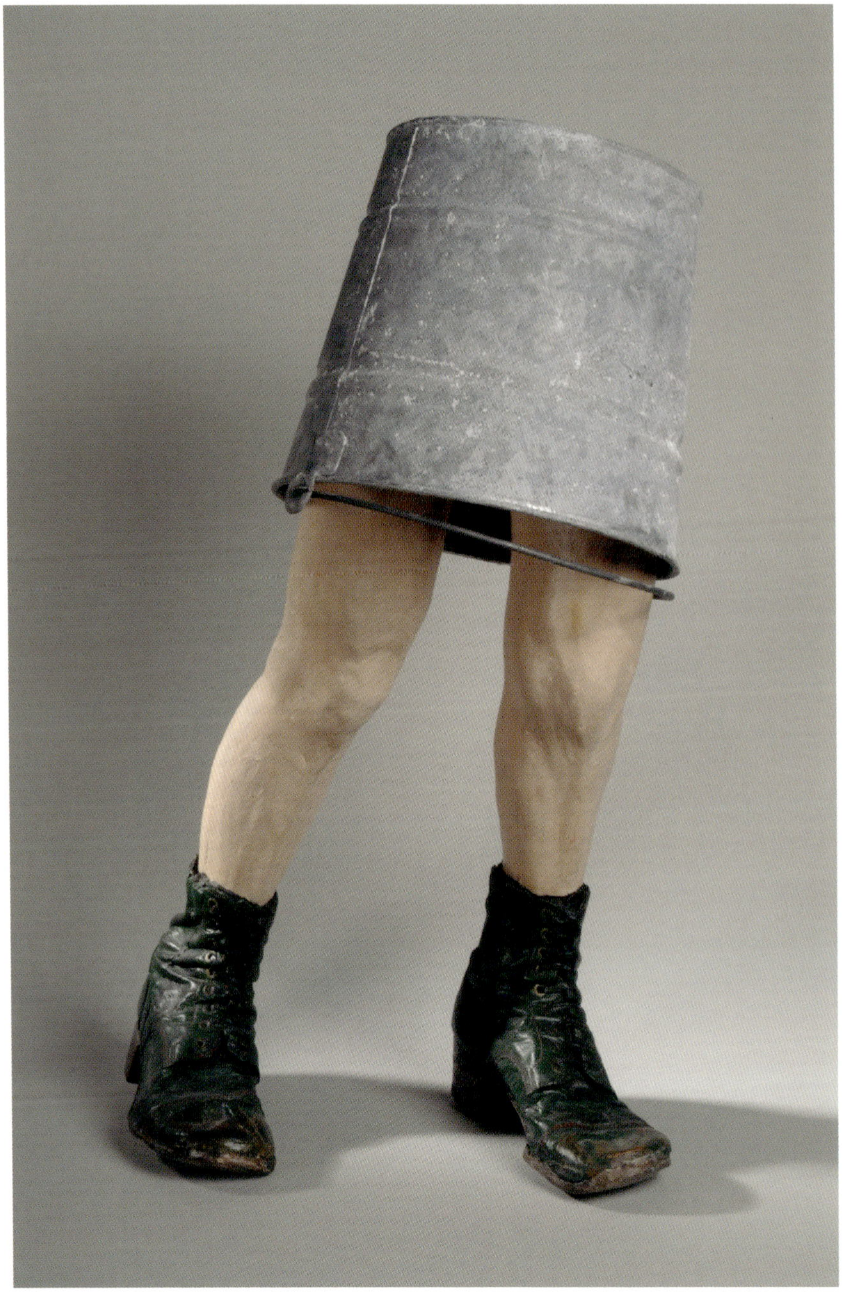

GRACE PAILTHORPE (1883–1971)

Dr Grace Pailthorpe was primarily a psychoanalyst. In 1935, she met the artist Reuben Mednikoff, who introduced her to the use of automatism in surrealist art and encouraged her to produce her own drawings and poems. Alongside Mednikoff's work, these became the basis of their research into the unconscious. Chosen to exhibit at the International Surrealist Exhibition held in London in 1936, their paintings were singled out for praise by André Breton, the 'pope' of surrealism, as 'the best and most truly surrealist of the works' exhibited by British artists. The pair also took an active part in the formation of the British Surrealist Group. In 1939, Pailthorpe published an essay on 'The Scientific Aspects of Surrealism' in the London Bulletin, the main outlet for surrealist ideas in Britain. However, by 1940, both Mednikoff and Pailthorpe had left the British Surrealist Group.

July 5, 1935–1 (Ancestors)
1935
Ink drawing on paper
30 x 39.5 cm
Provenance: Peter Nahum, London

Exhibited: *International Surrealist*, London, 1936 (280) Guggenheim Jeune, London, 1939, (13); *Sluice Gates of the Mind, The Collaborative Work of Pailthorpe and Mednikoff*, Leeds Art Gallery, Leeds, 15 January–8 March 1998

Literature: Herbert Read (ed.), *Surrealism*, Faber & Faber: London, 1936 (72); *Sluice Gates of the Mind, The Collaborative Work of Pailthorpe and Mednikoff*, exhibition catalogue, Leeds Art Gallery, 1998, cat. 6, illustration

November 3, 1937
1937
Watercolour on paper
29 x 39 cm
Provenance: Peter Nahum, London; Christie's, London, 15 November 2006

Exhibited: *Sluice Gates of the Mind, The Collaborative Work of Pailthorpe and Mednikoff*, Leeds Art Gallery, Leeds, 15 January–8 March 1998

Literature: *Sluice Gates of the Mind, The Collaborative Work of Pailthorpe and Mednikoff*, exhibition catalogue, Leeds Art Gallery, 1998, p.62 no. 21

November 16, 1937 at 2.30
1937
Oil on canvas
68.6 x 50.8 cm
Signed G.W. Pailthorpe (lower left) and inscribed *Nov.16.1937 2.30pm* (on the canvas overlap)
Provenance: Mayor Gallery, London; Peter Nahum, Leicester Galleries, London; Christie's, London, 15 November 2006

Exhibited: *British Surrealism – Fifty Years On*, Mayor Gallery, London, 1986, no. 100; *Angels of Anarchy and Machines for Making Clouds: Surrealism In Britain In The Thirties*, Leeds Art Gallery, 1986, no. 90 (Composition), illustration; *Surrealismi-Surrealism*, Retretti Art Centre, Finland, 1987, not numbered; *Sluice Gates of the Mind, The Collaborative Work of Pailthorpe and Mednikoff*, Leeds Art Gallery, Leeds, 15 January–8 March 1998

Literature: *British Surrealism – Fifty Years On*, exhibition catalogue, London, Mayor Gallery, 1986, no. 100, illustration; *Angels of Anarchy and Machines for Making Clouds: Surrealism In Britain In The Thirties*, exhibition catalogue, Leeds, Leeds Art Gallery 1986, no. 90, illustration; *Surrealisti*, exhibition catalogue, Milan, Palazzo Reale, 1989, p.440, illustration; *Sluice Gates of the Mind, The Collaborative Work of Pailthorpe and Mednikoff*, exhibition catalogue, Leeds Art Gallery, 1998, no. 20, colour illustration; *The Poetry of Crisis, The Peter Nahum Collection of British Surrealist and Avant-Garde Art 1930–1951*, 2006, Lot 80, colour illustration

April 22, 1940
1940
Oil on board
58.5 x 49.5 cm

Exhibited: *Sluice Gates of the Mind, The Collaborative Work of Pailthorpe and Mednikoff*, Leeds Art Gallery, Leeds, 15 January–8 March 1998; *Blast to Frieze, British Art in the 20th Century*, Kunstmuseum Wolfsburg, 2002

Literature: *Sluice Gates of the Mind, The Collaborative Work of Pailthorpe and Mednikoff*, exhibition catalogue, Leeds Art Gallery, 1998, cat. 40, colour illustration; *Blast to Frieze, British Art in the 20th Century*, exhibition catalogue, Kunstmuseum Wolfsburg/Hatje Cantz, 2002, plate 69, colour illustration

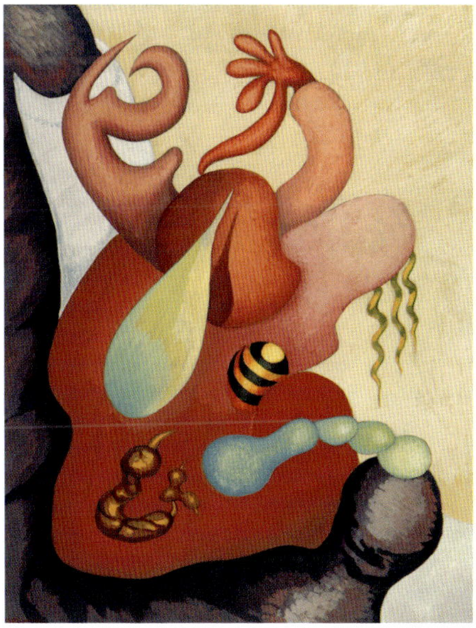

SIR EDUARDO PAOLOZZI (1924–2005)

Paolozzi is one of the most creative and innovative figures of our time. He was one of the first sculptors to realize that our visual life is made up largely of images and impressions which are manufactured: we live in a world of popular images from advertising and the media.

Paolozzi was a close friend of the photographer Nigel Henderson and both, like many of their contemporaries, were looking with interest to the French surrealists, but they were also dazzled by the wave of American popular culture which was starting to impinge on post-war British society.

Refreshing and Delicious
1949
Collage from the Bunk! lecture series in 1952 at the ICA
39 x 28 cm
Signed
Provenance: Sotheby's, London

In 1952, Paolozzi gave an illustrated lecture called Bunk! at The Institute of Contemporary Arts in London. The event is now recognized as the opening salvo of the Pop Art Movement. The images in his lecture were cut from American glossy magazines and celebrated popular culture – glamorous people, advertising. Twenty years later, when pop was coming to a close, Paolozzi made Bunk! a suite of prints based on the image used in his lecture. Bunk! looks back with nostalgia to the post-war era in Europe, when American culture became more influential.

Hermaphrodite (Metaphor Time)
1960–62
Collage
19 x 15 cm
Provenance: Sotheby's, London, 15 October 1992, Lot 402

Exhibited: Neue Nationalgalerie, Berlin, 1975; Badischer Kunstverein and travelling, 1975; Arts Council E. P. *Sculpture, Drawing, Collages and Graphics 1976–77*, p.91 illustration no. 56; Anthony d'Offay, E. P. Collage and Drawing 1977, illustration 25; Grob Gallery; Lit.E.P. Winfrid Konnertz, Cologne, 1984, p.106, no. 211, illustration

Head of an Actor (for Luis Bunuel)
1984
Bronze (unique)
Height: 33 cm (including base)
Provenance: the artist

Exhibited: *Contrariwise, Surrealism and Britain 1930–1986*, Swansea Festival Exhibition 1986, Glynn Vivian Art Gallery, Swansea, 20 September–15 November 1986; Victoria Art Gallery, Bath, 22 November 1986–3 January 1987; Polytechnic Gallery, Newcastle, 10 January–21 February 1987; Mostyn Art Gallery, Llandudno, 28 February–11 April 1987

Literature: *Contrariwise, Surrealism and Britain 1930–1986*, Swansea Festival Exhibition 1986, no. 114, illustration

Bandaged Head
c.1953–56
Bronze
23 x 26 cm
Provenance: originally bought from the artist by his friend the architect Cecil Elson CBE; Christie's, London, 6 June 2003, Lot 205

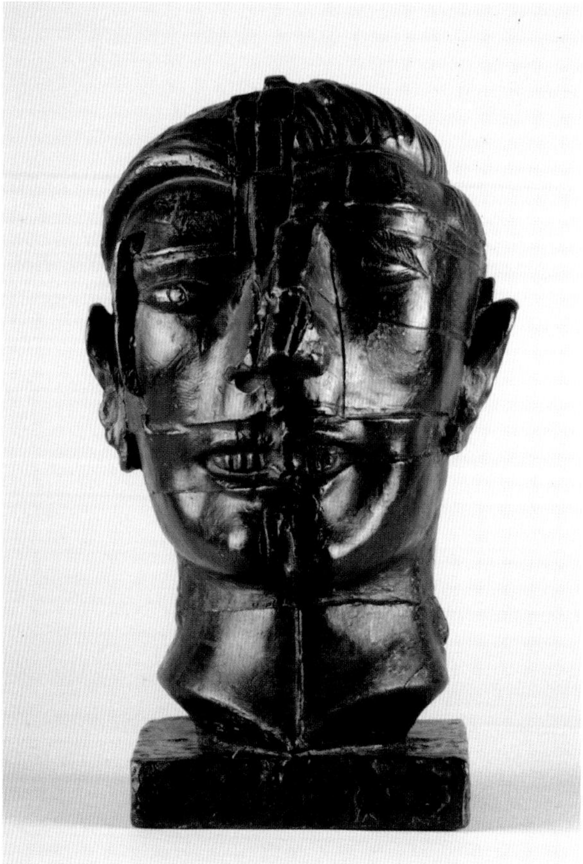

ROLAND PENROSE (1900–1984)

Throughout the 1920s, Penrose lived in France and forged friendships with many members of the surrealist group, as well as Picasso and Man Ray. In Paris, he met the British poet David Gascoyne, who was also a dedicated surrealist, and together they decided that it was time to bombard the British with surrealism. In 1935, they returned to London and formed the British Surrealist Group. In 1936, the International Surrealist Exhibition took place in London at the New Burlington Galleries. The exhibition, attended by over 25,000 people in under a month, was a huge success. As a result, Penrose set up a permanent showcase for British surrealism in the form of the London Gallery, with E.L.T. Mesens as director.

Penrose is one of the few British surrealists to explicitly depict and disjoin the female form which, in this case, is directly inspired by the American photographer Lee Miller, who Penrose met in 1937 and later married. In his work, the female body is often truncated and decapitated, raising issues of castration, anxiety and sadism.

Unsleeping Beauty
1946/47
Oil on canvas
Signed: Penrose
60 x 75 cm
Provenance: Bill Copley; Mayor Gallery, London

Exhibited: *Roland Penrose,* The London Gallery, 10 May–4 June 1949, no. 7; *Surrealism – A State of Mind,* California, 26 February–27 March 1967, no. 24

Literature: Michel Remy, *Surrealism in Britain,* Ashgate, 1999, colour illustration, p.303, no. 153; Antony Penrose, Roland Penrose, *The Friendly Surrealist,* Munich, London, New York, Prestel, 2001, listed: *Roland Penrose: The Major Works,* p.184, *1946 Unsleeping Beauty,* colour illustration p.113; Antony Penrose, *The Home of the Surrealists,* Lee Miller, Roland Penrose and their Circle at Farley Farm, London, Frances Lincoln Limited, 2001, p.59, colour illustration

Roland Penrose and Lee Miller visited Max Ernst and Dorothea Tanning at their new house at Sedona in the Arizona desert. Penrose was greatly impressed by the fantastic and spectacular beauty of the Arizona landscape. As an acknowledgement of his visit, Penrose has included a Max Ernst female figure in faint outline as part of the modelling of the mountain range. Two preparatory sketches exist for this painting and Penrose's son, Antony, writes about *Unsleeping Beauty*: 'Asleep in the Arizonan landscape, the fragmented body may be a reference to the way Lee lived her life in a series of watertight compartments, like those that protect ships from sinking'.

Perspex Cigarette Case
Late 1940s
Painted Europa and the Bull on one side and woman with straw head and ribbon in a deck chair with umbrella on the other side
7.5 x 13 cm
Provenance: given to Kathleen McCogan, a left wing journalist who was living with them in Hampstead

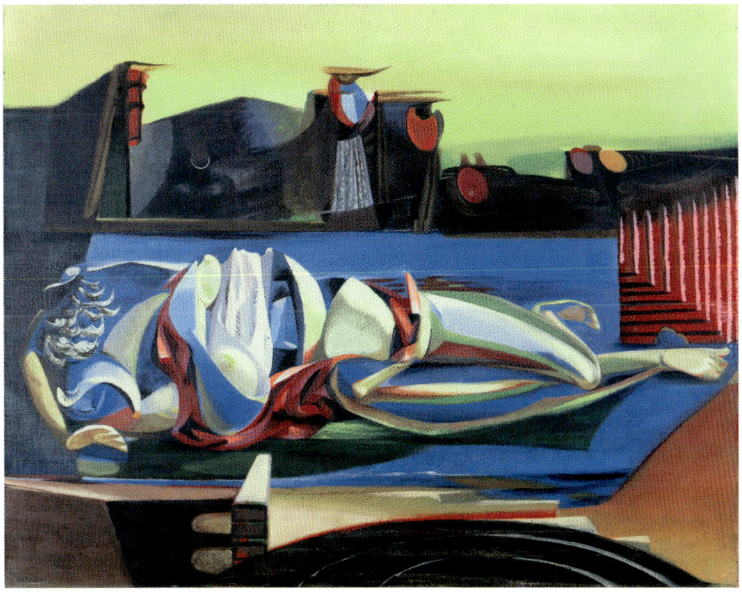

TOM PHILLIPS (born 1937)

Phillips is one of the most prominent contemporary British portrait painters, but he also writes and composes. In 1982, he published a translated and illustrated version of Dante's *Inferno*, and his opera *Irma* was first performed in 1973. One of his best-known publications is *A Humument*; a Victorian novel of which each page has been turned into an artwork. It is not just the finished work of art, but also the creative process itself that interests Phillips. This is reflected not only in his individual paintings, but even more so in his detailed documentation of each work's development.

Dante
Before 1985
Oil on canvas
48 x 38 cm
Provenance: Bonham's, London, 28 June 2000, Lot 101

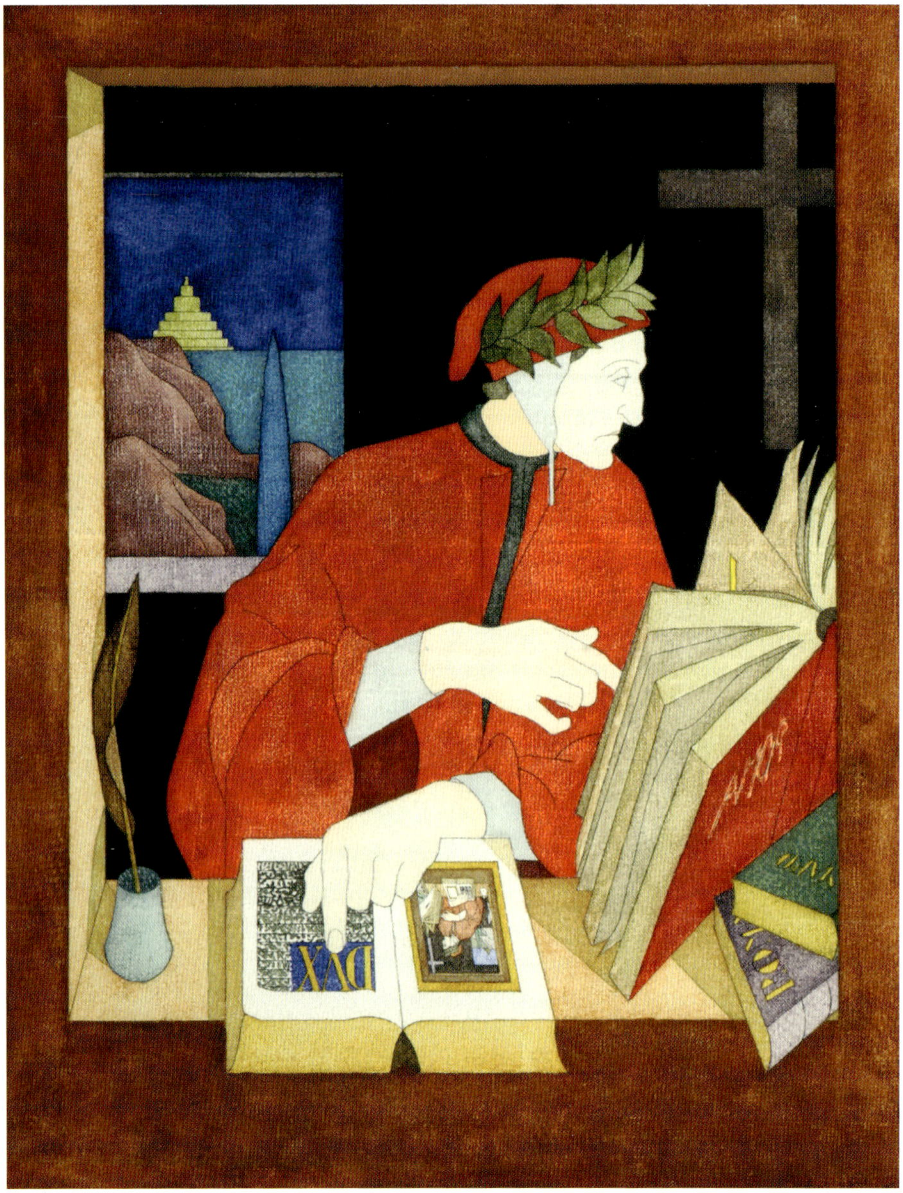

JOHN PIPER (1903–1992)

Piper is best known for his picturesque, architectural and landscape paintings, which are in the romantic tradition of William Blake and J.M.W. Turner. In the early 1930s, however, he produced dramatic abstract works, becoming a member of the 7&5 Group, alongside Ben Nicholson and Henry Moore. In the 1950s, he branched out, creating designs for stained glass, pottery, textiles and stage sets, as well as writing on art and architecture.

Forms on a White Ground
1935
Oil on canvas on board
50.8 x 60.1 cm
Signed, inscribed and dated on the reverse: John Piper 1935/oil/Forms on a White Ground
Provenance: Sir Clifford Norton, 1966; Christie's, London, 7 June 1991; Jonathan Clarke Fine Art, London with Marlborough Fine Art, London, 1996

Exhibited: Cologne Baukunst John Piper Obilder 1965; *John Piper in the 1930s, Abstraction on the Beach*, Dulwich Picture Gallery, London, 1 April–22 June 2003; Djanogly Art Gallery, Nottingham, 5 July–7 September 2003

Literature: David Fraser Jenkins and Frances Spalding, *John Piper in the 1930s, Abstraction on the Beach*, exhibition catalogue, London, Merrell, 2003, no. 36, colour illustration p.120

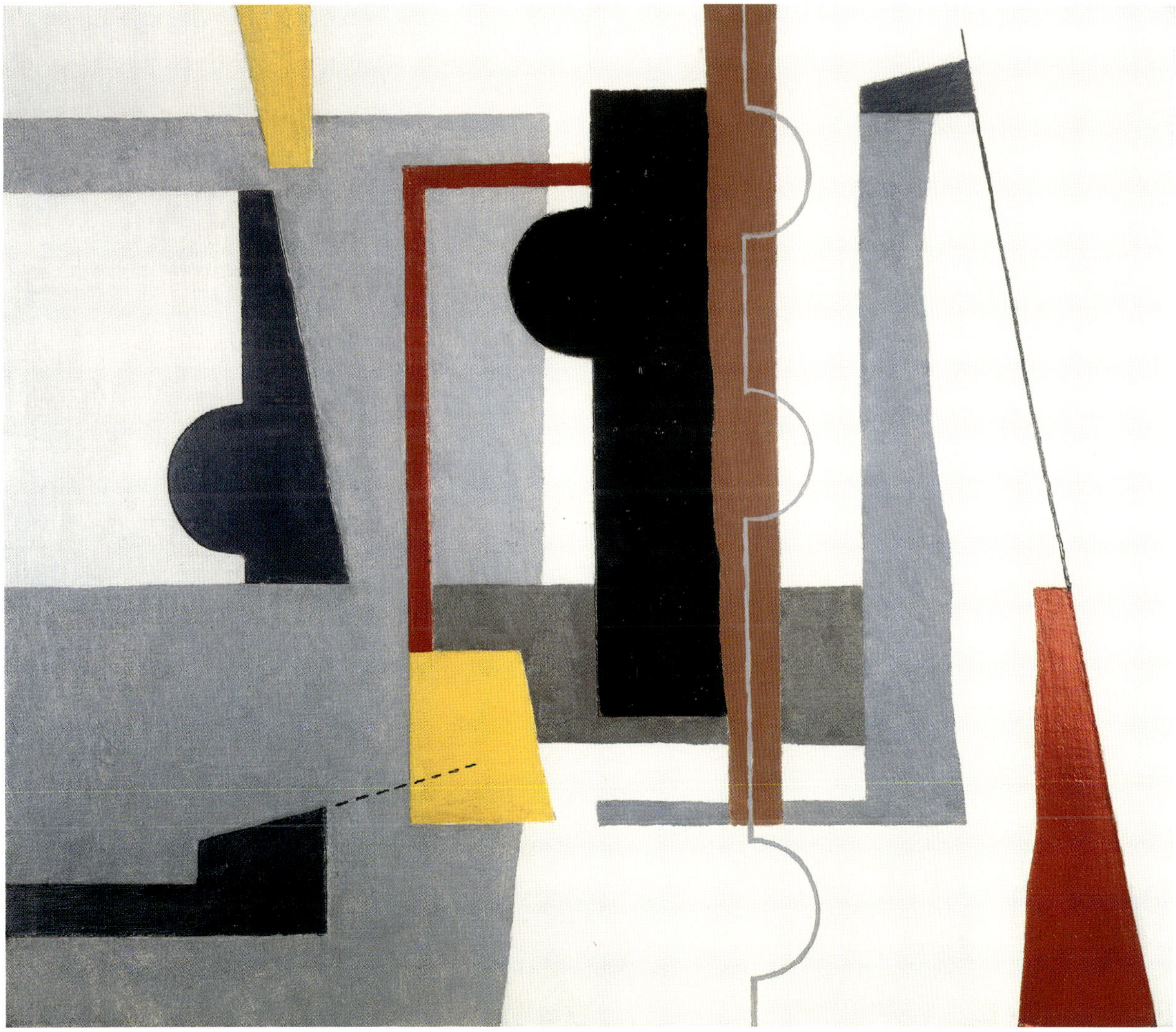

PETER ROSE PULHAM (1910–1956)

Born in 1910, Pulham studied at the Architectural Association School of Architecture and then at Worcester College, Oxford. He was a leading photographer in Britain until 1938, when he turned to painting. He became inspired and socialized in surrealist circles In the 1930s and 1940s.

Interior
Oil on board
50 x 76 cm
Provenance: Mayor Gallery, London

Exhibited: London Gallery; Zwemmer Gallery, London

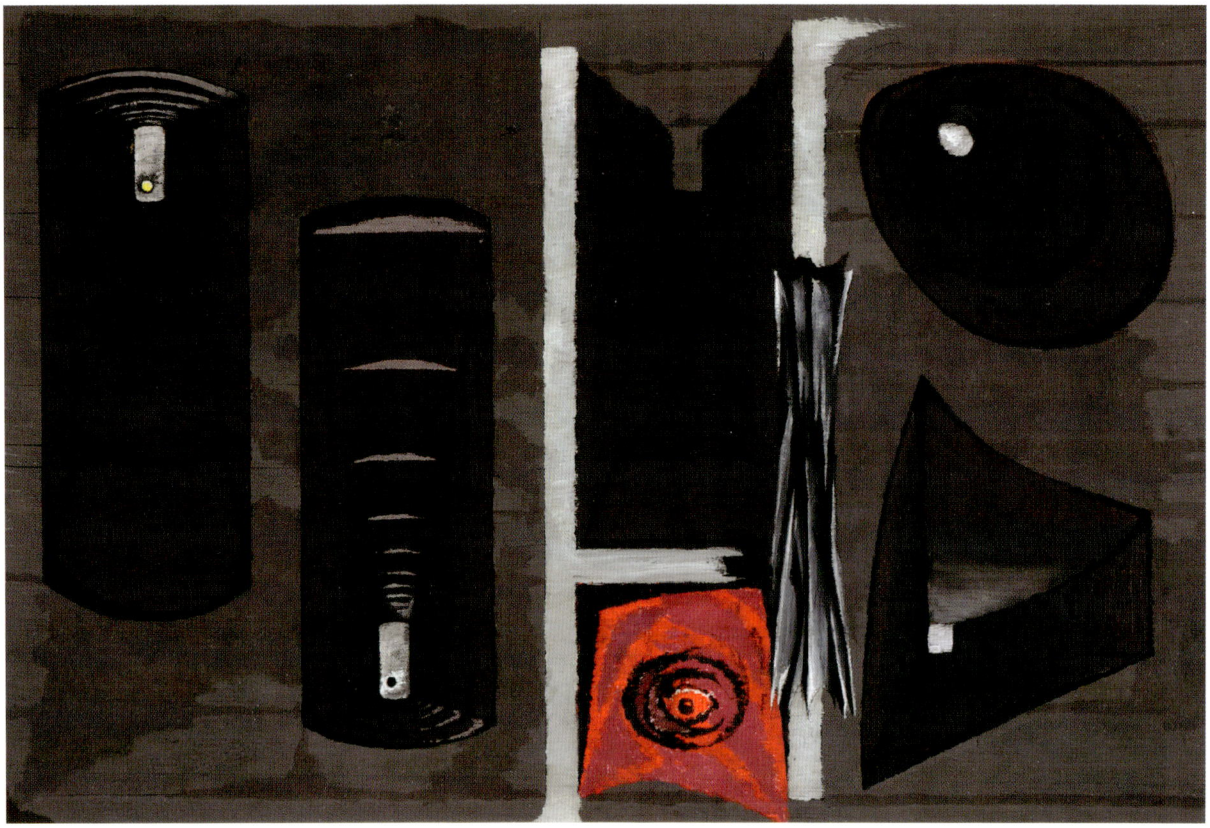

TONY PUSEY (born in 1953)

Paul Hammond and Tony Pusey were both instrumental in the re-launching of surrealist activity at the time of Melmoth. Pusey edited *Melmoth I* in 1980 and produced some of the most eccentric hybridizations of the organic and the inorganic. His creatures, endowed with eyes, noses, mouths, legs and hands, are never devoid of well-pronounced sexual parts.

Cat 2
Pen and ink
38 x 30 cm
Signed and dated: Tony 86

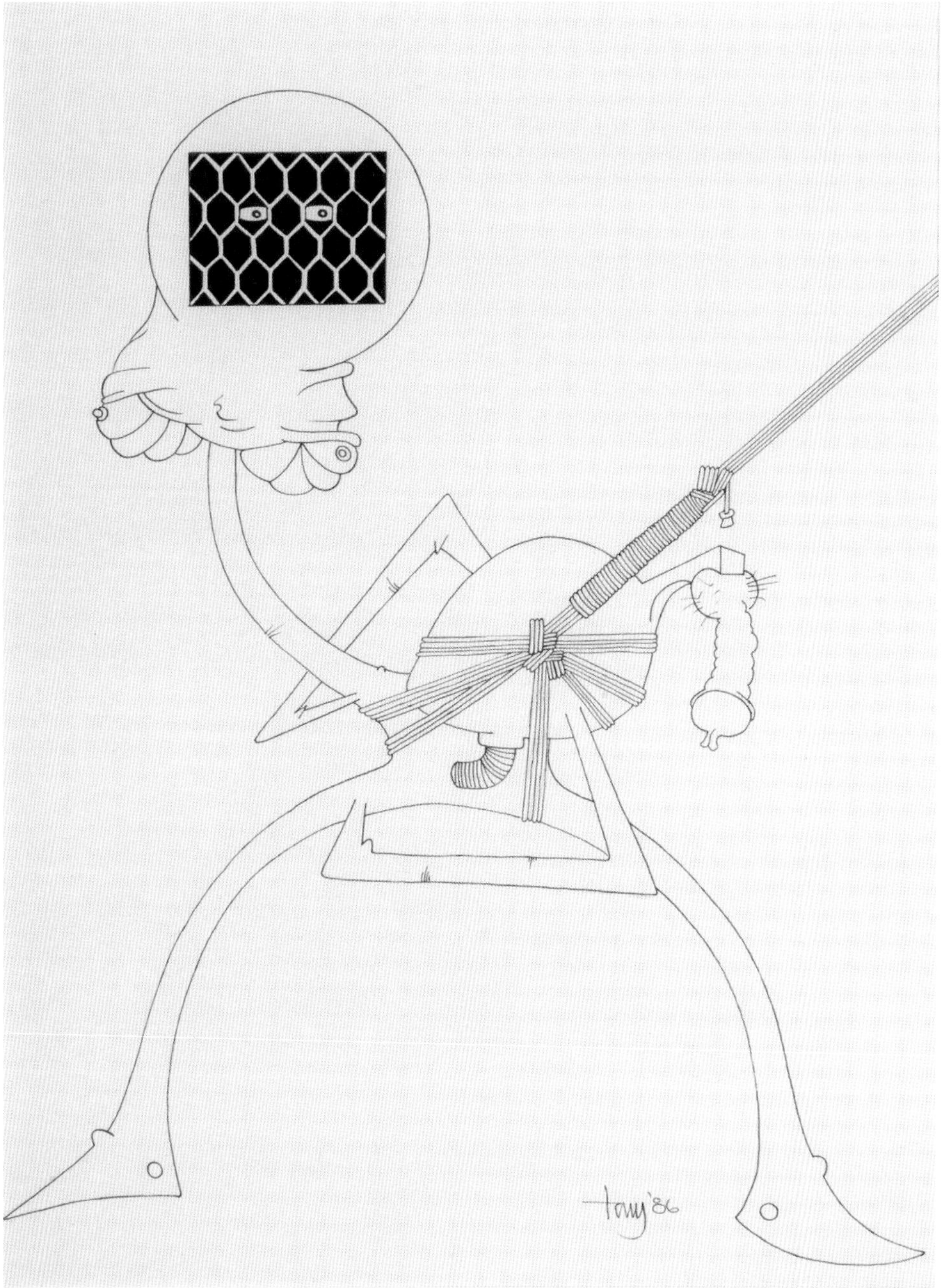

MAN RAY (1890–1976)

Perhaps best described simply as a modernist, Ray was a significant contributor to both the dada and surrealist movements, although his ties to each were informal. Best known in the art world for his avant-garde photography, his artworks took various forms and included photographs, paintings, objects and collages. A highly inventive photographer, he pioneered several techniques, including 'solarization', invented with his photographic assistant, Lee Miller, who became a photographer in her own right. He is noted for his photogams (photographic images made without a camera by placing objects directly onto the surface of a photo-sensitive material such as photographic paper and then exposing it to light) which he renamed 'rayographs' after himself.

Matchboxes
The 10 drawings; Woodpicks; Chalk
1959–60
8 x 5.8 x 3.6 cm
Four matchboxes mounted with photographs, each inscribed with their original contents; ampoule piles, felt, woodpicks, chalk, three silver prints (by Man Ray) and one colour print (photographer unknown), each containing various original items
Provenance: Sotheby's, London, 22 and 23 March 1995

Exhibited: *British Surrealism & Other Realities: The Sherwin Collection*, Museum of Modern Art (Mima), Middlesborough, 23 May–17 August 2008

Man Ray made a small number of matchboxes mounted with photographs, (executed in the early 1960s) of many of his well-known images. Some were used by the artist to store small items in his studio, others were offered as gifts to visitors to the studio when they asked for a light for their cigarette. The photograph of Picasso was taken in 1932 and printed later. The photograph of a watercolour by Man Ray is titled *Post-Columbian Art*.

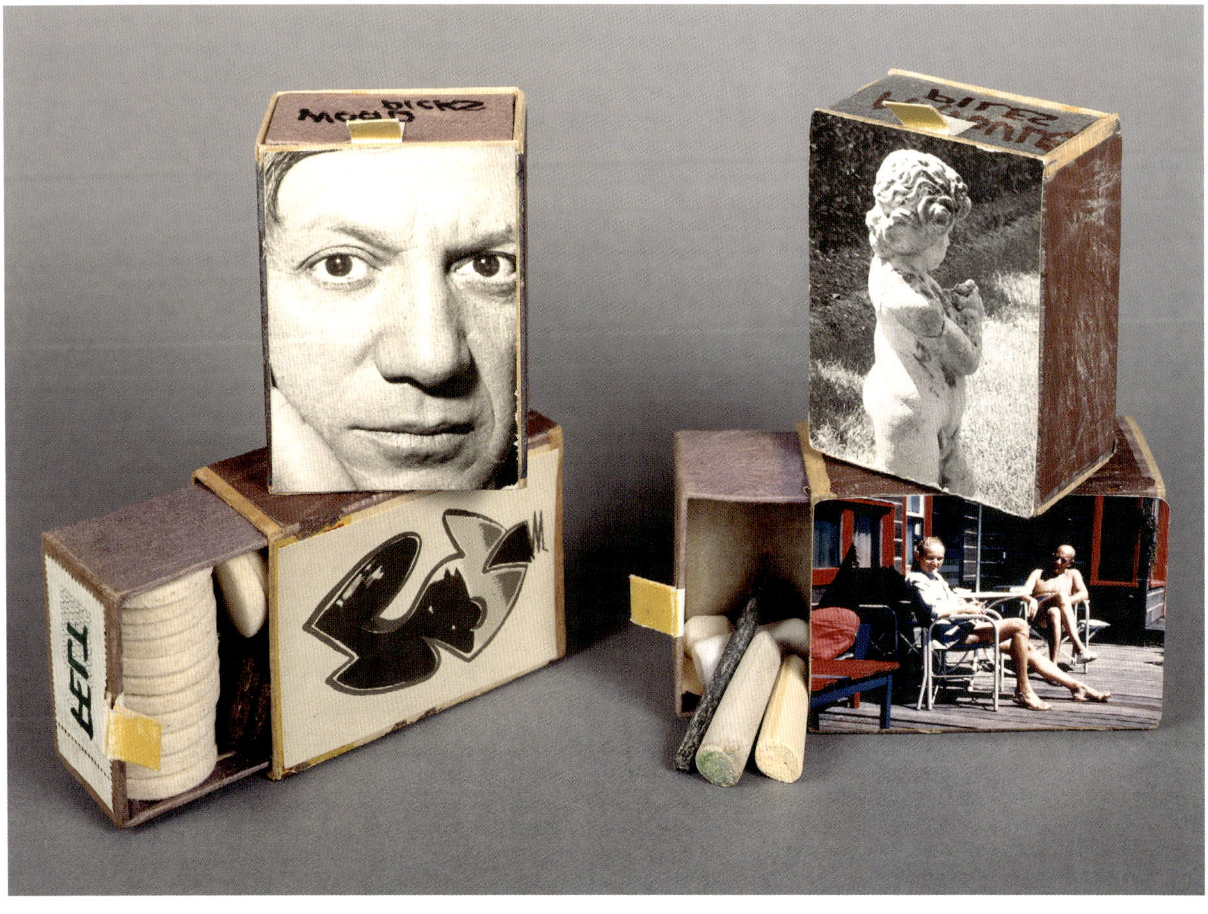

VICTOR REINGANUM (1907–1995)

In 1925, Reinganum went to Paris to study at the Academie Julien and was one of only six students accepted by Ferdinand Leger. Whilst in Paris, he was drawn to the work of the cubists, namely Braque and the purist paintings of Le Corbusier and Leger. The influence of these figures is visible in his precise handling of form and his rigorous structure that dictates every composition.

Angels Eggs
1938
50 x 25 cm
Oil on board
Provenance: the artist; Phillips, London, 4 June 1996

Exhibited: *A Salute to British Surrealism 1930–1950,* The Minories, Colchester, 6 April–5 May 1985; Blond Fine Art, London, 22 May–22 June 1985; Ferens Art Gallery, Hull, 6 July–4 August 1985

Literature: *A Salute to British Surrealism 1930–1950,* exhibition catalogue, Colchester, The Minories, 1985, no. 69

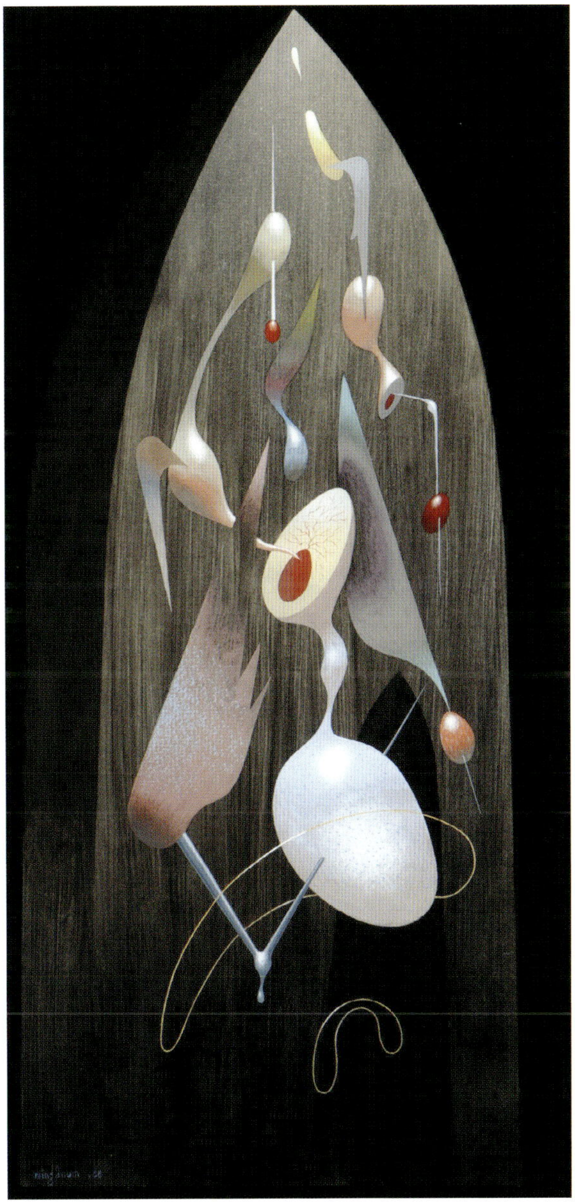

TONI DEL RENZIO (1915–2007)

Del Renzio played an important part in rooting the spirit of surrealism in England, silently reproaching Mesens for its lack of theoretical momentum. In March 1942, to counter the sense of disorientation afflicting the group, he organised the publication of *Arson*, which he described in the preface as 'a surrealist review, testimony of a vital life lived among the ruins not only of bombed houses but of exploited people'. In 1943, he married the painter and writer Ithell Colquhoun, who had been expelled from the surrealist group by Mesens for 'dabbling in the occult'. The marriage, together with the suspicion felt by Mesens that del Renzio was wanting to take over the group, created a rift between the two men.

Paranoiac Regression
1941
36 x 28 cm
Gouache on paper
Illustrated in *Arson*, del Renzio's magazine (one edition only) as a break away group from E.L.T. Mesens – an acrimonious parting of former friends.

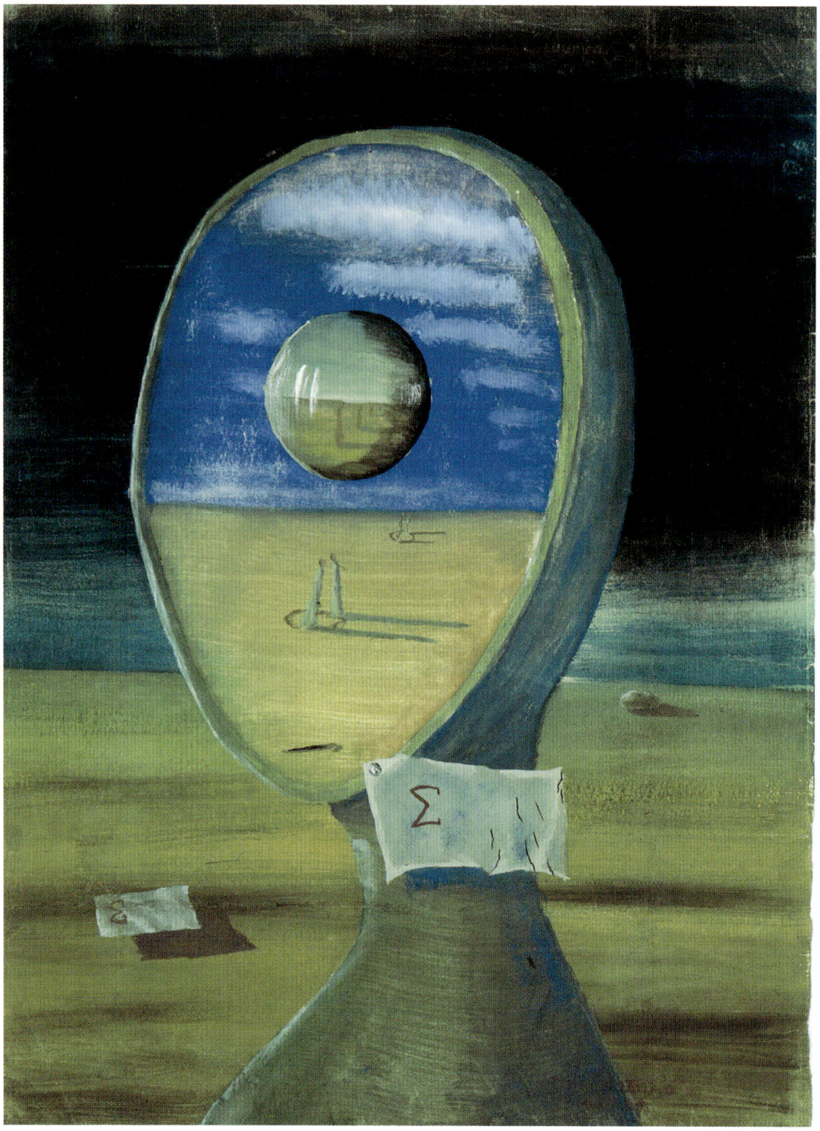

CERI RICHARDS (1903–1971)

Richards was born in Dunvant, near Swansea in Wales. After working as an apprentice to an electrician, he studied at Swansea School of Art from 1921 to 1924 and at the Royal College of Art, London, from 1924 to 1927.

In the 1930s, Richards was influenced by surrealism and he exhibited at the 1936 International Surrealist Exhibition in London. From 1945, Richards' work was influenced by Matisse and Picasso, after he saw an exhibition of their work. In addition to making wooden reliefs and painting, Richards produced book illustrations and designs for the theatre.

Bird And Beast
1944
Oil on canvas
26 x 46 cm
Signed: Ceri Richards
Provenance: Fischer Fine Art, London

Drawing For A Relief
1936
43 x 51.5 cm
Black ink and wash on paper
Provenance: Jonathan Clarke Fine Art, London

Exhibited: *Blast to Frieze, British Art in the 20th Century*, Kunstmuseum Wolfsburg, 2002

Literature: *Art in Britain in the 1930s*, Marlborough Fine Art, catalogue, London, 1965; *Blast to Frieze, British Art in the 20th Century*, Kunstmuseum Wolfsburg, 2002, plate 46, colour illustration; Marlborough 1965 *Art in Britain in the 1930s*

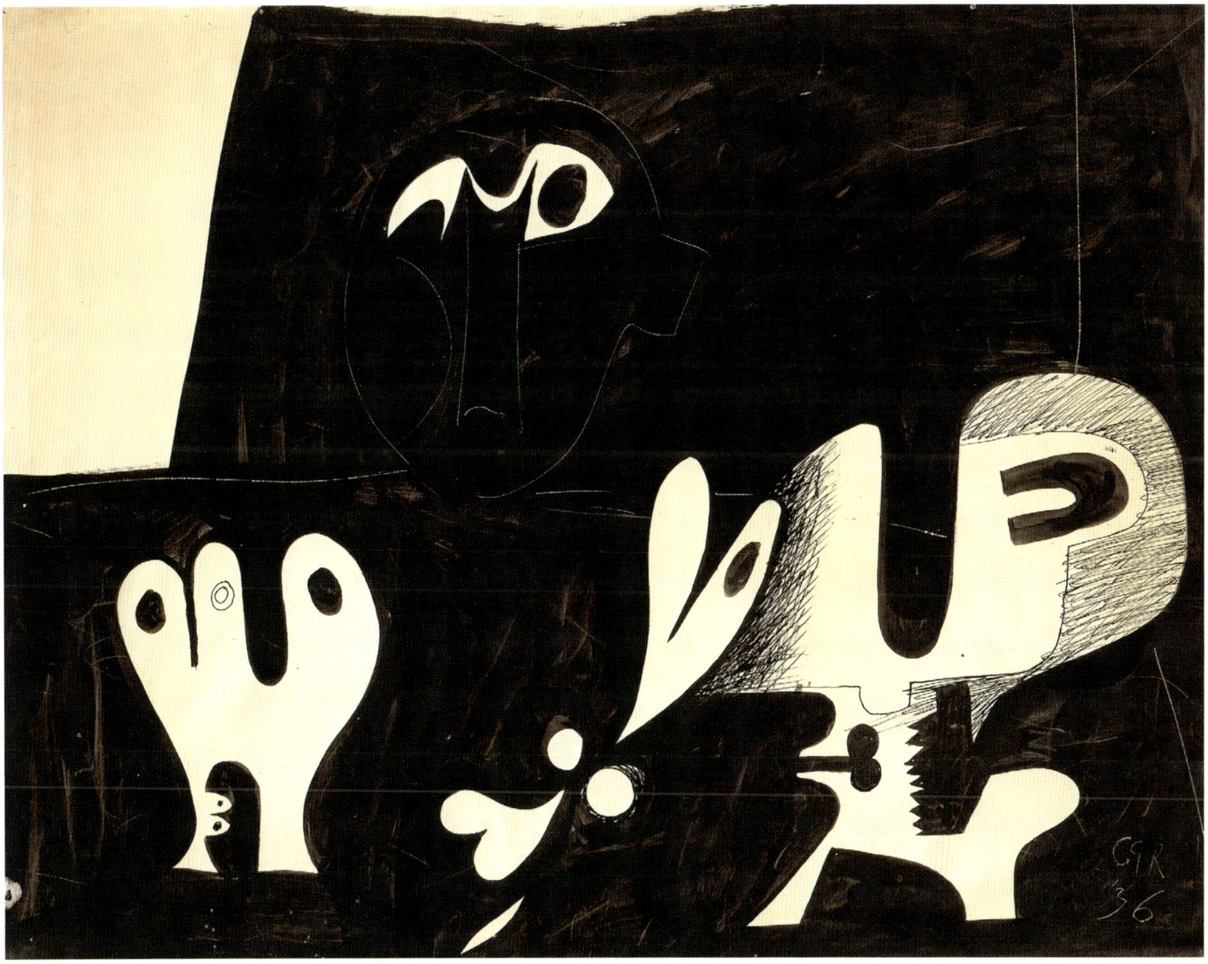

GERRIT THOMAS RIETVELD (1888–1964)

Rietveld was born in Utrecht in the Netherlands. After working in his father's joinery business, he apprenticed at a jewellery studio. In 1911, he started his own cabinet-making firm, which he maintained for eight years. In this same period, he studied architecture. Through his studies, he became acquainted with several founders of De Stijl. In 1917, Rietveld designed the *Red-Blue Chair*, which signalled a radical change in architectural theory. His unusual furniture designs led to several housing commissions, which he invariably designed in a Neo-Plastic style. The designs utilized the free and variable use of space and showed a profound understanding of dynamic spatial ideas.

Red-Blue Chair
1917
Painted wood
90 x 60 x 85 cm

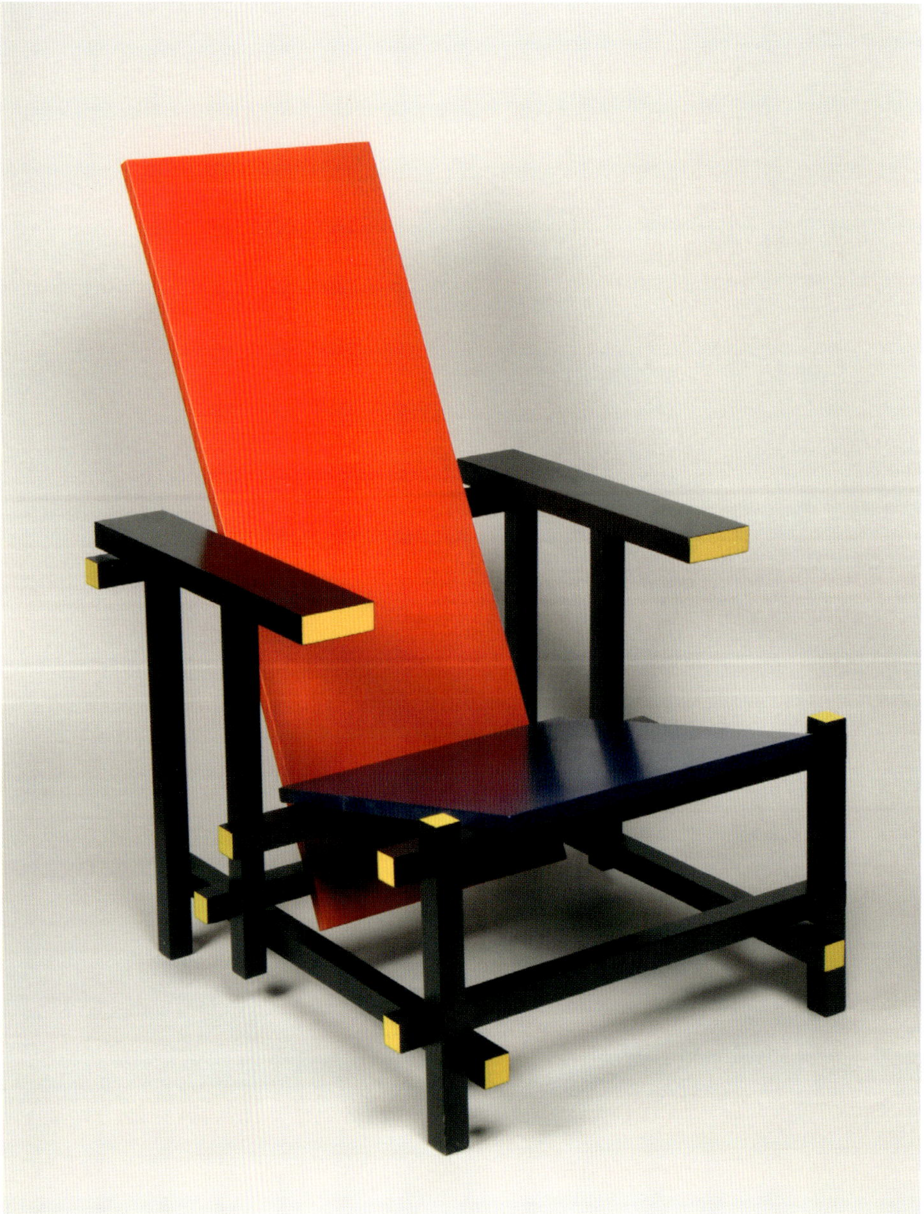

EDITH RIMMINGTON (1902–1986)

Rimmington joined the British Surrealist Group in 1937. She exhibited regularly with the surrealists and practised automatic writing and drawing, with some of her poems appearing in surrealist publications. Her paintings are noted for their delicacy and the precise application of paint. Many of her paintings feature images of poetic metamorphosis, with subjects relating to death and the sea, or feature disquieting sexual elements. By 1950, Rimmington had begun to experiment with photography, on which she concentrated in her later years.

Sisters of Anarchy
1940–41
Oil on canvas
30 x 35 cm

Minerva, metamorphosing into her owl being. Minerva, the Roman Goddess. Minerva the Owl was the symbol of wisdom and came to symbolise philosophy (Hegel). Edith Rimmington sees philosophy in anarchic terms.

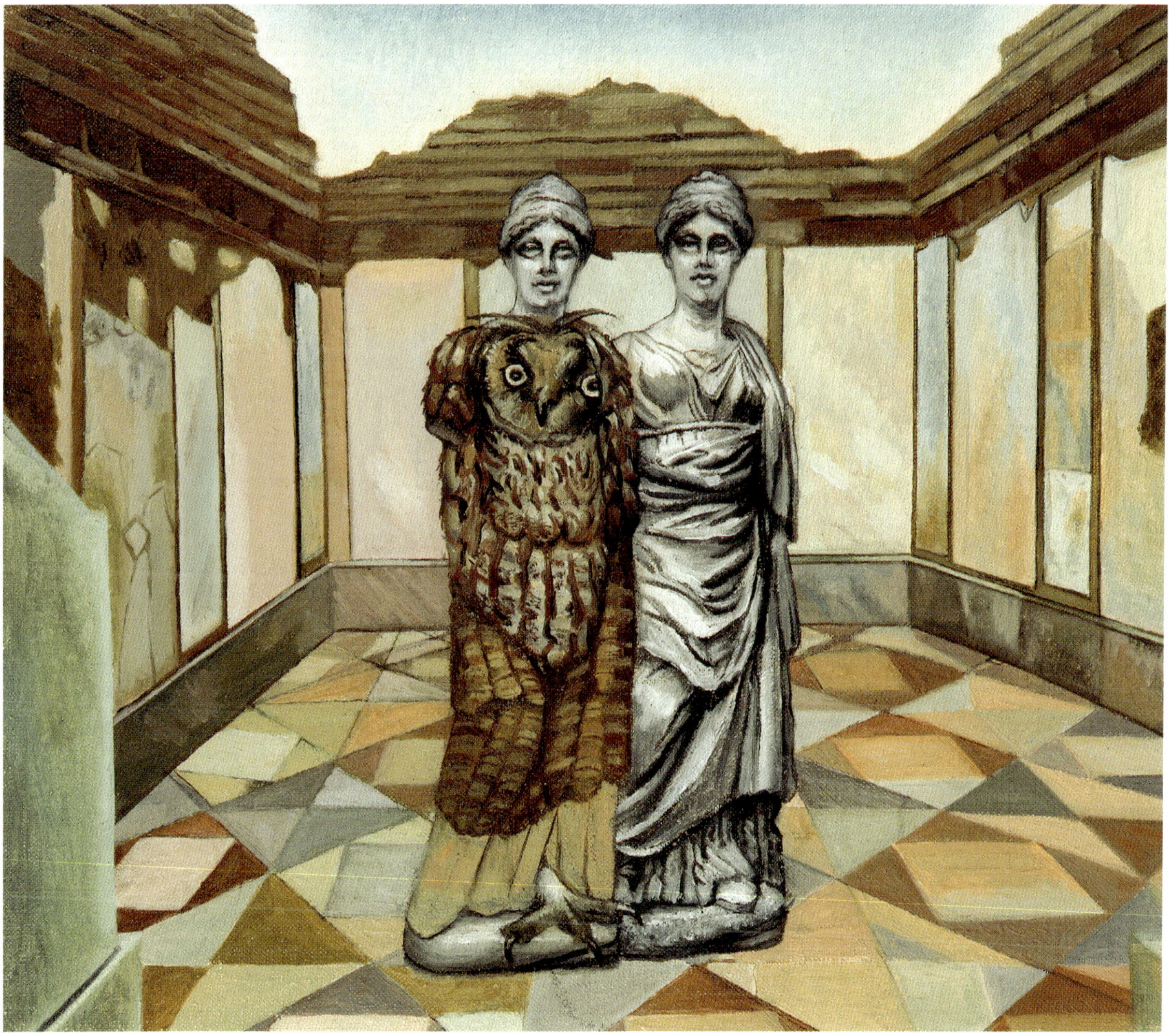

WILLIAM ROBERTS (1895–1980)

Roberts showed a sturdy independence, viewing the life around him with an almost Hogarthian eye for the antics of London's inhabitants. Many of his pictures of the 1920s contain acerbic and even grotesque elements, as he developed into an interpreter of city life on the street, in the cinema, at the music hall and on the dance floor. Retaining the stern architecture of his pre-war work and yet infusing it with a more robust feeling for the solidity of the human figure, Roberts treated his predominantly working-class protagonists with humour and dignity. He was a founder member of the influential Vorticist Group, a powerful recorder of the front-line battles of the First World War, and a unique observer of the foibles and activities of Britain at leisure.

The Wiring Party
c.1915–18
Black ink, wash and pastel on paper
28 x 38 cm
Signed
Provenance: Sotheby's, London, 1994

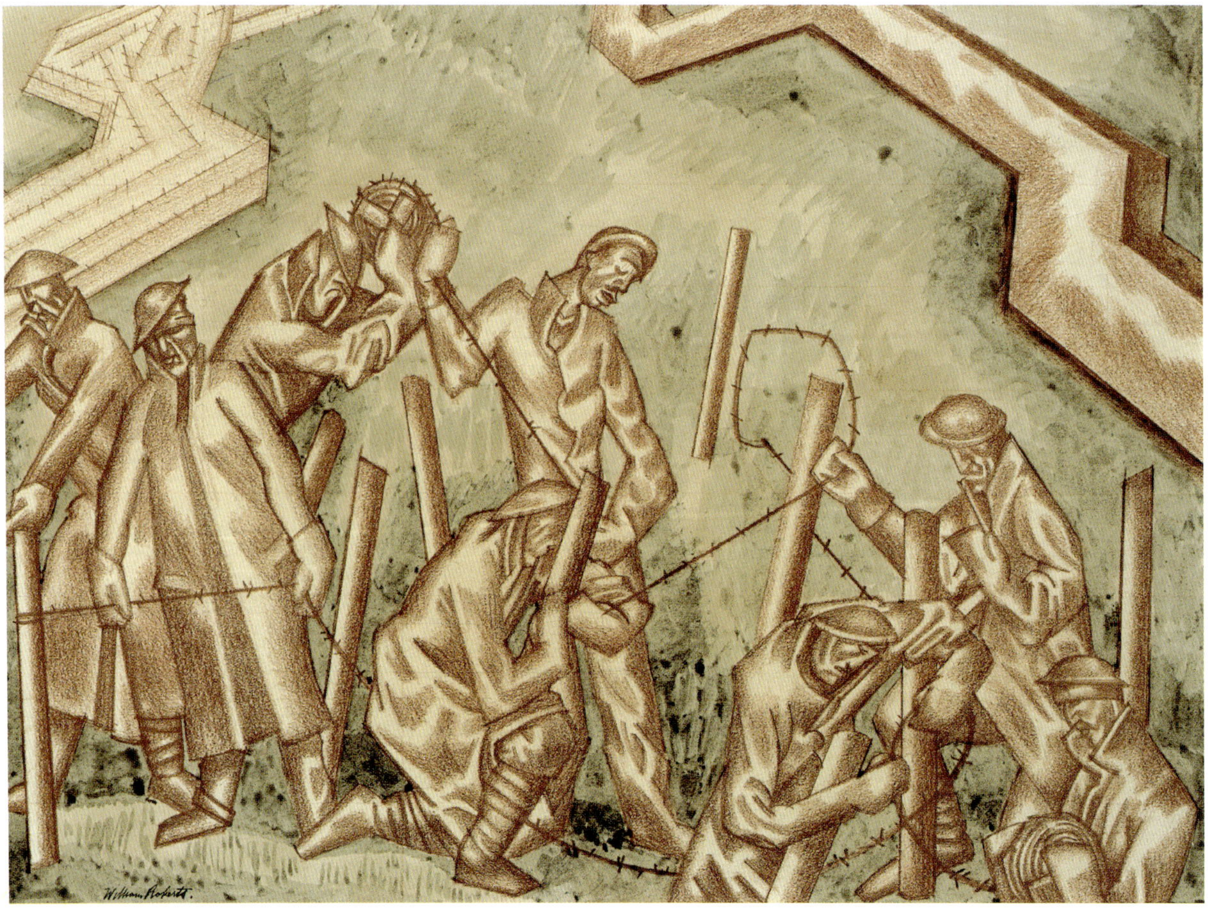

KURT SCHWITTERS (1887–1948)

Born and based for most of his life in Hanover, Schwitters began composing collages and assemblages from junk and everyday ephemera in 1919. He called these works 'Merz', a term derived from the cut-up letterhead of a bank used in one of his collages. He later used 'Merz' to refer to all his artistic activities, including painting, sculpture, typography and installation. He transformed the interior of much of his house in Hanover into a fantastic work of art – the so-called 'Merz Building'. He is often seen as a dadaist, but while dada defined itself as anti-art, Schwitters asserted that his work was art. The artist fled Nazi Germany in 1937, living first in Norway, before settling in England in 1940.

Mr. Churchill Is 71
1947
Collage and gouache
19.5 x 16 cm
Signed, titled and dated on the mount
Provenance: Ernst Schwitters (recorded under 1947/1064 Kurt Schwitters Archives, Sprengel Museum Hannover); Sotheby's, London, 9 December 1997, Lot 256

Exhibited: *VI Bien de Sao Paulo,* Sao Paulo, 1961, no. 84; *Blast to Frieze, British Art in the 20th Century,* Kunstmuseum Wolfsburg, 2002

Literature: *Blast to Frieze, British Art in the 20th Century,* exhibition catalogue, Kunstmuseum Wolfsburg/Hatje Cantz, 2002

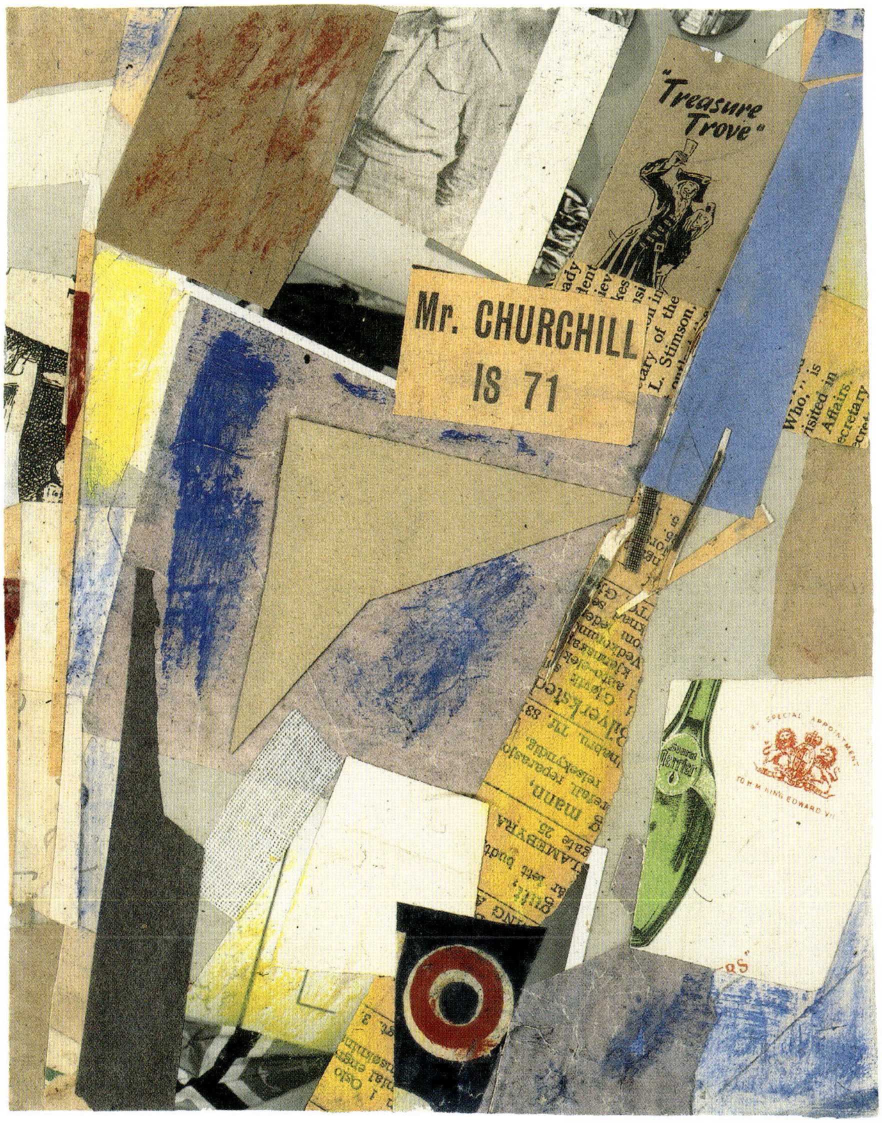

HUMPHREY SPENDER (1910–2005)

Humphrey Spender was a pioneer of the documentary photography style that suited the Mass Observation methods of gathering information. He first became aware of this form of candid photography while studying in Germany in the late 1920s. New technology and smaller cameras were making it possible for a photographer to be less noticeable in public. This allowed for more intimate social documentary.

He found the experience of taking documentary photos particularly stressful and disliked the intrusiveness of his work. After the Second World War, these anxieties persuaded him to all but abandon photography in favour of painting and textile design. Spender continued painting until his death in 2005.

Keep Moving
1952
Glass and mirror box
28 x 41 x 5 cm
Provenance: Leicester Local Authority (Education Department); Christie's, London, 25 July 1996, Lot 395

Designed for Pilkington's Glass of St. Helens as a possible 'mural' but not constructed

John Banting with Nazi Flag
1938
Photograph
38 x 28 cm
Provenance: the artist

Exhibited: *Contrariwise, Surrealism and Britain 1930–1986*, Swansea Festival Exhibition 1986, Glynn Vivian Art Gallery, Swansea, 20 September–15 November 1986; Victoria Art Gallery, Bath, 22 November 1986–3 January 1987; Polytechnic Gallery, Newcastle, 10 January–21 February 1987; Mostyn Art Gallery, Llandudno, 28 February–11 April 1987

Literature: *Contrariwise, Surrealism and Britain 1930–1986*, Swansea Festival Exhibition 1986, no. 132, illustration

Self Portrait
1980s
Photograph
38 x 28 cm

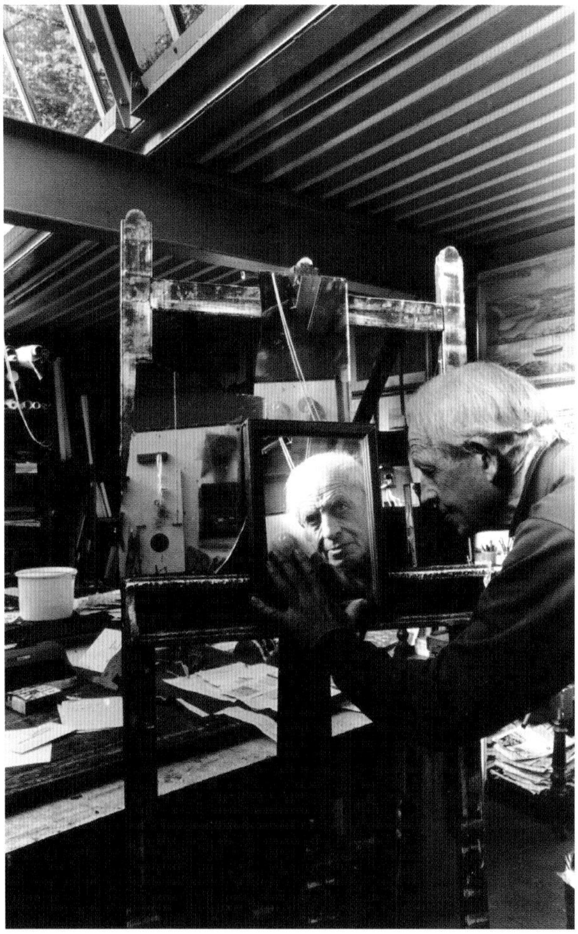

JOHN CECIL STEPHENSON (1889–1965)

Born in Auckland, Stephenson studied, among others, at the Leeds School of Art. In 1932, he began making his first abstract works, exhibiting during the next decade in many abstract and constructive shows in England, France and the USA. In 1934, he exhibited with the Seven and Five Society, along with the likes of Ben and Winifred Nicholson, Ivon Hitchens, Henry Moore, Barbara Hepworth and John Piper. From the 1950s, he returned to large abstract paintings, realizing many of the abstract compositions he had sketched out on a small scale in the previous decade, when materials had been in short supply.

Abstract
1934
Oil and collage
23 x 46 cm
Signed on the reverse: Cecil Stephenson 6 Mall Studios Parkhill Road Hampstead NW3. (Where Henry Moore and Ben Nicholson had studios).

The only part-collage (egg and sausage shape) known and incorporates various abstract shapes but with curls. Provenance: John Bruckland, Christie's, London, 26 March 1993

Bright Triangles
1938
Oil and tempera on canvas
102 x 76 cm
Signed on reverse

Various textures and abstract shapes, both solid and linear. Was Stephenson in competition with Nicholson to create different textures as suggested? Parkin Fine Art, Fischer Fine Art, Ex Camden Arts Centre, Herbert Read Exhibition, Leeds

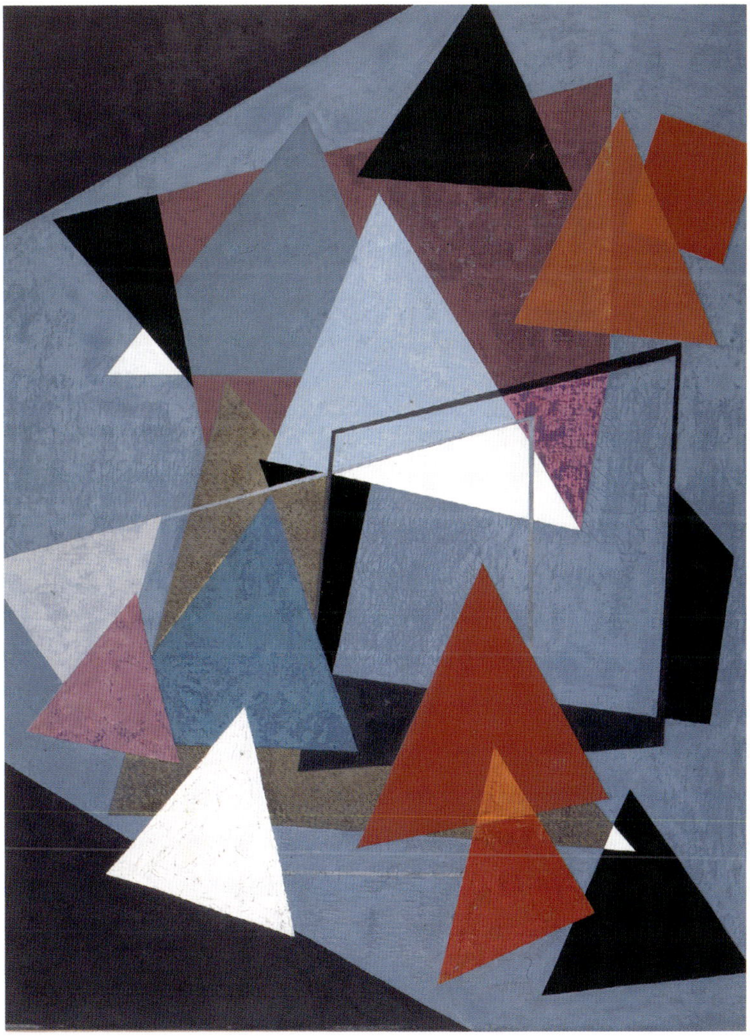

HARRY THUBRON (1915–1985)

Thubron's radical and reconstructive work in art education was legendary and many have said that he was one of the greatest teachers this country has ever known. He was Head of Fine Art at the Art Colleges of Sunderland (1950–55), Leeds (1955–64) and Lancaster (1966–68).

As a painter, sculptor and collagist, he is less well known and perhaps his own work as an artist was obscured by his commitment to his teaching practice. Although interested in Kurt Schwitters and Antoni Tàpies, it was the work of Paul Klee that Thubron most admired. Just as Thubron encouraged his students to experiment in a constructive manner, to exercise their intuition, to explore their own sensibilities, he described his own works as the result of emotive and imaginative experiences. His art served as a means of self-development and self-discovery.

Fanta
Collage on board
40 x 42 cm
Signed on reverse
Provenance: artist estate; Keith Chapman Gallery, London, 2009

Exhibited: Yorkshire Contemporary Art Show, Leeds, 1985, no. 23

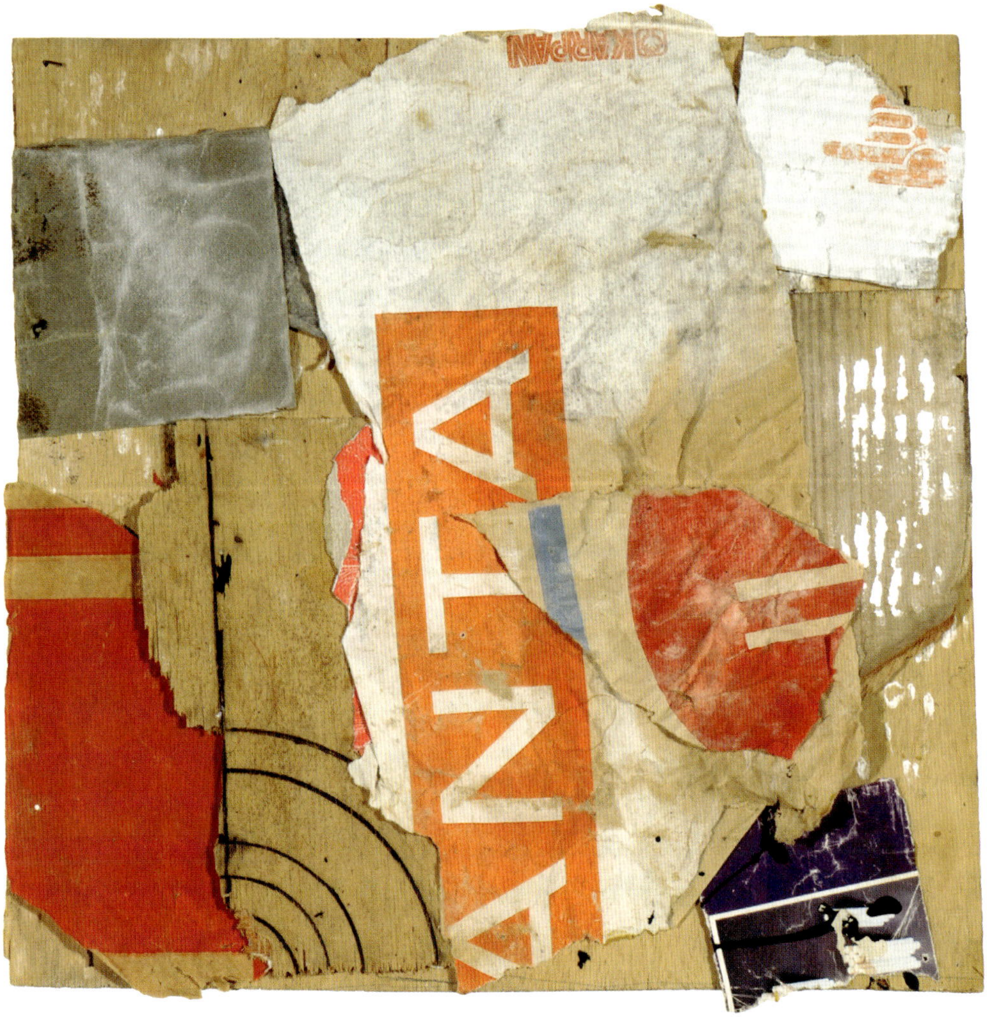

JULIAN TREVELYAN (1910–1988)

From his student days at Cambridge, Trevelyan had taken a keen interest in the surrealist movement. In 1930, he published the article *Dreams in Experiment*, edited by Humphrey Jennings, and while studying at Hayter's engraving school in Paris in 1931, he had encountered Picasso, Masson, Miró and Calder.

Trevelyan became a confirmed surrealist and exhibited at the International Surrealist Exhibition in 1936, but he was also closely involved in the Mass Observation Unit. He renounced his surrealist affiliations by formally resigning from the British Surrealist Group in 1938.

Ethiop Queen
c.1933
Oil on canvas
54 x 79 cm
Provenance: Jonathan Clark Fine Art, London

Hypnosis
1935
Oil on canvas
71 x 45 cm

Trevelyan left Cambridge on the advice of Jacob Bronowsky and worked with Stanley Hayter at Atelier 17, where he met Calder, from whom he purchased the first mobile that he sold. The mobile is now in the Tate but there is a reference to the mobile in the painting.

Captive in Eden
1936
Slate and paint
40.5 x 30.5 cm
Provenance: signed and dated on SLATE Engraved

Sold at auction 1951 at the Chenil Gallery, 'Art for Peace'.

Exhibited: *Blast to Frieze, British Art in the 20th Century*, Kunstmuseum Wolfsburg, 2002

Literature: *Blast to Frieze, British Art in the 20th Century*, exhibition catalogue, Kunstmuseum Wolfsburg/Hatje Cantz, 2002, plate 60, colour illustration

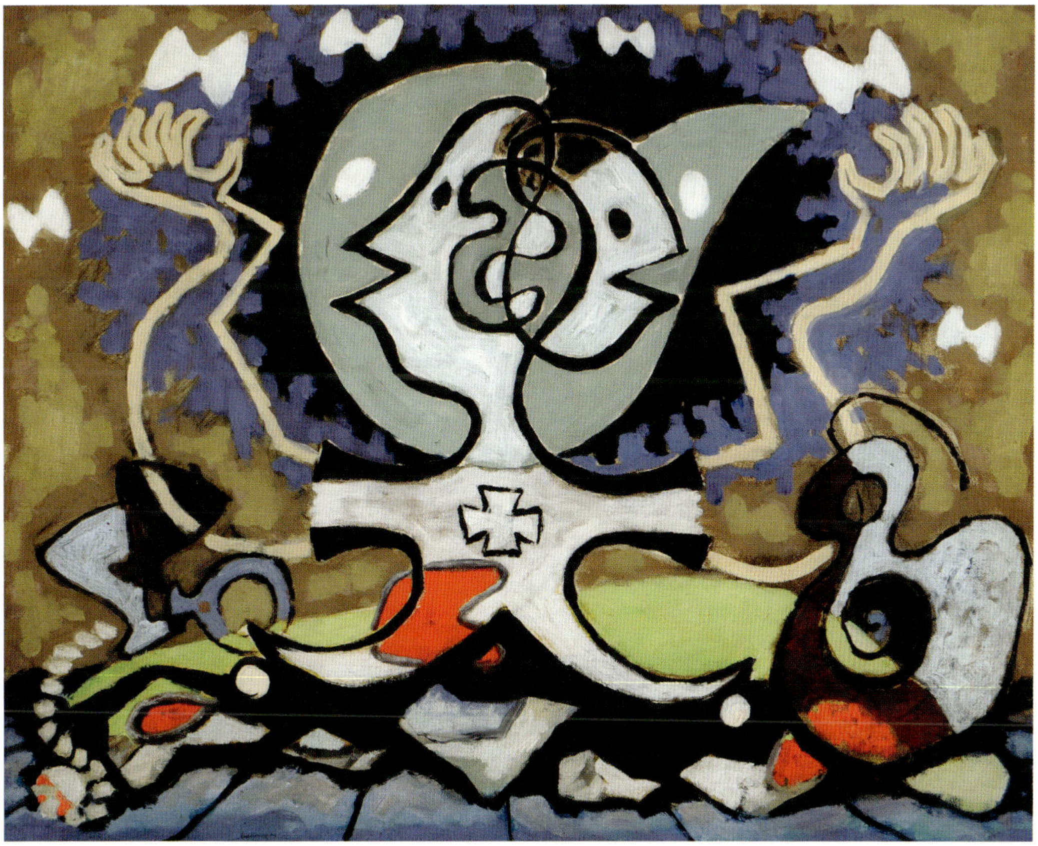

JOHN TUNNARD (1900–1971)

Tunnard studied at the Royal College of Art in London and worked as a textile designer early in his career. On moving to Cornwall in 1930, he devoted increasing amounts of time to painting. During the Second World War, Tunnard served as a coastguard and his paintings of this period show a preoccupation with navigational equipment, weather effects and distant horizons. Influenced by the work of Miró, Klee, and British abstract artists, Tunnard developed a distinctive style, which contained references to electrical appliances such as radars and radios. An accomplished jazz musician, the lines stretched across his pictures refer both to futuristic electrical equipment and stringed instruments. He participated in several surrealist exhibitions, but never officially joined the group.

Diabolo On The Quay
1936
Oil on canvas
45 x 61 cm
Signed and dated
Provenance: Julian Trevelyan R.A.; Mary Fedden; Christie's, London, 1996

Exhibited: *Blast to Frieze, British Art in the 20th Century,* Kunstmuseum Wolfsburg, 2002

Literature: *Blast to Frieze, British Art in the 20th Century,* exhibition catalogue, Kunstmuseum Wolfsburg/Hatje Cantz, 2002, plate 85, colour illustration

Composition With Anchor
1936
Pencil, black ink, watercolour, collage, black and coloured crayon on paper
35.5 x 23.5 cm
Signed and dated: John Tunnard 36
Provenance: Julian Trevelyan R.A.

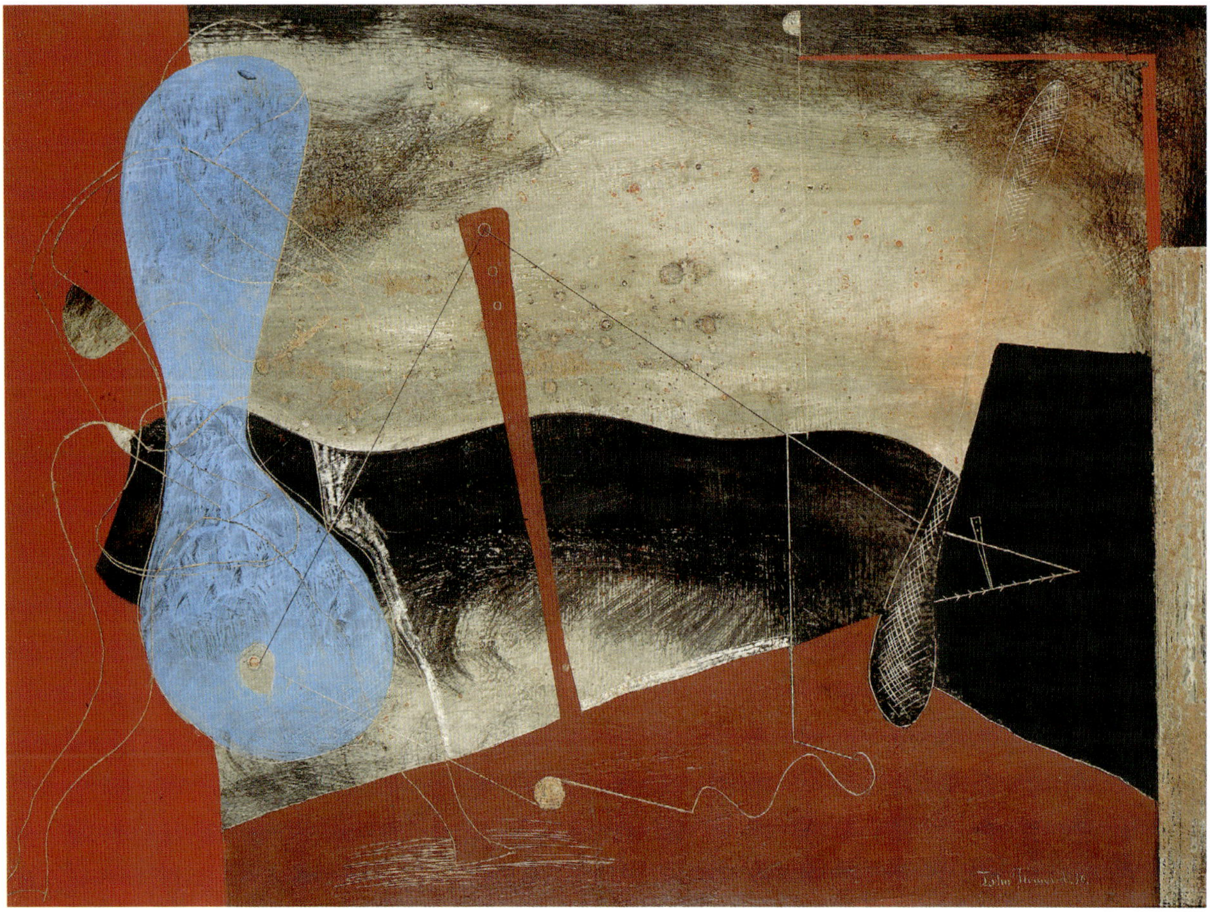

LEON UNDERWOOD (1890–1975)

Underwood was an artist, collector and writer. He was very interested in ethnography and non-western art, writing several books on various aspects of it. Throughout his life he travelled extensively to pursue his interest in cultures from which he drew inspiration. His responses to non-western art were motivated by a desire to achieve a sense of authenticity.

Mask of Apollo in Autumn
1933
Painted wood
Height: 27 cm
Provenance: estate of Leon Underwood; Christie's, London, 28 February 2007

Exhibited: *An exhibition of Sculpture, Painting, Drawings and Engravings by Leon Underwood,* Leicester Galleries, 1934 (1); *Mexico and After: Sculpture, Paintings, Drawings and Prints 1928–36,* Cardiff, National Museum of Wales, 1 August–16 September 1979 (10)

Literature: Ben Witworth, *The Sculpture of Leon Underwood,* The Henry Moore Foundation/Lund Humphries, 2000, no. 63 (Private Collection London)

The Herald of a New Day
1934
Polished brass, edition 1 of 2
Height: 75 cm including base
Provenance: Kate Murphy, Sotheby's, London, 7 November 1990

Exhibited: *Leon Underwood,* The Minories, Colchester, 1969

Literature: Christopher Neve, *Leon Underwood,* London, Thames & Hudson, 1974, p.151

The *Herald of a New Day* belongs to a series of dancing figures all produced in 1934. In all of them, the role of shine is an important one, as each surface explores luminosity to different degrees. It is also an essential component of the sculpture's ability to convey a sense of rhythm. All of them express dance and music: the Herald visualizes the ecstatic sound of a trumpet. Underwood first explored the expression of dance and rhythm using polished materials in 1932. He learned of the role of polished metal in Asian art from Gertrude Hermes. Both artists also responded to Brancusi's use of polished bronze and his condensing of anatomical detail to minimal forms.

Untitled (Foetus)
1924–25
Chalk
12 x 19 x 7 cm
Provenance: the carving was given to John Clark (Cosmo Clark) by Blair Hugh Stanton, 1926

Literature: Ben Witworth, *The Sculpture of Leon Underwood,* The Henry Moore Foundation/Lund Humphries, 2000, no. 16

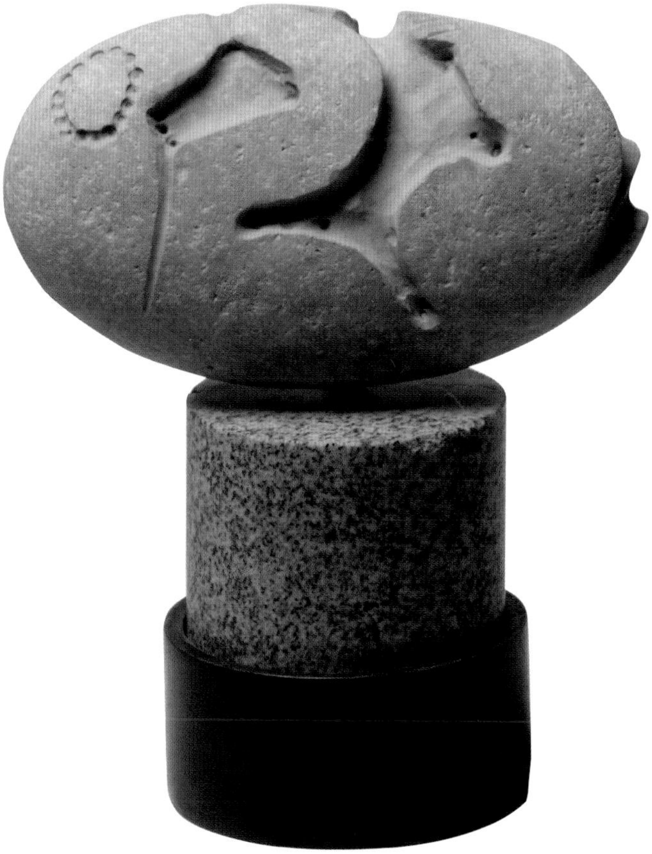

BOYD WEBB (born 1947)

His early photographic work was a kind of eccentric living painting, short fables in action with very simple props. The characters interacted in a fantasy world made of cardboard, polystyrene or plastic, in which the artificial constructed nature of environment was acknowledged and actually made it easier for the onlooker to get involved in the developing action. The brief stories performed are normally characterized by serious humour, in the tradition of Buster Keaton. His images evoke a fantastic and dreamlike universe and, in recent years, have come to comment on the balance between man and nature.

Prehensile Torpor
1977 3/3
Colour photograph
27 x 43 cm
Provenance: exhibited Jean & Karen Bernier, Athens; Sotheby's, London, 20 March 1997, Lot 115

Exhibited: *Contrariwise, Surrealism and Britain 1930–1986,* Swansea Festival Exhibition 1986, Glynn Vivian Art Gallery, Swansea, 20 September–15 November 1986; Victoria Art Gallery, Bath, 22 November 1986–3 January 1987; Polytechnic Gallery, Newcastle, 10 January–21 February 1987; Mostyn Art Gallery, Llandudno, 28 February–11 April 1987

Literature: *Contrariwise, Surrealism and Britain 1930–1986,* Swansea Festival Exhibition 1986, no. 143

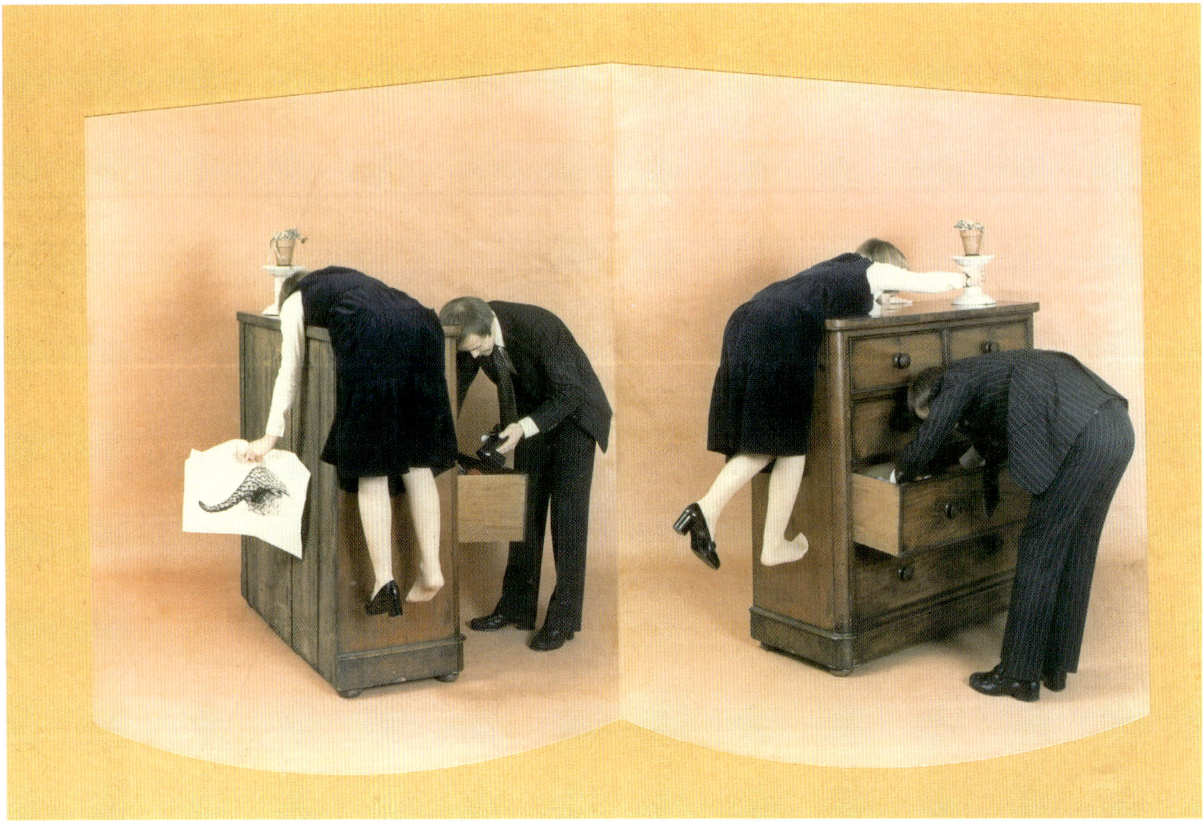

JOHN WELSON (born 1953)

John Welson produced his first surrealist paintings when 14 years old and has continued to work in the surrealist style. He met Conroy Maddox in 1973 and has been associated with the surrealist movement ever since. Welson has developed a constant, razor-sharp imagery contributing to all publications and exhibitions on present-day surrealism in Britain, as well as in exhibitions abroad. He co-edited *Surrealism – The Hinge of History* with Conroy Maddox and Paul Hammond in 1979. More recently, his works have been illustrated in *Manticore/Surrealist Communication*, the Leeds Surrealists Group's journal, which ran from 1997 until 2006.

Brittle Evening
April 11 1977
Oil on board
40 x 51 cm
Provenance: the artist

Brain Of Britain
17 May 1977
Collage
23 x 36 cm
Provenance: the artist

Interior
29 July 1978
Oil on board
49 x 64 cm
Provenance: the artist

Portrait of Óscar Dominguez
19 March 1978
Oil on board
38 x 32 cm
Provenance: the artist

Piano Hands
20 August 1980
Oil on board
19 x 23 cm
Provenance: the artist

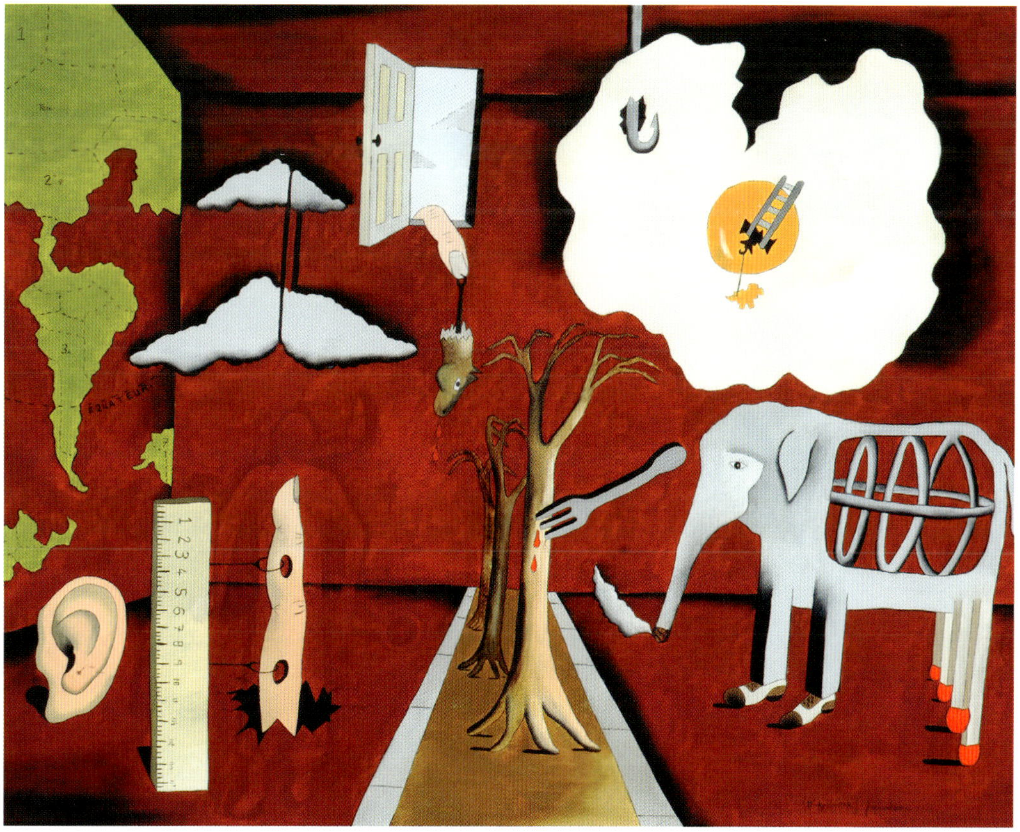

SCOTTIE WILSON (1891–1972)

Born Louis Freeman, Scottie Wilson was an Outsider artist known for his highly detailed style. He didn't complete many years of schooling, and while still in his teens joined the Scottish Rifles. Through two terms of military service, he went to France, South Africa and India.

He started his artistic career at the age of 44. His work was admired by the London Surrealists and collected by Jean Dubuffet and Pablo Picasso. Wilson relied on a relatively narrow range of visual elements – botanical forms, birds and animals, clowns (self-portraits), and 'Greedies' and 'Evils' (malignant personifications).

A British artist who grew up in Scotland, later moving to Canada before returning to his native England, he was an enigmatic character, and his drawings share this mysterious quality. Distinctive hatch marks provide texture in his works, populated by sinister 'greedies and evils' in his earlier pieces, later replaced with serenely decorative swans and fish. Although self-taught, Wilson was rather successful, in conventional terms, by the end of his life, though not even those who knew him realized how successful he was.

Despite receiving recognition for his work, he suddenly left Canada in 1945, returning to London. Only a few short months after his arrival, he had a solo exhibition at the Arcade Gallery in London, shown concurrently with *Surrealist Diversity* which included works by Picasso, De Chirico, Klee, Miró, and others.

Though conventional art galleries were taking interest in selling Wilson's work, he wasn't always fond of parting with his drawings. He would at times rent out vacant store fronts to display his pictures, or hang them in a bus, but not necessarily to sell. Instead, Wilson would charge admission for looking at his work, challenging anyone to find anything else like it in the world.

Town With Greedies, Moon And Bird
c.1945
Crayon, ink, gouache on paper
28 x 36 cm

Untitled
c.1945
Pen and ink on paper
28 x 19 cm

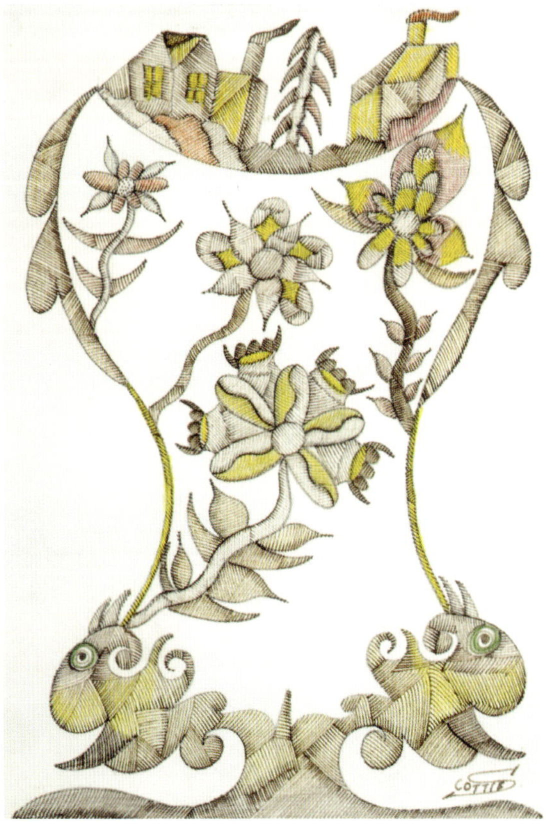

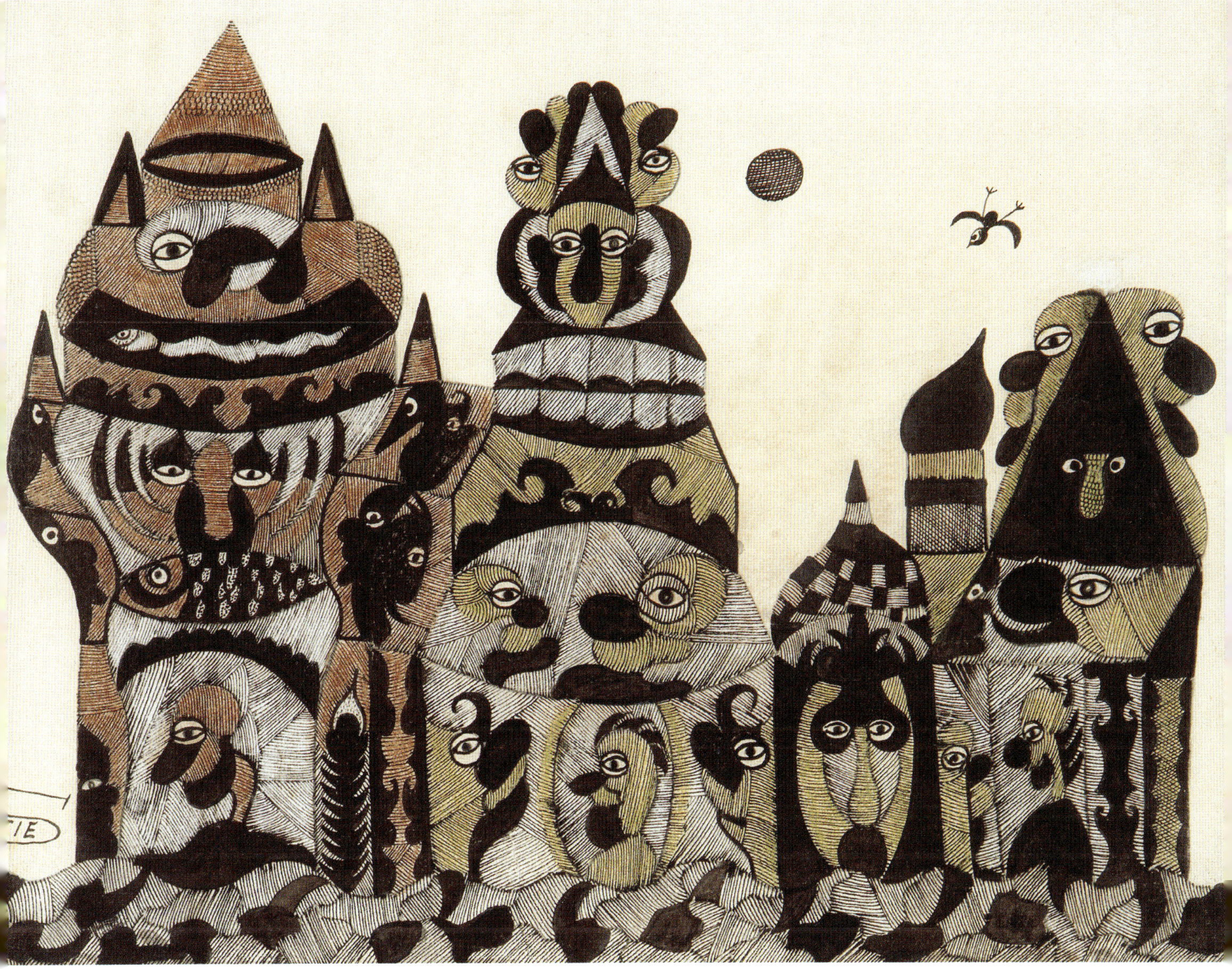

BILL WOODROW (born 1948)

In 1980, Bill Woodrow first devised his characteristic method of making sculpture, forming new objects from urban scrap, which he partially embedded in plaster as if they have been excavated. Collecting all manner of things, altering them and giving them a new context, allowed him an element of narrative in his work.

Playing with History, 2002
Aluminium, fabric
13 x 24 x 26 cm
Edition of 15
Summer Exhibition 2002, Royal Academy of Arts, London
About Face, Croydon Clocktower, Croydon, 2002

Playing with History, 2002
Ink on paper
23 x 31 cm
Unique

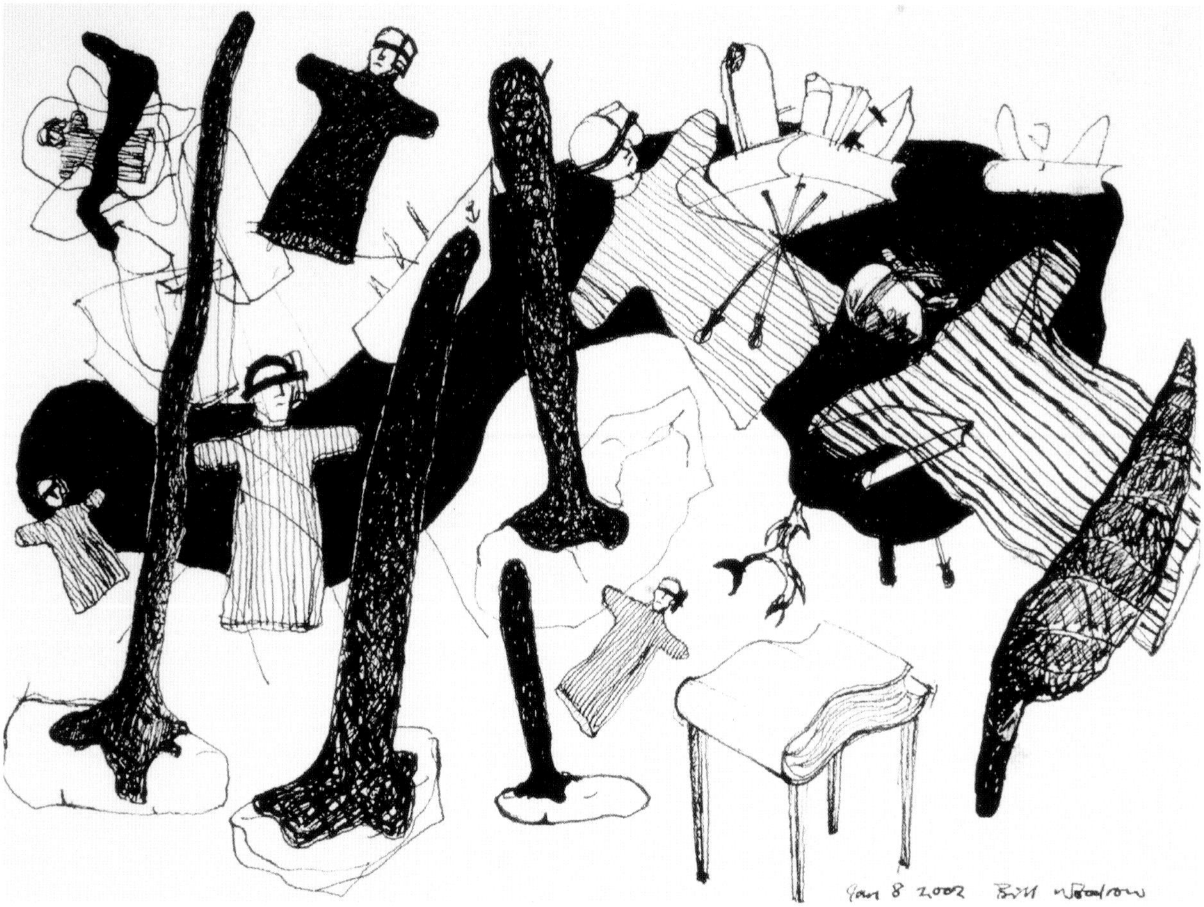

Copyright

Eileen Agar © the estate of Eileen Agar
Edward Allington © Edward Allington
Kenneth Armitage © the estate of Kenneth Armitage
John Armstrong © the artist's estate
John Banting © the estate of John Banting
Glen Baxter © the artist
Gilbert Bayes © The Fine Art Society, London
Pearl Binder © the artist's estate
Peter Blake © Peter Blake/DACS, 2009
Sir John Amherst Selby-Bigge © the estate of John Bigge
David Bomberg © the artist's family
Pauline Boty © the estate of Pauline Boty
Emmy Bridgwater © the estate of Emmy Bridgewater
Horace Brodzky © the estate of Horace Brodzky
John Buckland Wright © the artist's estate
Laurence Burt © Laurence Burt
Reg Butler © the estate of Reg Butler
Francis Butterfield © the artist's estate
Leonora Carrington © DACS, 2009
Geoffrey Clarke © Geoffrey Clarke
Cecil Collins © the estate of Cecil Collins
Ithell Colquhoun © the estate of Ithell Colquhoun, courtesy the National Trust, Bodmin
Hubert Dalwood © the artist's estate
John Davies © John Davies, courtesy Marlborough Fine Art, London
Anthony Earnshaw © the estate of Anthony Earnshaw
Sir Jacob Epstein © the estate of Sir Jacob Epstein
Max Ernst © ADAGP, Paris and DACS, London 2009
Merlyn Evans © the estate of Merlyn Oliver Evans
Gordon Onslow Ford © The Lucid Art Foundation
Sir Terry Frost © the estate of Sir Terry Frost
William Gear © the estate of William Gear
Thomas Samuel Haile © Marianne Haile
Paul Hammond © Paul Hammond
Stanley William Hayter © the estate of Stanley William Hayter/DACS, 2009
Nigel Henderson © the estate of Nigel Henderson
Gertrude Hermes © the estate of Gertrude Hermes
Patrick Heron © the estate of Patrick Heron/DACS, 2009
Roger Hilton © the estate of Roger Hilton/DACS, 2009
Damien Hirst © DACS, 2009
Arthur Jackson © the estate of Arthur Jackson
John Hoskin © the artist's estate
Patrick Hughes © DACS, 2009
Humphrey Jennings © DACS, 2009
Michael Kidner © Michael Kidner/ADAGP, Paris, 2009
Bryan Kneale © Bryan Kneale/ADAGP, Paris, 2009
Leon Kossoff © Leon Kossoff
Jacob Kramer © the artist's estate
Maurice Lambert © the estate of Maurice Lambert
Roy Lichtenstein © DACS, 2009
David Mach © David Mach
F.E. McWilliam © the estate of F.E. McWilliam
Conroy Maddox © the estate of Conroy Maddox
Rene Magritte © DACS, 2009
Man Ray © Man Ray, ADAPG, Paris and DACS, London
Mary Martin © the estate of Mary Martin/Annely Juda Fine Art, London
André Masson © ADAGP, Paris and DACS, London
Bernard Meadows © the estate of Bernard Meadows
Reuben Mednikoff © the artist's estate
Oscar Mellor © Oscar Mellor
John Melville © the artist's estate
E.L.T. Mesens © DACS, 2009
Juan Miró © DACS, 2009
Henry Moore © Henry Moore Foundation
Desmond Morris © Desmond Morris/ADAGP, Paris 2009
Alastair Morton © ADAGP, Paris
Richard Niman © Richard Niman
Grace Pailthorpe © the artist's estate
Sir Eduardo Paolozzi © Trustees of the Paolozzi Foundation/DACS, 2009
Roland Penrose © Roland Penrose Estate, England
Tom Phillips © DACS, 2009
John Piper © the estate of John Piper
Tony Pusey © Tony Pusey
Peter Rose Pulham © Peter Rose Pulham
Victor Reinganum © the estate of Victor Reinganum
William Roberts © the estate of William Roberts
Toni del Renzio © the artist's estate
Ceri Richards © the estate of Ceri Richards/DACS, 2009
Edith Rimmington © the artist's estate
Kurt Schwitters © DACS, 2009
Humphrey Spender © The Humphrey Spender Archive
John Cecil Stephenson © the estate of John Cecil Stephenson
Harry Thubron © the estate of Harry Thubron
Julian Trevelyan © the estate of Julian Trevelyan
John Tunnard © the estate of John Tunnard
Leon Underwood © the estate of Leon Underwood
Boyd Webb © Boyd Webb
John Welson © John Welson
Scottie Wilson © the artist's estate
Bill Woodrow © Bill Woodrow